CASS SERIES: STUDIES IN INTELLIGENCE
(Series Editors: Christopher Andrew and Richard J. Aldrich
ISSN: 1368–9916)

MI6 AND THE MACHINERY OF SPYING

Also in the Intelligence Series

MI6
and the
MACHINERY OF SPYING

PHILIP H.J. DAVIES
Brunel University

Foreword by
Michael Herman

FRANK CASS
LONDON • PORTLAND, OR

First published in 2004 in Great Britain by
FRANK CASS PUBLISHERS
2 Park Square, Milton park,
Abngdon, Oxon OX14 4RN

Simultaneously published in the USA and Canada by Routledge
270 Madison Avenue, New York, NY 10016

Transferred to Digital Printing 2005

Copyright © 2004 Philip H.J. Davies

British Library Cataloguing in Publication Data

Davies, Philip H. J.
    MI6 and the machinery of spying. – (Cass series. Studies in intelligence)
    1. Great Britain. MI6 – Management – History 2. Intelligence service –
    Great Britain – History
    I. Title
    327.1'241

ISBN 0-7146-5457-4 (cloth)
ISBN 0-7146-8363-9 (paper)
ISSN 1368-9916

Library of Congress Cataloging-in-Publication Data

Davies, Philip H. J.
    MI6 and the machinery of spying / Philip H. J. Davies.
        p. cm. – (Cass series–Studies in intelligence, ISSN 1368-9916)
    Based on author's thesis (Ph.D.)–U. Toronto.
    Includes bibliographical references and index.
    ISBN 0-7146-5457-4 (cloth) – ISBN 0-7146-8363-9 (pbk.)
    1. Great Britain. MI6. I. Title. II. Series.

UB251.G7D38 2003
327.1241–dc21   2003055262

Typeset in 10.5/12pt Sabon by FiSH Books, London

Printed and bound by Antony Rowe Ltd, Eastbourne

Contents

This work is dedicated in the first instance to my mother, and in loving memory of my father.

To John Wilfred Davies, who, as he was about to emigrate to Canada, was approached by two 'Men from the Ministry' types, who asked if he might be willing to pass back to them any information he might think to be 'interesting' once over there. He promptly pointed out the confidentiality clause in his contract with his future employers in Canada, and politely but firmly sent them on their way.

To Martha Alice Davies, who, as Staff Secretary in the engineering firm where they both worked, thoughtfully if recklessly 'fixed' her vocally left-wing fiancé's security clearance form.

They stacked the family bookshelves with Masterman and Winterbotham, Stevenson, Fleming and Albeury, and more besides, planting a seed which I hope will bear more fruit yet to come.

It is also dedicated to the memory of the late Ian MacIntosh, creator of the Yorkshire Television series *The Sandbaggers*, whose fiction about SIS went so far to inspire a search for the facts.

Figures

Photographs

Foreword

The last 25 years have seen 'intelligence studies' develop as a serious academic subject, but it is still finding its way. It has good historical and analytic literature, but there are many gaps, particularly over the secret intelligence agencies. There is little understanding of what makes them tick and how we should appraise them. So it is timely that Philip Davies now offers us a new lens upon them when intelligence reform is in the air and understanding of them is much needed.

I commend his book at two levels. At one, he uses publicly available material and confidential interviews to provide the most comprehensive account yet available of the Security Intelligence Service's internal organization: a research achievement in itself. And he does this without hazarding the Service's sources and methods, or sensitive details of its operational successes and failures.

At the second level he brings his social science training to interpret what he has found. It is part of the stock-in-trade of 'organization and management' studies that an organization's structure casts light upon its assumptions about objectives, priorities, challenges and responses. Properly looked at, wiring diagrams reflect organizational culture. But intelligence has not been examined in this way in the past, and Philip Davies now shows us that even Britain's most secretive agency can get the treatment – and with profit. His conclusions will come as a surprise to the reader who comes with preconceptions about 'proper' intelligence organization and how the SIS has measured up to it historically.

This is important not only in its own right, but also for demonstrating how effectively the study of intelligence can be linked with serious work on organization and management elsewhere. 'Intelligence studies', like its subject, risks becoming too inward-looking. Here we have a significant move towards developing closer links with other academic disciples, for benefit all round.

Much follow-up will be needed, but the book gives us the lens. It is innovative research and analysis of the best kind: the study of intelligence organizations will never be quite the same again.

Michael Herman
20 May 2004

Preface

Intelligence is about people and the study of people.
Sir Maurice Oldfield[1]

This study is concerned with that most prosaic aspect of a prosaic activity: the organization and administration of espionage. Back in the 1980s, Stuart Farson suggested that one could divide the study of intelligence into distinct national 'schools of thought', and pointed in particular to an American tradition that at the academic level tends to emphasize conceptual issues and ones of 'organizational efficacy',[2] essentially within the bounds of political and policy studies, and a British 'school' that is primarily historical.[3] He also hinted that, while there might be 'no single Canadian school of intelligence studies', what literature there was displayed influences of both the British and American traditions but went its own way, noting, for example, that 'the Canadian response to internal security was essentially to see it as an administrative problem not, as was the case in the United States, a political one'.[4] Like the 'Washinghall' systems in the Common-wealth capitals Ottawa and Canberra, the Canadian school of security and intelligence studies is a hybrid, partly or sometimes conceptual, and partly or sometimes historical, a combination that leads in its own direction quite distinct from either of the other two transatlantic precedents. This book may be considered an effort to import some of the more valuable conceptual tools of the American school into the historical approach of the British. It is, I suppose, a 'Canadian school' study of British intelligence.

As a result, the narrative herein follows two distinct trajectories. On the one hand, there is a historical account of the structural development of the British Secret Intelligence Service (SIS). On the other hand, there is an attempt to draw out certain themes and demonstrate the significance of certain trends and mechanisms that are meaningful from both a historical and a social-scientific point of view. The former of these places the study firmly not just within any putative 'British school of intelligence studies', but inside the much larger and much longer standing British 'machinery of government' tradition in political studies and public administration. Indeed, the machinery of government approach has often touched on intelligence within the British state, sometimes years or decades in advance of more popular or high-profile work. Hence, a 1957 Royal Institute of Public Administration study of Britain's central government dwells at some length on the emergence and function of the Joint Intelligence Committee and Joint Intelligence Bureau, as well as the wider and less secretive mechanisms of 'economic intelligence'.[5] This was six years before Lord Denning's inquiry would publicly avow the Security Service and publish the 1952 Maxwell-Fyfe Directive,[6] and 26 years before Lord Franks would take up the role and composition of the Joint Intelligence Organization again, and even then in only the very vaguest terms.[7]

There is also an attempt to analyse the developing structure of the SIS in terms of certain key concepts from the literature of organization theory such as span of control, centralization and decentralization, economies of scope and scale, and the contingency theory notions of organic and mechanistic management. These concepts often provide a basis to explain what sort of pressures might cause certain arrangements to be adopted, and allow us to identify when certain unexpected and even counter-intuitive principles of management have been adopted by the SIS. This, in principle, allows us to draw more general conclusions and ask further-reaching questions on the basis of the single-case study with conclusions and further questions relevant not only to the development of intelligence agencies in particular but of state-sector organizations in general during the last century.

The historically oriented, 'British school' reader can read and hopefully find some utility in the historical narrative developed herein without more than a cursory inspection of the more social-scientific aspects of the work, although I would encourage the historical 'British school' reader to take a little time over the theory (and would be even more adamant that the conceptually oriented 'American school' reader should work through the historical evidence in close detail). Most of the theoretical discussion occurs in the second part of Chapter 1, and in Chapter 7, but the relevance of many events in the narrative is established by reference to the concepts developed therein. Theoretical analysis in an exercise like this is not so much a retrospective social-scientific 'just-so story',[8] but rather an attempt to identify mechanisms and trends that might otherwise seem counter-intuitive. In today's high-tech management world, 'organic', 'network' and 'matrix' concepts of organization are par for the course. But, in 1946, the prevalent management doctrines were those of Weber, Taylor and Ford. People *really thought* that the only way to organize effectively was a rigid, regimented and compartmentalized bureaucracy. It is, therefore, a fascinating exercise to see SIS managers *forced* to improvise network relations between directorates, sections and even services even as they were trying to impose a Weberian bureaucratic model upon SIS – building an organic system despite themselves. This is the sort of historical development that is particularly *theoretically* interesting, and the history of SIS is replete with such occurrences.

This is not a detailed operational history of the SIS, although certain key operations and events are discussed in some detail. Others have compiled far more detailed accounts of the operations discussed here, and the reader is directed to their work in the text and the citations. Operations come and go; the questions asked in this exercise are 'How do people go about organizing and implementing *any operation* with which they are likely to be confronted?', 'How have those methods and organization changed since the SIS was established nearly a century ago?', 'How does the SIS fit into the machinery of government, and what does that tell us about the organization and methods of intelligence?', and, above all else, 'What might these things tell us about British Government itself?' Intelligence agencies do not exist in a vacuum; they are part and parcel of the overt machinery of government. As a result, one cannot do intelligence and security studies without doing political science, and one cannot do (or, at least *should not do*) political science without doing history. And that is why the following volume is as it is, a blend of the historical and the social scientific that I hope will more or less satisfy the intellectual requirements of both disciplines.

NOTES

1.   Attributed, Richard Deacon, *C: A Biography of Sir Maurice Oldfield, Head of MI6* (London: Futura, 1985), p. 189.

2. A. Stuart Farson 'Schools of Thought: National Perceptions of Intelligence', *Conflict Quarterly*, 9, 2 (Spring 1989), p. 56. Farson places the scholarly and process-oriented literature in distinction to another side of the American tradition concerned with issues of propriety and the kind of exposé that contributed to the Church inquiries in the 1970s.
3. Ibid., p. 61. Farson attributes the notion of the historical British school of D.C. Watt, noting also that like the American 'school', British scholarship has a populist *doppelgänger* of exposés obsessed with 'mole hunts' rather than propriety and public morality.
4. Ibid., p. 74.
5. F.M.G. Wilson, *The Organization of British Central Government* (London: Allen and Unwin, 1957), pp. 298–321.
6. Cabinet Office, *Lord Denning's Report* (London: HMSO, 1963, Cmd. 2152).
7. Lord Franks, *Falkland Islands Review* (London: HMSO, 1983) pp. 94–5.
8. A phrase for which I am indebted to Professor P.A.J. Waddington of the University of Reading.

Acknowledgements

The following work is the product of a decade's effort that would not have been possible without the aid, assistance and inspiration of a great many people. It would not have been possible without the support and vision of my doctoral supervisor, Dr Ken Robertson, of the Department of Sociology and Graduate School of European and International Studies at the University of Reading, who saw the potential value of such a project and agreed to oversee my Ph.D. work on the subject. On the basis of our first meeting in Ottawa in 1989, and a subsequent research proposal, Dr Robertson offered me an opportunity to do the two things I most wanted to – work on security and intelligence issues, and return home to England after 20 years abroad. For this alone I shall always be immensely grateful. As a supervisor of studies, Dr Robertson proved an example to learn from, knowing with sure judgement when to guide and suggest, when to be the voice of 'sober second thought', and when to stand back and let his research students use their initiative. More importantly, without Dr Robertson's network of 'old boy' intelligence contacts, and his willingness to give me access to them, this project would not have been possible. Dr Robertson also proved a dab hand at what some universities call 'pastoral responsibilities', seeing to the psychological well-being of his charges, of which I was in particular need during a difficult late 1995 and 1996.

That means that I also owe thanks to an assortment of people who directed me towards Ken as a potential supervisor, including Professor David Stafford at the University of Edinburgh's Centre for Second World War Studies, who also served as my External Examiner; Professor David Charters at the University of New Brunswick; and Professor Stuart Farson, now at Simon Fraser. It was Professor Stafford with whom I first discussed my thoughts on studying intelligence during his term as Director of the Canadian Institute of International Affairs at the University of Toronto, nearly 14 years ago. The transition from doctoral thesis to book monograph has been guided and overseen with great skill and tact by the editor, of the Intelligence Series at Frank Cass, Professor Richard J. Aldrich. I am particularly appreciative of Professor Aldrich's opinion, as a career historian, of the value and potential of a social science approach to the subject.

Professor Christie Davies served as my Adviser for three years before officially taking on the role in 1996, and finally acting as my Ph.D. Internal Examiner. Professor Davies is truly a master of academic lore, a guru of scholarship and the art of war. I have rarely met anyone who enjoyed their work, doing and *being* what they are, and for whom scholarship was so truly and evidently a vocation, as Professor Davies. Professor Davies is also one of an increasingly rare kind of wide-ranging scholar whose breadth of interests is matched only by their breadth of competence, far beyond the narrow confines of contemporary, conventional Americanized, 'professional sociology'. Such scholars-at-large are rapidly becoming an endangered species as their traditional collegial habitats are being eroded by the sprawling infrastructures of modern managerial and pedagogical bureaucracy.

I must express also my deeply felt thanks to the 12 former British SIS officers who agreed to be interviewed in the course of my research. They were all generous with their time, gracious hosts and infinitely patient with the inquisitorial pedantry of semi-structured interviewing. Many proved enthusiastic about the idea of the project, and went well beyond what I had a right to expect. Naturally, any errors or misrepresentations in the final product are entirely my responsibility.

The many other members of the University of Reading who provided valued help and advice were, from Sociology, Professor P.A.J. 'Tank' Waddington and Dr Tony Walter, Dr Mark Neil and Dr Bill Poole; from Economics, Professor Mark Casson and Dr Vivek Suneja; and from Politics, Dr Philip Giddings. Professor Christopher Andrew and Rupert Allason (better known as author Nigel West) both helped me contact a number of interviewees, and Rupert Allason also very generously gave me access to a number of his own primary sources. Other academics who provided advice and opportunities for me to present some of my results to other scholars included Yale's Professor H. Bradford Westerfield, Professor Wesley

ACKNOWLEDGEMENTS

Wark at Toronto, Dr Peter Jackson and Dr Jennifer Seigel also at Yale University, and Dr Sheila Kerr and Dr J.V.F. Keiger at Salford. Indeed, I must express particular appreciation to Professor Westerfield, whose verve and vigour as senior scholar has always been a great inspiration like that of Professor Davies – and who had faith in my work when my own confidence faltered.

To my wife, Dr Seetha Khartini Abdul Wahab, I owe the inevitable thanks and appreciation for her support during both my doctoral years, and the last two years struggling to wrestle my dissertation into readable form as a book. To my mother, Martha Alice Davies, the inevitable thanks any son owes an enthusiastic and supportive parent. Thanks also to my valued friend Dr Geoffrey Vaughan at the University of Maryland, Baltimore County, and my late aunt Margaret Wilbraham. Many thanks also to Lee Wilson at Darwin College, Cambridge, David White at Reading for providing me with last minute copies of articles and book chapters needed for the completion of this book. Special appreciation is also due to Christopher Murphy, currently completing his doctorate at the University of Reading on the organization and administration of the wartime Special Operations Executive, for copies of documents relevant to this work found during his own research.

I would also like to thank the University of Reading for the Postgraduate Teaching Studentship and the Committee of Vice-Chancellors and Principals, whose Overseas Research Scholarship funded this research.

PHJD
Brunel University 2004

1

Introduction

Intelligence is organization.

Sherman Kent[1]

The British Secret Intelligence Service, known variously as SIS, MI6, the Firm, the Office, the Racket and the Friends, has served the UK government for more than 90 years. Created at the end of the first decade of the twentieth century, it has been a vital part of the UK's true first line of defence, the national intelligence machinery, throughout the twentieth century.[2] It and its fellow intelligence and security agencies are almost certain to remain just as important, if not more so, in the next century as well.

The SIS is the oldest continuously operating organization of its type in the world, and as such it is perhaps one of the most instructive covert foreign intelligence organizations to study. Although it was preceded by its French equivalent in the Third Republic, and its founder turned very much to French advice when setting the agency up,[3] it really had to be built up almost entirely from scratch. The invention, innovation and improvisation that this required was not merely a question of building up networks of agents or assets almost (but not entirely) from zero, but also of solving problems of organizing and managing secret intelligence work, and incorporating that work and its product into the day-to-day operation of the British state. In many respects, it was often the problems of organization and integration, that is, of institutionalization and institution-building, that proved to be among the most daunting for its early leadership. Without an effective institutional structure to coordinate the work undertaken, there would have been little prospect of success in either the long or short terms for the officers in the field in getting the job done, or for their colleagues at headquarters in seeing that the information obtained reached the consumers in government who are any intelligence service's ultimate *raison d'être*.[4]

It is impossible, therefore, to understand how an organization, intelligence or otherwise, works without understanding its formal structure.[5] Organizational structure is the internal political lay of the land, a network of interdependencies and rivalries. It covers responsibilities taken, claimed or shirked and is, therefore, a central part of the practical, day-to-day rules of play for what one former SIS officer interviewed described – with an almost sociological turn of phrase – as 'doing spying'.[6] But even this sells the matter short, because this is only the *internal* function of organization in intelligence gathering. Formal, official organizational structure has an *external* function, which is to tie (or sometimes to fail to tie) the machinery of intelligence to the equally formal, and official machinery of central government. Those links can be many and varied, ranging from command and control of the agency through to communication links to convey the intelligence product to users on the overt side of government or issues and mechanisms of legislative and public accountability But, ultimately, how an activity is organized says a great deal about that activity, about how it is conceptualized and how it is undertaken by its participants. The organization of an intelligence service can, therefore, tell us a great deal about how that agency and its governmental and political masters go about 'doing spying'.

Structure is also a potential liability as well as an asset. Management literature is replete with examples of 'malorganization', its causes, and its costs and consequences. Intelligence agencies are no different. The American Central Intelligence Agency (CIA) has often been criticized for excessive bureaucratization. Likewise, both the Security Service (or MI5) and the Government Communications Headquarters (GCHQ) have been criticized for excessive bureaucratization in difficulties and crises with which they have been publicly confronted.[7] Variously weak and rigid structures, and over centralized and overly fragmented organizational structures have been identified as potential structural failings over the years.[8] As such, they on numerous occasions have been blamed for failures to provide sufficient warning or to maintain effective security.

The SIS is no exception, and indeed its organizational structure has figured more than most in accounts of its failures and shortcomings. Hugh Trevor-Roper's judgement of SIS in the Second World War, and its legacy to the inter-war period, is that

It was not a rational extension of an efficient bureaucracy of information. Perhaps it never had been. When it was set up, before the First World War, it had not been intended as such. It had been a piece of machinery to passively receive, rather than actively to collect, such intelligence as the friends of Britain, in foreign countries, might wish to secretly impart. ... As such, it no doubt performed its limited role well enough. But when it ventured outside those limits, it succumbed too easily to the inherent risks of all secret societies. It became divorced from the public bureaucracy; being recruited by patronage, it acquired some of the character of a coterie; and it preserved, as such coteries easily do, outmoded habits of thought.[9]

Numerous sources have also pointed to SIS's organizational weaknesses, inter- and intra-organizational turf wars being exacerbated by poor leadership and a divided wartime chain of command in the form of two feuding deputies to the then SIS Chief of Service Sir Stewart Graham Menzies.[10]

Perhaps most scathingly, Anthony Verrier has pointed the finger of blame at the SIS's failure to reform and reorganize effectively after the war as a fundamental reason that the Soviet penetration agent H.A.R. ('Kim') Philby could do as much damage as he did. The post-war reforms were nothing but trifling changes in which 'the personnel pack was reshuffled in order to promote the ambitious (Philby above all) and remove critics. No root and branch reorganization was considered or attempted.' As a result, the senior officers colloquially known as 'robber barons', that is, 'directors under C whose responsibilities were territorial and not functional' were unaffected. Therefore, 'The robber barons, safeguarding their perquisites and responsible for all tasks within them, were certainly immune from introspection about organizations and methods.'[11] The final blow was the failure to reform the then prevalent structure of counter-intelligence and counter-espionage under which, Verrier further argues, 'Broadway's counter-intelligence sections were, in practice, subordinate to the regional directors, whose requirement to produce material dominated all other considerations. *Penetration* of an enemy – or any other foreign – intelligence organization was a secondary requirement, a factor which enabled Philby to be a traitor secure from detection for many years.'[12] Verrier's judgements against the SIS, passed in 1983, have since been echoed throughout the last 20 years by other commentators, including journalists and amateur historians alike.[13]

Thus, SIS organization has consistently been portrayed as one of its underlying and most persistent shortcomings. However, few things in life are unalloyed good or evil, and if SIS developed in a particular direction, it is reasonable to ask what the thinking was behind a particular path of development, and given that thinking, were the failures unanticipated consequences of decisions which appeared otherwise reasonable, or were they by way of calculated risks which escaped their estimated boundaries of danger? If divided chains of command, amateurism, regional fiefdoms, turf wars and penetration were the *costs* of SIS organizational structure, what were the *benefits*? In the language of market economics, SIS organization has frequently been identified as a source of *comparative disadvantage*. But why did such a form of organization evolve and might that organizational structure have served as a comparative *advantage* in some ways which historians and critics have previously overlooked?

In his 1970 review of the British intelligence system, prepared against the background of a succession of scandals, revelations and allegations concerning the conduct of the American CIA, political scientist Harry Howe Ransom argues that 'the Secret Service [SIS], unlike the CIA, has not become a foreign policy boomerang often returning to embarrass and injure the government ... in contrast to the CIA, one rarely hears the suggestion that the Secret Service operates on the basis of its "own" foreign policy; one hears no debates as to whether the Secret Service ought to be disbanded; and there are few who would question whether the Secret Service is under responsible political control.'[14] Ransom does admit that far stricter conditions of official secrecy in the UK have meant that there is far less information on which to formulate any judgements, and he further qualifies that matter by adding that British foreign policy goals are necessarily less ambitious than those of the United States as are those of its agencies. Nonetheless, Ransom's suggestion raises the fundamental question: *if* the SIS has avoided becoming either boomerang or rogue elephant, what *institutional* or *structural* aspects of the agency and its role and working arrangements in the machinery of British government have served to restrain or circumscribe its activities to keep it from running out of control?

Organization charts are, of course, a staple of intelligence literature. Perhaps such a fascination is inevitable in the study of the arcane, reminiscent of Kabbalistic demonology, in which knowing the names of the assorted nether beings gives the would-be sorcerer

4

power over them. If nothing else, knowledge reduces the sense of powerlessness. Such charts may also appeal to the constitutionalist turn of mind, concerned as it is with rights and responsibilities, jurisdictions, powers, regulations and procedures. If so, it should be unsurprising that American intelligence literature is rich in wire-frame plumbing charts, from the excruciatingly detailed studies of Jeffrey Richelson (occasionally in consort with Australia's Desmond Ball)[15] to studies of the US intelligence community by former insiders[16] and the US intelligence community's accounts of itself.[17] However, as one reviewer of Richelson's and Ball's study of the UK–USA 'special relationship', *Ties That Bind*, has pointed out, mazes of wire-frame diagrams are of limited utility when divorced from their historical context.[18]

Popular historian Nigel West pointedly prefaces almost all of his intelligence books with a series of organization charts (including volumes on SIS), tracing the structural development of the subject of the agency in question over the interval covered by the book,[19] while Christopher Andrew regularly pauses in his *Secret Service* to perform a sort of 'the story so far' stocktaking of SIS organization.[20] Shortly before his death in 1994, Robert Cecil prepared an intricate, if somewhat entangled, organization chart of the SIS for the *Oxford Companion to the Second World War*.[21] West's, Andrew's and Cecil's accounts almost certainly reflect the British analogue to the constitutionalist idiom, the 'machinery of government' approach, which concerns itself with departments, divisions, and other matters of organization and methods. However, the Kabbalistic approach is also visible in the work of critics of the intelligence community. In 1982, journalist Duncan Campbell published a set of organization charts of Britain's intelligence and security agencies drawn from 'a handbook issued by American agencies to their own staffs', and of high probable accuracy.[22] By contrast, in his *In Defence of the Realm?* (1990), Richard Norton-Taylor provides supposedly contemporary organizational breakdowns for the various security and intelligence agencies both in the text and as organization charts – but in the case of the SIS, the text and the chart are completely different.[23]

Despite the prevalence of this fascination with the naming of names, and drawing of charts, very little *analysis* has been done upon this sort of organizational information. What does such information tell us about how and why an agency works, its relationships not only with itself, but with its twinned environments of the outside, operational world, and inside machinery of government? What kind of forces have acted to shape an organization in one particular way, as opposed to another, and ultimately, what does it really *mean*, what is the *consequence* of having one particular structure or another? And what does change in structure tell us about that agency, its environments and work?

INTELLIGENCE AND THE MACHINERY OF GOVERNMENT

One of the most interesting and instructive features of SIS's structural development over the decades is the degree to which it is not, and has never been, fundamentally *bureaucratic*. The term 'bureaucracy', of course, appears in many contexts and in many senses, but for all intents and purposes the most persistent sense is that of Max Weber's 'ideal type' of bureaucracy. This concept, or architecture of concepts, developed most fully in his *Economy and Society*, consists, roughly, of six major characteristics:

1. a strictly defined hierarchy and division of labour in which specialized officers cannot interfere in one another's work, juniors interfere in the work of their seniors and (less often noted) seniors meddle in the work of juniors
2. recruitment on the basis of expert training
3. promotion according to meritocracy (that is, by performance rather than personal affiliation or status), and conduct within the organization characterized by 'impersonality' and the primacy of general formal procedures over particular situations or cases
4. an explicit system of rules governing activities within the bureaucracy
5. a permanent system of written records or 'files'
6. a permanency of office such that when an incumbent departs from a post, the post continues under a new post-holder.[24]

As an 'ideal type', Weber's notion is not so much a description or checklist for any empirical organization, as an internally logically consistent way of going about organizing things and conducting oneself within that organizational context. This is a subtlety that has escaped many of Weber's critics,[25] and what it means is that people can conform to this approach to a greater or lesser degree, much as they might be influenced by the law or religious norms to a greater or lesser degree.[26] Bureaucracies, he noted, were best suited to large-scale, technically complex and highly routine situations where 'quick and consistent' decisions were more useful than slower ones that might be more thoroughly considered.[27]

As something of a counterbalance to bureaucracy, Weber saw organization on the basis of permanent consensus-driven bodies of equals such as a board of directors or a general staff. These he called 'collegial bodies',[28] and a number of commentators have seized upon these as constituting a 'limitation' upon the iron law of bureaucratic expansion.[29] Weber generally views collegial bodies as a less efficient precursor to bureaucratic forms, prone to factionalization and deadlock, and expensive in terms of inefficiency because of their slow deliberation process. This is, he argues, ultimately less cost-efficient than bureaucracy (for all its ills of procedural rigidity and secrecy). *However*, he also qualifies this with the observation that 'collegiality favours greater thoroughness in the weighing of administrative decisions' and even admits that 'where this is more important than precision and rapidity, collegiality tends to be resorted to even today'.[30] He further develops a sub-type of collegiality that he calls 'rationally specialized, functional collegiality', in which the membership is composed along lines of technical expertise like a bureaucratic division of labour, but where decision making is based on a consensus of expert opinion rather than submitting diverse assessments to a single, hierarchically senior decision maker.[31] As a result, any real-world organization could quite reasonably be expected to display the characteristics of both bureaucracy and collegiality, depending on when, where and to what degree it required quick, routine or 'well-considered' decisions.

In contemporary management theory, the notion of organizing according to expert consensus, interdisciplinary collaboration and what one research team called 'contributive working arrangements' has been termed 'organic' management, as opposed to the 'mechanistic' management of conventional bureaucracy. Organic management, 'network' structures and 'team'-based organization have generally been found to be characteristic of firms involved in industries subject to rapid change either in the market or technology.[32] Such 'collegiality' has been found to be typical, for example, of the electronics industry as far back as the 1950s, and the contemporary information technology industry is even more inclined this way. However, while management researchers did find that organicism suits variable and complex environments, it is difficult to implement in very large-scale organizations. This is because the same problems that Weber found limited the efficiency of collegiality. As a result, most large organizations employ a combination of mechanistic bureaucracy and collegial organicism, termed in current jargon a 'matrix' organization. Typically, this involves creating cross-functional organic bodies such as project 'teams' that draw personnel from across the bureaucratic hierarchy and a division of labour that provides an underlying, basic structure of the organization.[33]

The British SIS has always been highly collegial and organic in both structure and ethos. Initially, when the agency was very loosely structured on an ad hoc basis – as the first generation of officers and administrators found themselves making things up as they went along – there was a natural collegiality that was almost certainly a carry-over from the long acknowledged collegiality of British government life in general, and also a consequence of the very smallness of the headquarters offices and various regional bureaux. However, as the service grew and became more established, and efforts were made to impose some sort of organizational efficiency, collegial and organic arrangements began to appear as vaguely articulated 'work-arounds' that allowed the service to retain much of the original ethos and mode of work. As we shall see later, there were also very real and powerful pressures from its governmental environment that *forced* an emphasis on lateral coordination and communications. After successive reviews and reorganizations, one SIS Chief of Service, Sir Arthur Franks, explicitly adopted the notion of collegiality, at least at the level of the SIS board of directors.

The presence of collegial and organic structures in a secret service is, in many respects, a counter-intuitive phenomenon. In a field of activity where security and 'compartmentalization' – locking information up in hermetically sealed parcels of organizational structure – must be paramount, collaborative working arrangements would appear at best contradictory, and at worst self-defeating because of the risk of poor security. To be sure, there were points where interdepartmental consultation was detrimental to security (most notably during Philby's term as head of counter-espionage). But despite that, and the process costs of organicism, collegiality has remained so essential to the agency's mode of operation that, far from being reduced or phased out, it has become increasingly explicit, and increasingly fundamental. This inevitably invites the perplexed question, 'why?'

It would be tempting to suggest that collegiality and organicism of both ethos and structure must be some inevitable organizational-cultural overflow from the widespread collegiality of the UK central government. Indeed, there is something appealing in the idea of trusted chaps working things out together; a consensus of equals over a hot cup of tea that captures some essential Britishness of SIS. More-over, ethnocentrism aside, there might even be intellectual precedent for such an interpretation. The American scholars Hugh Heclo and Aaron Wildavsky noted the collegiality and network-oriented nature of Cabinet office and senior civil service life, crystallizing their findings in a compelling turn of phrase as the 'Whitehall village'.[34] Likewise, another American, the former IBM psychologist Geert Hoffstede, ran a series of surveys of IBM employees in different nations looking for differences in management preferences by country. The French, he found, preferred strict regulation and a rigid hierarchy; the Germans, a relatively flat hierarchy but strictly defined procedures that he compared to a well-oiled machine. Asians (in his data set, IBM employees in India) were oriented towards loosely defined procedures but a strict and severe hierarchy, which, he notes, resembles the traditional Asian family. But the British, his findings showed, had little taste for either hierarchy or formally defined procedure (less so even than supposedly egalitarian Americans, much to Hoffstede's surprise). The metaphor adopted by Hoffstede was that of the 'village market'.[35] The parallels between Heclo and Wildavsky on the one hand and Hoffstede on the other hand are too striking to ignore.

It would be tempting, therefore, to view the SIS structure as resulting from an endemic cultural preference, both ambient and pervasive, and this might be convincing, were there not obvious weaknesses in such an interpretation. In the first place, certain divisions of British central government have long been characterized by very strict bureaucratic structure. These are usually very large departments with a sizeable workflow of repetitive and routine tasks, such as the Department of Health or the Department of the Environ-ment. Evidently, the ethos of collegiality has not been sufficiently ambient or pervasive to mould them to its shape. Likewise, one might as easily observe of Heclo and Wildavsky's 'discovery' of organiza-tional process being implemented more in the canteen or Pall Mall club than the office a mere echo of sociologist Peter Blau's exposure of FBI work getting done over the water cooler or in the canteen when rigid agency procedures proved a prohibitive encumbrance to Hoover's 'special agents'.[36] Ethos and culture are vague and amorphous things, liable to be swept aside by circumstance, fad and even whim. It would be more compelling to look for structural reasons – from within or without – *forcing* SIS to adopt an organic structure, even when it tried to adopt a classic bureaucratic hierarchy, as it did in 1946.

As we shall see in greater detail below, structural reasons there are, and both from within and without. SIS has, for example, never been a large organization and it peaked in the latter half of the Cold War at perhaps 1200 persons.[37] The international arena in which SIS operates has always been a highly, and often rapidly variable environment. But, significantly, the institutional and, one might even say, constitutional status of intelligence in the British central government has provided perhaps the most inexorable force driving SIS into a flat, wide and collegial organization.

At a certain level, how one describes the status of intelligence in the UK government depends on what one means by intelligence. As former GCHQ and Joint Intelligence Committee (JIC) official Michael Herman has observed, there exist what he calls 'broad', 'middle' and 'narrow' views of intelligence.[38] At its broadest, intelligence constitutes the comprehensive pooling, evaluation and assessment of *all available* information, or 'all source analysis', to generate policy-relevant 'finished intelligence' for the overall guidance of decision makers in government.[39] At its narrowest, intelligence is, as academic Ken Robertson has put it, 'the secret collection of other people's secrets'.[40] At first glance, this would appear to be simply the kind of ambiguity one gets from approaching ordinary language concepts with too close a scrutiny. To be sure, etymologically, the development of the term 'intelligence' has always been a vague hotchpotch of espionage, news and analytical research.[41] However, the divergent senses of the term have a practical, institutional relevance, especially where machinery of government questions and the internal market for intelligence are concerned.

In the British Parliamentary system, the pooling of all available information, overt, covert and the merely confidential, and turning it into policy-oriented assessments is not so much *intelligence* as the basic function of the civil service. As Henry Parris has argued, the development of the British civil service as an advisory instrument to ministers answerable to Parliament evolved not merely as a matter of administrative expediency but as a substantive *constitutional* change.[42] The subordination of the civil service to ministers holding seats in Parliament did not appear whole cloth, but evolved over time as Ministers of the Crown were increasingly selected from the two houses of Parliament, and not merely from a royal coterie or network of elites. As ministers increasingly became parliamentarians, the civil service increasingly became subordinate to them and increasingly politically neutralized and removed from the public eye. Robertson, building on Parris, has even argued convincingly that British official secrets legislation evolved less to provide governmental clandestinity than to silence civil servants in the public sphere. This prevented them from constituting a rival presence in public politics, and allowed Parliament to monopolize decision making and responsibility.[43] In principle, then, the function of the civil service in the British government is partly as an executive mechanism, but chiefly as an information-collection, evaluation and policy-guidance mechanism for ministers.

The notion of the information and advisory roles of the civil service might seem painfully straightforward, and almost trivially true to most people familiar with the British system of government. However, it has some significant, non-trivial consequences when we try to understand how intelligence works in the British system. What is generally called all-source or finished 'intelligence' is in many respects the ordinary work of the ministries and departments of British government. This role has been captured most effectively by former Foreign and Commonwealth Office official Reginald Hibbert. According to Hibbert, the range of sources employed by the Foreign Office can be broken down into '50 per cent...drawn from overt published sources...privileged material which is not strictly speaking classified...is some 10 to 20 per cent...[and] material classifiable as confidential [which] is a product of normal diplomatic activity', leaving 10 per cent or so for secret sources.[44] He then argues:

> The Foreign office is itself a huge assessment machine...with its elaborate organization of over 60 departments, some geographical and some functional, it constitutes a capacious and versatile digestive system fed by the massive intake of information [composed of] the 50 per cent or so overt, the 10 per cent or so privileged, the 20 or 25 per cent confidential and the 10 per cent

secret. It chews the cud of this material day by day, reacts to it as it becomes available, 'in real time' as the expression goes, and applies it in the decision-taking and policy-forming process which is the end product of the system.[45]

The department as 'assessment machine' is not unique to the Foreign Office, and much the same can be said of any other branch of the central government from the Ministry of Defence to the Home Office and so forth. Hence, it is possible to say that intelligence in the *broad* sense is distributed among the different departments and ministries of State, who 'chew' their respective 'cud', assessing it and acting on it according to their jurisdictions and policy interests.

Because of the finished intelligence function of the civil service at large, the present author has argued elsewhere that at the level of all-source finished intelligence the British government is in fact highly *decentralized*. To be sure, there is a central, national all-source intelligence assessment mechanism in the form of the Cabinet Office's JIC, which combines information from the three intelligence and security agencies with that from the Hibbert spectrum of sources acquired by the Foreign Office, Ministry of Defence and so forth. However, the JIC (as will also be seen in greater detail below) was a relatively late arrival on the intelligence scene, and remains confined to generating 'high-powered reports for high-powered people' at the level of deputy- and permanent under-secretaries and ministers.[46] It is, in fact, only the collection of secret, unassessed *raw* intelligence that was originally centralized, and how and why this came about is very much a consequence of the decentralization of departmental analysis. Suffice to say at this point that the need for a national secret intelligence bureau sprang from the unwillingness of overt departments, such as the War Office, Admiralty and Foreign Office to be directly involved in anything as ethically uncertain and diplomatically hazardous – and potentially embarrassing – as espionage. The specifics of how this need for a separate agency drove the creation of the Secret Service Bureau in 1909, precursor to both SIS and MI5 (and the precedent on the basis of which GCHQ took shape), will be examined in detail below. For now, what is of central importance is the fact that the creation of central secret intelligence organs arose out of *demand* on the part of various departments and ministries for Hibbert's ten per cent secret material. The need for covert foreign intelligence arose out of the information needs of the overt machinery of government.

SUPPLY AND DEMAND IN THE WHITEHALL VILLAGE MARKET FOR
INTELLIGENCE

Indeed, the most significant feature of the British intelligence system, especially when viewed in terms of an internal market, is that it is primarily demand-driven. In the United States, former Deputy Secretary of State Henry S. Rowen has suggested viewing the market-like relationship between intelligence producer and intelligence consumer in terms of the commercial concepts of 'push' and 'pull' businesses.[47] Indeed, intelligence can be viewed as a variety of 'internal' market, with intelligence agencies collecting and disseminating intelligence in exchange for budgetary and other resource allocations. One aspect of this discussion has been directed towards the relative virtues of 'push' versus 'pull' architectures in intelligence administration, originally in the United States and more recently in Britain.[48] The distinction between 'push' and 'pull' is essentially that between arrangements in which intelligence agencies choose targets and priorities themselves – they are, so to speak, 'self-tasking' – and present their results to consumers in the overt machinery of government in the hope that they have chosen the correct targets and priorities (push), and arrangements in which the consuming departments choose those targets and priorities, and 'task' the intelligence-gathering agencies directly, giving those agencies little or no opportunity for independent action or taking the initiative concerning a potential target (pull).

The notion of a 'pull' architecture is also compatible with the essentials of American 'intelligence theory', as a 'pull' architecture is very much how intelligence is theoretically *supposed* to work, according to the contemporary 'theory of intelligence' and its concept of the 'intelligence cycle' (Figure 1.1). In the simplest and most common version, the intelligence cycle consists of four phases: tasking, collection, analysis and *then* dissemination. In the first phase, consumers review their information needs and 'task' collection agencies to gather the information needed to fill those requirements. That collection effort, be it from overt sources, or covert, human or technical sources, is then fed into the analytical process and the end product is 'finished' intelligence and in which form it is disseminated to the consumers.[49] In the British departmental model however, particularly as we have seen it described by Hibbert, the 'raw', unassessed intelligence is passed first to consumers, who then undertake their own analysis according to their own policy interests. The consumers then review what they now know and what they also need to know, and reformulate their intelligence requirements, and the cycle repeats. Hence, at the level of departmental requirements, the British approach to intelligence traditionally reverses the last two steps of the intelligence cycle (Figure 1.2). To be sure, central national assessment by the JIC conforms to the American model, but the majority of intelligence production has always been and remains chiefly for departmental purposes.[50]

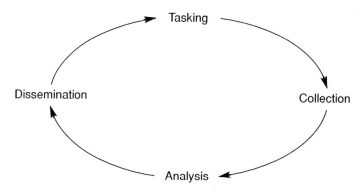

Figure 1.1: The US Intelligence Cycle

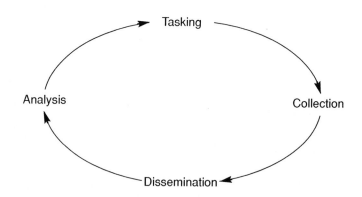

Figure 1.2: The UK Departmental Intelligence Cycle

14

Peter Scharfman, of the American think-tank MITRE, has argued that a 'pull' architecture should prove an unalloyed good, fundamentally superior to the 'push' architecture represented by a self-tasking agency. Under a 'push' architecture, he states, 'Intelligence analysts select from a vast quantity of information the things they believe the users need to know, then send the information to users they believe need to have it.'[51] According to Scharfman, both producer and consumer suffer under such an arrangement. The producer has the problem of assessing what information the consumer really wants and needs, must assess the appropriate distribution, and finally must judge whether or how often to revise a report or analysis. Clearly assessing who needs what information is the crux of getting the right information to the right people. Scharfman notes that overly wide distribution wastes the product on people who do not need or want to know about the subject reported upon, and, worse, encourages a tendency in them to ignore incoming reports,[52] although, surprisingly, he does not comment on the dangers to security of overly wide dissemination resulting in information leakage, no less a danger than that of creating uninterested or deprived consumers. From the consumer's point of view, Scharfman argues, the push architecture fails because 'intelligence arrives when it arrives, not when it is needed', and is less immediate and accessible to the reader than media reports.[53]

However, with a 'pull' architecture, the immediacy and directness of communication between producer and consumer mean that 'Decisions about which information gets to the consumer... will be made by the consumer rather than the producer, and... each user will be able to make his or her own decisions independently of the decisions made by other users who need intelligence information for other purposes.'[54] Under a 'pull' architecture, producers would be forced to 'tailor' their product to the consumers' needs, while the consumers will be able to reach independent conclusions derived from a common pool of intelligence data. The result, claims Scharfman, should be 'more analysis, better analysis, more help in a collaborative way from peers, less time lost "in process", and more use of analysis by the intended audience'.[55] The upshot of Scharfman's version of the push/pull market approach is that only the immediacy of modern high-speed, high-bandwidth communications and data processing, where consumers can search networked databases on intelligence and express their needs directly to producers through the miracle of electronic mail, can really permit the development of a 'pull' architecture.[56]

In the UK, however, the market for intelligence is a buyer's market and the forces of demand rather than supply prevail.[57] As a consequence, it turns out that the UK has been operating a 'pull' architecture in the case of SIS at least since 1919 (and thereby also in the case of the GCHQ's precursor, the Government Code and Cipher School[58]), in which case the question becomes one of why and how SIS has developed such an architecture so long ago, and without the putative benefits of contemporary information technology. The answer to this lies in the organizational politics of Whitehall, a set of conditions which has both imposed a demand-driven relationship upon the intelligence process and provided a pervasive organizational idiom of collegiality and organicism, of which the SIS is but a single example. As will become increasingly apparent below, SIS was never required to be, nor intended to be, an independent operational service in its own right (as would be, say, the Navy or various local police forces). Instead, it was intended to provide an operational armature working explicitly and only on the basis of the intelligence needs of Departments of State that were unwilling to risk the political and diplomatic consequences of having their accredited officials abroad getting caught spying. SIS was to exist and work on behalf of a plurality of highly independent and organizationally self-interested consumers. This in turn has driven the formation of a system of horizontal communications and 'contributive' joint working arrangements to convey the consumers' demands to SIS, and SIS' product back to the consumers.

In other words, if SIS is indeed collegially and organically structured, it is not merely because of its operational environment. It is because of the organizational politics and culture of Whitehall interdepartmentalism and the consumer-led nature of the British intelligence system, and a detailed and direct demand-driven relationship between SIS and its consumers has been feasible only because of collegial working arrangements both within SIS and between it and its consumers. Neither is the dependent nor independent variable; rather, the two mechanisms have developed hand in hand, each acting on the other in a positive feedback loop. Nonetheless, the process was initiated by consumers, and the weight of initiative and influence lies ultimately on their side, and not that of SIS.

REQUIREMENTS AND PRODUCTION: THE HEART OF THE SIS

The most persistent manifestation of the 'pull' architecture acting on SIS lies in the fundamental duality of both structure and process created by its *requirements* and *production* 'sides'. The distinction between requirements and production has historically been embodied in the central organizational distinction between operational sections, originally known as 'Group' or 'G Sections', and later as 'Production' or P Sections, and the 'Circulating', or later 'Requirements' or R Sections, sections which represent intelligence consumer wants and needs not merely to the SIS leadership but directly to the G/P Sections, bypassing the senior leadership entirely. The polarity between production and requirements took its original form in what the official history calls the '1921 arrangement', under which 'the intelligence branch in each of the three Services came to house one of its sections in the SIS, where it formed part of the HQ staff'.[59] These 'Circulating Sections' multiplied until 1946, when they were all renamed 'Requirements Sections' and placed under a single director of requirements, on an equal footing with the Production sections under their Director of Production. The Requirements Directorate would remain virtually unchanged until reorganized along geographical lines under Sir Maurice Oldfield around 1974, and even then the work was simply redistributed regionally while the essential mechanism remained the same.

The '1921 arrangement' provided both the conduit for a 'pull' dynamic, and a pressure towards organic and collegial working arrangements emerging from SIS's *governmental* rather than its *operational* environment. It did so by creating a system of horizontal communications between information collectors and their consumers, subject to a continuous dialogue to fine-tune the collection process and concentrate collectors' efforts within the parameters laid down by their consumers. Producer and consumer would meet day to day and face to face, providing precisely the immediacy and 'bandwidth' of communications required to provide an effective demand-driven system, even in the absence of any particularly sophisticated technology. Requirements came to be interwoven directly into the production process; not merely a permeable interface between producer and consumer, but an interpenetration of the two roles and sets of priorities into a single process. As we shall see below, it was through the 1921 arrangement link to the War Office that SIS first acquired the nickname 'MI6' in

1941. *The duality of requirements and production also provided an organizational core for the rest of the agency, with administrative, technical and other specialist bodies crystallizing around it, providing particular services in support of operations mounted in response to consumer demand.*

This is not to say that the requirements/production relationship worked with unbroken effectiveness and efficiency. On the contrary, the history of the SIS is littered with difficulties and drawbacks not merely those intrinsic to the running of a secret intelligence service, but also those particular to the operation of a 'pull' architecture. While, as Scharfman points out, consumers under a 'push' architecture may be confronted with an inadequate, ill-chosen and inappropriate supply of intelligence, under a 'pull' architecture, the collecting agency is always in danger of being overwhelmed by demands which exceed its resources or its ability to fulfil. The 'pull' agency is a potential victim of its consumers, especially where that agency is seen as being a vehicle of deniable actions which its consumers wish to undertake but are averse to the risk involved. As will be seen below, from its very inception, even before the proposal and implementation of the '1921 arrangement', SIS was envisioned not as an independent operational agency, but as a deniable – and expendable – covert extension of departments of State such as the War Office and the Admiralty. Just as the history of SIS has been one of continued collegiality and increasing organicism, it has also been a history of SIS being progressively brought back into the fold of avowed government and politics, from deniable and expendable 'screen' to legally sanctioned government agency more than 80 years later. And if, as has been suggested, it was a new generation of 'young Turks' in SIS who 'lobbied hard' for putting the service on a statutory footing,[60] in the wake of affairs such as Ordtec and Matrix Churchill,[61] it will almost certainly have been as much a matter of organizational self-defence as one of public accountability.

NOTES

1. Sherman Kent, *Strategic Intelligence for US World Policy* (Princeton: Princeton University Press, 1949), p. 69; Kent also observes in the same vein on that page 'Intelligence is an institution: it is a physical organization of living peoople which pursues the special kind of knowledge at issue.'

18

2. The term 'national intelligence machinery' is one of relatively recent vintage, appearing in the current published version of the Cabinet Office's Central Intelligence Machinery. See http://www.archive.official-documents.co.uk/ document/caboff/nim/natint.htm. Previous versions have simply referred to Central Intelligence Machinery, pivoting around the Cabinet Office Joint Intelligence Committee, as in the *Central Intelligence Machinery* booklets of 1993 and 1995 (London: HMSO). Even the JIC's designation has been variable, with the 1983 *Franks Report* referring instead to a Joint Intelligence Organization, in conjunction with unspecified 'Intelligence and Security Agencies' (London: HMSO, 1983). Unlike the American intelligence community which developed on the basis of a relatively concrete idea of where it stood in US institutional and constitutional political structure, the UK intelligence system has throughout displayed a much more ad hoc development, as will become increasingly apparent throughout the following historical narrative.

3. Alan Judd (Alan Petty), *The Quest for C: Mansfield Cumming and the Founding of the Secret Service* (London: Harper Collins, 1999), pp. 167, 230, 263–4.

4. This assertion depends really on the assumption that we are talking about intelligence in a liberal-democratic state. As authors such as John Dziak, *Chekisty: A History of the KGB* (New York: Ivy, 1988), pp. 1–4, 15–19 and Christopher Andrew have pointed out, intelligence in totalitarian states serves a very different purpose. Intelligence in autocracies is more to do with pursuing and suppressing dissidents and 'counter-revolutionaries' than policy.

5. The essential distinction between formal and informal modes of organization resides in the distinction between how people are supposed to do things on paper, 'officially', and how they 'actually' go about them in practice. Hence the notion of informal organization subsumes a whole gamut of profoundly different items such as the distinction between people's official status and their personal authority with their subordinates, the divergences between 'by the book' procedure and unofficial 'work-arounds' and the turning of blind Nelsonic eyes in the interests of efficiency and/or expediency. The classic studies which developed the notion of informal organization were Peter Blau's study of the US Federal Bureau of Investigation, Peter M. Blau, *The Dynamics of Bureaucracy* (Chicago: University of Chicago Press, 1963, 2nd edn) pp. 121–230 and Alvin W. Gouldner's examination of a gypsum mine (Gouldner, Alvin, *Patterns of Industrial Bureaucracy* (London: Routledge & Kegan Paul, 1995) *passim*).

6. i-15.

7. This complaint is leveled at GCHQ throughout Hugh Lanning and Richard Norton-Taylor's *A Conflict of Loyalties: GCHQ 1980–1991* (Cheltenham: New Clarion, 1991); for the Security Service, see the very stern evaluation that appears in the Security Commission report on Michael Bettaney, *Report of the Security Commission* (London: HMSO, 1985; Cmnd 9514).

8. See, for example, Harold Wilensky, *Organizational Intelligence: Knowledge and Policy in Government and Industry* (New York: Basic Books, 1976) *passim* but especially pp. 41–62, and Walter Laqueur, *A World of Secrets: the Uses and Limitations of Intelligence* (New York: Basic Books, 1985) *passim*.

9. Hugh Trevor-Roper (Lord Dacre) *The Philby Affair* (London: William Kimber, 1968), p. 69.

10. The feud between Claude Dansey and Valentine Vivian is a staple of wartime intelligence literature, featuring in H.A.R. ('Kim') Philby's often pernicious *My Silent War* (New York: Ballantine, 1983) p. 59 and *passim*, and similarly throughout Anthony Read and David Fisher's biography of Dansey, *Colonel Z: Secret Life of a Master of Spies* (London: Hodder & Stoughton, 1984) pp. 234–5, and Robert Cecil '"C's" War', *Intelligence and National Security*, 1, 2 (April 1986), pp. 176–9, the classic account perhaps being that in Ladislas Farago's *The Game of Foxes: British and German Intelligence Operations and Personalities Which Changed the Course of the Second World War* (London: Hodder and Stoughton, 1971), but it recurs in the literature.

11. Anthony Verrier, *Through the Looking-Glass: British Foreign Policy in an Age of Illusion* (London: Jonathan Cape, 1983) pp. 62–3.

12. Anthony Verrier, *Through the Looking-Glass: British Foreign Policy in an Age of Illusion*, pp. 62–3 infra.

13. See, for example, Richard Norton-Taylor's obituary of Sir Dick White, *Guardian*, 23 February 1993, and, far more recently, Tom Bower, *The Perfect English Spy* (London: Heinemann, 1994), pp. 165–84 and *passim*.

14. Harry Howe Ransom, *The Intelligence Establishment* (Cambridge, MA: Harvard University Press, 1970), pp. 203–4.

15. See, for example, Jeffrey T. Richelson, *Foreign Intelligence Organizations* (Cambridge, MA: Ballinger, 1988), essentially a book of 'org charts' for various non-US countries; also his *The US Intelligence Community* (Cambridge, MA: Ballinger, 1989), and, with Desmond Ball, *The Ties That Bind* (Boston, MA: Unwin, 1985).

16. See, for example, Scott D. Breckenridge, *The CIA and the US Intelligence System* (Boulder, CO: Westview, 1986) and Lyman B. Kirkpatrick, *The US Intelligence Community: Foreign Policy and Domestic Activities* (New York: Hill and Wang, 1973).

17. See, for example, the CIA Intelligence Directorate's 1996 Strategic Plan, *Analysis: Directorate of Intelligence in the 21st Century* (Washington, DC: Central Intelligence Agency, 1996); also the World Wide Web site of the new National Imagery and Mapping Agency (NIMA), which has recently taken over the once highly secret National Reconnaissance Office (NRO) and the overhead imagery elements of the CIA's Directorate of Scientific and Technical Intelligence (DSTI), downloadable http at: *http://164.214.2.53*, download date 12 October 1997.

18. Harry Gelber, review of Richelson and Ball's *Ties That Bind, Intelligence and National Security*, 2, 1 (January 1987), p. 198.

19. See, variously, the preface to West's *GCHQ: The Wireless War 1900–1986* (London: Weidenfeld & Nicolson, 1986), charts provided in *MI6: British Secret Intelligence Operations 1909–1945* (London: Grafton, 1988) pp. 19–23 followed in due course by a less graphical organization summary for 1946 in his *The Friends: British Post-War Secret Intelligence Operations* (London: Weidenfeld & Nicolson, 1988), p. 14. West follows the same pattern in his *MI5: British Security Service Operations 1909–1945* (London: Triad/Granada, 1981), pp. 25–33 and his subsequent *A Matter of Trust: MI5 1945–72* (London: Weidenfeld & Nicolson, 1982), pp. 12–15. Despite criticism for 'schoolboy errors' by Christopher Andrew and David Dilks, *The Missing Dimension: Governments and Intelligence Communities in the Twentieth Century* (Chicago: University of Chicago Press, 1984), p. 3, and despite the fact that the following study will necessarily expose a number of errors in West's work on SIS, his thoroughness remains commendable, and when the present author went through West's MI5 charts with a senior former Security Service official, he remarked that the charts were, for the most part, accurate, although West made some errors concerning the various incumbents in those offices in a couple of cases. In conversation with West, he remarked to the present author firmly that one cannot properly understand an intelligence service without understanding its organization, much the same hypothesis as is developed in this study.

20. Christopher Andrew, *Secret Service: The Making of the British Intelligence Community* (London: Sceptre, 1987), pp. 408, 488–90. Oddly enough, Andrew does not perform a similar stocktaking for either the Security Service or GCHQ.

21. Robert Cecil, 'MI6' in I.C.B. Dear and M.R.D. Foot (eds), *Oxford Companion to the Second World War* (Oxford: Oxford University Press, 1994), p. 745. Cecil, who held the senior position of PA/CSS during the war was well equipped to provide an accurate description, but the chart attempted to extend itself forward in time over the six-year duration of the war, as well as laterally across the division of labour and vertically up the chain of command. The result was somewhat overloaded, and hard to follow. Prior to his death, Cecil informed this author in conversation that he had provided the same chart to West during the preparation of the latter's *MI6*. West's final result deviates significantly from Cecil's, possibly because of West's attempt to synthesize Cecil's chart with the German report, 'Der Britisch Nachrichtendienst', reproduced in translation as an appendix to West's book. The original German report is currently on display at the Imperial War Museum; a cursory inspection of this volume in company with the author by one of the officers interviewed in this study elicited a muttered, 'Well, they got that wrong ... and that ...'

22. Duncan Campbell, 'Friends and Others', *New Statesman and Society* 26 November 1982. The overall accuracy of Campbell's charts was explicitly vouched for by i-29, while interview data from i-20 and i-28 will be seen to confirm and elaborate Campbell's information.

23. Richard Norton-Taylor, *In Defence of the Realm?* (London: Civil Liberties Trust, 1990); the chart on p. 62 is drawn from Campbell's 1982 publication, while the summary on p. 50 is drawn in part from Anthony Cavendish's description of SIS structure in 1948, and West's slightly muddled summary from the Friends of the SIS organization in 1946.

24. Weber, *Economy and Society*, translated by Gunther Ross and Klaus Wittich (London: University of California Press, 1978), pp. 956–8.

25. The misreading described is perhaps most clearly expressed in Michel Crozier, *The Bureaucratic Phenomenon* (London: Tavistock, 1964), pp. 175–8, in which he reviews both Weber and subsequent empirical sociologies of management and the workplace to conclude on p. 177 that 'Research has demonstrated that the ideal type of bureaucracy is far from being completely efficient.' Rosemary Stewart makes much the same mistake, but shrouds her misreading of Weber in reciting an unattributed set of criteria, taken all but verbatim from *Society and Economy*, but presenting the approach so thinly that it is, at best, a straw man of the original, which she then finds conveniently easy to knock down, in her *The Reality of Management* (London: Heinemann, 1963) pp. 5–19. Gouldner, in his 'Discussion of Industrial Sociology', *American Sociological Review*, 13 (1948), *passim*, develops his criticism of Weber and advocacy of the notion of informal organization on the basis of Weber's ideal type being a set of 'incomplete' hypotheses. Similar interpretations are developed by Charles H. Page, 'Bureaucracy's Other Face', *Social Forces*, 25 (1946), *passim*; T. Burns, G.M. Stalker, *Management of Innovation* (London: Tavistock, 1961), pp. 105–6, Peter M. Blau and Marshall W. Meyer, *Bureaucracy in Modern Society* (New York: Random House, 1987), *passim*; and, more recently, Jan-Erik Lane, *The Public Sector: Concepts, Models and Approaches* (London: Sage, 1993), pp. 49–54. Part of the problem may lie in the translation of Weber's work, described by one pair of translators (Hans Werth and C. Wright Mills) as almost incomprehensible 'gothic castles' even in the original. Nonetheless, German scholars have, as a general rule, displayed less discomfort with the essence of Weber's concepts of modernization and bureaucratization than Anglophone writers; see, for example, the works of Jürgen Habermas and Niklaus Luhman.

26. Weber refers at a number of points to bureaucracy being 'fully' and incompletely 'developed', that is, the degree to which any specific organization follows the internal logic of bureaucratic organization or alternative, outside considerations such as status, personal affiliation, or even leaving matters undefined to allow innovation and initiative – an aspect

of 'incomplete bureaucratization' that will become increasingly important shortly.

27. Weber, *Economy and Society*, p. 278.
28. Ibid., pp. 271–2.
29. See, for example, Martin Albrow *Bureaucracy* (London: Macmillan, 1970), p. 47.
30. Weber, *Economy and Society*, p. 277.
31. Ibid., p. 273.
32. T. Burns and G.M. Stalker, *Management of Innovation* (London: Tavistock, 1961), pp. 120–2. See also Paul R. Lawrence and J.W. Lorsch, *Organization and Environment: Managing Differentiation and Integration* (Boston: Harvard University Press, 1967), *passim*.
33. Kenneth Knight, 'The Compromise Organization'.
34. Hugh Heclo and Aaron Wildavsky, *The Private Government of Public Money* (London: Macmillan, 1974); this publication is one of the key works that have given rise to the 'policy networks' approach in political science, essentially a specialized branch line in the study of informal organization. See, for example, R.A.W. Rhodes and David Marsh, 'Policy Networks in British Politics: A Critique of Existing Approaches', in Rhodes and March (eds), *Policy Networks in British Government* (Oxford: Clarendon, 1992); or, more recently, Martin Burch and Ian Holliday, *The British Cabinet System* (London: Prentice-Hall/Harvester Wheatsheaf, 1996), pp. 81–105.
35. Geert Hoffstede, 'Motivation, Leadership and Organization: Do American Theories Apply Abroad?', in D.S. Pugh, *Organization Theory*, 3rd edn (London: Penguin, 1990), pp. 473–99.
36. Blau, *Dynamics of Bureaucracy*.
37. British Broadcasting Corporation, 'On Her Majesty's Secret Service', *Panorama*, BBC Television, 22 November 1993.
38. Michael Herman, *Intelligence Power in Peace and War* (Cambridge: Cambridge University Press, 1996), pp. 114–18.
39. Herman observes that 'distinguished US practitioners' tend to go with the broad definition, although senior British practitioners have expressed this view. See, for example, Jeffrey T. Richelson, *The US Intelligence Community* (Cambridge, MA: Ballinger, 1989), p. 1 or Michael Herman, *Intelligence Power in Peace and War* (Cambridge: Cambridge University Press, 1996), pp. 114–18.
40. K.G. Robertson, 'Intelligence, Terrorism and Civil Liberties', *Conflict Quarterly*, 7, 2 (Spring 1987), p. 46.
41. See, for example, Michael Herman, *Intelligence Power in Peace and War* (Cambridge: Cambridge University Press, 1996), pp. 9–10.
42. Parris, Henry, *Constitutional Bureaucracy: The Development of British Central Administration Since the Eighteenth Century* (London: Allen and Unwin, 1969).
43. K.G. Robertson, *Public Secrets* (London: Macmillan, 1987).

44. Reginald Hibbert, 'Intelligence and Policy', *Intelligence and National Security*, 1, 5 (October 1995), p. 112.
45. Reginald Hibbert 'Intelligence and Policy', p. 113.
46. Philip H.J. Davies, 'Organizational Politics and the British Intelligence Producer/Consumer Interface', *Intelligence and National Security*, 10, 4 (October 1995), pp. 113–32.
47. H.S. Rowen, 'Reforming Intelligence: A Market Approach', in Roy Godson, Ernest R. May and Gary Schmitt (eds), *US Intelligence at the Crossroads: Agendas for Reform* (London: Brassey's, 1995), pp. 233, 241.
48. Use of the push/pull paradigm was originally applied to intelligence in H.S. Rowen, *Reforming Intelligence: A Market Approach* (Washington, DC: Consortium for the Study of Intelligence, 1993). Reprinted in Roy Godson, Ernest R. May and Gary Schmitt (eds), *US Intelligence at the Crossroads: Agendas for Reform* (Washington, DC: Brassey's, 1995), with many thanks to Professor H. Bradford Westerfield of Yale University for securing me a copy of this piece. Michael Herman has also taken up the push-pull discussion in his *Intelligence Power in Peace and War* (Cambridge: Cambridge University Press, 1996), although his arguments and conclusions will be discussed in the conclusion of this study.
49. Walter LaQueur, *World of Secrets*, pp. 20–7. Michael Herman, *Intelligence Power in Peace and War*, pp. 284–6. Note that in recent years an alternative five-step version of the cycle has been in currency, consisting of: Direction (which amounts to tasking); Collection; Collation (in which raw intelligence is compiled into intelligence databases); Interpretation (that is, analysis) and Dissemination. See for example, John Hughes-Wilson, *Military Intelligence Blunders* (Robinson: London, 1999) pp. 6–15, or the CIA website www.cia.gov. For the sake of simplicity rather than currency, the older version is here employed.
50. I am indebted to Michael Herman for this description of the role of the JIC.
51. Peter Scharfman, 'Intelligence Analysis in the Age of Electronic Dissemination', *Intelligence and National Security*, 10, 4 (October 1995) pp. 201–2.
52. Ibid., p. 202.
53. Ibid., p. 202 *infra*.
54. Ibid., p. 203.
55. Ibid., p. 203 *infra*.
56. Ibid., p. 203 and *passim*.
57. For a more general examination of the demand-driven nature of SIS, GCHQ and the JIC (but not MI5), see Philip H.J. Davies, 'Organizational Politics and the Development of Britain's Intelligence Producer/Consumer Interface', pp. 113–32.
58. See ibid., and for greater detail 'From Amateurs to Professionals: GC & CS and Institution-Building in SIGINT' in Michael Smith and Ralph Erskine (eds), *Action This Day* (London: Transworld, 2001), pp. 386–402.

59. F.H. Hinsley, E.E. Thomas, C.F.G. Ransom and R.C. Knight, *British Intelligence in the Second World War: Its Influence on Strategy and Operations*, vol. I (London: HMSO, 1979), p. 17.

60. James Adams, *The New Spies: Exploring the Frontiers of Espionage* (London: Hutchinson, 1994), pp. 101–2.

61. In both situations, SIS was forced to disavow its British voluntary informants, or 'alongsiders', who were tried for export-control violations despite making those shipments with the knowledge of SIS and in support of SIS intelligence gathering for Whitehall on the Iraqi covert arms procurement network, and a number of whom eventually went to prison. See Richard Scott, *Report of the Enquiry into Export of Defence Equipment and Dual-Use Goods to Iraq and Related Prosecutions* (London: HMSO, 1996), 5 vols. Although the SIS testified in defence of Matrix Churchill's Paul Henderson, the defendants in the Ordtect trial refrained from invoking their SIS connections in court and were, as a result, convicted and sent to prison. Under the 1994 Act, any comparable operation breaching British legislation would have to be covered by an authorization signed by the Secretary of State, which could be cited in a court of law in defence of both the agent and SIS.

2

Origins and the First World War
1903–18

It is ridiculous to imagine that any clever Officer can at a moment's
notice be transformed into an efficient Intelligence Officer.
'Secret Service in the Event of a European War'[1]

ORIGINS OF A SECRET SERVICE

The manner in which the Secret Intelligence Service (SIS) came into
being is in no small way vital to understanding the fundamental
relationship between it and the rest of the British government. This is
because the very departmental interests and bureaucratic power
politics of Whitehall and Downing Street that drove its creation have
remained essentially the same *raison d'être* for the agency and its
basic terms of employment ever since. SIS was originally one half of
the Secret Service Bureau (SSB) of 1909, the other half being the
Home Section at nascent Security Service, MI5. As a result, the
conditions and rationale for the creation of the SSB were also the
conditions and rationale for the existence of SIS. Therefore, to
understand why SIS has developed the way it has, it is necessary to
look at the origins of the SSB.

The essential purpose of the SSB was never to function as an
independent operational entity comparable to the Admiralty or a
military GHQ. From its very inception, it was intended to act as a
sort of institutional 'cut-out' between the War Office and the
Admiralty (and later, more grudgingly, the Foreign Office) and the
outside world, where the dirty work of spying was actually done. The
central concern of the Cabinet decision that created the SSB was not
the creation of a secret service organization. Such a body already
existed in the form of the War Office 'Special Section', albeit on a

very humble scale and with chronically limited resources. Rather, the fundamental concern in creating the SSB, at least in terms of foreign operations, was to provide a screen, or institutional cut-out, between the intelligence-using departments of State in Whitehall and any operations in the field which might be detected and exposed. That function, as institutional cut-out and operational armature acting at the behest of the wider, overt British government has remained SIS's role to this very day.

Discussions of the origins of SIS and MI5 via the short-lived SSB have typically been somewhat paradoxical. On the one hand, they have commonly argued for a sort of political 'big bang' hypothesis in which the modern secret services were created out of a sudden groundswell of political concern, driven by a widespread 'spy scare' inspired by popular authors and journalists, which affected the political leadership of the day as moral panics are wont to do. On the other hand, the same authors are equally at pains to point out the roots of the SSB in the earlier War Office Special Section, created near the end of the Boer War and at various points in its short history labelled I3, MO3 and MO5.[2] Although originally created as a temporary arrangement, like previous campaign and theatre-level intelligence offices, MO5 survived the interval between the Boer War and the 1909 creation of the SSB in varying degrees of institutional health and capability. In 1905, it even began offensive intelligence efforts against Germany

During the nineteenth century, intelligence arrangements tended to be set up as required in campaign and theatre military commands, but as essentially ad hoc, short-term arrangements. Apart from postal interception by the Secret Department of the Post Office (abolished in 1840), there was no precedent for a permanent, central secret service. Specific officers were charged with setting up intelligence organizations during a campaign, such as in the fighting against Napoleon in the Iberian Peninsula,[3] but, here again, there was no continuity of personnel or administration between campaigns, and on each occasion the departments were dismantled after the war and capabilities and know-how had to be reassembled from scratch.

The crucial event in the initial creation of a permanent secret service department was the Boer War in South Africa. The British Army went into South Africa grievously ill-equipped in terms of intelligence as well as almost everything else. The War Office set up a field intelligence department in South Africa but this was shut down as soon as the conflict ended, just like its earlier predecessors. Concurrently, however, the War Office set up Section H in its Intelligence Department (ID) in London. Section H was responsible for 'Special Duties' including 'Secret Service', counter-intelligence and censorship. Section H was headed by Major James Edmonds (the future official historian of Britain's part in the First World War). Shortly thereafter, in 1901, as Christopher Andrew has noted, the Directorates of Intelligence and of Mobilization were amalgamated and Section H was 'superseded' by sub-section I.3.[4]

I.3 was, in its original form, a fairly sizeable concern by War Office standards with three sub-sections and more than thirty staff under the Assistant Quartermaster General, Colonel J.K. Trotter. Under Trotter, I.3(A) consisted of three officers, including two future heads of the section, Brevet-Lieutenant Colonel F.J. Davies and Brevet-Major G.K. Cockerill, and one clerk. It was tasked with a range of functions that included 'special duties' (a standard euphemism in War Office practice for secret intelligence, especially human intelligence), as well as censorship, interrogation of prisoners of war, ciphers and 'government telegraph code', licences for newspaper correspondents and finally, and, perhaps most tellingly, 'noting warlike stores'. In practice, I.3(A) was responsible for covert reconnaissance and planning agent-running operations. I.3(B) was responsible for the 'compilation of all maps for military purposes' and the various activities required for that compilation, while I.3(C) was the map room. I.3(B) was the most substantial subsection, composed of three officers, one superintending clerk, three military clerks, 15 lithographic draughtsmen, three lithographic printers, two stone grainers, and one photographer. These elements, then, inherited something of the very early Topographical and Statistical Department's role in intelligence history. Finally, I.3(D) was the intelligence department library, run by a librarian called Huddleston (plus one assistant and a bookbinder), who would remain in that position throughout the ensuing years including the First World War.[5] In many respects, I.3 was a surprisingly prescient creation, very much a central military intelligence department. It had access to information from agents and cable intercepts; in time of war, it would also have access to information from censorship (a highly productive area of collection in both World Wars) and from the licensing and debriefing of war correspondents. It also had what would now be termed an 'open-source intelligence' (OSINT) function through

Huddleston's library, which included in its work 'examination of English newspapers, and English and foreign general literary magazines'.[6]

In the wake of the Boer War and the subsequent Royal Commission, the Directorate of Mobilization and Intelligence was abolished, with mobilization moved to Training and intelligence absorbed into a combined Directorate of Operations and Intelligence. Under this transformation, I.3 became MO3. It has been argued that in the course of this restructuring, I.3(A) was dismantled and its officers returned to their regiments after the war, despite Trotter's plea for secret intelligence to be placed on a permanent footing.[7] If so, this was a very brief hiatus because in a year or so both Davies and Cockerill were back in harness in I.3's successor.[8]

Under the reorganization of intelligence, the work of I.3's map-making work and map room had been dispersed to the various geographical sections of the Directorate of Military Operations and Intelligence. What remained of I.3 was redesignated MO3, which collectively was known simply as the 'Special Section' and was divided into MO3(a) and MO3(b), under the control of Brevet-Colonel F.J. Davies, previously head of I.3(A). MO3(a) retained the special duties, submarine cables and wireless telegraphy tasks, and MO3(b) was now Huddleston's Library. MO3's administrative brief within the directorate was also expanded to include 'Correspondence relating to Appointments and Promotions in the Directorate, and to the employment of Officers and others in connection with it' and the 'Interior economy of the Directorate'. This division of tasks remained the same, even as Davies departed the section and was replaced by the head special duties officer Brevet-Major G.W. Cockerill around 1906, although MO3 was by now designated MO5. Later, in 1907, Cockerill was in turn replaced by the former head of Section H, Lieutenant Colonel James Edmonds.[9] Although a part of the War Office, the Special Section functioned as an inter-departmental secret service, operating also on behalf of the Admiralty and the Foreign Office, and drawing some of its operational funding from ad hoc disbursements from the Foreign Office portion of the Secret Vote, sometimes for as little as £2 to pay for a particular agent's services. When submitting its financial requests, MO5 also sometimes had to secure the signed support of representatives of the directorates of the War Office and Admiralty that the operation was necessary and its product actively sought by those departments.[10]

If the formative event in MO3's creation was the Boer War, that was also the formative event in its institutional thinking. MO3 was small, and its budget almost prohibitively limited; thus, its immediate concern was planning and preparation for an operational role in subsequent major conflicts, particularly the likelihood of a general war in continental Europe, as embodied in plans formulated and put down on paper in 1905. Built on the practical, operational experience of intelligence work in South Africa, Davies's MO3 plans for mobilization in the event of war were singularly prescient, including a range of methods and concepts that would characterize SIS operations not only during the First World War, but also for a long time thereafter. MO3 did not try to argue a case for a large-scale peacetime intelligence service. Instead, it echoed the prevalent view of the day that because Britain was an island with no extensive land frontiers to guard, it was not necessary to 'maintain an army of spies constantly in our neighbour's territory to report his slightest movements'. What was required, however, was to create a 'paper organization' and to 'earmark' potential intelligence officers who could be activated and 'put into efficient operation during that period of strained relations, which is practically certain to lead to war', leading to a fully mobilized wartime organization.[11]

There were three items in MO3's plan of 1905 that were prescient in the extreme. The first was a scheme analogous to the Third Country system that remains the standard operational doctrine in SIS to this day. The second was a proposed field organization that anticipated the operational infrastructure of Cumming's wartime MI1c in almost every respect. The third was a model of integrated tasking, collection, evaluation and even all-source analysis that both put intelligence collection into a more comprehensive context than previous ad hoc arrangements had imagined, and also anticipated the need for a tasking, collation and analysis architecture that would not systematically evolve until the interwar period.

MO3 proposed dividing the field organization between 'observers', 'carriers', 'collectors' and 'forwarders'. 'Observers' were described bluntly as 'spies, pure and simple'; in other words, agents. The notion of a 'carrier' included both that of a straight courier transporting information and that of a cut-out who provides a protective screen for the agent, relaying the observer's information back to the collector. Collectors, would-be intelligence officers and their collecting stations were to be responsible both for receiving

30

information from 'observers', and for evaluating and interpreting that material (what we would nowadays refer to as the 'take') in conjunction with information from all other sources available. The collector would have to 'sift the information received, discarding what is valueless, and condensing and editing what is useful. ... The Collector must also obtain information by other means in his power, and it will be his responsibility to carefully and systematically study every available newspaper published in the enemy's country, for the supply of which he must arrange.' The collectors would then pass their product either directly to the Directorate of Military Intelligence or to a senior government official, in all likelihood 'the nearest Ambassador, Minister, or salaried Consul', who would relay it by secure communications such as diplomatic bag.[12]

To a very real degree, the collectors were the key element in this scheme. They would be based in friendly or neutral countries, and then work across the frontier between that country and the hostile state that was the target. Just as in the Third Country scheme today, the resident station would not operate against its host government, but against neighbouring countries. They were responsible for local control of operations and recruitment of 'observers' and 'carriers', and had to be able to process the take their stable of 'observers' generated and turn it into what is in today's parlance called the 'product', meaningful, useable source reports. This also tied the collectors to their expected consumers in the War Office. MO3 concluded that potential collectors would have to be very carefully selected, because 'they must possess not only tact, patience, and an intimate acquaintance with the language, military organisation, and characteristics of the enemy with whom they have to deal, but also a knowledge of war and a previous military training which will enable them to sift information and accurately judge the military situation'. As part of the proposed 'earmarking' process, potential collectors should be drawn from 'that sub-section of the Military Operations Directorate which deals with the enemy's country', one member of which should be assigned the task in peacetime, mainly as a sideline over and above routine duties in the home geographical sub-section.[13] An almost identical arrangement would emerge after the war in the form of the '1921 arrangement'.

When Edmonds took over MO5 in 1907, he found that, far from getting its proposed manpower increases and funding for its earmarking programme and 'paper organisation', it had been starved of funds and reduced to barely a handful of officers. Nonetheless, international situation had deteriorated considerably in the previous two years, and, as a result, that same year he was authorized by the Director of Military Operations, Major-General John Ewart, to begin mounting operations in and against Germany, a development which drew vigorous support from the Director of Naval Intelligence (DNI), Rear-Admiral Edmond Slade, who had taken on the post of DNI only to discover that the Admiralty had no organized secret service at all.[14]

Despite the emphasis on foreign intelligence in its 1905 scheme, Edwards's MO5 found itself responsible for both offensive intelligence collection and defensive counter-intelligence work against foreign espionage against Britain (counter-intelligence in the empire was the immediate task of the relevant colonial governments and administrations[15]). Therefore MO5 and its War Office and Admiralty consumers also concerned themselves with attempts to detect and monitor German secret service activities directed against and within Britain. In December 1908, the Admiralty forwarded a request to MO5 that one of its officers, retired Special Branch officer William Melville (who also handled MO5 human sources on the continent) and an assistant go to Dover to try to detect the expected arrival of the 'chief of the German Secret Service at Brussels', who was expected to make a secret visit to the UK from Ostend over the Christmas week. When Melville requested the assistance of the local CID, the request was turned down by the head of the local CID on the grounds that 'if [their] assistance came to light, there might be awkward questions asked in Parliament'. An MO5 minute on the incident in February 1909 complained that 'Without the assistance of all the Departments of State there can be no effective system of contre-espionage [sic].'[16] Even with the support of the War Office and the Admiralty intelligence branches, MO5 seemed a voice in the wilderness where the rest of British government was concerned.

Planning for a larger-scale, offensive intelligence capability was not confined to the military minds at MO5, however. The Foreign Office was also engaged in the formulation and consideration of plans for a foreign intelligence system in 1905. However, where MO5 thinking focused on operations in support of military requirements, the Foreign Office approach focused on economic information. Economic intelligence was not a new notion to the British government, but previously the emphasis had been upon state-gathered OSINT in support of British private commercial enterprise abroad.[17] Since 1901, the Board of Trade had maintained a 'Commercial Intelligence Branch', the function of which was to gather commercial information abroad which could be provided in support of British firms trading in the foreign countries it covered.[18] The Foreign Office's proposals were, however, of a different order, directed as they were towards 'the establishment of a permanent organisation for obtaining information of all the contracts made by foreign governments for the supply of such stores as may be required in the active operations of war, and of the collection of such stores in such places, or under such circumstances, as may indicate their intended application in premeditated operations'.[19] As a result, the proposed organization would be located within the Foreign Office's Commercial Department.[20]

Foreign Office thinking also proposed a version of the Third Country scheme, and shared MO5's concerns that a new intelligence organization would have to 'grow under prudential guidance, and cannot be suddenly launched into existence as a complete and manifestly active institution'.[21] However, unlike MO5's plans to expand its own collection capabilities, the Foreign Office approach was more inclined to seek information and assistance from non-governmental, British interests already active abroad, such as private firms and business associations. Lloyds and the London Chamber of Commerce were viewed as institutions that might be able to provide the Foreign Office organization with information circulating in the business community. There was even the suggestion that private firms should be employed to collect information on the new agency's behalf, one proposal suggesting that 'in one or two of the more important capitals, it might be possible, by the expenditure of a small sum annually, to persuade British private enterprise contractors to establish agencies for the purpose of obtaining information concerning the requirements of foreign governments, treating the question as a matter of ordinary business, and tendering for the supply of such articles as may be included within their ordinary sphere of business.'[22] Apart from relying on the generosity of the British business community abroad, and possibly hiring commercial firms to act as collectors, it was also cautiously suggested that the new agency might approach 'foreign consular agents, preferably from the minor powers, requesting from them services similar to those which it is proposed be rendered by our own consular agencies.

33

These foreign gentlemen could best be approached by their British colleagues resident in the same countries with them.'[23]

Where MO3's plans of 1905 were greeted with an almost complete lack of interest and absence of practical follow-up, the Foreign Office approach ran aground on traditional diplomatic dismay at something as unsavoury as spying. At least one British Minister abroad, Alan Johnstone in Copenhagen, was tactfully aghast, responding to the proposal that he thought it 'undesirable that members of His Majesty's Embassies and Legations should be in any way connected with Espionage in the country in which they are temporarily resident'. While he acknowledged that the mooted scheme involved operating against a third country, and not that hosting them, he remained earnest that 'Embassies and Legations should have as little as possible to do with such matters; which should be left to specialists. Any connection of a diplomatist with espionage which got to the ears – say of the German Foreign Office – would militate very significantly against such diplomatists in future times in Germany.' In good diplomatic style, Johnstone quickly qualified his condemnation of the scheme with the disclaimer that 'I pretend by no means to be right in this matter, and can only record my honest conviction'.[24]

There are two crucially important aspects of both the MO5 and the Foreign Office intelligence plans in understanding the origins of the SIS. In the first place, both schemes were formulated in or around 1905, well before 'spy mania' had really built up momentum, and hence could not be ascribed in the first instance to pressure resulting from agitation by William Lequeux and his ilk. In the second place, both proposals were concerned with *offensive intelligence collection*, and not merely with defensively countering a perceived, foreign espionage threat. The implication of these two features, especially the emphasis on offensive collection operations, is that there was already an established demand for espionage in existence in British defence and foreign policy circles. Such a demand for foreign intelligence necessarily sprang from very different motives than simply a defensive fear of German espionage against Britain, even if both 'spy mania' and the need for foreign intelligence certainly sprang from common roots in the increasingly fraught international situation. That demand for offensive intelligence remained relatively unfulfilled because of the lack of resources and infrastructure, and perhaps because of a lack of political will to create that infrastructure.

34

As is so often the case, where demand cannot be met by available supply, there develops a 'black market' for the goods in question. In this case, once the Committee of Imperial Defence convened a subcommittee on the matter of espionage in 1909, the Foreign Office was to discover that British diplomatists had been conducting precisely the kind of secret service work abroad that it had been at pains to oppose four years earlier. Among those revelations was the fact that British vice-consuls in Germany had been going around the country taking photographs of military installations, noting the movements of warships and so forth on behalf of the Admiralty.[25] While that persistent need for covert foreign intelligence might not have driven the creation of a CID inquiry into foreign espionage in Britain, it ultimately lay at the heart of that inquiry's conclusions and recommendations.

Exactly what prompted the formation of a 'Sub-Committee of the Committee of Imperial Defence Appointed by the Prime Minister to Consider the Question of Foreign Espionage in the United Kingdom' remains somewhat unclear. The general consensus appears to be that a combination of spy and invasion scares, fed and amplified by the alarmist fiction of figures such as William LeQueux, led to a swell of panic which included the politicians and officials on the CID and in MO5, or at least that the phenomenon led to public pressure, especially in the Tory press, upon these individuals, amounting to a conviction that 'something should be done'.[26] There can be no doubt that much of the information presented to Haldane's CID subcommittee was exaggerated, erroneous and, in some cases, even fraudulent.[27] It might indeed be charitable to suggest that Edmonds, in his presentations to the sub-committee, simply erred on the side of caution, but although the danger of German espionage may have been the central rationale for the inquiry, it was not the sole or even major component of its conclusions. Even as the Haldane Committee weighed the evidence of foreign spies afoot in Britain, it also noted that:

> It was represented to the sub-committee that our organisation for acquiring information of what is taking place in foreign ports and dockyards is defective, and this is particularly the case with regard to Germany, where it is difficult to obtain accurate information. The Admiralty and the War Office also pointed out that they are in a difficult position when dealing with foreign spies who may have information to sell, since their dealings have to be direct and not

through intermediaries. They are therefore compelled to exercise precautions in order to prevent the Government from becoming involved, which would be unnecessary if an intermediary who was not a Government official was employed in negotiations with a foreigner.[28]

One can see in these words both the sobering news of the 'black market' in espionage involving British officials abroad, as well as the kind of concerns that had informed the Foreign Office and MO5 proposals for a foreign intelligence system. This extract is particularly telling when one examines the actual, substantive proposals that resulted from the Committee's deliberations.

At the end of its deliberations, the Haldane Committee concluded that Britain needed a new, single Secret Service Bureau (SSB) the functions of which were

> (a.) To serve as a screen between the Admiralty and War Office and foreign spies who may have information that they wish to sell the Government.
> (b.) To keep in touch with the Home Office, who would nominate an officer for the purpose, with the county and borough police, and, if necessary, to send agents to various parts of Great Britain with a view to ascertaining the nature and scope of espionage that is being carried on by foreign agents.
> (c.) To serve as an intermediary between the Admiralty and the War Office on the one hand, and the agents we employ in foreign countries on the other.[29]

The peculiarity of these recommendations lies in the fact that a CID inquiry into the threat from espionage in the UK by foreign countries ended up proposing arrangements by which the UK could go about conducting its own espionage against those same foreign countries. Item (b) certainly provided for a counter-intelligence role, but both items (a) and (c) were concerned with foreign intelligence, and, perhaps more interestingly, cast the role of the SSB not as independent intelligence service but as 'screen' and 'intermediary' working on behalf of the Admiralty and the War Office. In other words, *two out of the three priorities for the proposed SSB concerned foreign intelligence, and not domestic counter-intelligence*, this foreign intelligence to be collected on behalf of the Admiralty and the War Office. This alone places a question mark over the adequacy of the prevalent 'spy mania' explanation for the creation of the SSB. Had counter-espionage and defence been the only priority at work, items (a) and (b) would simply have been surplus to requirements. A more plausible reading of events might be that the invasion and spy scares which had been building up since the Boer War provided a window of opportunity for the War Office and the Admiralty to mobilize support within government and the civil service for the kinds of changes and expansions to the machineries of intelligence and defence that they had been advocating and inconsistently pursuing since the turn of the century. As a result, any upgrading of intelligence machinery in 1909 was no more than consistent with phenomena such as the naval arms race and the colonial confrontations that were part and parcel with the escalating tensions presaging the general war in Europe that had been widely anticipated since the late nineteenth century.

The appearance of the SSB, and in due course its Home and Foreign Sections, therefore, was, to a very real degree, one more manifestation of the slide to war which so characterized the first decade of the twentieth century. While MO5's proposals for an upscaled secret service on the Continent in the event of a general war may have appeared stillborn to their authors in 1905, the events of the next half decade after 1909 would lead to the development of a wartime SIS that conformed to MO5's plans in almost every respect. Unfortunately, the brief burst of political will that had created the SSB proved short-lived. Once the bureau had been created, its masters in Whitehall and Downing Street seemed more than a little at a loss about what to do with it. As a consequence, the organization languished until that long-anticipated general war in Europe finally broke out.

By November 1909, the SSB was established, absorbing and taking over the work and resources of MO5a, but leaving MO5b unaffected. The financial arrangements which had prevailed for MO5a were slightly modified. The Foreign Office would continue to fund the new bureau, but the moneys would be channelled through the War Office rather than separately, as had previously been the case.[30] Once established, the Admiralty and the War Office each provided its own appointee to start setting up the bureau. The War Office appointed a serving officer, Captain Vernon Kell, while the Admiralty turned to a retired naval commander, mainly active only in terms of planning and evaluating the Navy's 'boom defence' system,

Mansfield Smith-Cumming. Almost immediately after their appointment, the two divided work between them such that domestic counter-espionage was to be handled by Kell, and foreign offensive espionage, the remit of Cumming. According to evidence from both Kell's and Cumming's diaries, it was quickly felt by the two officers that the two sides of their work had very little in common. Each began looking for separate quarters for his work, and, by 1910, the bureau found itself, de facto, if not yet *de jure*, divided by the mutual consent of both parties involved, into two separate organizations.[31]

One needs to be as clear as possible about what the creation of the SSB entailed in machinery-of-government terms. MO5 was not abolished on the creation of the new bureau, but continued under the new leadership of a future director of military intelligence (MI), and a crucial influence in the later development of the SIS, Colonel William J. MacDonogh. All that had in fact happened was that the 'special duties' part of MO5's remit had been hived off to the new bureau while the rest of its work description continued unchanged. Now more prosaically but less clearly designated the 'Miscellaneous Section', MO5 still housed the General Staff library (still run by Huddleston, aided by one assistant, two military clerks and a bookbinder),[32] and therefore acted as the main centre for information, and hence intelligence, storage, collation and dissemination. This had two implications for the development of the new bureau, and especially Cumming's foreign secret service side. The first implication was that MO5 was to act as the main War Office customer for Cumming's department, laying requirements upon his nascent organization in parallel with those from NID. The second, and more difficult, implication was that MO5 retained the records and institutional experience of the previous seven years of special duties work. The upside of this was that MacDonogh arranged for Edmonds to meet with both Cumming and Kell, and give them a skeletal training in agent running, clandestine communications, and the other rudiments of tradecraft his section had acquired or developed.[33] The downside was that MacDonogh proved completely unwilling to allow 'special duties'-related documentation to leave his offices for inspection by Cumming at the bureau's initial offices at Victoria Street, and was vaguely uncooperative about allowing Cumming access to them at all, even on War Office premises.[34] No such restraints were imposed upon the War Office's appointee, Kell, and for much of his first year, Cumming feared that the War Office was determined to oust him from his position.[35]

A more persistent problem was that of trying to accommodate two different customers, each with voluminous demands for secret intelligence, and always under a profoundly limited budget. In particular, while the Admiralty requirements focused on ongoing and timely reporting of developments in German shipyards and naval technology, the War Office was more concerned with early warning indications of an impending outbreak of war.[36] These two requirements necessitated very different kinds of agents, and each would probably have been sufficient to swallow up the complete resources of Cumming's department. As a result, Cumming spent much of his time shuttling between the Admiralty and the War Office, playing both ends against the middle as it were, while occasionally turning to the Foreign Office as a relatively neutral mediator and referee. The Foreign Office enjoyed much of its neutrality in these discussions on the grounds that it was not actually a consumer of the Foreign Section's product (it was determined that political intelligence should remain solely a Foreign Office domain), even though it funded Cumming's work.[37]

Despite briefing from Edmonds, eventual on-site access to MO5's operational files and even inheriting a small stable of agents, Cumming found himself, otherwise, an agency of one man. For much of the first year, he was forced to meet agents in Britain and on the Continent himself, and was reliant on contacts in the War Office and the Admiralty passing likely potential agents to him.[38] He did eventually acquire a part-time deputy in the form of an NID officer, who divided his time and efforts between the Foreign Section and his home department, and would eventually set up Cumming's first foreign residency in Brussels in 1913.[39] Cumming's ability to find and recruit really good agents was also hobbled in part by rivalry for control of what agents could be found between the Admiralty, MO5 *and* Kell's Home Section, and himself, and in another part by his limited access to UK government facilities abroad. The Foreign Office's determination to retain exclusive control of political intelligence, and its sensitivity to diplomatic nicety that defeated its own foreign intelligence proposal, also meant that Cumming was forbidden access to members of the consular service abroad. This proved a major stumbling block, as consular officers would naturally have had the best access to both British and foreign nationals whom

Cumming might have recruited as agents.[40] Despite these limitations, Cumming's Foreign Section achieved a surprising degree of success, especially in terms of German war preparations.[41]

THE FOREIGN SECTION AND THE FIRST WORLD WAR

With the outbreak of the First World War, and that conflict's evolution into a European land war rather than a maritime and colonial campaign, the operational and intelligence emphases shifted from the Admiralty to the War Office. Under mobilization, both the Foreign Section and the Home Section found themselves once again sub-sections of the War Office in general, and back within MO5 in particular, the former as MO5j and MO5t respectively.[42] However, in the War Office reorganization of 1915/16, in which the Directorate of Military Intelligence was finally re-established, the two sections were placed under the DMI. The Home Section became MI5, while the Foreign Section became a sub-section of the MI secretariat as MI1c (although it continued to be funded by an allocation from the Foreign Office Secret Vote).[43]

The Foreign Section's transfer to the War Office and its designation as MI1c has recently been a matter of some uncertainty, particularly in light of Alan Judd's recent assertions (based primarily on Cumming's diary) that the transfer was little more than a War Office (read: MacDonogh's) claim to suzerainty over Cumming's agency and its work. It was, he argues, 'never accepted' inside SIS itself, and then adds that there were *two* entities identified as MI1c, one the Secret Service proper, and the other a War Office section run by a Colonel Dansey responsible for military agent networks on the Continent and liaison with the Secret Service.[44] However, even a brief inspection of the *War Office Lists* of the period shows that SIS was listed throughout as MI1c, with Cumming and his immediate senior staff resident in London given as its members. As a result, even if SIS did not view itself as MI1c, the rest of the British government almost certainly *did*. Moreover, the only Dansey listed in the Directorate of Military Intelligence is the only Major C.E. Dansey (almost certainly Claude Dansey, who will figure ever more centrally in the history of SIS), and he was, as late as 1917, attached to Kell's MI5. In that capacity, he was in charge of MI5c, given as 'Military policy connected with control of civilian passenger traffic

Captain Sir Mansfield Smith Cumming, the first 'C'

to and from the United Kingdom. Passes and permits for the "zone des armées". Port Intelligence.'[45] As we shall see below, this latter range of functions would necessarily have brought him into regular and close contact with Cumming's department because SIS was responsible for counter-espionage and, increasingly, movements control abroad. As a result, by late 1917, Dansey had moved horizontally to become fully employed by Cumming at MI1c.[46] Therefore, regardless of the Secret Service's preferred self-perception, in machinery-of-government terms, SIS was indeed *formally* subordinate to the DMI, although given the service's inter-departmental responsibilities, that was undoubtedly more a matter of form than content.

Having operated prior to the war on a very limited scale, with only a single foreign residency in Brussels, and everything else done directly from London, the ex-Foreign Section now had to scale up its operations, and integrate them into the machinery of wartime military organization. The resulting MI1c field organization conformed almost exactly to the scheme developed in the 1905 MO3 report. It set up bureaux, 'collecting stations', in neutral countries, and ran networks of agents through cut-outs and couriers – 'Observers' and their 'Carriers' – across the borders into enemy territory. As in the 1905 proposal, much of the collation work was done at the bureau before being forwarded to London or the theatre GHQ, and, to a large degree, the local bureaux came under the immediate authority of the theatre command or Foreign Service Head of Mission. The only major feature of MI1c bureau organization which did not have a precedent in the MO3 proposals was counter-espionage.

The initial wartime organization of Cumming's MI1c was tenuous at best, and highly decentralized. Cumming's dislike of 'bureaucratic routine' is a standard of SIS history,[47] and the surviving first-hand accounts of MI1c work during the war uniformly point to an organizational structure in which the bulk of the day-to-day administrative work and operational responsibility was in fact farmed out to the regional 'bureaux' abroad. Indeed, in December 1914, the staff at Cumming's headquarters at Whitehall Court consisted of only 'four officers [including Cumming], four clerks, two typists...one messenger and two "outside men"'.[48] Several environmental factors seem to have operated to create this system beyond any preferred informality of organization. A major consideration was that British military and diplomatic administrations were themselves highly decentralized, particularly under the authority of the theatre GHQs in Europe and the Mediterranean. The immediate subordination of the foreign bureaux to them, rather than to Whitehall Court or the War Office, derived generally from the overarching authority of the theatre GHQs. Of course, any direct central control from London would moreover have been severely limited by the relatively unsophisticated wireless telegraphy of the day.

A typical regional bureau arrangement existed at the Rotterdam bureau, in which the offensive intelligence side was divided into a Naval Section and a Military Section, alongside the defensive counter-Espionage Section, with the Military Section concerned with operations about German military activities and passing its product to the British military attaché for local assessment, and the Naval Section performing the equivalent tasks concerning German naval matters. There were also a finance officer and a general office 'factotum'.[49] A similar pattern can be discerned in the development of the Aegean Intelligence Service (AIS), set up by Compton Mackenzie for MI1c after the Allied occupation of Greece (Figure 2.1). In the eastern Mediterranean, the Eastern Mediterranean Special Intelligence Bureau (EMSIB), integrated into the GHQ at Alexandria (from 1917, in Cairo), organized its remote offices into an A Bureau, handling espionage, and a B Bureau, dealing with counter-espionage, with one or two staff to handle administration.[50] In 1917, after the Allied occupation of Greece, the EMSIB branch based at Syra absorbed the other Aegean bureaux, was made independent of Cairo and became answerable instead to the British Naval Authority under the Vice-Admiral of the Eastern Mediterranean Squadron. In this capacity, the new Aegian Intelligence Service (AIS) under the control of Compton Mackenzie (previously responsible only for the counter-espionage B Bureau at Athens and later Syra) was organized along much the same lines as it was under EMSIB, but with a number of extensions to its internal formal organization.

Under Mackenzie, the AIS consisted of five sections: A Section, responsible for offensive espionage; B Section, dealing with counter-espionage; C Section, dealing with the predominantly maritime concerns of submarines and contraband; D Section, handling finance, personnel and relations with the MI1c headquarters in Whitehall Court; and MC Section, handling passport control, a function the Syra bureau had taken on by default because of the central role of its counter-espionage work in granting or withholding of travel permits

43

(see below).[51] Thus, apart from the passport control duties, the AIS moved in 1917 towards essentially the same organizational structure as the Rotterdam bureau, essentially on the basis of the specialized interests of the GHQ consumers the two bureaux were servicing.

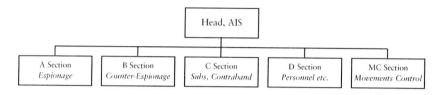

Figure 2.1: The Aegean Intelligence Service (AIS) in 1917

Organizations rarely function in practice as they have been expected to during planning. In the case of SIS, evidence rapidly began to accumulate that there was a sizeable omission in pre-war thinking about collection operations, an omission deeply rooted in Cumming's own approach to the agency. That omission was counter-intelligence.[52] Compton Mackenzie recalled his first superior in Athens, who used the cryptonym 'V', complaining to him that 'Contre-espionage in a neutral country is always unsatisfactory. C will never allow much money for it.'[53] Later he added that 'C doesn't like spending money on contre-espionage, for after all…the real object of C's organization is to obtain information about the enemy.'[54] V may have overstated C's aversion, as Cumming certainly accepted that his personnel would engage in 'a little second rate CE work'.[55] In any event, regardless of Cumming's preferences, counter-espionage proved to be both qualitatively and quantitatively a sizeable portion of the work undertaken by MI1c's foreign bureaux. Throughout his memoirs, Mackenzie stresses his conviction that counter-espionage was crucial to the secure running of offensive intelligence lines,[56] and the card indices and black lists compiled and maintained by bureaux in neutral countries were essential to the military movements control system.[57] One indication of the scale of work undertaken in counter-espionage or 'B' work in Greece was that Mackenzie's Athens B Section found itself in danger of running out of file cards when its list of names topped 400 in 1915 – but two years later it routinely dealt with a card index that 'by now contained over 20,000 names, and the relevant information in files could not

ORIGINS AND THE FIRST WORLD WAR

have occupied less than a quarter million typewritten pages'.[58] Despite this, counter-intelligence and counter-espionage were viewed by Cumming as a side issue and would continue to be treated as such until the end of his term as chief.

By 1916, Cumming counted among his assistants Lieutenant Colonel F.H. Browning, Cumming's deputy chief and Brevet-Major T.B. Traill.[59] Commander Percival 'Pay' Sykes, RN, was already in harness as the MI1c financial officer, a position he would hold well into the Second World War.[60] In October, the headquarters staff had grown to 60 persons[61] organized mainly around geographical sections controlling the work of the various foreign bureaux.[62] Despite Cumming's resistance to counter-espionage, the volume of this work and its tendency to cross borders and jurisdictions led to the creation of a 'central bureau' whose function was to collect and collate the information generated by the different regional bureaux' counter-espionage operations,[63] and which may have been the precursor of the agency's Central Registry. The headquarters complement also included a small Air Section housed at separate premises that may have dealt with monitoring German airfields, sabotage and homing pigeons, the last of which SIS increasingly relied on for communications with its train-watching networks behind enemy lines.[64]

MI1c efforts were complicated, however, by the fact that it did not hold a monopoly on human intelligence operations. Prior to the outbreak of war, the Foreign Section's operators had, on a number of occasions, been endangered by 'amateur' clandestine reconnaissance missions by military officers for the War Office.[65] During the war, the recently formed Intelligence Corps found itself deprived of its usual means of reconnaissance and gathering of tactical intelligence by the Continental breadth of the trench line which spanned from neutral Switzerland in one direction to neutral Netherlands and the North Sea in the other. As a result, the War Office set up two human intelligence-gathering organizations to gather what information they could about enemy forces and movements at a tactical level, a General Staff organization working through the Netherlands out of Folkestone, and the other run by the War Office out of London. The result of this proliferation of HUMINT organizations was a considerable degree of confusion, line-crossing and devalued information collection, even though the two military units were supposed to be confined to strict geographical jurisdictions, and there was supposed to be a fundamental difference between Cumming's organization, which was geared to *strategic* intelligence, and the two War Office units geared to *tactical* intelligence. As a result, there developed an extended campaign of what would today be termed 'turf wars' between the various organizations, a fact which mitigated against their acquiring sufficient, timely or reliable information.[66] There was also a separate human intelligence network run by NID under Admiral Sir Reginald 'Blinker' Hall, but this was set up in consultation with Cumming and operated without any particular friction between the two departments.[67]

Friction with the other War Office agent-running operations and perceived underproduction of the kind of intelligence required led almost inevitably to a confrontation not merely between SIS and its consumers but between the consumers themselves. Whether or not SIS was guilty of genuinely failing to produce intelligence that adequately met the requirements laid upon it, qualitatively or quantitatively, is a chronic problem in evaluating the agency's work throughout its history. In times of real crisis, the demand for intelligence is potentially unlimited, and no volume can be 'sufficient'. SIS was not without productive sources such as the Belgian White Lady (*Dame Blanche*) network that watched trains,[68] or the well-placed and reliable German marine engineer Herman Krueger known by his Dutch station controllers by the symbol TR 16 or simply (albeit inaccurately) as 'the Dane'.[69] MacDonogh had been pressing for de facto if not *de jure* control of the new service since serving as head of MO5, and, as DMI, his determination had redoubled. He had developed a series of proposals to tighten the responsiveness of Cumming's organization to its consumers in general and MI in particular. At a meeting on 22 October at the War Office that Judd notes, 'Cumming attended but was not allowed to speak', MacDonogh, according to Cumming's diary, said that he wanted a revision of the MI1c's internal organization that would 'do away with divisions by Geographical [*sic*], and substitute sub-divisions, so that the military would be self-contained and his Military staff would be able to control more directly the Agents (Head) in the field'. MacDonogh also criticized the state of MI1c's administrative machinery, complaining that it 'lacked a good organization section resembling that in MI5'.[70]

MacDonogh's plans for MI1c reached potentially far further than just a reorganization along functional lines. He had a more ambitious scheme in which the Foreign Office, the War Office and the Admiralty would attach representatives to SIS to articulate their home departments' needs, albeit under Cumming's overall control. This scheme, as we shall see below, has generally been regarded as the most significant transformation in SIS internal organization in its history, although existing literature has always attributed it to the deliberations of the post-war Secret Service Committees of 1919 and 1921. The official history even goes so far as to label it the '1921 arrangement', although it attributes the idea to the Secret Service Committee of 1919. Alan Judd's recent biography of Cumming (based on closed SIS papers including Cumming's diary) makes a convincing case for dating the substance of the '1921 arrangement' four years earlier, attributing it not to a committee but to MacDonogh in 1917. Judd even goes as far as to term the scheme the 'MacDonogh Reforms', echoing the judgement that the staff secondment scheme was vital to the future evolution of SIS. However, Judd's own formulation of events is far from clear on the degree to which MacDonogh's scheme was implemented. He shows, for example, that Cumming's initial attempts to accommodate MacDonogh's ideas mainly involved reorganizing his own internal staff along the proposed functional lines. Out of a meeting between himself, Browning and Claude Dansey (who had evidently by now made his transfer from MI5 to the Secret Service) Cumming proposed a functional division composed of 'Air: Smith; Economics: Browning; Military; Dansey...; Sommerville Naval and for Organization a good, strong character whom [MacDonogh] will get for us'.[71] The liaison section secondment scheme was not yet, therefore, in question, as these were all MI1c personnel.

On 29 November, Cumming received instructions to revise his internal organization along the proposed functional lines, and on 2 December found himself 'trying to fit the new Sections and dependants into the rooms at our disposal so as to keep the flocks around their shepherds. Trying to let every officer retain the Secretaries he is accustomed to working with and make each Section complete in itself with an adequate staff.'[72] At the end of it, Cumming's headquarters staff was reorganized into a range of functional sections (Figure 2.2) 'with such titles as Economic, Air, Naval, Military, Political, while other sections were responsible for personnel, movements, cover, liaison, escape plans, communications and secret devices'.[73] Under the discussions that gave rise to the MacDonogh scheme, the SIS also

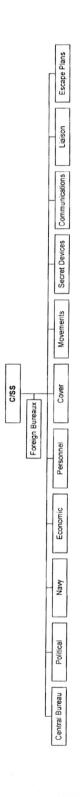

Figure 2.2: SIS in 1918

received authorization to gather political intelligence on behalf of the Foreign Office. In March 1918, Cumming set up an 'intelligence bureau' for the Foreign Office manned by Sir William Tyrrell, formerly senior clerk at the Foreign Office and private secretary to the Foreign Secretary,[74] who would 'receive all our reports and be solely responsible for their distribution'.[75] Judd has noted Cumming's lack of resistance over this external intrusion into the internal management of his service, although it is imperfectly clear whether this was out of any genuine agreement with the MacDonogh scheme or simple defeatism.[76] His agency, after all, had been in a chronically weak political position since its inception. It is worth keeping in mind, however, that, as we have seen in Rotterdam and Syra, a number of his foreign bureaux were already organized along similar lines. As with the MacDonogh scheme in London, this was to accommodate the specialized needs of the theatre military and naval authorities as represented by the local Service Branch attachés. In other words, the adoption of functional 'reporting sections' was not a wholly radical and unprecedented development in SIS management practice. With its consumers at least partially appeased, at least for a time, the MacDonogh scheme provided Whitehall Court's internal organization for the remainder of the war, and created the foundation for the basic internal structure which characterizes SIS to this day.

There is an old saying that one should begin something as one intends to continue it. In the case of SIS, the agency began very much as it was doomed to continue, whether it wished to or not. It was not to provide for any new kind of activity, but to provide a 'screen' mainly for the Admiralty and the War Office to maintain a vaguely, plausibly deniable distance for secret service work they would have been engaged in anyway. The rationale for the creation of SIS, therefore, was not a desire to begin spying at last, but a desire to minimize the political and diplomatic risks associated with spying – particularly the spying that was already going on through a sort of internal black market in intelligence. This is particularly clear in the confusion surrounding who should contact, run and pay agents during the first year or two of the SSB's creation. The use of Cumming's side of the bureau as an operational armature, rather than a 'screen', developed later. By the same token, once the consumers began to employ the SIS as a mechanism for extending the reach of covert human intelligence collection, rather than as an acutely subordinate intermediary in the conduct of that work, they began to express anxiety about the agency's comprehension of their exact intelligence requirements. The early history of SIS is, therefore, characterized by one persistent paradox. That paradox was that *SIS's consumers in Whitehall were almost exactly as unwilling to delegate responsibility for spying to a separate agency as they were unwilling to go about doing it themselves and risk getting caught.*

If anything is to be drawn from the early days of its development, and the considerations and conclusions of the Haldane Committee, it is that the Foreign Section of SIS was never envisioned as being an independent organization, not even from the beginning. From its very inception, SSB was to be a piece of governmental machinery working on behalf of, and according to the demands and priorities of those parts of the machinery of government that were to be the consumers of its intelligence product. SIS was to be beholden to others, from the very outset. It was precisely that beholden nature that shaped the agency's experience of the First World War, less in terms of its operational work than in the nearly impossible task of satisfying customers frantically in need of raw intelligence in a runaway crisis and war that had escalated, and deteriorated, beyond all expectations for four years. The post-war reflection, reviews and reorganization that led off the inter-war years might try to ameliorate some of the dilemmas and difficulties incumbent upon SIS's role in British government, but as we shall see in the remainder of this tale, they could not really be resolved and done away with. When an organization is little more than a screen, armature or servant, it is all too easy for the demands of its masters to exceed its abilities. And that is a problem of those masters, not the agency. But no real solutions would be forthcoming until SIS's masters in Whitehall and Downing Street were willing to see their own role in the problem.

NOTES

1. HD 3/124, PRO.
2. See, for example, F.H. Hinsley, E.E. Thomas, C.F.G. Ransom and R.C. Knight, *British Intelligence in the Second World War: Its Influence on Strategy and Operations*, Vol. I (London: HMSO, 1979), p. 16; and Nigel West, *MI6: British Secret Intelligence Operations 1909–1945* (London: Grafton, 1988), p. 29. The 1909 SSB figures also in the service's oral tradition; see Nigel Clive, *A Greek Experience 1943–1948* (Wilton, Wiltshire: Michael Russell, 1985) p. 20.

3. For discussions of the successive, fixed-term, campaign intelligence arrangements, see, for example, Christopher Andrew, *Secret Service* (London: Sceptre, 1987), pp. 21–66; Thomas Fergusson, *British Military Intelligence 1870–1914* (Frederick, MD: University Publications of America, 1984); or Jock Hasswell, *The First Respectable Spy: The Life and Times of Colquhoun Grant* (London: Hamish Hamilton, 1969). With reference to the Secret Department of the Post Office, see K. Ellis, *The Post Office in the Eighteenth Century* (Oxford: Oxford University Press, 1958).

4. C.M. Andrew, *Sacred Service*, pp. 60–2.

5. *War Office List*, 1903, p. 47.

6. Ibid., 1908, p. 46.

7. It has been suggested by Christopher Andrew that I.3a was abolished and its officers returned to their regiments (*Secret Service*, p. 62). This seems unlikely.

8. The question of I.3's transition to MO3, especially I.3a, is a matter of some vagueness in the literature and documentary record. Andrew maintains firmly that it was dismantled and its three officers 'returned to their regiments' (*Secret Service*, p. 62). However, the *War Office Lists* of the period create a firm impression of unbroken continuity, with Davies replacing Trotter as Head and Cockerill remaining in harness in MO3a. This impression is particularly strong if one examines I.3 as a whole, and not simply I.3(A) on its own, where, apart from the dispersal of map-making, the section remained relatively unaffected by the amalgamation of operations and intelligence. To complicate matters, PRO historian Louise Atherton asserts briefly and obscurely that MO5, 'established during the Boer War... was reactivated', *Top Secret: An Interim Guide to Recent Releases of Intelligence Records at the Public Record Office* (London: PRO, 1993), p. 10, but it is unclear whether she means I.3 was 'reactivated' or Section H was reactivated in the form of the I.3/MO3 lineage. Moreover, Fergusson in his British Military Intelligence refers to Trotter as being the first head of MO3 (p. 222), as would almost certainly be the case if I.3 were simply reconstituted as MO3 rather than abolished and reconvened. In the last analysis, while there may have been a break between Section H and I.3a, it is unlikely that a comparable discontinuity existed between I.3 and MO3. If there was one, it must have been a hiatus so brief as to be almost notional.

9. *War Office Lists* for 1905 and 1907. Andrew, *Secret Service*, pp. 88–9; Michael Smith, *New Cloak, Old Dagger: How Britain's Spies Came in From the Cold* (London: Gollancz, 1996), p. 44.

10. Letter to the Undersecretary of State at the Foreign Office, 1 June 1909, in HD 3/139 PRO. See also, for a more sizeable funding request in 1908, a request from Edmonds to the Foreign Office, countersigned in support by representatives of both the War Office and Admiralty, also in HD 3/139. See also Hiley, 'Failure of British Espionage Against Germany', *The Historical Journal*, Vol. 26, no. 4 (1983), p. 874.

11. 'Secret Service in the Event of a European War', cover letter dated 17 October 1905, HD 3/124, PRO.
12. Ibid.
13. Ibid.
14. Andrew, *Secret Service*, pp. 89–90.
15. See, for example, Richard Popplewell's excellent history of Indian political intelligence, *Intelligence and Imperial Defence: British Intelligence and the Defence of the Indian Empire 1904–1924* (London: Frank Cass, 1995).
16. MO5 minute foliated with Edmonds's Intelligence Division accounts for January 1909, HD 3/139, PRO.
17. The very notion of national intelligence operations conducted in support of private sector interests resurfaced at the end of the Cold War in debates over the post-Cold War role of the intelligence services.
18. 'Historical Sketch of the Department of Overseas Trade' in BT 61/60/8, PRO.
19. 'Proposal for an Intelligence Organization', cover letter dated 17 October 1905, HD 3/124, PRO.
20. Ibid.
21. Ibid.
22. Ibid. It is impossible to ignore how this aspect of the report foreshadows the intelligence and commercial affiliations which would become the centre of almost frantic public and political attention during the 1990s in the 'supergun affair', the Matrix Churchill trial and the subsequent Scott Inquiry.
23. 'Proposal for an Intelligence Organization'.
24. 'Secret Memorandum', 17 October 1905, HD 3/128, PRO.
25. Hiley, 'Failure of British Espionage Against Germany', p. 875.
26. These two hypotheses are developed by both Andrew in his *Secret Service*, pp. 69–101, and more recently Michael Smith in *Old Cloak, New Dagger*, pp. 45–7.
27. Andrew and Smith both trace examples of this, Andrew in particular pointing to a set of probably false invasion plans provided to MO5 by a French informant, which Edmonds himself would eventually admit to being so many years later (*Secret Service*, pp. 98–9). However, such exaggeration is really no different from the dubious, hawkish estimates and propaganda tactics employed by the US Department of Defense to secure development funds throughout the Cold War. In other words, *Tous qui changes, tous qui restes les même choses.*
28. 'Report and Proceedings of the Sub-Committee of the Committee of Imperial Defence Appointed by the Prime Minister to Consider the Question of Foreign Espionage in the United Kingdom', CAB 61/8, PRO.
29. Ibid.
30. Sir Edward Grey to Sir Charles Hardinge, 4 November 1909, in HD 3/138, PRO; Judd, *Quest for C*, pp. 73, 87.

31. Judd, *Quest for C*, pp. 103, 151–3, 168; Andrew, *Secret Service*, pp. 101, 123.
32. Judd, *Quest for C*, p. 89; *War Office List 1910*, p. 48.
33. Judd, *Quest for C*, pp. 97, 116–17.
34. Ibid., pp. 99–101, 102. An interesting item here is that once Cumming did get access to MO5's papers in 1909, MacDonogh apparently lent him a copy of 'the "scheme" made out some four years ago', i.e., in 1905, almost certainly the MO5 scheme described above. On p. 132, Judd argues that Cumming came up with the Third Country system for deploying agents into 'hard target' states from neighbouring neutral ones, in a 1910 report to MacDonogh, but he must already have encountered the technique in the 1905 'scheme', and cannot, therefore, be said to have developed the method himself.
35. Judd, *Quest for C*, p. 115.
36. Ibid., p. 151.
37. Ibid., pp. 87, 123.
38. This occurred repeatedly throughout the first year or so of the Foreign Section's existence; see, for example, Judd, *Quest for C*, pp. 119–22, 127.
39. Ibid., p. 124.
40. Ibid., p. 111.
41. Andrew, *Secret Service*, pp. 126–30; Judd, *Quest for C*, pp. 131–228. It is notable the degree to which evidence compiled by Andrew and Judd reverses the previously pessimistic assessment developed by Nicholas Hiley in his 'Failure of British Espionage Against Germany, 1907–1914'.
42. Michael Occleshaw, *Armour Against Fate: British Military Intelligence in the First World War* (London: Columbus, 1989), p. 146; F.H. Hinsley and C.A.G. Simkins, *British Intelligence in the Second World War: Counter-Espionage and Security* (London: HMSO, 1990), p. 4 and Andrew, *Secret Service*, p. 259.
43. Andrew, *Secret Service*, p. 211. Andrew has described this arrangement as 'an administrative anomaly', but, as War Office 'Special Section' documents released into the PRO under the 'Open Government' initiative in 1993, and Judd's recent biography of Cumming clearly indicate, this was precisely the funding arrangement adopted in 1909 to fund the SSB, and evidently the 1916 arrangements represent continuity rather than discontinuity.
44. Judd, *Quest for C*, pp. 302–3, 389.
45. *War Office List 1917*, p. 84.
46. *War Office List 1918*, p. 110.
47. Andrew, *Secret Service*, p. 408.
48. Judd, *Quest for C*, p. 290.
49. Henry Landau, *All's Fair: The Story of British Secret Service Behind German Lines* (New York: Putnam, 1934), p. 43.
50. Compton Mackenzie, *Greek Memories*, (London: Cassell, 1939), p. xii;

Mackenzie notes that the Athens office of EMSIB was organized in this fashion 'as usual', and also in *Aegean Memories* (London: Chatto & Windus, 1940), p. 51 he notes that the Salonica branch had the same organization until it was 'purged' by GHQ in Egypt during late 1916, eliminating the A Bureau and reducing the counter-espionage, B Bureau to a skeleton staff.

51. Mackenzie, *Aegean Memories*, pp. 262–7.
52. The idea of counter-intelligence appears a somewhat fraught matter in the jargon of intelligence. In early usage this century, one was generally most likely to see the French *contre-espionnage* or its more Latinate equivalent, *contra-espionnage*. In current parlance, one is more likely to encounter *counter-intelligence*, but even this is sub-divided into counter-espionage, that is, penetrative espionage against a hostile intelligence service, and counter-intelligence proper, which involves monitoring and intercepting hostile intelligence operations on the ground. Throughout the following, the contemporary usages of 'counter-intelligence' and 'counter-espionage' will be employed, except in quotations from the period.
53. Mackenzie, *First Athenian Memories* (London: Cassell, 1931), p. 13.
54. Ibid., p. 75.
55. Judd, *Quest for C*, p. 393.
56. See, for example, Mackenzie, *Greek Memories*, p. 102.
57. Ibid., pp. 1–7, *Aegean Memories*, pp. 263–6; Landau, *All's Fair*, pp. 161–2.
58. Mackenzie, *Aegean Memories*, p. 263.
59. Judd, *Quest for C*, pp. 354, 390; Michael Occleshaw, *Armour Against Fate*, p. 390.
60. Landau, *All's Fair*, p. 43.
61. Judd, *Quest for C*, p. 354.
62. Ibid., p. 389.
63. Mackenzie, *Greek Memories*, p. 129.
64. Judd, *Quest for C*, p. 354.
65. Andrew, *Secret Service*, pp. 130–2.
66. Detailed accounts of these 'turf wars' have been provided by both Andrew, *Secret Service*, pp. 195–258, and Michael Occleshaw, *Armour Against Fate*, pp. 144–80 and *passim*.
67. Andrew, *Secret Service*, p. 179.
68. For the White Lady network, see variously Henry Landau *All's Fair: The Story of British Secret Service Behind Enemy Lines* (New York: Puttna, 1934) *passim* as well as his *Spreading the Spy Net* (London: Jarrolds, 1938) *passim* also. See also Judd, *Quest for C*, pp. 359–69.
69. Krueger, aka TR 16, makes a brief appearance in Landau's *All's Fair*. However, the only detailed description of this German working for British intelligence appears in Chapter 12 of Judd's *Quest for C*. According to Judd (pp. 342–4), TR 16, almost certainly Krueger, continued to provide intelligence to the Dutch station until his capture shortly before the

outbreak of the Second World War – and reported execution five weeks after the outbreak of war. Judd also notes (p. 345) that SIS officialdom blamed Krueger's arrest and execution on information published by Landau, although Judd attributes the failure to 'a combination of ill-luck and neglect of elementary procedure: allowing one agent to learn the identity of another'.

70. Judd, *Quest for C*, p. 389.
71. Cumming's diary, quoted in Judd, *Quest for C*, p. 392.
72. Ibid., p. 393.
73. Judd, *Quest for C*, p. 391; note also that Paul Dukes recalls reporting to Cumming's 'Political Section' for his work in the newborn USSR around 1918, in his *The Story of ST 25: Adventure and Romance in Red Russia* (London: Cassell, 1938), p. 30.
74. *Who Was Who, 1941–1950*, pp. 1174–5.
75. Cumming's diary quoted in Judd, *Quest for C*, p. 419. Judd adds, rather speculatively, that 'this sounds like a form of assessment unit, a foreshadow perhaps of the later Joint Intelligence Committee'. This is incompletely consistent with his reference to Tyrrell tasking Sir Paul Dukes in subversive efforts in 'Red Russia' (and, indeed, Dukes refers to himself being tasked by the head of the SIS Political Section, and even gives a cautious and elliptical, unnamed description of Tyrrell in that capacity).
76. Judd, *Quest for C*, p. 393, records Cumming's own assessment as follows: 'I don't quite see the way clear, but if it will keep each man to his own business it ought to improve the present system which allows agents to send in anything from abroad so long as there is plenty of it – all trade stuff with a little second rate CE work.'

3

The Inter-war Years, 1919–39

The attention of the Committee has been drawn to the difficulties imposed on our Secret Service by lack of funds. . . . If the allowance under its head is not augmented, and very largely augmented, the organization cannot be expected to fulfil its functions, and this country will be most dangerously handicapped.

'Defence Requirements: Programmes for the
Defence Services', 1936[1]

INTRODUCTION

If the period prior to the First World War was the period that led to the creation of the Secret Intelligence Service (SIS), it was the inter-war period in which it most developed the trappings of a truly modern secret service. It was during this interval that the agency acquired that distinctive internal tasking and dissemination architecture the official history terms the '1921 arrangement', which remains almost unique to the agency 90 years later. As a result, the years from 1919 to 1939 are the crucial period for understanding the fundamental relationship between the SIS and its masters in Downing Street and Whitehall, and its essential status and function within the machinery of British central government.

In terms of the SIS experience of the era, the inter-war years can be divided into two distinct chronological phases, and two distinct structural trends in its internal organization. The two historical phases are a bit more than a decade of post-war demobilization, recession and retrenchment between 1919 and 1932, and a second interval of just less than a decade of escalating international tensions between 1932 and 1939, terminating with the outbreak of the

Second World War. The two structural trends within the SIS were the establishment and progressive elaboration of the intelligence producer–consumer interface in government on the one hand, and the technical and technological elaboration of the business of spying on the other hand. The former of these was very much imposed from without, a consequence of the struggle for control of human intelligence operations that resulted from the First World War 'turf wars'. The latter was a result of internal initiatives, chiefly on the part of the SIS's second Chief of Service, or 'C', Admiral Sir Hugh 'Quex' Sinclair. Cumming may have been the founding father of the SIS, but it was Sinclair who displayed a real vision of how a national intelligence service should work, what it should be capable of, and what it needed to be able to do to fulfil those requirements. Where Cumming had been ambivalent about the role of any counter-intelligence or counter-espionage effort, Sinclair was determined to incorporate those functions centrally within SIS's work and organization. Cumming's MI1c had dabbled passingly and amateurishly in political operations in the nascent Soviet Union, but Sinclair sought to create a permanent subversion and sabotage arm within his agency. Where Cumming's headquarters had been loose and informal, Sinclair's displayed real attempts to formalize and rationalize administration and finance. Under Sinclair, the SIS took on the desperately secret work of opening foreign diplomatic bags on behalf of the Foreign Office. When the Passport Control Organization that Cumming had worked so hard to acquire as standing cover for his post-war foreign bureaux looked as if it might have been compromised, Sinclair set up an auxiliary field organization under a notionally dismissed officer to provide a back-up capability. Finally, it was Sinclair who confronted the new technologies and intercontinental scale of secret intelligence operations through the creation of a covert, secure clandestine radio network that linked SIS HQ to its stations abroad and their agent networks in the field. But, in the last analysis, no amount of rationalization or innovation by the new C was going to be enough to compensate for the crippling effects of recessions and international depression, and the comprehensive financial retrenchments of an increasingly economically beleaguered succession of governments, especially once confronted with the rapid escalation of tensions with what would become the Axis powers.

TASKING, OPERATIONS AND DISSEMINATION: THE '1921 ARRANGEMENT'

The end of the First World War prompted a comprehensive review of Britain's defence and intelligence needs, including the intelligence services. When Cabinet convened the first of a series of Secret Service Committees in 1919 to review post-war intelligence needs, the committee was confronted with the dual problems of a failure to fulfil consumer intelligence requirements on the one hand, and operational hazards from poor interorganizational coordination in the field on the other hand.[2] According to the official history of British intelligence in the Second World War, one of the main conclusions of the Secret Service Committee of 1919 was that to 'safeguard the interests' of the agency's major consumers, 'the intelligence branch in each of the three Services came to house one of its sections in the SIS, where it formed a part of the HQ staff'.[3] Thus, the service branches, and in due course the Foreign Office and others, would have a direct input to operational targeting and planning, and would also have members of their staff indoctrinated into SIS's sources of information. The official history of British intelligence in the Second World War refers to this consumer liaison system as the '1921 arrangement', although, as we have already seen, Alan Judd has compellingly argued that the essence of the 1921 arrangement had already been formulated in what he calls the MacDonogh reforms of 1917. The details Judd provides from Cumming's diary strongly suggest that the original, functional reorganization of Whitehall Court into 'reporting sections' was *internal*, and that the consumer liaison dimension of the MacDonogh reforms was not fully implemented during the war, although it was certainly on the books for progressive or future implementation. Of course, it is also possible that the 1919 report served as an enabling document for arrangements that already existed de facto. After all, the SIS was staffed almost entirely by personnel seconded from the service branches, and it would be very difficult to distinguish between staff seconded for operational purposes and those seconded for liaison purposes, because even the former would have been liable to report back to their home departments. At any rate, in the absence of having the 1919 report available in the public domain, it would appear that the real substance of the 1919 decision was the complete implementation of the MacDonogh scheme, but it provided as a quid pro quo (perhaps to appease Cumming's defenders in the Admiralty and possibly the Foreign Office) an SIS monopoly on human intelligence operations. Military Intelligence won the campaign to tie SIS to its customer departments, but lost the right to run HUMINT operations of its own.

A second quid pro quo for the SIS's central role was that each of the Service branches would take turns providing the Chief of Secret Service (CSS), or 'C' (a title retained from Mansfield-Cumming even after his death).[4] However, this particular aspect of the arrangement was not observed in practice. When Mansfield-Cumming died in 1923, he was replaced not by a representative of either of the other two Service branches but by the Director of Naval Intelligence (DNI), Admiral Sir Hugh 'Quex' Sinclair. Sinclair (who, as DNI, had overseen the workings of the government Code and Cypher School [GC & CS]) arranged for SIS and GC & CS to be brought closer together, bringing GC & CS under his control as C and into SIS HQ at Broadway Buildings in 1925. Under this combined arrangement, the SIS Circulating Sections also served to issue consumer requirements to GC & CS as well as SIS.[5]

The series of consumer liaison sections seconded to the SIS have become a standard in the literature on the internal organization of the SIS between the wars. They were known as the 'Circulating Sections', and, in the existing literature are usually, at the time of the Second World War, described as follows:

Section I Political (Foreign Office)
Section II Air (Air Ministry)
Section III Naval (Admiralty)
Section IV Military (War Office)
Section V Counter-Espionage
Section VI Industrial/Commercial (MEW)
Section VII Finance
Section VIII Radio/Cypher.[6]

To be sure, the 1917 reorganization had created functional 'reporting sections' for Political, Military, Naval, Air and Economic intelligence that sorted and collated raw information forwarded from the agency's foreign bureaux. It is unclear whether or not the Circulating Section designations were in use at the time of the original MacDonogh reforms the 1921 arrangement. This is because the assigned numerals do not reflect the chronological order in which the various Circulating Sections appeared – Section V, for example, did not exist until 1931. But it can be ascertained that these designations *were* in use by 1932, at the very latest, from SOE papers released into the Public Record Office in the early 1990s.[7] To complicate matters further, Sections V, VII and VIII were not technically 'Circulating Sections' at all. Section V was operational, concerned with counter-intelligence and counter-espionage operations abroad. Section VII was Percival Sykes's internal finance department, and Section VIII (not added until 1938) was also operational, providing a network of short-wave radio stations to carry SIS intelligence traffic on a global scale. As a result, in order to understand the development of the 1921 arrangement, one has to concentrate chiefly on Sections I, II, III, IV and VI.

The War Office liaison section, Section IV, retained the designation MI1c within the reconsolidated Directorate of Military Operations and Intelligence throughout the inter-war period. It was given in the *War Office Lists* of the period simply as 'Special Duties'. After the war, under the original 1919 implementation of the 1921 arrangement, it was a fairly sizeable section within Whitehall Court. It included three officers, Brevet-Major Stewart Graham Menzies, formerly of the British Expeditionary Force's GHQ intelligence branch during the war; Major L.A.C. Vigors; and Captain J.W.F. Wyld, who had been on Cumming's staff since 1918 at least.[8] It steadily dwindled in size as post-war austerity set in, with Vigors departing in 1920, and Wyld (now listed as 'Extra-Regimentally employed') leaving around 1921. By 1922, it was manned by Menzies alone, and would continue to be so until his promotion to C at the beginning of the Second World War.[9] Menzies also eventually doubled as unofficial deputy chief under Sinclair on top of his primary function as 'IV'.[10]

The Admiralty's relationship with the SIS developed along similar lines. In the wake of the First World War, the Naval Intelligence Directorate (NID) underwent a comprehensive review, and was cut back quite significantly. The extent of the NID's global and London-based presence was such that the review took a number of years to complete.[11] Under the eventual post-war form of the NID in 1924,[12] the SIS liaison was designated Section 3 (NID3; it would hold much the same designation as Section III within the SIS). NID3 was answerable to the head of NID1b which grouped together 'special intelligence' (SIS) with the naval intelligence organization abroad (mainly its naval attachés and intelligence centres) and a sub-section

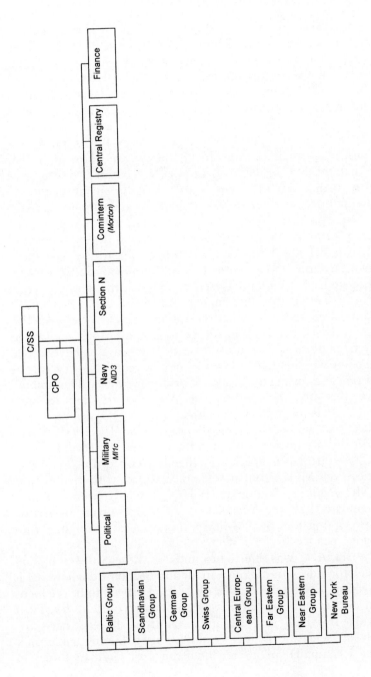

Figure 3.1: SIS in 1923–24

handling 'special enquiries re persons'.[13] The original appointee to the Naval Section was a Captain Sommerville, and one of his first tasks was to prepare a report on the quality of the 'Naval Secret Service' provided by Cumming's organization.[14]

While the War Office and Admiralty aspects of the 1921 arrangement appear, in many respects, to have essentially involved Service Branch officers taking over their respective 1917 functional reporting sections, the development of Section I was much less continuous. According to the official history, the Foreign Office insisted that the SIS 'be kept operationally separate from its own political reporting system and only then that 'in so far as the SIS engaged in political intelligence, it should do so as a supplier... to the Foreign Office, under Foreign Office control'.[15] As we have seen above, the prohibition of the SIS performing foreign political espionage on behalf of the Foreign Office appears to have been withdrawn around 1917, with the SIS Political Section being established under Sir William Tyrrell in 1918. In this sense, Foreign Office liaison anticipated full implementation of the 'MacDonogh scheme', and well ahead of either service branch. However, in 1919, Tyrrell returned to the Foreign Office to become Assistant Under-Secretary of State.[16] As a result, the section appears to have lapsed until Malcolm Woolcombe's appointment two years later in 1921; he was later replaced during the Second World War by David Footman.[17]

During the inter-war period, the Air Ministry had its own intelligence division under its Directorate of Operations and Intelligence[18] but did not set up an SIS presence until 1929/1930. The reasons for this are unclear, although the fact that the Directorate of Military Operations oversaw intelligence concerning 'military aeronautics' via MO1 from 1925 on, coupled with the already existent MI1c/Military Section at SIS HQ, may have been a factor.[19] However, in late 1929, the decision was taken to set up an Air Section at the SIS alongside the Military, Navy and Foreign Office secondments, headed by F.W. Winterbotham and designated AI1c.[20] Within the SIS, AI1c was referred to initially as the Air Section, and then, under the adoption of the Circulating Section designations, it became Section II. Winterbotham's Air Section proved to be the locus of a great deal of innovative thinking and activity within the SIS. It was Section II which first began to address the SIS need for technically and scientifically literate intelligence gathering, undertook a revitalized campaign of air reconnaissance of German forces in

1939 by setting up an SIS air photographic unit employing freelance pilot Joseph Cotton,[21] and would provide the setting for the first SIS scientific intelligence section, IId, shortly after the outbreak of the Second World War (discussed in greater detail in the next chapter).

The final development in terms of strict consumer liaison functions was that of the section handling commercial, industrial, economic and financial intelligence. The development of Section VI is less clearly defined in the literature on the SIS than that of the other consumer liaison sections. Under the MacDonogh reforms of 1917, Whitehall Court included an Economic Intelligence Section collating information needed by the War Trade Intelligence Department (later the Ministry of Blockade) and Service Branch sections involved in the enforcement of the blockade. War trade and blockade intelligence ceased to be issues after the war, and in so far as the Economic Intelligence 'reporting section' carried on, it did so without any single primary consumer. As we have seen above, the Department of Overseas Trade (DOT) had a long-standing intelligence function, and may have had some interest in the SIS product. If so, the interest would have been short-lived because, by the mid-1920s, it had abandoned trade intelligence as its main function in favour of organizing trade fairs abroad to promote British exports.[22] For much of the inter-war period, therefore, economic intelligence was a much diminished sphere of customer demand. The Second World War Economic Intelligence Section did not have any institutional *raison d'être* until nearly a year before the outbreak of that war.

The development that put the Economic Section on the same footing as Sections I, II, III and IV was the creation of the Industrial Intelligence Centre (IIC), originally set up at 54 Broadway and staffed with SIS personnel. The function of the IIC was to handle intelligence regarding the economic and industrial war-fighting potential of potential adversaries on behalf of the Industrial Intelligence in Foreign Countries (FCI) sub-committee of the Committee of Imperial Defence (CID).[23] It was originally installed at Broadway with an SIS officer called Desmond Morton as its head. Why it was initially housed at the SIS is unclear; in 1932, Morton observed in support of the Centre's relocation to the DOT that 'the work of the IIC in no way resembles that of "secret service". ... The IIC is not responsible for obtaining information in the first instance i.e. it is not a "secret service", and has no official or unofficial agents reporting to it.'[24] Indeed, the unit relied chiefly on information from overt sources, either published or acquired through the various Whitehall Departments with whom it also dealt as consumers of its assessments. The IIC was an analytical, not an operational entity, an early step in the evolution of the contemporary, interdepartmental, 'all-source' analysis of intelligence that has increasingly dominated the consumer side of the intelligence equation since the Second World War. Despite these profound differences from the SIS, and the limitations already upon the Secret Service, the IIC was set up at SIS HQ and staffed with SIS personnel.[25] Morton had been attached to the SIS since 1919,[26] in which capacity he appears to have controlled the anti-Soviet section that would figure so centrally in the 1924 Zinoviev letter affair (discussed below),[27] while the Deputy Head, F.F. Clively, had served as a Passport Control Officer in Prague from 1925 to 1931 and had then been posted to Passport Control headquarters prior to his attachment to the IIC in 1932.[28]

The demands on the IIC increased rapidly during the 1930s, leading to increases in staff size that, in 1935, made continuing housing it at Broadway unfeasible. The Treasury representative on the FCI suggested that an informal subcommittee should meet 'and examine how best to provide staff for the IIC'.[29] The conclusion was that the IIC should be relocated to the DOT. On 26 August 1935, Morton wrote to Sir Edward Crowe, Comptroller of the DOT, reminding him of discussions in March of that year concerning a possible transfer of the IIC to the DOT. Apart from the steady expansion of the IIC, he argued, 'there is also the question of relieving C of the burden of payment for the existing staff', and it had been suggested at the time that the costs of rehousing the IIC at Overseas Trade would be absorbed from savings at the DOT during the 1935–36 financial year. Despite those discussions, he complained, 'I have heard nothing from Jones (J.H. Jones at the DOT) since then, but the financial pressure on C has certainly not been lightened by recent events.'[30]

The reason for Jones's reticence was simply that the DOT was less than enthusiastic about acquiring the IIC. His view, expressed in a 1937 paper on IIC staffing, was that 'The IIC has to be attached to some Government department, but there is no particular reason why it should have to be attached to the DOT except that every other Department seems likely to be excluded for special reasons.' Presumably, the 'special reasons' Jones so tactfully refers to were that the other government departments were for the most part consumers of the IIC's assessments. They were, therefore, partly in competition for access to the IIC's scarce resources and for one of its consumers to have controlled the IIC might have constituted a conflict of interest for both the IIC and that department. Jones's assertion that there was 'no particular reason' that the DOT should take on the IIC seems somewhat idiosyncratic in view of the DOT's original intelligence function. The department had originally been established in 1900 as the Commercial Intelligence Branch of the Board of Trade, rechristened the Department of Commercial Intelligence in 1916. In this capacity, we have already encountered the pre-1914 form of the DOT in the background of the 1905 Foreign Office intelligence scheme. In its original incarnations, the DOT had been created to gather (mainly open-source) information which would be of value if provided to British firms competing with foreign ones in overseas territories. In 1919, it acquired the title 'Department of Overseas Trade', and although, throughout the inter-war period, it progressively shifted its attention to foreign trade fairs, it continued to train and post 'intelligence officers' abroad.[31] There appear, therefore, to have been very real reasons for governmental commercial and industrial intelligence work to have been consolidated under one institutional roof in the DOT.

During the following four years, the IIC expanded considerably to keep up with demand. Morton went to considerable lengths to promote the cause of industrial intelligence in general, and his centre in particular, within the Whitehall village. The official historian of the Second World War economic blockade and the Ministry of Economic Warfare (MEW), W.N. Medlicott, has even argued that the very notion of 'economic warfare' originated with Morton and the IIC. Medlicott also notes of Morton that 'he became an "honorary" member of the Joint Intelligence and Joint Planning Committees of the Chiefs of Staff; members of the IIC lectured regularly to the three Staff Colleges and to the Imperial Defence College, and Morton himself was nominated as an unofficial instructor assisting their war games and consulting with the Commandant and professorial staff.'[32] It was in this context that, in 1937, Morton was invited by the CID subcommittee planning for the creation of a wartime Department of Economic Warfare to develop a scheme for an economic warfare intelligence branch.

In composing his proposal for an 'Economic Warfare Intelligence Branch', Morton consulted with the relevant departments in Whitehall, including the Security Service, the GC & CS and the SIS, submitting his first draft proposal in March of 1938.[33] The proposal suggested that, for the planned directorate, 'enquiries to and information from secret sources will pass through a "special liaison officer" who will also handle information from the GC & CS'.[34] With the establishment of the MEW on the outbreak of war, the IIC moved from the DOT to the MEW to form the basis of the latter's intelligence branch. A document from the 'first month of the war' noted that the intelligence branch included a 'Liaison Intelligence [LI] Section', with sub-sections dealing with the police, the military, and other bodies which might generate industrial and economic intelligence as a by-product. The wartime LI section included a 'Secret Sources' sub-section consisting of two officers 'supplied by SIS', but there is evidence that by this time these arrangements had already been operating for at least a year.[35] The Economic Intelligence Section at last had a main consumer in the same fashion as the political and service intelligence branch section. Under the pre-war Circulating Section scheme, it was designated Section VI, and was headed by retired Engineer Rear-Admiral Charles Limpenny, a former ADC to the King.[36]

The Circulating Sections did more that simply set requirements for raw intelligence in the form of wish-lists, and evaluate the content of agent reports from field stations abroad. C Sections (not to be confused with the designation of the Chief of Service as 'C') also originated operations which the operational G Sections were required to execute. Group Captain Winterbotham noted about his experience in setting up Section II: 'I discovered that people who had the required technical knowledge and were willing to sell it to a foreign country were hard to find ... the sort of people I required were a considerable cut above the run-of-the-mill agent whose job was primarily to report on what he saw and seldom what he knew.'[37] During the war, R.V. Jones would form the more scathing opinion, that the 'average SIS agent was a scientific analphabet'.[38] Winterbotham concluded: 'I should not only have to find the right people, but also train them in the sort of intelligence I required. Then from knowledge of the motives of the agent involved in selling me the information, I should have to assess its accuracy.'[39] In the event, of course, Winterbotham went beyond even this, travelling to Germany to meet and glean information from senior Nazi officials in person.[40] Such extreme measures were, of course, the exception rather than the rule.

The practice of the C Sections planning operations to be mounted via the agency's operational side was not a peculiarity of F.W. Winterbotham and the Air Section, however. In 1938, the Director of Naval Intelligence, John H. Godfrey, was approached by Lord Melchett, who suggested to Godfrey that the Jewish athletic organizations, or 'Maccabees', might be used as the basis for a clandestine network in Romania. Contacts were made with a businessman in the Palestinian Jewish community willing to go to Romania to make a start. 'At this moment', records Godfrey, 'it was decided that the whole project should be turned over to C, which meant that nothing else was done about it.'[41] Non-completion of the operation notwithstanding, the Maccabee affair illustrates again how SIS consumers could and would issue the service with very specific operational plans (and even contacts).

The development of the Circulating Sections may have been the core feature of the 1921 arrangement, but, in fact, it constituted only one side of a broader SIS internal structure that was driven by it. On the other side was the SIS operational side that fulfilled the requirements laid down by the agency's consumers. The operational side of the SIS consisted of essentially three elements. The first element was the headquarters operational side made up of numbered G Sections, headed by G Officers, and divided up along regional lines. The second element was the field organization of stations abroad that operated under a hard-won measure of official, although technically not *diplomatic*, cover in the form of the Passport Control Organization (PCO), a cover which wore steadily thinner as the inter-war decades dragged on until it collapsed completely in the Venlo incident in November 1939. The third element was a later addition in the shape of an auxiliary field organization created by Sinclair precisely because of suspicions that the PCO system had been compromised. This auxiliary presence was known as the Z Organization. In practice, the Z Organization was never fully integrated into the tasking and dissemination system of the 1921 arrangement, and was eventually – and disastrously – consolidated with the PCO system on the outbreak of the Second World War.

After the First World War, the operational side of Cumming's service adopted a geographical structure, divided into regional 'Groups', each Group overseeing a range of foreign stations generally operating under PCO cover. In 1923, these were the Baltic Group, the Scandinavian Group, the German Group, the Swiss Group, the Central European Group, the Far Eastern Group and the Near

Eastern Group, with the New York station operating on the same level of seniority as the regional groups. Under the Baltic Group came Estonia, Finland, Lithuania and Latvia. Under the Scandinavian Group came Denmark, Sweden, Norway and Poland. The German Group dealt with Germany, The Netherlands and Belgium (and the Rhine separately), while the Swiss Group oversaw stations in Switzerland, France, Italy, Spain and Portugal. The Central European Group consisted of Austria, Slovakia and the Czech lands, Hungary, Bulgaria and Yugoslavia and Romania. The Near East Group had stations for Turkey, Egypt and Palestine, Greece and southern Russia, and the Far East Group covered Vladivostok, Hong Kong, Singapore, Canton, Shanghai, Harbin, Tokyo and Vancouver.[42] By 1932 (at the latest), the various Groups were known as G Sections and given Arabic numerals (G1, G2, G3, G4 and so forth), headed by G Officers.[43] The number of G Sections may have dwindled as the scale of the SIS operations was curtailed by financial constraint. Certainly, by the outbreak of the Pacific war, the Far East Group had contracted from the eight stations above to three (Hong Kong, Shanghai and Singapore),[44] and it would appear likely that by 1939 SIS global effort had been consolidated into just four G Sections.[45]

SIS's acquisition of the PCO as cover is generally portrayed as having been a 'grudging provision' by the Foreign Office. There tend to be two interpretations of this development. On the one hand, the fact that this was all that was provided is taken as a reflection of chronic Foreign Office neglect of the SIS.[46] On the other hand, it is seen as a compromise between the SIS stations' need for some sort of official status abroad and the Foreign Office's concern that SIS might lead to embarrassment for the Foreign Office if their activities were ever exposed, mitigated by the Foreign Office's desire to exercise some sort of de facto control over those activities to reduce that risk.[47] Christopher Andrew has demonstrated that the process by which the SIS acquired PCO cover was both less fraught and more gradual than was previously believed, but even he is vague about how the PCO system shifted from being the operational arm of the interdepartmental Aliens and Nationality Committee, concerned initially with monitoring the movements of subversives and international revolutionaries (and 'initially' forbidden to deal with secret service agents), to becoming primarily concerned with visas and the SIS. Eunan O'Halpin has suggested that the shift in emphasis came 'as the panic about Bolshevism receded'.[48] However, what both the 'grudging support' and the compromise and control hypotheses omit is the fact that, prior to 1919, the Foreign Office was simply in a limited position to provide cover for the SIS abroad. Until after the First World War, the Foreign Office 'was for staff purposes a Home department'.[49] Its only foreign presence in 1914 was six commercial attachés, apart from which it had virtually no dealings abroad; this was the preserve of the diplomatic and consular services. The Foreign Office and the Diplomatic Service were not amalgamated until immediately after the First World War (and the Consular Service would remain separate until 1943/44),[50] and that, of course, is when SIS finally did receive some official cover through the PCO system. As for the matter of SIS operational control of the passport system, Cumming, as will become apparent shortly, had been manoeuvring for a piece of that action since the middle of the First World War.

Cumming's interest and claim to some portion of the passport control system lay partly in the practicalities of movements control and the monitoring of 'subversives' abroad, and partly in the bureaucratic politics of movements control that took shape on the cusp between the end of the First World War and the inter-war years. In 1919, the wartime military movements control system was in the process of being replaced by an international passport and visa system. The British side of this was handled by the interdepartmental Aliens and Nationality Committee, through the Passport Control Subcommittee set up in February 1919 and composed of representatives from the Foreign Office and MI1c, the War Office, MI5 (Vernon Kell), the Metropolitan Special Branch (headed by Basil Thompson), the Board of Trade, the DOT and the Ministry of Labour. The Cabinet Office approved the committee's proposal of a Passport Control Department under the Foreign Office, although the Foreign Office had very little interest in the problem of monitoring revolutionaries and subversives. Initially, supervision of the PCO system was handled by a subcommittee made of up officials from the SIS, MI5, the Home Office Aliens Branch and Basil Thompson, who, since March 1919, had become head of his own civilian Directorate of Intelligence which had been carved out of the Special Branch.[51] The head of the new PCO from July 1920 was Herbert Spencer. Spencer came to the new department from MI5a, where he had been responsible for 'Military policy connected with the employment of alien workmen on war service',[52] and in which capacity he had, on occasion, attended meetings of the Aliens and Nationals Committee in

Kell's stead. From February 1920, he attended as a representative of the Foreign Office, and from July of that year he was duly acknowledged as the head of the PCO.[53] His official title was Chief Passport Control Officer (CPO), and his offices were housed with the rest of the SIS, at the time at 2 Whitehall Court. Because the PCOs were officially accredited to the countries where they were stationed, they were subject to a prohibition against operating against their host country, and so stations in one country operated against neighbouring countries.[54] This restriction, since referred to as the 'Third Country Rule',[55] finally formalized a principle that had been advocated both by MO3 and Cumming since before the First World War.

How and why Cumming and the SIS secured operational control of the PCO is, to be sure, unclear, from the documentary record available. However, one factor which should not be discounted is that by the end of the First World War, MI1c played a central role in the passport control process, and, in some theatres, *already had* full operational movement control. This was because MI1c's counter-espionage information was a crucial input in identifying those whom travel controls were designed to keep out of British and Allied territory, especially in neutral countries where movement control could not be directly run by the War Office or the Admiralty. According to Henry Landau, in charge of the wartime Rotterdam bureau's Military Section, no visa was issued to a Dutch national until the individual had been checked out by the head of the bureau's Counter-Espionage Section. As for citizens of neutral states, they were checked against the existing British blacklist (which prohibited entry to persons suspected of trading with the enemy, and was also partly a product of the SIS war trade intelligence collection), and information about their intentions 'was not only obtained through recognized business channels such as banks, but in many cases the applicant was watched for a long time by our agents'. Landau comments of this surveillance work, with a certain salacious glee: 'Every movement was followed. I often laughed over the indiscretions of some of the individuals – in the hands of their wives the information would have been devastating.'[56]

Mackenzie's wartime Eastern Mediterranean Special Intelligence Bureau (EMSIB) was even more deeply involved in passport control, which, during the Allied occupation of Greece, became the basis of a sustained 'turf war' between the Foreign Office, the naval and military authorities, and MI1c. Prior to the occupation, Mackenzie's

B Bureau had no executive powers to act on the suspect files it was accumulating. During the violence in Athens resulting from Allied moves towards the country prior to the occupation, Mackenzie's office had been stormed, and he and his intelligence work were often the subject of vitriolic accusations in the 'Ententophobe' press. As a result, his office was relocated to Syra, where it continued to operate as before, while an Allied government of occupation was installed in the Greek capital.

The presence of an Allied administration now made travel controls based on CE information feasible in the form of an International Passport Bureau in Athens. With a card index of suspects which had been accumulating since 1915, the Syra office was a natural entity to take on the task of screening travellers for the Passport Bureau, and ironically it was C, who had previously resisted any involvement in CE, that now proved determined to keep at least some degree of travel control in Secret Service hands. In a March 1917 telegram to Mackenzie, C stated, tellingly, that 'The Foreign Office, Naval and Military Authorities are of one mind in deciding 1st that you cannot go back to Athens, and 2nd, that Passenger Control cannot be worked from Syra. ... The Naval Authorities take the view that Control work is not part of secret service and they do not regard favourably any Military Control that is not under the Vice Admiral. I feel therefore, *if we are to retain any of this Control in our hands* that we must send an officer to Athens of sufficient standing to hold his own.'[57] There was, it seems, a positive interest on Cumming's part in retaining a piece of the action in travel control. In March 1917, Hall, as the Admiralty's Director of the Intelligence Department (DID), appears to have tried work out a deal acceptable to both sides. According to Hall, port control would be under the authority of the vice admiral while Mackenzie would become overall head of secret service operations in Greece, both A and B Bureaux, under the direction of the Vice Admiral, 'his reports being furnished simultaneously to yourself, London, and where necessary, to Cairo'.[58] On 14 May, the British Head of Mission, Sir Francis Elliot, sent a telegram to the Foreign Office to the effect that 'As the International Passport Bureau is about to be re-established at Athens, this will necessarily be the central British office for this purpose under my supervision. The materials and staff necessary to secure its efficiency will be supplied by Mackenzie.'[59] As a result, when Mackenzie set up his new Aegean Intelligence Service (AIS), this combined organization

71

was to include an MC (presumably standing for 'Military' or 'Movements Control', Mackenzie does not specify which) section processing intelligence information for the International Passport Control Bureau, partly because EMSIB was filling an administrative power vacuum, but also through a concerted effort by Cumming to keep a measure of MI1c involvement and control of the process.

Certainly, Cumming did not waste any time in deploying his own officers abroad into the Passport Control Officer (PCO) role. Henry Landau took up his post-war position as PCO Berlin immediately after demobilizing his wartime agents and a three-month leave of absence, and firmly maintains that his SIS duties were coupled with his position as PCO from the outset. Landau has described how he was posted to Berlin from the beginning with a dual intelligence and passport control remit. He recalled: 'In London I was informed by the Chief [Cumming] that . . . I was to open an office in Berlin, and in addition to my duties which he would give me to perform, but which would develop after I had got settled, I was to direct and organize passport control there.'[60] Before returning to Germany, Landau paid a visit to the Home Office, which presented a 'multitude of forms and rubber stamps, whose use was explained to me with the assurance that a supply of them was waiting for me at the British Mission'.[61] As Andrew has argued that PCOs were initially forbidden to deal with Secret Service agents,[62] it would appear that any prohibition of PCOs engaging in espionage abroad may have been either a very short-lived and transitional provision, or at least a practice (like the Third Country Rule) observed mainly in the breach.

The limitations and difficulties experienced by PCOs in their SIS capacity has been subject to extensive discussion elsewhere,[63] the problems ranging from financial scandals to diplomatic spats and the refusal of the Foreign Office to extend diplomatic privilege to PCOs. Some diplomats even refused to have a PCO appointed to their mission. Within a couple of years of the PCO system being implemented, the border controls in Europe were progressively relaxed until the number of PCOs required, and the number of potential SIS residencies available, shrank from 54 in 1922 to 22 in 1923. Although the Passport Control Organization was self-funding, meaning that PCO salaries were paid out of visa fees, and not out of the dwindling SIS budget,[64] those salaries were not particularly good. This meant that the SIS had to recruit mainly from former servicemen who already had a basic military pension. The financial strictures of life as a PCO appear to have resulted in at least one penetration by the German *Abwehr*, which recruited a cash-strapped Dick Ellis in Berlin as a source;[65] one PCO interviewed by another researcher admitted to having run a range of notional agents and pocketing their payments from London.[66] There was also a succession of financial scandals in the 1930s, causing one PCO to commit suicide.[67]

Apart from the Ellis case (which did not come to light until the inquiries into Soviet penetration during the 1960s), the PCO cover was hopelessly blown by the outbreak of the Second World War. The Hague station's agent network had been penetrated by the *Abwehr* from 1935 onwards, to be sure,[68] but Christopher Andrew argues that Compton Mackenzie blew their cover in 1932.[69] Mackenzie's information was, however, retrospective to circumstances prevalent in First World War Greece. Any compromise by Mackenzie was considerably exacerbated two years later by Henry Landau's memoir *All's Fair*. Besides recounting his wartime work in The Netherlands and his own post-war appointment as PCO Berlin, Landau states that he was replaced as PCO by Captain Frank Foley. He then very lamely tries to claim that Foley (who was still PCO when Landau went to print, and would still be so on the outbreak of the Second World War) was not, in fact, doing any secret service work, but, rather, 'someone else whom I recommended highly relieved me of my secret service work'.[70] Foley, of course, was the Berlin head of station, although he would perhaps ultimately become better known as the British 'Oskar Schindler' for, in his capacity as PCO, issuing visas to thousands of beleaguered Jews before the Nazi government shut down both his visa and secret service work on the outbreak of hostilities.[71]

Although the PCO system produced significant revenue, the SIS did not benefit from those funds. In 1921, when it was at its most profitable with 28 offices abroad, Cumming assured the Aliens and Nationality Committee that 'while the money derived from visas was not applied directly to maintaining the secret service, the Passport Control Offices enabled a useful liaison to be maintained with foreign police'.[72] This continued the practice of cultivating contacts with host-nation police developed by Cumming's wartime bureaux, a practice apparent in Leslie Nicholson's memoir *British Agent*,[73] and a post-war SIS officer would observe during an interview that the host nation's security service was considered the SIS head of station's 'first point of contact'.[74] The official history briefly summarizes the operational function of the PCOs as acting 'for the most part as post-boxes, and the secret service work continued to be carried out by private individuals paid out of secret service funds'.[75] This description does not conform to the accounts of former intelligence officers.[76] However, what the official history *might* be referring to is the fact that the informant networks run by stations consisted of a primary agent, with a network of sub-agents beneath him or her, linked to the SIS station only by clandestine communication routes such as cut-outs, dead- and live letter boxes, and secret writing sent to an accommodation address.[77]

The third element of SIS field organization appeared late in the inter-war period. Set up in 1936, the Z Organization, or Z Network, was a system of SIS residents abroad using commercial rather than official cover for their intelligence-gathering activities. The reasons for the creation of the Z Organization remain somewhat unclear, and are divided between two alternative explanations. Claude Dansey's biographers Anthony Read and David Fisher assert that Dansey proposed the organization to Sinclair on the grounds that he possessed 'anti-Nazi contacts in the *Abwehr*' who had alerted him to the penetration of the Hague station.[78] Christopher Andrew, however, has suggested that the project arose out of Dansey's personal network of contacts in the British business community, and as a way of overcoming the limits placed upon the PCO system by ambassadorial hostility (there was, for example, no PCO at Bern at the insistence of Sir George Warner, the British Minister there[79]), limited finances, and the flood of refugees overwhelming the PCOs in Europe.[80] Of these two accounts, Andrew's seems the most likely, given the very limited state of SIS counter-espionage knowledge of the potential enemy indicated by the official history.[81] The Z Organization also received limited official support from Sir Robert Vansittart during the last year or so of his incumbency as Permanent Under-Secretary at the Foreign Office.[82]

To set up the organization, Dansey was notionally dismissed by C for financial irregularities while Rome PCO (an entirely plausible story given the trials and tribulations of PCOs noted previously), and the organization was set up at Bush House. From here, the Z Organization recruited contacts from Dansey's acquaintances in the British business community, journalists, and even the film producer Sir Alexander Korda. However, the quality of access achieved by Z operators does not appear to have been particularly high, even when compared with the underfunded efforts of the official SIS stations. Leslie Nicholson, recounting his work as the Riga PCO, has painted a less than flattering picture of his Z Organization opposite number, 'Daniel'. Nicholson accuses 'Daniel' of simply dealing with what he terms 'the dubious professional agents' who used to gather at a café near the Riga Stock Exchange, and whom Nicholson considered 'agents provocateurs' or at least 'disreputable and suspect'.[83] Wesley Wark has suggested that Nicholson's aversion to 'Daniel' may simply have been 'a turf war' between PCO and Z officer,[84] but a former Z officer during an interview remarked that information provided by the Z Organization was often little better than what one might have acquired from the newspapers of the day.[85]

NEW OPERATIONAL FUNCTIONS

During the inter-war period, the SIS began to expand its operational functions beyond basic process of human intelligence gathering. The SIS's new operational tasks built in part upon its existing human intelligence capability, in part in support of that capability, and in other parts independently of that role. In the mid-1920s, the agency moved into the exceedingly delicate field of clandestinely opening and inspecting foreign diplomatic bags through its Section N. During this period, Sinclair sought to recombine offensive intelligence and counter-intelligence by trying to have MI5 absorbed by his SIS. This failed in the first instance, and the SIS's own domestic operations against Soviet espionage and Soviet-backed communist agitation eventually led SIS into a new 'turf war' with MI5 and the Metropolitan Special Branch. From these events, the foundations were laid for a counter-espionage service-within-a-service, Section V. Two other semi-autonomous sub-services were the formation of the first standing covert action section in British secret service history, Section D (which would eventually be hived off to become part of the wartime Special Operations Executive), and the Radio Section (in turn hived off post-war to become the Diplomatic Wireless Service). All of these, however, reflected an aggressive effort by Sinclair to create a secret service equal to its times in vision if not in resources.

Section N has always been one of the most sensitive and traditionally least discussed features of SIS work and organization.[86] Its purpose was to intercept foreign diplomatic bags, clandestinely open them and photograph the contents on behalf of the Foreign Office. Section N was probably set up around 1924 under Sinclair.[87] A great deal of mythology has developed around how these bags were acquired, supposedly due to the 'inadequate courier system employed by many states, and to the indiscipline of the couriers themselves',[88] conjuring up images of a courier awaking 'from a passionate embrace, or alcoholic or drugged slumber, or a combination of all three, to find his bag at his side, apparently intact'.[89] In practice, the process of interception was generally far more prosaic, since many of the smaller European nations routinely entrusted their diplomatic bags to the British Foreign Office for transportation.[90] Run by a man who was, among other things, Menzies's stockbroker, David Boyle, Section N is reported to have employed a 'team of thirty seamstresses' housed in Palmer Street, who opened the bags 'in a fashion calculated to avoid detection',[91] although more technology-intensive methods were used to attack the official seals in the bags. The latter part of the work came to grief at least once during the Second World War when, according to Kim Philby, 'on one occasion, the red seals in a Polish bag turned purple under treatment, and nothing could be done to restore them. The Poles were regretfully informed that the bag in question had been lost'.[92] The incident of the Polish seals embodies precisely the kind of risk which the Foreign Office would not be willing to take on its own recognizance, but which it could task the SIS to take on its behalf in its classic institutional cut-out role as 'screen'. In his capacity as head of Section N, Boyle was known just as B, and the product of his section as TRIPLEXXX (triple-X).[93]

As noted above, despite Cumming's aversion to counter-espionage, it was a task which the SIS had been forced to take on during the war. At the end of the First World War, the DMI suggested that MI5 and MI1c should be amalgamated under the Foreign Office and staffed with officers from the Service Branches. Mansfield-Cumming rejected this on the grounds that 'there was no real connection between counter-espionage and the work of the SIS'.[94] The Foreign Office supported this argument, and the proposal was defeated. However, Mansfield-Cumming's successor, Admiral Sinclair, shared very few of his predecessor's views on the ambit of a secret intelligence service, and after taking over the post in 1923 he promptly commenced a sustained campaign to absorb MI5. At this time, MI5 was in a somewhat weak position. Although it had survived the challenge to its role from Basil Thompson's short-lived Directorate of Intelligence, it was becoming increasingly detached from the War Office (Maurice Hankey would, in 1940, describe MI5's interdepartmental status as being 'something of a lost child'[95]) and was therefore without a specific Minister of State to champion its cause as the Foreign Secretary might that of the SIS and GC & CS.

The counter-espionage situation in the UK government remained in this transitional state when, in 1924, the Zinoviev letter scandal broke in the press. The Zinoviev letter affair has been a standard problem in literature on British intelligence for decades, and various amateur and professional historians have tried their hands at demonstrating its authenticity or otherwise, its source and authorship, and how it made its way into the press, although the most recent account (and probably as close to definitive as can be achieved, given the present state of the documentary trail and demise of most of the participants), has been that issued by the Foreign Office historian, Gill Bennett.[96] Authentic or not, the letter urged the Communist Party of Great Britain (CPGB) to mobilize the 'proletariat' in support of a new Anglo-Soviet treaty and preparation for an armed insurrection and revolution. Once acquired by the SIS, it subsequently found its way not only to the usual stable of consumers, but also to the *Daily Mail*.

As a result of the furore, the Secret Service Committee was reconvened under Sir Warren Fisher with Sir Eyre Crowe and Sir Maurice Hankey. The Committee interviewed Sinclair, the Chief Commissioner of the Metropolitan Police, the Assistant Commissioner, both Kell and his deputy Holt-Wilson, the head of Indian Political Intelligence, a member of the Scotland Yard section handling liaison with the SIS (SS1), the Assistant Commissioner in charge of Scotland Yard's Special Branch, the directors of Naval and Military Intelligence, an Air Vice Marshall with equivalent responsibilities (Air Intelligence [AI] would not be formally set up until the end of the decade) and Sir Russel Scott, who had recently conducted an investigation of Scotland Yard. The report of the Committee records that 'the highly efficient chief of the Secret Intelligence Service strongly urged amalgamation of all [intelligence] branches under one head' because of 'the difficulty of maintaining proper contact between five different organizations housed separately, and dotted at irregular intervals along a line starting at Olympia and ending only at Westminster Bridge' as well as the risk of different organizations employing the same agents. However, 'the main body of opinion represented by the witnesses was more conservative in character'.[97] Hence, while the committee started with 'a mild predisposition in favour of amalgamation', it eventually decided that, in view of 'the heterogeneous interests, liaisons, traditions and the responsibilities of the different Services, and the marked reluctance of the majority of those concerned to advocate any drastic change, a coalition would, if it were not an actual failure, be no great improvement'.[98] This risk-averse reasoning ended Sinclair's attempts to take over MI5.

The section that secured the letter was a small section set up in the first instance to penetrate the Soviet-backed Communist International (Comintern), and so, in a somewhat literal reading of the SIS brief, lay within the jurisdiction of foreign intelligence. In pursuit of this requirement, the SIS found itself running operations against Comintern activity in the UK, including the penetration of the CPGB and attempts to detect Soviet espionage within the UK as well,[99] and these activities did not sit so easily within that jurisdiction. The section was evidently headed by Desmond Morton, whom Bennett notes, in his account of the Zinoviev letter affair, was 'in charge of evaluating and disseminating on these [Soviet] matters' and was, moreover, running agents that were 'supplying information to SIS without the knowledge of Departments that were supposed to deal with domestic intelligence, MI5 and Special Branch'.[100] As the official history notes, the confusion and friction which had persisted after the 1925 Secret Service Committee 'came to a head in 1931 when Scotland Yard and MI5 had both taken exception to SIS operations against Communist targets in the United Kingdom'.[101] The resulting turf war prompted the convening of a Secret Service Committee in 1931, again under the supervision of Sir Warren Fisher, assisted this time by the Permanent Under-Secretary of the Foreign Office, Sir Robert Vansittart, the Permanent Under-Secretary of State (PUS) of the Home Office, Sir John Anderson, and Sir Maurice Hankey. On the basis of the 1931 inquiry, the division of labour between the SIS and MI5 was finally and formally established, giving MI5 jurisdiction in British and Colonial territory and the SIS jurisdiction outside the three-mile limit.[102] Under the terms of the 1931 agreement, the SIS anti-communist section was transferred to MI5, where it became M Section[103] while a counter-espionage (CE) Circulating Section was set up in SIS under the designation Section V.

78

The officer chosen to set up Section V was a former Indian police officer, Colonel Valentine Vivian. Throughout most of the inter-war period, the CE Section remained very small, consisting only of Vivian, an assistant and a secretary. Not until 1938 would the section receive an additional officer in the form of Felix Cowgill, brought in as an anti-communist specialist and potential successor to Vivian.[104] According to John Curry's MI5 official history, this meant that 'Section V was established... as a Circulating Section to serve as a channel between SIS and MI5, in the same way as other Circulating Sections served as channels to the Foreign Office, the War Office and so on',[105] but this is a somewhat incomplete description. Almost from the outset, Section V had an operational brief beyond that of any of the other C Sections. Although it was some time before Section V began running agents of its own, it quickly found itself responsible for security and counter-intelligence work abroad, Vivian being tasked by Vansittart to investigate a Foreign Office security leak (the 'Cicero affair') in Rome in 1937.[106] On the whole, however, Vivian's section concerned itself with acting as conventional Circulating Section, targeting the Comintern in the first instance and foreign espionage services as a somewhat distant second preference, and passing relevant information between SIS and MI5.

For the most part, these operations were handled by the SIS G-side on the basis of Section V tasking and information. Despite its limited assets, Section V's work led to the seizure in 1931 of the Far Eastern Bureau of the Comintern and the Secretariat of the Pan-Pacific Trades Union Secretariat.[107] The SIS also successfully penetrated the Brazilian communist movement in the mid-1930s on the basis of which Curry's history of MI5 records that 'the Brazilian government was fore-warned and was enabled to take action to forestall the revolutionary attempt in the capital'.[108] Section V would not become an agent-running body in its own right until the Second World War. Prior to the penetration by GC & CS of *Abwehr* ciphers in late 1940, very little was known about the Axis intelligence services, and in 1937 the Section issued a warning to its overseas stations that it very much needed information on the German, Italian and Japanese intelligence services. In 1938, it set up a station of its own in The Netherlands, to work closely with the French, Dutch and Belgian authorities, with another officer being posted to Belgium in 1939.[109] However, as already noted, by 1935, the Hague PCO agent network had been penetrated by the *Abwehr*, which was also routinely filming the comings and goings of its officers.[110] By the time the section had begun to mobilize, the damage was already done.

Section D's function was that of sabotage and subversion behind enemy lines in the event of a war; this function was under Major Lawrence Grand, who bore the cryptonym D, just as the C Section Heads bore the title 'I', 'II', 'III', 'IV' or 'V'. Section D was not the SIS's first foray into political action, but it was the first attempt to create a permanent infrastructure for planning and implementing covert action. The SIS had first become involved in covert political action as MI1c in 1918–19, in the wake of the October Revolution in Russia. The work was directed by the headquarters Political Section created in 1917,[111] although this work did not continue under Section I under the 1921 arrangement reforms. Moreover, while Morton's anti-communist section had worked against the Comintern abroad, it had been dissolved in 1931 with its domestic work transferred to MI5, and Morton moved sideways to head up the new Industrial Intelligence Centre. It was not until Sinclair's administration that a separate headquarters machinery was re-established to handle sabotage and subversion, running in concert with the War Office's arrangements for irregular warfare being developed by Colonel Holland at MIR. Roughly speaking, the distinction between Section D and MIR was that MIR was concerned with irregular operations performed by British service personnel in uniform, while Section D was to undertake actions for which the UK government would want to be able plausibly to deny responsibility.[112]

On 20 March 1939, Grand and Holland put up a paper to Lord Gort, Chief of the Imperial General Staff, outlining their proposed arrangements and division of labour. At a meeting with the Foreign Secretary, Lord Halifax; the Permanent Under-Secretary of the Foreign Office, Alexander Cadogan; and C, it was agreed that initial steps could be taken to implement Section D plans to counter Nazi influence in smaller European countries under German control or in immediate danger, provided such actions were undertaken with Prime Ministerial authorization.[113] However, until the actual outbreak of war, Section D remained more or less notional, confining itself to originating plans and techniques for possible sabotage, and subversion methods and operations, and possibly some limited liaison with exile and dissident political organizations on the Continent.

Christopher Andrew has rightly noted the capacity of Sinclair's SIS to pioneer new areas with respect to Section D and Section II's programme of aerial reconnaissance. However, an additional area of very real secret service innovation which is often overlooked is Sinclair's initiation of a proprietary, secure, international, short-wave radio network. The Radio Section was set up in 1938 with the appointment of Richard Gambier-Parry, and in either late 1938 or early 1939, it was amalgamated with a pre-existing Codes (sometimes referred to as 'Cipher') Section that generated one-time pads for the PCOs abroad. The resulting combined Communications Section was set up alongside the Circulating Sections as Section VIII.[114] Gambier-Parry's task was to assemble a clandestine W/T network to link the SIS in the UK with its stations and sources on the Continent, both by importing transceivers and recruiting engineers to build them.

One example of Gambier-Parry's wireless development programme was that of Harold Robin, who would eventually become chief engineer in the Diplomatic Wireless Service.[115] Robin had been introduced to a colleague called Peter Hope by Gambier-Parry in 1938. Hope had been contracted to operate a small commercial radio station in Liechtenstein at the time and employed Robin to build the station's transmitter. The two communicated regularly via their own (in Robin's case, unlicensed) 250-watt transceivers, which allowed immediate communications 'hence avoiding the cost of telephone calls'. In this way, 'Hope made contact on 29 August and said "drop everything and return to London at once!"' Robin made his way post-haste back to the UK, where Hope instructed him to report to Gambier-Parry directly. At this point, he was required to sign the Official Secrets Act and 'was immediately instructed to build an additional transmitter for an MI6 outpost at Woldingham, Surrey, where a few Czechs and Poles were already sending coded messages in Morse to their native lands.'[116] The SIS also needed a transmitter built in the West Country, clear of the *Luftwaffe*'s expected target areas in England, and a transmission facility, including 100-foot-high transmission towers, was assembled on rented farmland near Cirencester. The Radio Section's main facilities were at Whaddon Hall and Hanslope Park.[117]

Gambier-Parry was assisted by Major E.H. Maltby, who is probably best known for his cameo appearance in Leslie Nicholson's *British Agent*. Nicholson counted among his sources a Latvian engineer, ALEX-2, who had installed a short-wave transceiver for the Riga station in the form of a maritime radio found in a breaker's yard. However, with the announcement of the Molotov–von Ribbentrop pact, preparations were made for another agent, ALEX-1, to use either this or another, smaller transceiver supplied by the SIS (there appears to be some uncertainty in the various accounts of this event). 'In the spring of 1939 a telegram arrived from Warsaw announcing the arrival of a senior colleague on tour from London, and whom I had not met and whose name was unfamiliar to me', recalls Nicholson. 'I was asked to meet his train the following day and the telegram ended: *Will be wearing Old Etonian tie.* How typically English, I thought. I felt sorely tempted to cable back: *Regret unfamiliar with O.E. colours,* but I thought better of it.' With the situation on the Continent worsening, Maltby was touring the region's stations to check on the state of Section VIII's radio network in the field. Nicholson also recalls that Maltby 'gave me one bad moment. We had been talking till quite late one evening at the borrowed flat when he seized on the wireless set. Muttering something about "hoping I didn't mind" he whipped off the back, fiddled around with some wires, connected up a Morse tapper and started rattling off a code message to London. I was rather shaken by such expertise and I had an awful vision of it doing irreparable damage to Anglo-Latvian relations – and to [ALEX-2's] wireless set.'[118] Kenneth Benton, who served as Nicholson's deputy PCO in Riga, recalls of Maltby's visit that he and Maltby had originally tested an SIS-supplied radio set on the Riga Strand one night. Benton recalls that 'It took [Maltby] some time to get what he called a thumping clear signal from his operators at Hanslope, and a Morse message which acknowledged his reply but he did it.'

ADMINISTRATION AND SUPPORT

After accounting for Sections V, VI and VIII, one is left with the persistent puzzle of Section VII. Why was the agency's Principal Financial Officer designated a Circulating Section (apart from the facetious response that he was in the business of circulating money to and from the Treasury Department)? The most common response of respondents to this query amounted to a shrug or roll of the eyes, one officer arguing, 'I agree that inclusion of VII is anomalous; but Sykes was a Section head and it was simpler to list him alongside the others instead of inventing a new category',[119] concluding bleakly, 'Do not look to the [SIS organization] chart for consistency or coherence.'[120] Much the same might be said of grouping the Radio Section with the

Circulating Sections, although the same officer offered the limited, if vaguely facile, justification of this on the grounds that Section VIII 'circulated' ciphers to the rest of the organization. Of Sykes, Nicholson recalls that 'he treated public money as if it were his own and seemed to begrudge almost every penny we spent'.[121] If this was so, it was because of the financial pressures already upon the SIS, with Treasury-led cuts whittling its finances to the degree that Sinclair made his now famous complaint that the SIS budget was less than the cost of operating a single destroyer in home waters.[122] Sykes would make routine inspections of the stations,[123] although after the financial scandals in the 1930s a programme of unannounced spot inspections was reportedly adopted.[124] But the answer to this curiosity is also profoundly indicative of the relative disarray of the agency's administrative support machinery. Recruitment, personnel and even training were in even worse disrepair.

At the height of the First World War, there may have been sections for escape routes, communications (cipher), secret devices and personnel, but their continuation in peacetime proved less clear cut. Personnel management and recruitment, for example, was far less structured, verging on the notional, and personnel record-keeping was fragmentary at best. For example, during the transfer of the IIC from the SIS to the DOT, it was noted that 'No paper record exists' of Morton's and his staff's service with the SIS. This is surprising in view of the duration and active nature of Morton and Clively's terms with the service. Likewise, the SIS had not even kept a 'paper record' of the agreement in 1931 between Maurice Hankey, Sir Edward Crowe and Sinclair that Morton should be appointed head of the IIC.[125]

Technical research for 'secret devices' needed for human intelligence operations had been a mainstay of SIS efforts since before the First World War. There is an account of Mansfield-Cumming's seeking advice from scientists at the University of London about secret writing materials in 1915,[126] and, according to Paul Dukes, the SIS of 1918 possessed a 'laboratory' dealing with 'inks and all that',[127] while Judd has noted the development of a 'secret devices' section after the MacDonogh reforms of 1917. Benton has provided one of the few appearances of this section in the published literature, recalling that it provided 'a special device supplied by our Technical Aids Section in Broadway, which dispensed with the conventional Morse tapper. A metal panel was used, with channels containing a series of electrical contacts, each of which corresponded to a digit from 1 to 9. By means of a contact being slid along the selected channel, the correct series of dots and dashes was supplied to the transmitter.'[128] There was also a section providing cover documentation, such as forged passports and identity papers, that, one interviewed officer recalled, was by the mid-1930s simply known as 'Docs'.[129]

Contrary to popular impression, training was not completely absent from the SIS during the inter-war period, although it was limited, and inconsistently implemented. Leslie Nicholson notes that upon recruitment in 1929 he was 'put through a fairly hectic course to familiarize [him] with communications, codes and ciphers, and to learn about the financial arrangements'.[130] He was granted time to pick up some advice from then Vienna PCO Thomas Kendrick. After examining the Vienna station's files to little effect, he finally approached Kendrick:

'Could you give me any idea of how to begin?... Are there any standard rules?... or could you give me some practical advice?' He thought for a bit. 'I don't think there are, really; you'll just have to work it out for yourself. I think everyone has his own methods and I can't think of anything I can tell you.' This was appalling.[131]

Apart from doing 'a bit of homework on the political set-up in Eastern Europe', he received no detailed brief on requirements other than the broad need for 'information on every subject under the sun, political, military, industrial, economic, social scandal in high places'.[132] Nicholson's experience was also echoed by one of the officers interviewed whose career had begun in the 1930s. He noted that their only formal training was in codes and communications, while the techniques of targeting and recruitment were left untouched.[133] Another classic horror story of SIS indoctrination and training has been published by Kenneth Benton. Joining Kendrick's Vienna Station in 1937, Benton had no idea he had been recruited by the SIS until a member of Kendrick's staff presented him with a letter to translate from the German. Benton recalls,

I opened the letter... and said, 'Look I can't do this; it is in Czech.' She said, 'Oh, I'm sorry, hang on for a moment.' At the back of my desk there was a little open bottle of colourless liquid, with a brush, and she dipped the brush in the liquid, passed it over the whole front of the letter and to my amazed eyes red writing appeared at right angles to the Czech text and it was in German. Then she did the same on the rear side, so I had two sides of what was in fact a German report.[134]

The only exception was the Z Organization, in which Dansey not only trained his officers in clandestine communications but also brought in a retired Scotland Yard officer to teach counter-surveillance tactics. According to one former officer, they 'had a tame detective, an ex-CID man called Auger, who would take one "round the streets". He gave tips on how to lose someone if you were being followed. Then you had to plan a route, he would follow you and you had to try and shake him on your way to your destination. Afterwards he would submit a report on your performance.'[135] This officer also recalled being posted initially to the Z Organization's headquarters to see how the department worked and to 'learn the ropes'. Unfortunately, the Z Organization was a very separate creature from the main infrastructure of G Sections and PCOs, and any benefits that might have accrued from Dansey's approach to training and fielding officers were not felt by the rest of the service. The SIS would not develop an effective agency-wide training programme until it appropriated the practice from the wartime Special Operations Executive (SOE), first by putting its own agents through SOE training facilities in Britain and Canada and later by absorbing and asset-stripping SOE wholesale after the Second World War. The real irony here is that SOE was itself originally a part of the SIS as Section D, although the original 'D School' would not take shape until 1940.

CONSEQUENCES AND COSTS OF THE 1921 ARRANGEMENT

The inter-war period can be said to have been the critical period during which the SIS took on the institutional architecture which would continue to characterize it – and, indeed, distinguish it – into the 21st century. The central feature of this architecture was the '1921 arrangement' (although that actually took shape in 1919), which created the distinction between the agency's operational side, the Group or G Sections, and its tasking and dissemination side, the Circulating or C Sections. This turned the SIS into an explicitly consumer-led, demand-driven intelligence agency, in which staff seconded from, or representing, its consumers in Whitehall provided explicit intelligence requirements and sometimes equally explicit operational requirements. It should, however, be understood that none of this was the result of any conscious organizational design, at least on the part of the SIS, but rather resulted from divergent, departmental demands for control of intelligence production, and the horse-trading and logrolling of the 1919 and 1921 Secret Service Committees. Although the 1921 arrangement tied the SIS closely to its consumers, the requirements issued via the C Sections often turned out to be vague and poorly defined.[136] Ill-defined or not, requirements laid upon the agency steadily escalated throughout the inter-war period as international tensions escalated, and as the official history notes:

> the SIS was not a strong enough organization to settle priorities between the requests that were made of it, or even able to resist demands for assistance which went beyond its resources. When those demands became insistent and conflicting, as they did during the 1930s, it was overstretched by user departments.[137]

Problems of surplus demand were exacerbated by the steadily increasing financial strictures placed upon the SIS by a financially beleaguered Treasury. In other words, Whitehall wanted more and more intelligence, but was less and less inclined to pay for it.

Some have pointed the finger of responsibility at the Foreign Office for neglecting an organization it variously viewed as potential embarrassment and potential competitor, but, to be fair, the overt armed services fared little better during the same period.[138] As the official history of war production points out, government inter-war defence expenditure was guided by a CID assessment 'that it should be assumed for the purpose of framing estimates of the fighting services that at any given date there will be no major war for ten years'. The CID and the Treasury continued to employ the 'ten-year assumption' as late as March 1932.[139] Moreover, Britain had suffered a succession of economic and financial setbacks throughout the inter-war period, including the 1919 post-war recession, the 1925 gold standard crisis and the transatlantic consequences of the 1929 stock market crash. G.C. Peden has compellingly argued that the Treasury's reticence over defence spending was not merely a function of departmental intransigence, but a consequence of pressure placed upon the Treasury by successive inter-war governments pursuing a series of severe austerity programmes.[140] The same can easily be said of the SIS's budgetary ills during the same period. Between 1919 and 1922, the SIS experienced a 28 per cent[141] cut in its budget. Almost as if to add insult to injury, the PCO more than paid for itself yet its revenues were not available to supplement the SIS operating budget.[142] Even the overall heightened tensions on the Continent that prompted the expansion of the IIC, and the Abyssinian crisis in particular, were not enough to drive increased expenditure. In 1935, the same year the IIC moved to the DOT because the SIS could no longer house it, Sinclair made his complaint that the entire operating budget of the SIS was less than the cost of operating a Royal Navy destroyer in home waters.[143] In 1936, the Defence Requirements Committee (which included the SIS's major armed service customers) petitioned Fisher's Treasury on the SIS's behalf for £500,000, but to no avail. The only temporary respite in the cutbacks was 'some increase', as the official history puts it, in the wake of the Austrian *Anschluss*, and during this year Sinclair took the initiative of introducing Sections VI, VIII and D. Restraint returned afterwards, and, as discussed further below, struggles among the SIS, the Tizard Committee and the Treasury delayed implementing a new scientific sub-section to Section II until the outbreak of war.

The persistent cutbacks had a significant impact on the SIS's operational ability and the quality of its product. By the outbreak of war, at least the War Office, Air Force and Foreign Office were chronically dissatisfied with its performance. The War Office complained about an inability to meet 'urgent needs' for information about Germany, the Air Force discounted 80 per cent of the SIS product on the German Air Force as inaccurate, and the Permanent Under-Secretary of the Foreign Office even felt the need to circulate a minute on the matter. They were all perfectly aware that the SIS was simply so under-resourced it could not possibly fulfil the growing and increasingly immediate demands being made upon it.[144] Hence, the SIS's problems at the outbreak of war were less ones of mismanagement and cronyism than a consequence of decreasing finance, with dwindling resources coupled to both increased consumer demand *and* increased operating costs. In many respects, it is less surprising that the SIS may have achieved what little it did than that it survived at all.

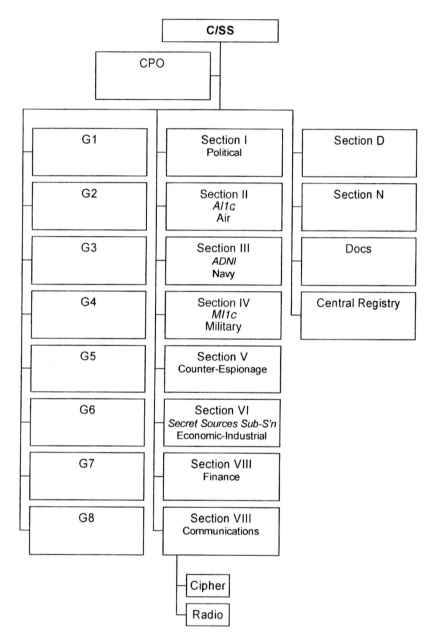

Figure 3.2: SIS in 1939

NOTES

1. Paper in the proceedings of the CID Sub-Committee on Defence Policy and Requirements, Defence Requirements Enquiry, of March, 1936 in CAB 16/123, PRO.
2. The interorganization a coordination problem would, of course, be repeated in terms of SIS/SOE relations during the next World War.
3. Hinsley et al. *British Intelligence in the Second World War: Its Influence on Strategy and Operations*, vol. I (London: HMSO, 1979), p. 17.
4. Ibid., footnote.
5. A.G. Denniston, 'The Government Code and Cypher School Between the Wars', *Intelligence and National Security*, 1, 1 (January 1986), p. 57.
6. This is a corrected version of the arrangement which may be found in Nigel West, *MI6: British Secret Intelligence Service Operations 1909–1945* (London: Grafton, 1988), pp. 19, 145–8; Philip Johns, *Within Two Cloaks* (London: William Kimber, 1979), p. 40; Robert Cecil 'MI6', in I.C.B. Dear and M.R.D. Foot (eds), *Oxford Companion to the Second World War* (Oxford: Oxford University Press, 1994), p. 745. In all of these versions, Section II is given as 'Military' and Section IV as 'Air'; however, H.A.R. 'Kim' Philby refers to Section IV as being 'Military' in his *My Silent War* (New York: Ballantine, 1983), p. 75. During interviews, most of those who claimed to be able to recall the Circulating Section/Requirements organization claimed that II had been Air and IV Military; this was particularly stressed by one former Air Section officer. This also seems the most likely arrangement in view of the organizational status of the Second World War escape and evasion organization, MI9 vis-à-vis the SIS. MI9's resident escape and evasion networks in western Europe were controlled by a section called IS9g, which was subordinated to the SIS field organization. For most of the war, they held the operational designation P15; however, initially IS9g was under the War Office SIS liaison as MI6d (see 'Attachment A: Historical Record of MI9', p. 94 WO 208/3242 in the Public Record Office); within the SIS, this original section was designated 'IVz' (see James Langley, *Fight Another Day* (London: Collins, 1974); see also M.R.D. Foot and James Langley, *MI9* (London: Bodley Head, 1979), where it is referred to as '4z', p. 44), and Section 5.11 below. Moreover, in Anthony Cavendish's post-war order of battle, the Air Section appears as R2 and the Military Section as R4; see Cavendish, *Inside Intelligence* (London: Collins, 1990), pp. 40–1. Finally, and most recently, among published sources, Philby's reports to his Russian controllers, reproduced in Nigel West and Oleg Tsarev's *The Crown Jewels* (London: HarperCollins, 1998), state that 'Section II...performs the same type of work for the Air Ministry [as Section I]...the other circulating sections...are: Section III Admiralty; Section IV, War Office; Section VI, Ministry of Economic

Warfare', p. 302. The most compelling item was a copy of an SIS internal document in the possession of one of the officers interviewed, which explicitly identified R.V. Jones as IId, and therefore the Air Section as Section II.

7. SIS Minute Sheet, Form R1, revision date February 1932, in XC22483, HS 2/240, PRO.

8. *War Office List 1918*, p. 100.

9. *War Office Lists 1919–39* give Menzies as attached to MI1c on 'Special Duties'; prior to 1919, MI1c 'Special Duties' are under Cummings name. As Andrew notes in *Secret Service*, the date of Menzies's entry into the SIS is also given in his entry in the *Dictionary of National Biography 1961–1970*, p. 749.

10. Christopher Andrew, *Secret Service* (London: Sceptre, 1987), p. 487; Anthony Cave Brown, *C: The Secret Life of Stewart Graham Menzies, Spymaster to Winston Churchill* (New York: Macmillan, 1987), pp. 139–40.

11. Documents pertaining to the post-First World War contraction and reorganization of the NID can be found in ADM 116/1842; in particular, note that although the pressure to contract appeared in 1919, the Admiralty was still mulling over its tasks, which it viewed as having 'increased a thousandfold due to demands made by other departments, as a result of...war experience' in 1921, and arguing with the Treasury over the scales and functions of its presence at home as well as abroad. See 'Draft Reply to the Treasury Re Reduction in NI', 1921, and the undated NID 10388/21 'Naval Intelligence Operations Abroad', both in ADM 116/1842 PRO.

12. Admiralty papers dealing with the post-First World War reorganization and contraction of the NID can be found in ADM 116/1842 PRO.

13. 'Organisational Chart of Intelligence Division, Naval Staff, Admiralty', ADM 116/1842, PRO.

14. Alan Judd (Alan Petty) *The Quest for C: Mansfield Cumming and the Founding of the Secret Service* (London: HarperCollins, 1999), p. 382.

15. Hinsley et al., *British Intelligence*, vol. I, p. 16.

16. *Who Was Who*, 1941–1950, pp. 1174–5.

17. Hinsley et al., *British Intelligence*, vol. I, p. 16; Andrew, *Secret Service*, pp. 211, 408, 488–9.

18. Hinsley et al., *British Intelligence*, vol. I, p. 9.

19. Keith Jeffery, 'British Military Intelligence Following World War I', in K.G. Robertson (ed.), *British and American Approaches to Intelligence* (London: Macmillan, 1987), p. 83, from *War Office List 1925*. The possible role of MO1 in delaying the need for AI1c was also suggested by Michael Smith during preparation of his *New Cloak, Old Dagger: How Britain's Spies Came in from the Cold* (London: Gollancz, 1996).

20. F.W. Winterbotham, *The Nazi Connection: The Personal History of a Top-*

90

Level British Agent in Pre-War Germany (London: Wiedenfeld & Nicolson, 1978), pp. 15–19; R.V. Jones, *Most Secret War* (London: Hamish Hamilton, 1978), p. 93.

21. See, for various accounts of this work, Winterbotham, *The Nazi Connection*, pp. 188–202; Hinsley et al., *British Intelligence*, vol. I, pp. 28–30, 496–9; Andrew, *Secret Service*, pp. 654–6.
22. 'History of the Department of Overseas Trade', BT 61/60/8, PRO.
23. For details on the origins and work of the IIC, see Wesley Wark, *The Ultimate Enemy* (Oxford: Oxford University Press, 1986), pp. 159–87 and *passim* and Hinsley et al., *British Intelligence*, vol. I, pp. 30–4.
24. Desmond Morton to J.H. Jones, DOT, Notes A and B, FIN 28, BT 61/60/9, PRO.
25. Letter from J.H. Jones to Secretary of the Treasury, 12 August 1936, FIN 51; FIN 28, both in BT 61/60/9, PRO.
26. FIN 51 in BT 61/60/9, PRO.
27. Wark, *The Ultimate Enemy*, p. 159.
28. FIN 51, BT 61 60/9, PRO.
29. 'The Staffing of the Industrial Intelligence Centre', ICF 279, BT 61/60/9, PRO.
30. Morton to Sir Edward Crowe, 26 August 1935 in ICF 279, BT 61/60/9, PRO.
31. 'History of the Department of Overseas Trade', BT 61/60/8, PRO.
32. W.N. Medlicott, *The Economic Blockade*, vol. I (London: HMSO, 1952), p. 16.
33. 'ATB and (EPG) 13 and 14, Item 2(b) Organization of an Intelligence Service, Interim Report' with cover noted from Morton to Jones dated 31 March 1938, FCI 968, BT 61/69/2, PRO.
34. FCI 968, BT 61/69/2, PRO.
35. The cover note to Section D's (see 4.9) October 1938 Oxelsund report states that an 'abridged version circulated to Sec. VI + III', HS 2/263, PRO. However, Morton's March 1938 proposal for his Economic Warfare Intelligence Branch (ICF 968) refers to GC & CS's circulating its commercial SIGINT from its 'Trade Section' to the Department of Economic Warfare via the proposed 'DEWI special liaison officer', clearly indicating that the GC & CS Trade Section (see Denniston 'The Government Codes and Cypher School Between the Wars', p. 63) predated Section VI and was itself already extant in March 1938. It is also possible that Morton's suggestions may have been by way of a sort of 'enabling act', acknowledging arrangements which had existed for some time. Another possible point at which Section VI might sensibly have been implemented was in 1935, after the move from Broadway to the DOT removed Morton from regular access to SIS reports.
36. Johns, *Within Two Cloaks*, p. 48; West, *MI6*, p. 147; Limpenny's 1940 *Who's Who* entry indicates his one-time posting as ADC to the King.

91

37. Winterbotham, *The Nazi Connection*, pp. 18–19.
38. Jones, *Most Secret War*, p. 100.
39. Winterbotham, *The Nazi Connection*, p. 19.
40. Ibid., p. 19 and *passim*.
41. 1947 Report on Intelligence Methods, pp. 7–8, ADM 223/475, PRO.
42. A chart for the 1923 SIS field organization from Cumming's papers can be found on the cover leaves of Alan Judd's, *Quest for C*.
43. SIS Minute Sheet, Form R1, revision date February 1932, in XC22483, HS 2/240, PRO. Distribution header on the SIS minute sheet includes item 'Seen G (G. Officer to Initial)' and the right margin space headed 'Action Proposed (For use of G. Sections)'. Andrew, *Secret Service*, p. 408. Philby also notes that at the time he joined SIS, field operations were overseen by G Sections; see *My Silent War*, p. 54.
44. Telegram from Commander-in-Chief Far East to Air Ministry of 6 January 1941, CAB 81/900, PRO.
45. West, *MI6*, p. 144. West's account here is a little uncertain, with an unexplained reference to the G side as 'YP' (Y generally referring in UK practice to wireless interception), and conflating the pre-1941 and post-1941 G and P (Production) designations.
46. This position has been repeatedly made by Robert Cecil in, for example, his 'The Assessment and Acceptance of Intelligence: A Case Study', in K.G. Robertson (ed.), *British and American Approaches to Intelligence*, pp. 168–9, and his interview with Bob Cuddihy in the documentary video *MI6: The Inside Story* (First Independent, 1995).
47. This interpretation is developed by Nigel West in his *MI6*, pp. 56–7.
48. Eunan O'Halpen, 'Financing British Intelligence: The Evidence Up To 1945', in K.G. Robertson (ed.), *British and American Approaches to Intelligence*, p. 204.
49. D.N. Chester and F.M.G. Wilson, *The Organization of British Central Government 1914–1956* (London: Allen & Unwin, 1957), p. 194.
50. Ibid., p. 195.
51. Andrew, *Secret Service*, pp. 346–7.
52. *War Office List 1917*, p. 84.
53. Spencer appears in minutes of the Aliens and Nationals Committee's 8th Meeting (18 July 1919) in Kell's stead, at the 24th Meeting (20 February 1920) as representing the Foreign Office, but not until the 30th Meeting (30 July 1920) as the Head of the Passport Control Organization. Minutes and Proceedings of the Aliens and Nationality Committee, Vols 3–4, HO 45/19966, PRO.
54. Andrew, *Secret Service*, pp. 408, 495.
55. Interview with i-20.
56. Henry Landau, *All's Fair: The Story of British Secret Service Behind German Lines* ((New York: Puttnam, 1934), pp. 161–2.
57. Telegram published in Compton Mackenzie, *Aegean Memories* (London:

Chatto and Windus, 1940), p. 105, emphasis added.

58. DNI to Vice Admiral, Eastern Mediterranean Squadron, March 1917, published in Mackenzie, *Aegean Memories*, p. 107.

59. Quoted in Mackenzie, *Aegean Memories*, p. 235; emphasis mine.

60. Landau, *All's Fair*, p. 227.

61. Ibid., pp. 227–8.

62. Andrew, *Secret Service*, p. 347.

63. Ibid., pp. 491–2; West, *MI6*, pp. 88–91; John Whitwell (Leslie Nicholson) *British Agent* (London: William Kimber, 1966), *passim*.

64. O'Halpen, 'Financing British Intelligence', p. 205.

65. Nigel West, *A Matter of Trust: MI5 1945–72* (London: Coronet, 1987), pp. 178–9; Peter Wright, *Spycatcher: The Candid Autobiography of a Senior Intelligence Office* (Toronto: Hodder & Stoughton, 1987), pp. 329–30.

66. Information from Nigel West. See footnote 139, Chapter 5, above.

67. Andrew, *Secret Service*, pp. 495–6; West, *MI6*, pp. 88–91.

68. F.H. Hinsley and C.A.G. Simkins, *British Intelligence: Security and Counterintelligence*, vol. IV (London: HMSO, 1990), p. 57; Andrew, *Secret Service*, p. 607; Anthony Read and David Fisher, *Colonel Z* (London: Hodder & Stoughton, 1984), p. 171.

69. Andrew, *Secret Service*, p. 497.

70. Landau, *All's Fair*, p. 234.

71. Andrew, *Secret Service*, pp. 535–6, and see particularly Michael Smith's biography of Foley, *Foley: The Spy Who Saved 10,000 Jews* (London: Coronet, 1999).

72. Minutes and Proceedings of Aliens and Nationality Committee, vols 3–4; 34th meeting, 10 June 1921. HO 45/19966, PRO.

73. Whitwell, *British Agent*, pp. 62–4.

74. Interview with i-20.

75. Hinsley et al., *British Intelligence*, vol. I p. 17, footnote; sourced to the Hankey Report of 11 March 1940.

76. See, for example, Whitwell (Nicholson), *British Agent*, pp. 61–2 and *passim*; informed officers also made it quite clear that they were directly involved in the targeting and recruitment of agents as Heads of Station.

77. For descriptions of these practices, see, for example, Whitwell (Nicholson), *British Agent*, pp. 60–2.

78. Read and Fisher, *Colonel Z*, p. 171.

79. Andrew, *Secret Service*, p. 409.

80. Ibid., p. 537.

81. Hinsley and Simkins, *British Intelligence*, vol. IV, p. 11.

82. Andrew, *Secret Service*, p. 540.

83. Whitwell, *British Agent*, pp. 106, 109.

84. Welsey Wark, 'Our Man in Riga: Reflections on the Career and Writings of Leslie Nicholson', *Intelligence and National Security*, 11, 4 (October 1996), p. 634.

85. i-015.

86. When Robert Cecil was preparing the SIS organization chart for the *Oxford Companion to the Second World War* and submitted the article for inclusion, the Foreign Office insisted that he remove any mention of Section N. Conversation with Robert Cecil.

87. The earliest reference to Section N in the secondary literature refers to the section's being headed by David Boyle in 1924. Brown, C: *The Secret Life of Stewart Graham Menzies, Spymaster to Winston Churchill*, pp. 210–11 and footnote. The existence and role of Section N was confirmed by several former SIS officers interviewed.

88. Philby, *My Silent War*, p. 63.

89. Brown, C, pp. 141, 144; Philby, *My Silent War*, p. 63.

90. Philby, *My Silent War*, p. 64; interview with former SIS officer with Section N experience.

91. Brown, C, p. 211, footnote.

92. Philby, *My Silent War*, p. 64.

93. Nigel West and Oleg Tsarev, *The Crown Jewels*, p. 328.

94. Hinsley et al., *British Intelligence*, vol. I, p. 18.

95. Hinsley and Simkins, *British Intelligence*, vol. IV, p. 8.

96. A considerable volume has been written on the so-called Reilly–Lockhart affair. Sidney Reilly prepared his own version of events before finally disappearing into a trap set by Dzerzhinsky's V-Cheka and its notorious 'Trust'. The volume was published posthumously by his wife, P. Reilly as *The Adventures of Sidney Reilly* (London: Ellis, Matthews & Marot, 1931). Two other figures directly involved, the Foreign Office's Robert Bruce-Lockhart and George Hill, under War Office direction recorded their own accounts in *Memoirs of a British Agent* (London: Putnam, 1932; Macmillan, 1985) and *Go Spy the Land* (London: Cassell, 1932), respectively. A carefully researched historical study of the Reilly and Dukes efforts can be found in Andrew, *Secret Service*, Ch. 6 *passim*, and a Soviet view of the affair in David Golinkov, *The Secret War Against Soviet Russia* (Moscow: Novosti, 1981), includes the subsequent interrogations of Reilly and his ally General Boris Savinkov. Less reliable versions can be found in Robin Bruce Lockhart's *Reilly, Ace of Spies* (London: Futura, 1983; edited as a companion to the ITV television series of the same title by Linda Hawkins, London: ITV Books, 1983), and in Michael Kettle's frequently speculative *Sidney Reilly: The True Story* (London: Corgi, 1983). Most recently, and with access to Soviet archives, the Foreign Office historian Gill Bennett has produced *History Notes: A Most Extraordinary and Mysterious Business: The Zinoviev Letter of 1924* (London: Foreign and Commonwealth Office, 1999), probably as close to a definitive account as is likely to be achieved given the state of the surviving papers on both sides.

97. 1925 Secret Service Committee Report, reproduced in Bennett, *History Notes: A Most Extraordinary and Mysterious Business*, p. 110.

98. Hinsley and Simkins, *British Intelligence*, vol. IV p. 7; the 1925 Secret Service Report has also been published as an appendix to Bennett's FCO account of the Ziniviev Letter affair, *History Notes: A Most Extraordinary and Mysterious Business: The Zinoviev Letter of 1924*, pp. 105–14, the tract referred to by Hinsley and Simkins appearing on p. 110.

99. The existence of this section is firmly established in John Curry's official history, *The Security Service 1908–1945* (London: Public Record Office, 1999), p. 143. Although a central player in the Zinoviev affair, it is referred to only elliptically in Bennett's FO account, *History Notes: A Most Extraordinary and Mysterious Business, the Zinoviev Letter of 1924*, *passim*.

100. Bennett, *History Notes: A Most Extraordinary and Mysterious Business* p. 38. Note that while Bennett here is referring to a particular agent Morton apparently 'shared' with Sir George Makgill, it is evident from Bennett's account that this informant was not unique and that Morton had a ' whole file' of Communist internal correspondence (p. 31). Although a brief curriculum vitae of Morton appearing in Board of Trade files surrounding the transfer of the IIC to the DOT cited above states that Morton had worked for the SIS from 1919, it does not indicate in what capacity. Wark, *The Ultimate Enemy*, p. 159, also remarks tentatively upon Morton's concern with Soviet affairs prior to setting up the IIC.

101. Hinsley and Simkins, *British Intelligence in the Second World War*, vol. IV: *Security and Counter-Intelligence*, p. 7.

102. Ibid., p.7; Currie, *The Security Service*, pp. 48, 101–3.

103. Curry, *The Security Service 1908–1945* (London: Public Record Office, 1999), p. 101.

104. Robert Cecil, 'Five of Six at War', *Intelligence and National Security*, 9, 9 (April, 1994), pp. 345–6.

105. Curry, *The Security Service 1908–1945*, p. 101.

106. David Dilks, 'Flashes of Intelligence: The Foreign Office, the SIS and Security Before the Second World War', in Christopher Andrew and David Dilks, *The Missing Dimension: Governments and Intelligence Communities in the Twentieth Century* (Chicago: University of Chicago Press, 1984), pp. 105–18; a more detailed account appears in Andrew, *Secret Service*, pp. 568–72.

107. Curry, *The Security Service 1908–1945* (London: Public Record Office, 1999), p. 104.

108. Ibid., p. 105.

109. Hinsley and Simkins, *British Intelligence*, vol. IV, p. 11.

110. Read and Fisher, *Colonel Z*, p. 171, quoting Hans Giskes, the *Abwehr* counter-espionage officer who would also eventually run the NORDPOL double-cross against SOE during the war.

111. Paul Dukes, *The Story of ST 25: Adventure and Romance in Red Russia* (London: Cassell, 1938), p. 30.

112. See, for example, M.R.D. Foot, *SOE in France* (London: HMSO, 1966), pp. 2–4; Foot, *SOE: and Outline History* (London: BBC, 1985), pp. 14–15; J.G. Beevor, *SOE: Recollections and Reflections* (London: Bodley Head, 1981), p. 13.

113. Foot, *SOE in France*, p. 3.

114. This is indicated from Gambier-Parry's entry in *Who Was Who, 1961–1970*, p. 410.

115. Ellic Howe, *The Black Game: British Subversive Operations Against the Germans During the Second World War* (London: Queen Anne Press/Futura, 1982). According to the acknowledgements, Robin assisted Howe extensively in assembling his account of British subversive actions during the Second World War, and so it can be assumed that Howe's account derives directly from Robin's recollections (p. xi).

116. Howe, *The Black Game*, p. 77.

117. Howe, *The Black Game*, pp. 77–8; Kenneth Benton, 'The ISOS Years: Madrid 1941–3', pp. 369–70; West, *MI6*, p. 147.

118. Whitwell (Nicholson), *British Agent*, pp. 85–6; original emphasis. A somewhat more prosaic version of Maltby's visit appears in Benton, 'The ISOS Years', p. 369. Wesley Wark, '"Our Man in Riga": Reflections on the SIS Career and Writings of Leslie Nicholson', pp. 638–40, has recently noted the conflict between Nicholson's recollections concerning ALEX 2's salvaged transceiver and Benton's account, according to which the transceiver was an SIS product supplied to ALEX 1, who was eventually to act as a stay-behind agent. Wark suggests that the Riga station may have started out with ALEX 2's piece and then been supplied with a new unit by SIS, either by diplomatic bag or during Maltby's tour of inspection. This seems likely since the ALEX 2 unit, described as being 'the size of a butcher's refrigerator', would have been too large and unwieldy to manhandle up to the friend's apartment where the incident with Maltby's Morse tapper took place.

119. Correspondence with i-01.

120. Similar sentiments were uttered by i-09 during interview, although his attitude appears to have been that SIS did not have to worry about such things.

121. Whitwell (Leslie Nicholson), *British Agent*, p. 40.

122. Hinsley, et al., *British Intelligence*, p. 51; given that the current budget is around £200 million, with current salaries and fuel costs the same might almost be true today.

123. Whitwell, *British Agent*, pp. 40–1.

124. West, *MI6*, p. 91.

125. FIN 28 Note A of 15 May 1935, BT 61/60/9, PRO.

126. Andrew, *Secret Service*, p. 225.

127. Dukes, *The Story of ST 25*, p. 36.

128. Benton, 'The ISOS Years', p. 369.

129. Interview with i-15.
130. Leslie Nicholson (writing as John Whitwell), *British Agent*, p. 20.
131. Whitwell, *British Agent*, p. 26.
132. Ibid., p. 20.
133. Interviews with i-011; i-019.
134. Kenneth Benton, 'The ISOS Years: Madrid 1941–3' *Journal of Contemporary History*, 30, 3 (July 1995), p. 362.
135. Interview with i-015.
136. Hinsley et al., *British Intelligence*, vol. I, p. 56, Whitwell (Nicholson), *British Agent*, p. 20.
137. Hinsley et al., *British Intelligence*, vol. I, p. 18; acknowledgements to Mike Smith of the *Daily Telegraph* brought this quotation to my attention.
138. M.M. Postan, *British War Production* (London: HMSO, 1952), ch. 1, *passim*.
139. Ibid. p. 1.
140. G.C. Peden, *British Rearmament and the Treasury 1932–1939* (Edinburgh: Scottish Academic Press, 1979), *passim*.
141. From £125,000 to £90,000; Hinsley, et al., *British Intelligence*, vol. I, p. 50.
142. Minutes of Proceedings, 34th Meeting of the Passport Control Committee, 10 June 1921, in HO 45/19966/31848.
143. Hinsley et al., *British Intelligence*, vol. 1, p. 51.
144. Ibid., p. 55.

4

War Without and Within, 1939–45

I wondered whether, as an intelligence officer of the old school, he [Menzies] was quite the right choice to deal with the changed face of espionage and the multitude of new men and tasks which must be met.

H. Montgomery Hyde
Secret Intelligence Agent[1]

The SIS that emerged out of the inter-war period was an organization that was designed primarily as an intermediary between intelligence consumers on the wider, overt machinery of government and whatever intelligence sources might be available. This role of screen or cut-out was certainly the original *raison d'être* for the Secret Service Bureau in 1909, and the subsequent 1921 arrangement (or, as Judd would have it, the 1917 MacDonogh reforms) created a series of formal structures that reinforced that basic relationship. The 1921 arrangement also created a headquarters infrastructure based more on horizontal communication between producers in the Group Sections and consumers represented by the Circulating Sections than on a direct, vertical chain of command under C. Both the centrality of consumer influence and the tendency towards what organization theorists call a 'flat' and 'wide' structure would prove crucial to the fits and starts of organizational development in the SIS during the new crisis in Europe and the Second World War.

The wartime development of the SIS can be broadly divided into three main trends. The first trend was the foreseen, planned (albeit more in theory than in practice) expansion of the organization under wartime mobilization. This involved adapting its operational side to meet both increased intelligence demand from consumers and the operational circumstances that emerged out of the first months and year of the war. The rapid German advance in Europe swept away most of the agency's resident presence on the Continent, and forced it to find new ways of penetrating Axis and occupied territory. The emergence of large-scale, sustained campaigns in the Middle East and North Africa (and later the Far East) forced SIS HQ, by noir at the Broadway Buildings, to devolve much of its work and control to theatre-level commands. Grand's sabotage and subversion Section D and Richard Gambier-Parry's radio and cipher Section VIII that had existed to varying degrees on a theoretical or skeletal basis rapidly became sizeable concerns with responsibilities well beyond their original, narrowly visualized briefs. Unsurprisingly, just as increased consumer demand involved expanding the operational side, so it also required an expansion of the consumer liaison side to cope in part with an anticipated flood of wartime material from the mobilized group side and in part with an anticipated diversification of secret functions, such as escape and evasion and covert political operations.

Much of the first trend involved coping with setbacks from the way the early stages of the war developed. The second trend was adapting new and emerging opportunities for intelligence work. The most significant such opportunity was almost certainly the successful attacks on the German Enigma codes by the Government Code and Cipher School (GC & CS), then still under the control of C. This source of intelligence, generally known as ULTRA (although there were a variety of different systems broken under different code names during the course of the war), affected many aspects of the SIS's internal organization, as well as the structure and process of GC & CS. The SIS found itself responsible for providing a secure wireless system for conveying ULTRA to theatre commands abroad, and the *Abwehr* ULTRA and hand-cipher breaks, collectively known as ISOS, opened the door to a vast range of counter-espionage human intelligence better known operations abroad run by the SIS in concert with the side of the domestic 'Double-Cross' campaign headed by MI5. The SIS also found itself mounting operations in Europe with or through the exiled intelligence services from occupied states such as Czechoslovakia, Poland and France.

The third trend that emerged throughout the wartime period was the failure of the model of a wide, flat internal organization that might have worked with a headquarters staff of 65 at the end of the First World War, and of probably only 25 by the outbreak of the Second World War, but was ill-suited to anything larger. That intrinsic organizational problem was intensified during the first years of the war by the unenviable combination of rapidly escalating consumer demand and rapidly dwindling capability for production, as Europe collapsed in the first year of the war, and the Pacific empire collapsed under the Japanese onslaught in the second. Of these three trends, it was probably this third one that virtually brought the agency to its knees at the mid-point of the war, and raised serious questions about its future existence afterwards.

MOBILIZATION AND THE OUTBREAK OF WAR

The Second World War began badly for the SIS. Financial constraints between the wars had severely limited its ability to install stay-behind intelligence networks, and installing new networks in an occupied Continent was a difficult and painstaking process, with numerous setbacks. There were major problems that were, to be frank, self-inflicted. One of these was the wholesale compromise and effective collapse of the PCO system even before Continental Europe was overwhelmed by Germany's blitzkrieg. For reasons which remain entirely unexplained, Sinclair, on the outbreak of war, merged the PCO with Dansey's Z Organization. The Z Organization had arguably been set up as a backup system just because of the risk that the main organization had been compromised. Admittedly, the Z Organization's reliance on business contacts and commercial cover meant that its prewar advantage of cover and mobility evaporated with the closure of occupied European borders, but combining the two served to undercut completely any back-up role the Z Organization might have played during the collapse of SIS's Continental assets. Shortly after the amalgamation of the two systems, both the Hague Head of Station and the former Hague Z officer who had become his deputy were captured by the Nazi *Sicherheitsdienst* (SD), in the notorious Venlo incident on 9 November 1939.[2]

If the consolidation of the PCO and the Z Organization escapes easy explanation, so also does the decision in 1940 to divide the chain of command under C, and not merely to divide it but to do so ambiguously. In November 1939, Sir Hugh 'Quex' Sinclair died while still in office as C, even as the Venlo incident was coming to a head. At this point, something of a struggle broke out for control of

100

the SIS. Claude Dansey, who had been running the Z Organization from Geneva, viewed himself as the most senior and best qualified candidate for the post of Chief, and returned to Britain in pursuit of the position. In many ways, Dansey could make a plausible case, since, as we have seen, he had been with the SIS since 1917, and with MI5 before that. However, he had been formally out of the chain of command since the mid-1930s and had departed under something of a cloud (albeit a notional one). The Admiralty supported Rear-Admiral John H. Godfrey, Director of Naval Intelligence (DNI), a stern critic of the SIS, against the War Office's candidate, Stewart Graham Menzies, head of Section IV and Sinclair's unofficial deputy. Perceiving the impossibility of obtaining the succession, Dansey put his support behind Menzies. To complicate matters further, Winston Churchill proposed his own candidate in the form of Captain Gerald Muirhead-Gould, then commanding the HMS *Devonshire*. However, as David Stafford has observed of these events, 'even on the most generous interpretation Muirhead-Gould possessed no obvious qualifications for the top job in British intelligence' apart from flattering Churchill over his stance on rearmament.[3] In terms of Whitehall politics, the Admiralty had now provided the Chief twice in succession, in violation of the terms of the 1919 and 1921 Secret Service Committees, and Churchill's intervention spurred the Prime Minister, Foreign Secretary and Permanent Under-Secretary of the Foreign Office to unite behind Menzies. Menzies clinched the matter by producing a letter written by Sinclair nominating him as the new C.[4] Despite his efforts to acquire the post of Chief, Menzies then took a series of decisions that were to weaken profoundly his own control of the SIS for the remainder of the war.

In January 1940, Menzies appointed Dansey as his Assistant Chief of Service (AC/SS) and the head of Section V, and Valentine Vivian as Deputy Chief (DC/SS), but, as Robert Cecil has pointed out, 'without clearly defining duties or precedence'.[5] In principle, appointing at least one deputy made considerable sense since the lack of an obvious successor in 1939 had tied up a great deal of senior time and effort in the SIS and its consuming departments for nearly a month. Moreover, the SIS was due for a rapid expansion as a result of wartime mobilization, and no single senior head of service could possibly run the entire agency single-handed. However, Menzies's actions had the unanticipated consequence of splitting the chain of command in two, each officer nominally C's immediate junior, but

101

each struggling for seniority over the other in a pitched campaign of mutually exclusive empire building. Robert Cecil has suggested that this was because Menzies was not strong enough to keep a tight reign on a ruthless and ambitious Dansey.[6] Whatever Menzies's actual reasoning, the end result was an ongoing round of internecine bureaucratic hostilities.

The result of this undefined arrangement was that the two officers appear to have moved into their vice-chiefdoms with little more than enhanced versions of their original responsibilities. Vivian maintained ultimate responsibility for Section V over its new head, Felix Cowgill. Dansey, however, as an operational officer, held sway over the G Sections and most offensive intelligence collection abroad.[7] After a year, Vivian minuted C to the effect that he was becoming increasingly marginalized, complaining that SIS officers fell into three categories: those who treated his position with doubt and reservation, expressing concern that he was almost exclusively tied up with CE work deriving from Section V; those who were under the impression that his authority had been confined to the short-lived evacuation of headquarters personnel to Bletchley Park, the SIS's 'War Station' or 'Station X', shortly after the outbreak of war; and, finally, those who were completely unaware of his promotion.[8] Vivian further complained that he had virtually no access to the 'policy, plans, methods or results' of a number of the group and circulating sections, as 'I am rapidly losing my touch with SIS policy and performance generally, except in so far as I am kept in the picture by my talks with CSS...the Section I Weekly Summaries, the daily bundle of "flimsies", and the G2, G4, IVa, IVb and Sec. VI papers which those sections sometimes, but not consistently, refer to me.'[9] Vivian's detachment was worsened by the fact that Section V remained housed away from Broadway. After the initial Bletchley Park evacuation, it moved to Prae Wood, St Albans, where the Central Registry had also been moved out of the way of immediate threat from German bombs. It was not until 1943, when Section V moved back to London, to be housed at Ryder Street, that coordination would improve.[10]

The nature of the conflict was more than merely structural; it was reflected and intensified by the incompatibility of the two personalities. Dansey has been described variously as 'corrupt, incompetent but with a certain low cunning',[11] and as 'the only real professional in MI6'.[12] Philby describes Vivian as being 'mortally afraid' of Dansey,[13] but, if so, he was not alone. Philip Johns, variously IIIc, and Head of Station Lisbon and Rio de Janeiro before transfer to the Dutch section of the SOE, recalls that there was 'a love/hatred feeling for [Dansey] in the organisation, but he was unquestionably a pillar of strength'. Johns's personal impression was that 'provided one could tolerate his pungent wit, often deliberately assumed to provoke a subordinate, he could be a most likeable character and a good, helpful friend.'[14] James Langley, who headed the escape and evasion networks in Broadway from 1941 onwards, has recounted one incident of Dansey in all his acerbic glory, as he briefed Langley concerning his responsibilities as the SIS liaison for MI9, the joint-Service escape and evasion organization: 'Just listen to me and don't ask any silly damned questions. The likes of you in France and Belgium are causing me considerable trouble, which is being made worse by the apparent inability of the RAF to remain airborne over enemy territory. My job, and that of my agents, is to collect information about German intentions and activities, not to act as nursemaids to people who seem totally incapable of doing much to get back on their own.'[15] Dansey was no less hostile to counter-espionage (despite starting his secret intelligence career in Kell's MI5),[16] one officer recalling that he referred to it contemptuously as 'ragoût de la concierge'.[17]

While Dansey proved an aggressive manager, Vivian, whatever his weaknesses, was, according to Philby, a 'stickler for correct procedure'. Philby further acknowledged that 'his sermons on the subject told me more about the intricacies of government machinery than I could have learned from the slapdash "result getters" such as Dansey or Cowgill'.[18] Indeed, it was Vivian who displayed a critical awareness of the weaknesses of the flat, wide and loosely integrated SIS organizational structure in his memorandum to Menzies, arguing that the Deputy Chief's role should be 'to form a coordination point, short of CSS himself, for the whole SIS machinery which would (a) save CSS a spate of constant references which he ought never to have to deal with and (b) integrate the present collection of independent units, known as SIS, into an organized and coherent whole'.[19] Vivian's concerns, however, would be ignored throughout the war, until the eventual programme of review and reorganization heralded by the European war's drawing to a close. In the meantime, however, Menzies did little to resolve the conflict between the two deputies, perhaps because of the enormous pressures upon him with GC & CS overloaded both on the supply and demand sides[20] and customer dissatisfaction with his performance and that of the SIS. Indeed, Menzies took measures to insulate himself further in 1943 by assigning a Principal Staff Officer (PSO/CSS) in the form of the former IIIb, Christopher Arnold-Forster,[21] who was not technically in the chain of command but whose task, according to one officer from the period, amounted to handling the personnel and administrative 'dirty work' that Menzies preferred to avoid.[22]

With the start of a new general war, the demand for secret intelligence was bound to rise exponentially, as it had in the previous war. Consequently, there had to be alterations and extensions to the 1921 arrangement to meet consumers' new needs. With the outbreak of war, the Service Branch directorates of intelligence began programmes of expansion and reorganization leading, in turn, to the expansion and reorganization of their liaison sections attached to the SIS HQ. The programme of expansion reflected two different sorts of process: on the one hand, Service intelligence departments were gearing up for an anticipated increased volume of information, while, on the other hand, new functions were being set up and installed in their home departments, and a number of these had implications for the SIS. Air Intelligence (AI) and Naval intelligence both began their expansion programmes before the actual outbreak of war, while the War Office reorganization did not take place until 1940. SIS also had to mobilize and bring in new recruits to handle its wartime operations. Both the SIS's endogenous expansion and the attachment of newly mobilized officers brought in through the Circulating Sections resulted in a considerable influx of new, young personnel, leading to the now notorious conflict between the old, pre-war 'professionals' (some of whom had been in harness for decades) and the new 'amateurs' often recruited from or shortly after having graduated from university.[23]

One of the first C Sections to undergo structural alterations to meet the needs of the new conflict was Section II, Winterbotham's Air Section. Prior to and at the outbreak of war, the AI liaison had grown from being simply Winterbotham and his personal staff to including the SIS air photographic unit and a scientific intelligence sub-section called IId. Photoreconnaissance was a short-lived undertaking, taken over by the RAF proper in the spring of 1940.[24] By comparison, scientific and technical intelligence was to become a permanent feature of SIS infrastructure.

The origins of the SIS scientific intelligence section lay well before the outbreak of war in the creation under Sir Henry Tizard of the Committee for the Scientific Survey of Air Defence in 1935. One of the committee's conclusions was that Britain's intelligence departments were 'obtaining very little information about foreign scientific and technical developments'. What was immediately proposed, therefore, was that 'a scientist should be attached for a trial period to AI in order to stimulate the flow of information'.[25] AI reported this intention to the JIC in February 1939, and expressed the hope that other service branches would follow suit, but they did not.[26] The scientist in question, R.V. Jones, was attached to Winterbotham's AI1c/Section II,[27] wherein Jones bore the title IId.[28] Although the preparations for a scientific intelligence liaison were announced in February, Treasury resistance to the expenditure implied delayed the actual implementation of the AI plan until September 1939, by which time, of course, war had already broken out.

As noted above, the Circulating Sections were, technically, sections or sub-sections of their respective Service Branch intelligence directorates attached to the SIS HQ in order to direct operations undertaken along the lines of their respective Service Branch requirements. However, the status of IId and the scientific intelligence section was still more ambiguous than that. The bulk of IId's brief lay in acting as a channel for scientific intelligence from *all sources* to the Tizard Committee and the Air Ministry Directorate of Scientific Research, including both SIS HUMINT and GC & CS SIGINT. This diverged from the original 1921 arrangement in that it gave IId a plurality of sources, and a brief for analysis as well as collation and dissemination. In a 1945 report to the JIC on wartime scientific intelligence, Jones described the ambiguous status of IId as being 'anomalous' and a happy 'accident'. Paradoxically, despite the need for compartmentalization and secrecy, Jones concluded that the '"free" atmosphere of SIS organization, as compared with the "Civil Service" atmosphere of the normal departmental offices, undoubtedly provided better conditions for Intelligence work. The success of Scientific Intelligence was therefore partly due to the liberality of C in allowing the section to use his accommodation and facilities, and ACAS(i) [Assistant Chief of Air Staff, Intelligence] in allowing one of his sections to spend most of its time outside his offices.'[29] The strength of IId's location was, therefore, the very emphasis on lateral communications and collegial ethos in SIS that would later prove so difficult to sustain.

In April 1941, AI underwent an internal reorganization, with its functional sections promoted to full Directorates or Deputy Directorates, and under these new arrangements Jones became Assistant Director of Intelligence (Science) (although his position in the SIS hierarchy remained unchanged), and a small staff of scientists was provided to support his work.[30] In keeping with the 'free', face-to-face organizational culture at Broadway, as IId's work expanded, it acquired a growing staff of scientists that were organized into various informal teams by Jones to handle the specific scientific topics as they emerged.[31] IId dealt directly with AI, both the SIS operational G-side officers and the agency's senior command, and even directly with Churchill and members of the War Cabinet on a number of occasions.[32] As the war progressed, Jones would find his section fulfilling scientific and technical intelligence services not just for the Air Ministry, but for other consuming departments as well.[33] Jones's work began with a review of source reports already compiled by the SIS on scientific matters, which he found sparse, ill-informed and often grossly implausible.[34] After the brief windfall of the so-called Oslo Report,[35] IId's functions developed into an increasingly complicated range of scientific concerns ranging from German radar technology through magnetic mines to the development of the so-called V Weapons and the German nuclear programme.

Jones, throughout his tenure in scientific intelligence consistently advocated and agitated for the creation of a separate 'scientific intelligence service' which would bring collection, interpretation and analysis together under one roof. He argued this in opposition to what he calls in his memoirs 'Buckingham's system' of handling scientific intelligence, with reference to Deputy Director J. Buckingham at the Admiralty's Directorate of Scientific Research. It was partly Buckingham's opposition to Jones's view of scientific intelligence that stalled his initial proposal in December 1939. Buckingham rejected Jones's scheme on the grounds that assessment of any scientific intelligence gathered by an intelligence agency should be undertaken not by that agency but by experts in the Service Branch scientific directorates. Jones rejected Buckingham's argument as fallacious, remarking that 'plausible as it seems the scientific experts in one country are not necessarily as good at assessing intelligence as independent intelligence officers'. Jones's doubt about customers' own scientists was that if introduced to a new, enemy development they would reject the information either because they had not thought of it before or because earlier 'careless work' had made the development seem intrinsically unfeasible.[36] In other words, Jones expected any scientists *other than* members of an intelligence service to be more prone to what is now termed 'mirror imaging' than members of the intelligence community. Jones's criticisms of Buckingham's approach are probably overly severe because, as we have already seen, it essentially reflected the existing role of SIS within the 1921 arrangement.

Jones remarked of his 1941 promotion: 'Scientific Intelligence was now established as a branch having its place alongside, and inter-locked with the more traditional divisions of Naval, Military and Air Intelligence, as we had the beginnings of a Scientific Intelligence organization.'[37] There was, however, a minor exception to IId's central interdepartmental role in scientific intelligence. For a brief period, the Admiralty tried a separate arrangement for scientific intelligence concerning chemical warfare preparations by the Axis states. Under this separate process, the head of Section III received any intelligence on chemical warfare generated by the G side of the service, and forwarded it to the chemical warfare research facilities at Porton Down. Jones has since argued that the Section III arrangements served as an experimental 'control' for IId. In his reading of events, the results of the Section III control validated his own position, but only on the basis of a single instance where Section III and Porton Down failed to recognize indications that the Germans were developing nerve gas. Jones attributes this to the passive role of Section III as a collating office serving a remote body of 'experts'. Of course, as Jones himself admits, it may simply have been that 'III', while a 'splendid Naval Captain', 'knew little of science' and cannot really, therefore, have been the most effective conduit for the information reaching the Porton Down scientists.[38]

While MI1c had remained unchanged throughout the inter-war period, and AI1c had begun to grow in the last 18 months before the outbreak of war, the Naval Intelligence Direcorate (NID) experienced a progressive structural attrition throughout the inter-war period, and this attrition was reflected in its provision for liaison with the SIS and GC & CS. As noted above in 1924, the NID's structure had included four sections for liaison with SIS and GC & CS, one at the SIS and three dealing with GC & CS, as well as a very wide range of functional and geographical departments. However, by 1939/40, the functional sections had been consolidated into groups of staff under three Assistant Directors of Intelligence, for Secret Service liaison, security, and technical intelligence functions respectively, with the numbered geographical sections under a single Deputy DNI.[39] NID3 had ceased to exist as a separate entity within Naval Intelligence, with Section III simply answering directly to the relevant ADNI. In May 1940, proposals were made for the four junior NID directorships to be replaced with two Deputy Directors, Home (DDNI(H)) and Foreign (DDNI(F)). DNI John Godfrey proposed promoting the ADNI responsible for Secret Service liaison, a Marine Colonel called Craig, to DDNI(F) on the grounds that Craig already performed a number of functions outside the Secret Service brief and because, since the fall of Continental Europe, 'the Secret Service work has shrunk to very small proportions and is unlikely to revive in the near future. ... By agreement with the Head of the [Secret Service] arrangements are being made to deal with this aspect of Intelligence work, which as far as the Admiralty end is concerned, will be divided between the two DDNIs if approved.'[40]

By May 1941, under the new reorganization, the Admiralty liaison to the SIS and GC & CS came under a new Coordination and Liaison Section, NID17. NID17 included the NID attachments to the Joint Intelligence Committee (JIC), the Interservice Security Board, and the Joint Planning Committee, as well as 'Special Liaison Duties' covering GC & CS (referred to as the Government Communications Bureau [GCB]), the SIS, and SOE (given in 1940 papers as SO2).[41] As the range of NID liaisons multiplied through the war, adding the Joint Intelligence Staff and IS(O) to the Divisions commitments, the liaison duties were broken up between two different NID sections. The GC & CS and SIS liaison sections were excised from NID17 in November 1944, and placed in their own section, NID12a, as 'Naval Section, Government Communications Bureau' and 'Naval Section, London' respectively, an arrangement which prevailed until October 1945 at least. However, when the SIS and SOE were forced to set up their joint water-bus programmes for infiltrating agents and officers into enemy-held territories, this function was eventually given a separate NID designation as NID(c).[42]

The 1940 reorganization of Military Intelligence took the form of both an expansion of the SIS HQ secondment staff and an upgrading of the War Office status of that staff. In 1939, the Military Circulating Section was still known within the War Office as MI1c, a single officer (Menzies) manning the 'Special Duties' sub-section of MI1, the

Military Intelligence section responsible for 'Organization and Coordination of Military Intelligence, League of Nations Questions'.[43] Under the 1940 reorganization, a greatly expanded MI Division was divided between three deputy directors, one for 'Organization' (DDMI(O)), another for 'Information' (DDMI(I)), and another handling security (DDMI(S)). The DDMI(O) title was not particularly representative of that officer's functions, which encompassed not just the organization and coordination section, MI1, but also a number of intelligence collection and liaison sections. These included communications security and interception through MI8; the escape and evasion organization MI9; MIL, which handled military attachés, liaison with home departments of government and liaison with and from Allied forces; and, finally, as 'Special Duties', the War Office liaison to the SIS. Special Duties was now designated MI6 – *the first time this title was ever used with reference to SIS.*

Under the new system, 'Special Duties' had been expanded from a solitary officer to the sizeable complement of '1 GSO1; 3 GSO2; 1 GSO3; 4 Intelligence Officers (Captains); 1 Intelligence Officer (Lieutenant)'.[44] Despite this extended presence, and the Circulating Sections' central role at Broadway Buildings, Military Intelligence remained dissatisfied with its degree of influence over both the SIS through MI6 and the Security Service through MI5. A 1941 Military Intelligence report proposing another series of reforms to the Directorate complained that 'MI5 and MI6 fulfil the purpose of liaison with the Security Service and the Secret Service respectively but it is regrettable that the Army Council should have in general little or no say in the use to which the available funds are put, the selection of personnel or the disposition of those services on whose efficiency military security and information depend.'[45] This would continue to be the chief complaint at MI throughout the war.

Section VI's work similarly increased as the blockade effort was stepped up. In response to this, Limpenny, as VI, expanded his section from a single deputy (Bruce Otley) to three sub-sections: VIa, handling 'general' economic information; VIb, specializing in banking and finance; and VIc, dealing with international trade information.[46]

As before the war, Circulating Sections also continued to originate projects which were implemented by the service's operational side. Philip Johns, for example, has recalled how, during a brief appointment to Section VI in 1943, he worked on an operation which he termed 'Ship Swap'. 'Ship Swap' was not an intelligence

109

operation against an Axis target but rather was intended to provide clandestine support for Allied transatlantic shipping by covertly acquiring Axis ships which had taken sanctuary in Spanish ports. SIS arranged for them to be purchased via third parties in neutral countries who would then sell them to the British. The operation was to be implemented through the SIS's field organization, particularly in the western hemisphere.[47]

The geographical, operational side of SIS, the G Sections, underwent a series of changes as the war developed, but during the first year of the war those changes were mostly negative. As noted above, the security of the PCO organization and its field stations abroad had been called into serious question by the Venlo incident in 1939, but this was merely the beginning of a comprehensive disintegration of the SIS's European system. To be sure, the Passport Control Office was well and truly bankrupt as cover by the outbreak of war, but the real reason for the loss of its pre-war European capability had more to do with the rapid Nazi sweep across Europe, combined with the territorial acquisitions made by Stalin's Soviet Union under the Molotov–von Ribbentrop Pact. The SIS lost its Vienna Station with the Nazi *Anschluss* and the Prague station after the German invasion in 1938. After that, the German invasions of Poland and Norway, the loss of the Low Countries and the collapse of France in 45 days and Denmark's exit from the war meant that the SIS resident staffs had to flee back to the UK or face the same fate as Best and Stevens, the officers captured at Venlo. The Baltic states were lost to Soviet invasion. By the end of the first year of war, all the SIS really had left on the Continent were the stations in neutral states such as Switzerland, Sweden, Spain and Portugal. The loss of the Continental residencies had two implications. The first and more obvious was the loss of production capability. The second was the practical problem of trying to find a way around the lost collection machinery and developing new ways to penetrate occupied Europe and the Axis states. In principle, this was very much back to the early days of SIS experience in the First World War, but this time The Netherlands (conveniently close to both Britain and enemy territory) was not available to run a new generation of Danes and Dame Blanches. The problems of infiltrating and running networks in 1939–40 were of a different order from those in 1915–16, and a new operational system needed to be set up to reflect that.

At the outbreak of war, the SIS's operational side consisted of eight regional 'Group' or 'G' Sections that oversaw foreign stations abroad. The loss of much of the SIS's overseas presence meant three of these groups were now essentially non-existent. The solution adopted was essentially to relocate what had been foreign stations back to the UK, and use British territory as the staging point for launching operations on the 'Third Country' model. As a result, three of the eight G Sections were abolished, and broken up along country rather than regional lines, and designated A Sections for obscure reasons. A1, which handled Germany, was run by former Berlin PCO Frank Foley; A2 was The Netherlands and Denmark; A3 was Belgium; A4 dealt with France and Poland and was run by ex-Paris PCO, 'Biff' Dunderdale with a junior officer acting as liaison with the exiled Polish *Deuxième Bureau*; and a second French section, dealing also with Gibraltar and Tangier, was under the control of Dansey's former deputy in the Z Organization, Kenneth Cohen, aided by John Codrington as A5a.[48] This left G2 running operations in the Far East, North America and South America, G4 controlling stations in Aden, Iraq, Iran, East and West Africa; G5 controlling Spain and Portugal residencies; G7 controlling Egypt, Malta, Palestine and Turkey; and G8 controlling Sweden, Finland and the Soviet Union.[49] The grouping together of the French and Polish functions resulted from the fact that, in the initial stages of the war, the SIS's main network in Europe was the INTERALLIE circuit set up in France by the escaped Polish intelligence officer, Roman Garby-Czerniawski.[50] Prior to the penetration and collapse of INTERALLIE, that network involved efforts by both the exiled Polish and French secret services, as well as the SIS.

During 1940 and early 1941, however, the work of G4 and G7 would be devolved to a new regional Middle East SIS headquarters under the Middle East GHQ, while G2's work would be parcelled out between similar theatre commands in Delhi (later Kandy) and an expanded New York residency that would become Sir William Stephenson's British Security Coordination (see below), leaving only G5 and G8 alongside the country A Sections. Most of Broadway's operational side was no longer acting as a conduit between widely scattered foreign stations, but was now concerned directly with recruiting, infiltrating and controlling agents, that is, with the actual production of intelligence. The relocation of the field stations from the major European capitals back to London meant that the SIS offices in the UK would have to transform themselves into an

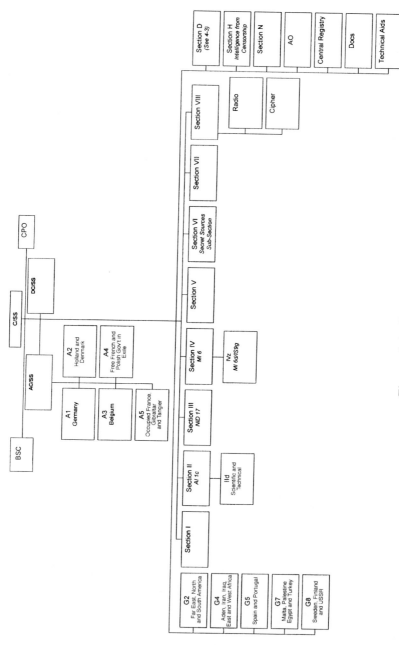

Figure 4.1: SIS in 1940

operational headquarters, deploying agents onto the Continent by sea or air. As a result, the SIS operational side was reorganized by the end of 1941 with the former foreign stations working from the UK reconstituted as country-based Production Sections, consecutively numbered from P1 to P15.[51] P1 was France but it was subdivided into P1a (French North Africa), P1b (Non-Free/Vichy France), and P1c (Free French liaison).[52] P2 handled the Iberian Peninsula,[53] P3 handled Switzerland (although most Swiss operational control went directly to Dansey),[54] P4 handled Italy, P5 handled Poland and the Polish networks in France, P6 handled Germany and liaison with the Czechs on their sources such as Paul Thummel (A54), P7 handled Belgium,[55] P8 dealt with The Netherlands,[56] P9 handled Scandinavia, P13 handled the Baltic States[57] and P15 was MI9's western European escape line section IS9g. However, Yugoslavia fell within the jurisdiction of the Interservice Liaison Department in Cairo, and so was probably housed there, and not in London, with P4 relocating to Cairo when ISLD (Cairo) took over control of operations in Italy in 1943.[58] This scheme would characterize the operational side of the organization for the remainder of the war, with some minor chopping and changing driven by the ebb and flow of the war effort.

In view of the collapse of Europe, no amount of mobilization or improvisation was going to be sufficient to compensate for the setbacks in 1939 and 1940. Confronted with both escalating intelligence demand and dwindling supply, the first wartime review of SIS efficiency took place in December 1939 under the supervision of Lord Hankey, Minister without Portfolio. Hankey's review covered the full range of covert functions, not just intelligence, and he produced reports not only on the SIS and GC & CS, but also on matters such as operational security within the UK, the coordination of irregular activities by Section D and its War Office opposite number MIR, and the intelligence failures leading to Germany's surprise invasion of Norway in early 1940.[59] Hankey found that, for the most part, it was the Service Branches which displayed the greatest dissatisfaction with the SIS product, while the Foreign Office and the newly established Ministry of Economic Warfare (MEW) were for the most part satisfied with what the SIS was providing. Despite the existing consumer-liaison machinery already central to Broadway's organization, Hankey suggested even closer liaison between C and the Service Directors of Intelligence. Menzies countered that such arrangements should be made outside the

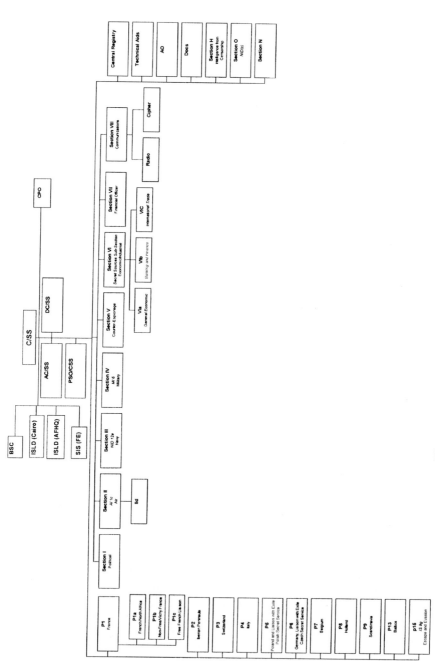

Figure 4.2: SIS in late 1941/Early 1942

context of the Joint Intelligence Sub-Committee of the CID, but apparently no such meetings ever took place.[60] Instead, in May 1940, the SIS, MI5 and the MEW were taken into the JIC as full members. This development was a two-edged sword. While it gave the SIS a forum in which to deal directly and routinely with its consumers at a senior level, it also involved agreeing to a certain degree of JIC authority over matters of the coordination of intelligence, a major concession on the part of the SIS, which had consistently tried to avoid being integrated into the routine machinery of Whitehall committees.[61] As the JIC progressively became the central executive body overseeing the coordination and administration of intelligence under the War Cabinet during the following years, the SIS would find itself increasingly having to answer to concerns raised in the JIC, and accept decisions taken by that body concerning the SIS.

As we have seen in the previous chapter, the central tasking, dissemination and operational structure that had emerged from the 1921 arrangement was not the only operational system developing at the SIS HQ. Grand's sabotage and subversion section also had to mobilize on the outbreak of war, but this led to a traumatic and persistently troublesome series of organizational changes for Menzies's SIS. From the very beginning, Section D also found itself subject to considerable constraint at the behest of the main SIS organization. As Bickham Sweet-Escott has recalled in his memoir of Section D and SOE work, in coordinating D work with that of the SIS's main field organization there was a fundamental conflict from the outset. A man, he observes, 'who is interested in obtaining intelligence must have peace and quiet and the agents he employs must never...be found out' while by contrast, 'the man who has to carry out operations will produce loud noises if he is successful, and it is only too likely that some of the men he uses will not escape'.[62] It would be impossible to conduct paramilitary operations without placing intelligence ones at risk. Therefore, Section D had to install its own field organization abroad, independently of the PCO system, a process which had begun in 1938. By the time it was hived off from the SIS and combined with its War Office and Foreign Office opposite numbers to create SOE, it constituted virtually a complete service within a service.

When Section D was carved out of its parent agency, its various tasks had already crystallized into a large number of internal specialist sections grouped into four major departments or divisions.

These four main divisions were Administration, Plans, Supplies and Execution. There is very little in the public record concerning Administration, and Plans probably included Guy Burgess's (according to Philby) short-lived D/U, which specialized in developing potential schemes and operations.[63] Supplies and Execution were the most sizeable divisions. The Supplies division was divided into four main functions: propaganda, communications, personnel and a section concerned with technical divisions, chiefly weapons and munitions. The propaganda sub-sections included those writing pamphlets for clandestine dissemination, preparing broadcasts for transmission by foreign stations, 'interpreting the Section as a whole to the BBC', disseminating press stories to foreign publications by telegraph and mail bulletins, and, finally, a sub-section handling contacts with foreign dissident parties and other friendly political organizations. Communications included a section handling travel arrangements for Section D officers going abroad under varying degrees of cover, and a telecommunications section that worked in concert with Gambier-Parry's Radio Section (Section VIII).[64] The Supplies division had one section handling technical research in weapons and explosives, and another section that clandestinely acquired arms abroad for friendly opposition groups in enemy-occupied or threatened territories.[65] The technical research section was effectively two sections D/X and D/D under a common head. D/D dealt with 'research and development of an engineering nature, small mechanisms and devices', including firearms, while D/X was the Laboratory Section dealing chiefly with explosive and incendiary devices (and it was responsible for developing the first time-delay fuses, although MI (R) in the war office had a parallel development, the long-lead fuse, as well).[66]

The Personnel Section had two main sections within it; a training establishment sometimes referred to as the 'D School', and a section responsible for handling German refugee groups.[67] Section D was well ahead of the rest of the SIS in its creation of the 'D School', whose purpose was training potential agents in 'propaganda, organisation of subversive cells, the art of spreading rumour and propaganda, the use of arms and explosives, wireless telegraph etc.'.[68] This was set up initially at Brickendonbury Hall, near Hertford, with a Royal Navy captain as school commandant, and including amongst its instructors George Hill, a participant in Reilley's early inter-war escapades in Russia.[69]

The Execution division was geographically organized, and, by 1940, its subsections included D/H (Hungary, the Balkans and the Middle East),[70] D/K (Abyssinia and propaganda in the Middle East),[71] D/G (Sweden),[72] D/J (Norway),[73] and a clandestine letter-opening department cooperating with Censorship abroad designated D/L.[74] Section D's initial operational remit was enormously broad. For example, in 1940, the D/H organization (Hungary) had as its four main operational requirements, '1. To maintain contact with the Polish organization centred at Budapest, and to hand over to it supplies of materials and devices for use by the Poles in Poland. 2. Sabotage. 3. Propaganda. 4. Developments of contacts with anti-German elements in Hungary.'[75] D Section's operations had to be cleared by both D and an assistant, D/T.[76] Section D, however, was a sizeable enterprise, and there almost certainly remain other elements of its organization that have not yet come to light in published accounts and papers in the Public Record Office.[77]

It is generally asserted that Section D's only actions prior to the creation of the SOE were the rescue of some £1.25 million worth of diamonds from Amsterdam in 1940,[78] and a series of what Sweet-Escott has described as 'Scarlet Pimpernel missions', including the rescue of General de Gaulle and his family by flying boat after the collapse of France in 1940.[79] D/G saw its Swedish field organization collapse after its local head, Alfred Rickman, was arrested by the Swedish authorities in April 1940.[80] Section D also undertook a limited programme to develop a network of stay-behind cells in the UK in the event of a German invasion, although this appears to have been somewhat haphazardly pursued, and Sweet-Escott recalls that 'one of our emissaries arrived, complete with black hat and striped trousers, in a remote Scottish village, and, on asking the postmaster if he would accept a parcel of stores, was promptly handed over to the police',[81] although a far more extensive programme of this type was mounted by Holland at the War Office in the form of MIR's 'auxiliary units'.[82]

Because of documents released to the Public Record Office since the original 'open government' initiative in the early 1990s, there is now evidence of a considerable body of work done by Section D in terms of political rather than paramilitary operations. According to a 1941 Section D internal history, the Section was very active in contacting and supporting Continental dissident and opposition groups, and the history concludes that the section, 'incidentally to its

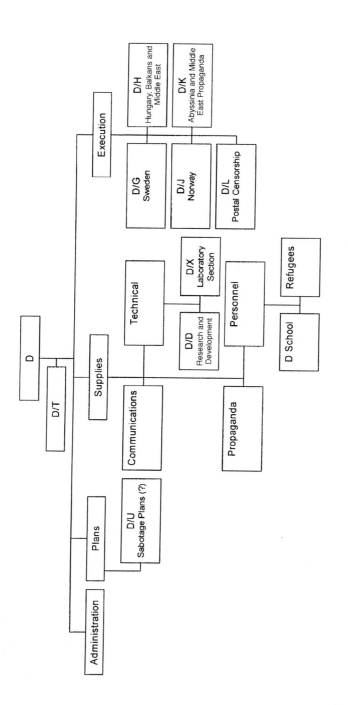

Figure 4.3: Section D in 1940

main purposes', was able to maintain a 'regular flow of information from four main sources', consisting of 'the constant expeditions of Section Officers or Agents into all the countries of Europe...the intimate relations which the section has established with virtually every anti-Nazi and anti-Fascist organisation in Europe...the development and exploitation of the Secret Censorship [and] the Section's contacts, albeit at second-hand, with the sabotage and propaganda sub-agents actually resident in enemy or enemy-occupied countries'.[83] With the general emphasis in SOE histories on successful (and unsuccessful) acts of sabotage, subversion and similar derring-do, clandestine political operations remain one of the most underdeveloped features of wartime secret service history. Such a bias has almost certainly contributed to a systematic undervaluation of Section D's achievements during its early years within the SIS.

Grand's unit saw itself as 'an integral though distinct branch of the SIS'. While it may indeed have generated a flow of raw intelligence for the use of Broadway's Circulating Sections as a by-product of its other work, it was not part and parcel of the G Section and PCO organization that made up the operational side of the 1921 arrangement. Despite this, it was in many respects almost as demand-driven as the main body of the SIS, particularly on the basis of requirements laid upon it by Section VI. This is apparent in the section's own account of its work, according to which the Planning division 'brought [Section D] into daily contact with all the Service Departments and many of the State Departments, particularly the Foreign Office and Ministry of Economic Warfare'. As a result, 'From the Ministry [of Economic Warfare] the Section...received unnumbered targets, so that among the Section's sabotage projects many have been designed to complement or round off the blockade.'[84] The fact that Section D was so often tasked by the MEW also may cast a slightly clearer light on the reasons for placing the combined Special Operations organization under the MEW in 1941. It certainly is a motive rather less Machiavellian than M.R.D. Foot's attribution of the arrangement to 'a somewhat meaner chord' of internal War Cabinet politics in which 'it was generally supposed by the senior men in the [Labour] party...that now that Labour had joined Churchill's wartime coalition, one secret service at least would be placed under a Labour minister'.[85]

In the language of the 1921 arrangement, the MEW could very reasonably be said to have been Section D's main 'consumer'. Much as the 1921 arrangement acted as a mechanism of constraint as well as impetus, so Section D's reliance on 'customers', such as the MEW, for 'requirements' in the form of targets also acted as a constraint. For example, when it briefed Desmond Morton at the former IIC, now the MEW Intelligence Branch, on its plan to attack the iron ore trade through Oxelösund, Sweden, to Germany, Morton stressed that it should undertake no actions 'which could possibly be attributed by the Germans to the British' on the grounds that the Swedes had made it clear that they would abandon their neutrality in favour of the Germans.[86] The project was subsequently abandoned.

One of Lord Hankey's conclusions during his 1940 review of the intelligence agencies discussed above was that the work of MIR and Section D should be combined under a single Minister, on the grounds that their work was both complementary and, on occasion, overlapping.[87] Hankey's conclusions were taken up by a meeting on 1 July which consisted of the Foreign Secretary, Hankey, the Colonial Secretary, the Minister of Economic Warfare, Desmond Morton (who was now acting as Churchill's personal representative on intelligence matters) and the Permanent Under-Secretary of the Foreign Office, his Private Secretary, the Director of Military Intelligence and C. What all parties (including Menzies) agreed on at this meeting was that sabotage and subversion needed to be undertaken by a single organization under what the Colonial Secretary described as 'a Controller armed with almost dictatorial powers'.[88] Although Menzies had agreed to the principle of special operations being placed under a single, separate agency, and the actual transfer of Section D to the new service was made by a War Cabinet decision on 22 July 1940, Menzies apparently did not learn of this until the beginning of September.[89] The new organization was divided into SO1 which handled propaganda and was derived chiefly from the Foreign Office 'Electra House' group; SO2, which dealt with sabotage and subversion, and was composed of Section D and MIR; and a short-lived SO3 planning section. It was placed under Hugh Dalton, Minister of Economic Warfare, and a new head was chosen in the form of Sir Frank Nelson, formerly the Consul at Basle.

On Nelson's takeover, one of the first decisions taken was the dismissal of Lawrence Grand. This is a matter of some ambiguity in the literature, typically confined to vague references to agreement between Dalton and Nelson that the man should go.[90] However, SOE documents released to the Public Record Office have since made it clear why Grand could no longer be kept on at the new organization, and it is worth quoting this evidence at some length. On 15 September 1940, within days of his learning about Section D's transfer to the new SOE, Menzies met with Grand. According to the minutes of that meeting, the two agreed that

> D is a separate secret organisation, forming part of a larger organisation under Mr. Dalton. ... At the same time D is intimately associated with C both on historical and practical grounds [and therefore] C will continue to afford D such facilities for the use of SIS ciphers and communications as the requirements and security of SIS will permit. ... If D's agents collect intelligence other than that specifically on D's affairs, it will be passed on to C *before being circulated anywhere*, even within the D organisation itself. Conversely, if any of C's men is in a position to perform or recommend some act of subversion, C will get in touch with D before taking any action. ... D is at liberty to take the initiative in recruiting agents, but can *only definitely engage them with the knowledge and (subject to appeal) the approval of C or C's representative.*[91]

By so agreeing, of course, Grand effectively signed away SO2's operational autonomy by giving the SIS a stranglehold on any planned action. Such an arrangement would, of course, have thoroughly undermined SOE's autonomy, and Grand was duly dismissed.

When the D networks were transferred to the newly formed SO2 in late 1940, they were often transferred lock, stock and barrel, even retaining their original SIS Section D designations. This was particularly true in the Balkans and Scandinavia.[92] SO2 also found itself dependent upon the SIS's communications infrastructure abroad, with the SIS fending off a plea for SO2 to run its own communications on the grounds that its methods were still insecure.[93] The new SO organization also suffered from pressure from the Ministry of Information, which believed that propaganda, be it white, grey or black, naturally came within its own remit, and not that of the MEW, and therefore lobbied to acquire control of SO1. In August 1941, SO1 and SO2 were hived off from one another, SO1 becoming the Political Warfare Executive, under the

Major General Sir Stewart Graham Menzies,
'C' during World War II

ultimate control, not of the MOI, but the Foreign Office, while SO2 became the Special Operations Executive proper, remaining under Dalton and the MEW.[94]

During the first 18 months of the war, the SIS's ability to produce Continental intelligence had been crippled, mainly by the loss of its Continental stations, and not only their sources but their liaison with Continental intelligence bodies (some of which were actively seeking to resist the German occupation). As a result, SIS requests for transportation in order to put agents onto the Continent tended to carry a lower priority with the RAF and Admiralty than the SIS would have liked.[95] Therefore, a new section was created to acquire clandestine means of transport in 1940, primarily fishing smacks for slipping agents ashore.[96] SO2 (as SOE then was) was also developing its own flotilla for much the same function based on the River Helford in Cornwall. At the same time, the security and intelligence agencies were confronted with a stream of refugees from Norway after the German invasion, as well as the need to infiltrate their own agents into the same country. A meeting in October 1940 between the SIS G Officer responsible for Sweden and Denmark, G3, the head of the German A Section A1 (Frank Foley), and representatives of SO2 noted that the flood of refugees required proper controls and that therefore 'an officer acceptable to SIS, MI5 and SO2' should be stationed permanently in the Shetlands to examine their credentials and undertake initial interrogation, partly for security reasons and partly to identify potential agents. From there, the officer would also forward refugees that London might need for further interrogation. Finally, he would arrange the supply of accredited ships to carry agents and stores, and ensure proper security, keeping the crews apart from the rest of the local population.[97]

One of Foley's juniors, A1(3) Leslie Mitchell, was subsequently assigned to handle the joint SIS/MI5/SO2 task in the Shetlands.[98] The joint SIS/SOE 'water bus' arrangement was eventually placed under the control of SIS officer Frank Slocum, with the designation O.[99] O also came under the supervision of the Admiralty, who viewed maritime irregular operations as lying within their jurisdiction,[100] under the NID designation NID(c).[101] The SIS itself created a Transport Section to handle its side of these operations, although it failed to provide regular service until spring 1942, at which point the Admiralty finally provided a Motor Torpedo Boat (MTB) flotilla, and an RAF Special Duties Squadron (from summer 1940 to spring 1941,

No. 419 squadron; after that No. 138 squadron) was flying frequently to France by August 1941, with aircraft available for operations in the Far East somewhat later.[102] From spring 1943, Slocum had, in addition to his status within the SIS, a position in the Admiralty chain of command as Deputy Director, Operations Division (Irregular), DDOD(I).[103]

The degree of coordination of the flotillas to the Middle East and North Africa was not as close as the UK-based units until the end of 1942. The official history claims that difficulties between the various separate 'water bus' units in North Africa were resolved in the spring of 1942 when the SIS, MI9 and SOE units were combined into a single 'Coast Watching Flotilla',[104] but the SOE archives indicate that the SOE side of this work was later subordinated directly to Slocum in London in December of that year. In December, SIS in Algiers forwarded a complaint to Broadway that the SOE had 'made certain private arrangements with the captain of a French submarine, without the knowledge of Naval authorities'. Although the complaint proved inaccurate, the freebooters proving to be the American Office of Strategic Services (OSS) instead, the result was that the SOE's North African operations were brought under the direct control of NIDc in London.[105]

Further economies of scale between the SIS and the SOE also appeared in the form of shared resources for the training of agents and the acquisition of special equipment. In both of these cases, the result was not head-on conflict but rather the joint use of common facilities. The development of training facilities had begun with the so-called 'D School' organized under Grand before Section D's transfer to SO2. Although initially set up to train clandestine operators for special operations, these schools trained their people not only in weapons and sabotage techniques, but in clandestine communications, W/T and interrogation resistance, skills required by SIS agents as well. As a result, some measure of SIS/SOE cooperation was achieved on the matter of permitting the SIS to send its agents to the SOE Special Training Schools (STS).[106]

Although the SIS and SOE possessed separate document production (forgery) facilities and the SIS had its own Technical Aids Section, both employed a common link with the Ministry of Supply to acquire special equipment or 'Q devices' from contractors in the private sector. That common link was the Ministry of Supply (MOS) official Charles Fraser-Smith, whose work ranged from negotiating with commercial suppliers and a sceptical Treasury, which had to pay for all of the equipment, to wandering around Paddington looking for second-hand Continental clothes and accoutrements.[107] Fraser-Smith found himself liable to be tasked by the SIS, the SOE or MI9, and much of his contact with SIS was through the naval liaison officer at MI9 HQ in Beaconsfield.[108] However, despite having a common need for the same kind of resources acquired through the same kind of presence in the MOS, Fraser-Smith recalls in his memoirs feeling like the rope in a tug-of-war between the two agencies,[109] much as the RAF Special Duties squadrons and Slocum's water buses had to serve both competing users. The common need for essentially comparable technical and scientific support led to the proposal in 1944 by SIS Far East branch, the Interservice Liaison Department Far East (ISLD) (FE), of a Joint Scientific Laboratory in the Far East. The SOE was originally doubtful, warning the ISLD initially that it would not commit funds to what one officer, in April 1944, scathingly called a 'bucket shop'.[110] However, by August, the SOE's objections had been resolved, and a joint directive was issued for the creation of Higgins's Joint Scientific Laboratory, which would provide services to ISLD(FE) and SOE (that is, its Far East division, Force 136), as well as the OSS, and Indian censorship. Executive control lay with the head of the ISLD, Colonel Bowden-Smith, while Gavin Stewart, an SOE officer, was to act as Bowden-Smith's deputy in Calcutta.[111]

As in the previous war, an important area of SIS activity was the operation of escape and evasion routes behind and out of Axis occupied territory, and this provided a second point of intersection between the SIS and the work of MIR. On the outbreak of war, the JIC approved an outline scheme developed by Holland at MIR for an escape and evasion organization, technically an interservice body but organized in the first instance under MI administration as MI9. MI9 covered a range of functions from escape measures for British servicemen to the extraction of intelligence through the interrogation of Allied escapers and captured Axis prisoners of war. The need to create escape routes, or 'ratlines' as they came to be known, necessarily implied some sort of coordination with the SIS, which would either be maintaining any surviving intelligence networks or recruiting new ones in the areas out of which servicemen would probably have to escape.

The MI9 section responsible for organizing and running the 'ratlines' was set up in spring 1941 under the auspices of the MI9 training school, Intelligence School 9 (IS9). This delay of some 18 months resulted from SIS doubts about the risks posed to its own networks by escaping Allied servicemen. M.R.D. Foot and James Langley have argued that the reasoning was analogous in some respects to SIS concerns about SOE actions disrupting their intelligence operations, and accuse the SIS of not pausing 'to think things through'.[112] However, a post-war report on MI9 noted that the SIS concern was drawn from experience, its representatives frequently referring to the loss of one of their agents during the First World War, the Nurse Edith Cavell, who was discovered while assisting an escaping prisoner of war, an incident which 'seemed to dictate the whole attitude of SIS towards the Section. They were determined to prevent evaders and escapers from involving them in any way.' Rather more philosophical about the problem than SOE, MI9's historian remarks: 'This attitude may have been correct from their own security aspect, but it was a terrific handicap to those trying to build up an organisation.'[113]

SIS support for yet another secret organization cutting across and potentially compromising its European networks was very limited throughout 1940, and it was not until April 1941 that any arrangements were made for direct coordination between MI9's escape line programme and SIS intelligence operations in the form of a notional branch of the MI9 school called IS9g. IS9g's task was the recruitment, organization and support of dedicated escape and evasion circuits, and because of the need to avoid line-crossing, it 'was controlled in its actions by the over-riding [sic] authority of SIS, and was, in fact, started as MI6(D), with an office in Broadway and a staff of one junior officer and two clerks'.[114] The SIS designation of MI6d was IVz, an office initially held by James Langley.[115]

According to Langley, even his title IVz and nominal attachment to the War Office liaison section were all but incidental, the designation originally being intended for an officer who, according to Colonel Heydon-Home at Section IV, had never shown up on mobilization. In Langley's recollection, Dansey telephoned Heydon-Home to ask what IVz's task was originally supposed to have been, the Colonel responding, 'How the hell do I know if he never turned up?' According to Langley, Dansey responded

'Well he has now. Captain Langley is his name and he will be seconded to me.' The telephone backfired several times and Uncle

126

Claude [Dansey] said soothingly 'I don't suppose you do want him. Don't worry, he will be paid by us. All you have to do is inform the War Office that IVz has now turned up and has been seconded for special duties.'[116]

In due course, Langley was joined by other officers such as Airey Neave and Donald Darling.[117]

Once IVz successfully began to recruit and maintain its own, independent agent networks, the section was subsequently transferred to the SIS's operational production side as P15.[118] In this capacity, P15 was divided into three sub-sections. The headquarters section was responsible for 'Policy regarding the carrying out of escape & evasion [sic] plans in Western Europe [and] Training of agents under MI6', while one sub-section was responsible for 'operational work in Belgium and Holland' and the other for 'operational work in connection with escape and evasion in France'.[119] The post-war report concluded that while the 'rather negative form of support' from the SIS in terms of keeping escape and intelligence lines rigorously compartmentalized caused such difficulty that any future such organization would be better off separate from the SIS, SIS training and methods constituted a good example for any future escape and evasion organization.[120]

The expansion of the Circulating Sections, the mobilization of Section D and the installation of IS9g all reflected more or less planned elements of wartime mobilization. Section D's departure to become part of SOE may not have been planned, but the existence of parallel plans and organizations at the War Office, Foreign Office and Broadway made some kind of rationalization and consolidation almost inevitable. Beyond this, most of what was developing was improvisation in the face of crisis. Any attempt to enhance the field organization in response to escalating demand was undercut by the rapid collapse of Continental Europe and the retreat and relocation of the SIS's foreign stations to British soil. Indeed, the very rapid flux in fortunes during the first year and a half of war was the most significant pressure acting on the formal organization of the SIS operational side, not just in Europe but in remote theatres such as the Middle East, North Africa and, from late 1941, the Pacific.

During the inter-war years, the SIS had long since abandoned the First World War pattern of highly autonomous foreign stations acting as regional secret services in their own right, under the immediate day-to-day control of local British military and diplomatic authorities, in favour of a London-centred command and control system. This centralization was intensified by the retreat of its European residencies to the UK-based A Sections. However, in four theatres of operations in the Second World War, the SIS abandoned central control in favour of a return to regional HQs similar to those described by Compton Mackenzie and Henry Landau. In the Americas, the Middle East, North Africa, and the Far East, the SIS set up regional, semi-autonomous agencies which acted as operational headquarters, subject only to loose administrative oversight and technical support from London. However, the reasons behind these developments differed in each theatre. The SIS organizations in the Middle East and North Africa were subject to requirements and control chiefly from their theatre commands from the Middle East Command and African Forces HQ (AFHQ) respectively. Theatre-level command, however, was only one of three considerations for the Far East SIS. In the Far East, the need for a theatre-level SIS head-quarters was combined with poor management on the ground prior to and at the outbreak of war and far longer lines of communication than any other theatre of operations. The North American SIS, British Security Coordination, was a very different matter, as it served a double purpose; it was an administrative more than an operational headquarters for both the SIS and SOE, and a channel of liaison between the British and American security and intelligence services.

The SIS already had a small cluster of stations in the Middle East prior to Italy's entry into the war, at Athens, Jerusalem, Istanbul and Cairo.[121] However, with the outbreak of fighting in the Middle East, there arose the need to coordinate SIS work under the regional GHQ; therefore, the SIS dispatched what the official history circuitously refers to as 'senior men' to GHQ Middle East in Cairo,[122] led by Captain Cuthbert Bowlby, RN working under the cover designation as the Inter-Service Liaison Department (ISLD).[123] Despite getting off to a slow start, failing to achieve a great deal by the end of 1940,[124] it began to pick up in 1941 and 1942, with ISLD setting up new stations in Tehran, Baghdad, Damascus and Beirut.[125] Although the ISLD's first point of contact was the GHQ Director of Military Intelligence (DMI (ME)), it also maintained its own three-man collation section.[126] According to one officer interviewed, the ISLD collation group was supposed to deal with everything from military order of battle to political intelligence,[127] while Nigel Clive, who was an ISLD

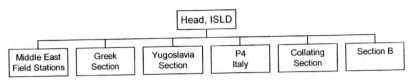

Figure 4.4: ISLD (Cairo) circa 1943

clandestine operator in wartime Greece, was absolutely convinced that his lengthy political reports on the various partisan groups were ignored by the Cairo headquarters, whose 'whole professional upbringing had schooled them to treat politics as an arcane art, best left to others'.[128]

When Greece and Yugoslavia fell to Axis forces, the Athens and Yugoslav stations retreated to Cairo, where they became part of the ISLD headquarters.[129] ISLD also had a role in the GHQ (ME) security organization, Security Intelligence Middle East (SIME). SIME required SIS authorization to set up counter-intelligence bodies or mount operations within the SIS jurisdiction (much as it did from the Security Service within mandates and colonial territory), and SIS Cairo had maintained a liaison officer at SIME from the latter's inception in December 1939.[130] After GC & CS began to break the *Abwehr* Enigma codes in December 1940, Section V set up an office in November 1941 at ISLD Cairo, called Section B.[131] Potential friction arising from potential duplication and overlap between B Section and SIME was avoided because of the existence of pre-existing joint arrangements, ones which apparently worked very well.[132] ISLD's only links with London were the distribution of ISOS from Section V; officers' salaries, which were paid at armed service regulation rates by Section VII; and the provision of W/T facilities and operators by Section VIII.[133]

The Algiers ISLD began in the UK with an SIS unit that was attached to Allied Forces HQ at Norfolk House, and provided information to the Anglo-American Combined Intelligence Section during preparation for operation TORCH, the landings in Algeria.[134] After the TORCH landings, the new regional SIS HQ under AFHQ in Algiers adopted the ISLD designation as well.[135] With the defeat of Axis forces in the Middle East and North Africa in 1943, ISLD Cairo took over control of ISLD Algiers.[136] The invasion of Italy expanded ISLD jurisdiction to that country. It set up a station there concerned with infiltrating intelligence cells and W/T operators into northern

Italy.[137] Within a few months, ISLD Italy had 20 radio sets under its own control and another ten under the control of the Italian intelligence service, which was, by 1944, effectively under SIS control.[138] However, although ISLD Italy was operating in Continental Europe, it experienced no day-to-day control from Broadway, but instead came under the direct control of Advance AFHQ in Italy, and was answerable within the SIS chain of command to ISLD Cairo.[139] For a time in 1944, ISLD Italy also controlled the SIS's Yugoslav operations, being immediately closer to the Balkan coastline than ISLD Cairo.[140] ISLD Italy did not, however, have control of counter-espionage, which was handled instead by three Section V Special Counter-Intelligence Units (discussed below).[141]

ISLD (FE) took shape in the first instance from a review of intelligence organization in the Far East by the Commander-in-Chief Far East, Admiral Sir Robert Brooke-Popham. At the outbreak of war, the SIS maintained only three stations in the Pacific. Singapore, Hong Kong and Shanghai were all that was left of Cumming's 1923 Far Eastern Group of nine residencies. These three stations were subject to the direct control of a very distant Broadway, and weakly at that, with little or no coordination between the three. Menzies, aware of the limitations of his Far East organization, had already dispatched a representative in the form of businessman Geoffrey Denham. Denham's task was to conduct an internal review during (but not before) Brooke-Popham's January 1941 review. Brooke-Popham's investigation resulted in a scathing assessment wired back to the Chiefs of Staff on 6 January to the effect that the SIS constituted the 'weak link' in British Far East intelligence.[142] According to Brooke-Popham, the three stations left were producing little information of any use, and, worse still, the 'identity of principal officers at Shanghai, HK and Singapore is known to many'. They employed an assortment of amateurs with no real knowledge of the kind of technical, military and political information they were required to gather. Brooke-Popham concluded: 'I am aware that a representative is being sent out to investigate but consider that action is required at once. I recommend immediate appointment of head for SIS organisation in Far East to supervise and coordinate work for existing three sections and with power to make changes in personnel without delay.'[143] Brooke-Popham and Denham agreed that the latter should take on the role of regional head of the SIS Far East organization, attached to the Far East Combined Bureau in Singapore.[144]

With the Japanese offensive in late 1941 overrunning Hong Kong and Singapore by 1942, the SIS retreated to India, where it was based in New Delhi, with a forward station in Calcutta. It was at this point that SIS Far East (FE) adopted the SIS Cairo designation, ISLD.[145] ISLD (FE) remained in Delhi until 1944, when, under a new head, it relocated to Kandy, Ceylon (Sri Lanka), where Mountbatten's South East Asia Command (SEAC), created in 1943, had relocated along with SOE's Force 136 (SOE FE) in early 1944.[146] Like ISLD Cairo, ISLD (FE) was answerable directly to the theatre GHQ, in this case, SEAC, and received no operational direction from London. From December 1943, the coordination of all the various UK and Allied 'clandestine services' came under the oversight of SEAC's P (Priorities) Division, which sought to coordinate not only SIS and the Special Operations Executive, but also the British agencies with the work of the American Office of Strategic Services (OSS). To process the raw intelligence gathered by ISLD cells behind enemy lines into source reports for SEAC, ISLD (FE) maintained its own collation section, which was also empowered to collate all raw intelligence generated by any of the other clandestine services operating under SEAC's control.[147]

British Security Coordination (BSC) was a very different institution from any of the three ISLD sub-organizations, and its nature has been clouded by a great deal of myth-making, much of which was at the personal behest of its overall head, Sir William Stephenson.[148] Essentially, BSC expanded around the offices and functions of the New York Passport Control Office. As noted above, the first point of contact of any PCO had always been the security and intelligence services of the office's host state. It was this liaison role which distinguished BSC from the three ISLDs. In the first instance, Stephenson's brief was threefold: 'to investigate enemy activities, to institute adequate security measures against the danger of sabotage to British shipping and other property, and to mobilize American public opinion in favour of aid to Britain'.[149] BSC began its development beyond the basic PCO machinery with its move to the International Building of the Rockefeller Center. Stephenson was furnished, initially, with an Assistant PCO and a senior SIS officer to oversee the SIS side of the office's extensive brief.[150] The SIS work was, however, constrained by the fact that the New York station was forbidden to take action which might tip the scales of American neutrality, and it was allowed to operate within the US only via the Federal Bureau of

Investigation (FBI).[151] The counter-sabotage function provided the office's overt rationale, given in its official registration as a foreign agency under the name 'British Security Coordination' (a name reportedly suggested by FBI director J. Edgar Hoover), with Stephenson as Director of Security Coordination.[152]

BSC expanded rapidly during 1940, until, by the end of 1941, it consisted of four distinct divisions under the Director of Security Coordination: Secret Intelligence, Security, Special Operations, Statistics and Analysis, and Communications. The Secret Intelligence Division, confined in North America to liaison duties, posted officers to Latin America in parallel with the small and understaffed SIS stations there[153] (although operational control of the Latin American stations was via Broadway, not BSC)[154] and, in 1941, the expansion of Section V's work led to the creation of a Counter-Espionage Section under that Division.[155] Counter-sabotage work was handled by the Security Division. Its work was undertaken by Consular Security Officers, appointed to all of America's major ports by March 1941, a programme extended at the request of the Home Defence Security Executive (HD(S)E) to 45 South American ports over 1941–42. Although much of the Consular Security Officer (CSO) work was taken over by US authorities with the entry of the United States into the war, the Security Division also added a network of Industrial Security Officers in South America working with the FBI to oversee the security of shipments from their place of manufacture to their embarkation.[156] In either late 1940 or early 1941, the Security Division also took over the British Purchasing Commission's Credit Investigation and Shipping Security Sections that would eventually form the basis of the BSC's Statistics and Analysis Division.[157]

In December 1940, BSC acquired a Special Operations Division, representing SO2 (later SOE), and setting up a training facility in Whitby, Ontario, Canada,[158] in the form of Special Training School (STS) 103, better known as 'Camp X'. Finally, in 1941 the BSC was instructed to set up a North American end to Section VIII's growing short-wave network under a new Communications Division. Although the BSC was forbidden covert collection work in the United States (the CSOs and Industrial Security Officer (ISOs) were overt functions), a collateral benefit of the BSC's contacts with American politicians and officials was that it provided a source of what might essentially be considered confidential but *open source* information about the currents and trends in American politics.[159]

Unlike any of the three ISLD bodies which existed to serve the needs of powerful theatre GHQs and their commanders-in-chief, the BSC's *raison d'être* depended upon the continuity of London's need for it as a liaison channel. While the various ISLD branches had nominal monopolies on producing secret intelligence under their respective GHQs (challenged, perhaps, by the ability of SOE and MI9 to produce HUMINT as a by-product of their particular tasks), there was no comparable natural monopoly for BSC. Liaison via New York was not even necessarily the most direct means of communicating between London and Washington once liaison personnel were posted directly to the two capitals. As a result, BSC found its role under threat on a number of occasions. From spring 1941, the UK government had established a British Joint Staff Mission in London, which included a Joint Intelligence Committee (Washington), JIC (W), including in turn an SIS officer,[160] and from that point on, intelligence liaison work began to gravitate towards Washington. Although the UK–USA cooperation on signals intelligence was routed via BSC's Communications Division, the actual liaison work between British and American cryptanalysts took the form chiefly of teams sent either to Washington from Britain or to London and Bletchley Park from the United States. The pressures on BSC mounted throughout 1942 and 1943. SO1 (PWE) duties had never been included within Stephenson's brief, even though the BSC had been running its own pro-British and anti-Axis propaganda campaign both in the US and through radio broadcasts to the Far East.[161] In summer 1942, PWE posted its own Political Warfare Mission (PWM), not to New York, but to Washington under David Bowes-Lyon, and in due course PWM took over BSC's overt propaganda duties.[162] This progressive loss of independence resulted in Stephenson's commissioning an internal report in June extolling the achievements and importance of BSC, an effort to protect his status within the emerging transatlantic intelligence community.[163] An additional point of what one commentator has called 'bureaucratic danger to the BSC' occurred in March 1943, resulting in a second report being prepared and issued to London to try to forestall a move afoot within the SIS to strip BSC of its operational control of so many aspects of British intelligence in the western hemisphere. In many respects, the size and extent of BSC by and after 1943 was as attributable to Stephenson's campaign of empire building as it was to any operational or governmental need for such an entity.

133

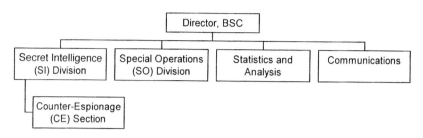

Figure 4.5: BSC from 1941

Spring 1943 also saw the crux in the debate concerning whether the BSC should represent MI5 as well as the SIS and SOE. In August 1942, the Director-General of the Security Service (DGSS), Sir David Petrie, had proposed, and it had been nominally agreed, that BSC should also represent the Security Service, in the form of an officer attached to the Counter-Intelligence Section, chiefly to undertake liaison with the FBI.[164] However, this was not acted on immediately, and during this period relations between BSC and the FBI soured considerably. As a result, in December 1942, Hoover attached a liaison officer to the US embassy in London to provide a direct link with MI5. Petrie now reversed his previous decision, and proposed instead to post an MI5 representative directly to Washington. In April 1943, a short-lived Secret Service Coordinating Committee created to mediate the various turf wars between Britain's assorted secret organizations decided to send an SIS officer to the BSC to assess the feasibility and desirability of routing MI5 liaison via New York. The review proved favourable, but the final outcome in September 1943 was a compromise, in which the first point of contact between MI5 and the FBI was the FBI representative in London, with additional contact through intermittent visits by Security Service officers to the US, on condition of agreement from the BSC. BSC still continued to carry out operational work on behalf of MI5 through its Security Division, especially security vetting. Nonetheless, by that September, BSC's campaign of expanding responsibility had halted, offensive operations in the Americas were fading in importance as the tide in North Africa turned back towards Continental Europe, and BSC was no longer the sole, or even the primary, channel of liaison between British intelligence and its American opposite numbers.

CRISIS, OPPORTUNITY AND IMPROVISATION

As noted above, the war had indeed begun badly for SIS and its new Chief, Menzies. There were momentary breaks in the generally bleak situation, such as the INTERALLIE network, but the recovery of human intelligence was a very slow and prosaic affair. The other side of Menzies's empire, GC & CS was a very different story. The production and impact of breaks against Axis Enigma codes (amongst others) have been extensively examined and have, indeed, led to an extensive revision of our understanding of the conduct of the war. However, ULTRA and its assorted relations had a range of implications for the work of the SIS that have not been closely examined nor fully appreciated. After all, it was SIS liaison with the Poles and the French that provided many of the initial steps in the attack on German cryptography, it would be SIS short-wave transmitters that had to carry the ULTRA product to consumers in the various theatres of operations, and ULTRA also served to transform counter-espionage human intelligence operations in the now-famous Double-Cross programme.

During the first few months of the Second World War, much of the London SIS organization was evacuated from the threat of German bombing to Bletchley Park, which at the time held the designation Station X.[165] When, from January 1940, GC & CS began to break German Enigma traffic (initially *Luftwaffe* signals), the problem developed of how to handle and disseminate such a delicate source securely while still disseminating it to the people who needed it. As the original breaks were German air force, the handling of the first Enigma product came under the auspices of Section II, and F.W. Winterbotham. Menzies assigned Winterbotham the task of formulating a secure dissemination system, and out of this assignment he developed the Special Communication Unit and Special Liaison Unit (SCU/SLU) arrangements which would characterize ULTRA distribution to theatre commands throughout the war. In his *Ultra Secret*, Winterbotham recalls: 'We already had our own highly efficient Secret Service short-wave radio network and through it we could communicate directly with our organization in most parts of the world.' He was, of course, referring to the Radio Section under Gambier-Parry's Section VIII. He claims responsibility for suggesting that it could handle the secure dissemination of the ULTRA product, suggesting to C that 'if this could be expanded to include enciphering

135

and transmission to the main overseas commands in the field, I should then be allowed to form small units of trained cipher and radio personnel and attach these people to the commands in question, with the double purpose of providing an immediate link for the information and having an officer on the spot charged with seeing that all the necessary precautions were carried out for its security'.[166] However, it has to be pointed out that there was very little in the way of alternatives to Gambier-Parry's division.

Under the resulting arrangements, the cryptanalysts at Bletchley, after deciphering, translating and interpreting the intercepts, prepared a paraphrase of the content of the intercept. This would be transmitted by a coding and transmission facility built on the grounds of the Bletchley Park estate,[167] received by the appropriate SCU, and the decrypted paraphrases held and distributed to consumers by the SLU. Thus, Section VIII became responsible for the secure handling of ULTRA throughout the war, although operational control of the SCU/SLU system belonged to GC & CS.

The initial SIS evacuation to Bletchley Park proved temporary, and most SIS staff returned to Broadway except for Section VIII's coding section, which, like GC & CS, remained at Bletchley (the main Section VIII transceiver centre was located at Hanslope Park). Under the Head of Codes, Captain Edward Hastings, and his Assistant Head of Codes were two separate coding sub-sections. The main coding section handled SIS communications traffic, while a special coding section handled the production of ciphers used to carry ISOS, the product of GC & CS's success against *Abwehr* Enigma and hand ciphers.[168]

Section VIII transmitters also served SO1 (later the PWE), under the euphemism 'Research Units'. Engineers from the Radio Section installed transmitters carrying black propaganda at Gawkcott, near Buckingham, and at Potsgrove, near Milton Bryant, and finally installed transmitters for an SO1 facility known as 'Simpsons' at Wavendon Tower.[169] All told, in 1940–41, Section VIII installed around 20 clandestine RUs for SO1. However, while the Radio Section was responsible for installation and day-to-day functioning of the hardware, the RUs came under the administrative and operational control of SO1. According to Ellic Howe, black propaganda became something of a 'cottage industry', with '"home workers" bringing their products (broadcasting scripts) to the "factory", i.e. "Simpsons", where they were recorded on sixteen-inch, glass-based discs of

American manufacture...then dispatched to one or other transmitting stations where Gambier-Parry's "technicians" delivered the finished product to listeners in Europe.'[170] The most formidable addition to this arm of the Radio Section's capability was a powerful 600-watt transmitter intended to overcome German radio jamming of PWE's broadcasts in what Gambier-Parry described in a memorandum on the project as 'counter-battery work in propaganda'. This transmitter, code-named Aspidistra, was based at Ashdown Forest, Crowborough, in Sussex. The Aspidistra transmitter and related components were acquired in the United States under the auspices of BSC. Robin Hope was seconded to the BSC for a few months in 1941 to familiarize himself with the workings of the Aspidistra units being supplied by RCA.[171] Aspidistra, once installed, did triple duty, not only carrying PWE propaganda but also supporting the BBC Overseas Service and RAF Fighter Command.

Section VIII carried traffic to and from agent networks run for the exiled Polish and Czechoslovakian secret services out of the Woldingham station in Surrey,[172] although both these agencies already possessed extensive agent networks and W/T facilities in their own right (partly as a consequence of the early Polish success with INTERALLIE). However, SIS insisted on retaining exclusive control of the W/T traffic of other European services that, as the official history tactfully puts it, were 'less well founded', such as the Norwegian, Dutch and Belgian.[173] Between late 1940 and 1942, SIS also controlled SO 2/SOE w/t, until SOE activities began to exceed Section VIII's capacity. By the end of 1941, it had become apparent that the volume of intelligence-related, transatlantic w/t traffic (including the Enigma product) was becoming sufficient to warrant a separate short-wave link of its own. As a result, BSC was tasked to set up a communications division to link it with the UK headquarters of the SIS and SOE. The development of this short-wave trunk, code-named HYDRA (with reference to its many-headed cluster of antennae), has been traced in detail by David Stafford, who records that, originally, 'it was an improvised station constructed from radio parts acquired somewhat haphazardly from all over North America'. Its initial transmitter was a 2500-watt unit in 1942, augmented a few months later by a much larger, water-cooled, 10-kilowatt unit, originally used by a commercial radio station in Philadelphia. Both of these were installed at STS 103, the BSC field school at Whitby, Ontario. The chief engineer at BSC's communications division also developed a high-speed cipher machine which became known as the Rockex, a name attributed to GC & CS director Edward Travis, playing partly on the idiom of the British standard coding machine named 'Typex' (Type-X), and partly on the fact that BSC was based at the Rockefeller Center, home of the famous Rockettes dance troupe. HYDRA offered the advantage of a far higher transmission rate than the transatlantic cable (although in 1943 high-speed encryption system was installed on the cable), and in due course became the communications links for transatlantic SIGINT cooperation under the 1943 BRUSA agreement, as well as the main SIS/SOE transatlantic trunk.[174] Finally, Hydra provided a training facility for w/t operators being trained at STS 103.[175]

By 1944, the Foreign Office began taking a proprietary interest in the SIS transceiver network. In a March letter to the Air Ministry's Director General of Signals, W.M. Codrington, noted: 'For some time now we have been using a Foreign Office controlled wireless organisation (Gambier-Parry) as the channel for direct cipher communication between the Foreign Office and certain missions abroad.' He referred to the SIS network simply as 'Government Wireless'.[176] There had even been debate between the foreign missions and the Foreign Office about whether or not British firms abroad should be allowed to use Gambier-Parry's 'Diplomatic Wireless' (as it was known in Foreign Office circles) as an alternative to the often unreliable wartime commercial telegraph services.[177] Although originally an SIS entity, Section VIII was rapidly outgrowing its original master, providing, as it did, the only source of global, secure, civilian (as opposed to military) governmental short-wave communication.

Among the cryptanalytical successes of December 1940 was the penetration of *Abwehr* traffic, breaking first its Enigma code, the product of which was code-named ISK ('Intelligence Service, Knox', after Dilwyn Knox, an alumnus of Room 40 who was leading the team attacking the *Abwehr* Enigma) and later its hand cipher was called ISOS ('Intelligence Service, Oliver Strachey', after another Room 40 alumnus), both of which were usually treated together under the ISOS label. The availability of ISOS was a critical advantage in British counter-espionage, both at home and abroad. This had both costs and benefits. On the plus side, it provided comprehensive information about both the *Abwehr* and its operations, and also a check on the credibility of Double-Cross agents with their German controllers. On the negative side, the availability of ISOS, and the scale and pressure of work resulting led to a sustained turf war between the SIS and MI5 over the control of counter-espionage. This time, instead of the SIS trying to subsume MI5, MI5 was seeking to take over Section V.

Section V started the war grossly undermanned and under-resourced, with only three officers and a secretary. To exacerbate matters, while the rest of SIS had returned to Broadway from Bletchley after their temporary evacuation on the outbreak of war, Section V and the Central Registry had both been relocated to Prae Wood, St Albans, presumably to remove them from the main centre of German bombing, but this also removed Section V from both Broadway and MI5. Both wartime mobilization and the increasing volume of ISOS decrypts, intercepted by the SIS-controlled Radio Security Service (RSS) and decrypted by GC & CS, resulted in internal pressures to expand Section V's ability to process the materials. Meanwhile MI5's demand for ISOS and the need to coordinate the domestic side of the developing Double-Cross programme, as the British played Abwehr's agents back on their German controllers, with SIS's foreign counter-espionage work applied an external pressure. A measure of expansion was achieved by having MI5 release staff to work at Section V's offices at St Albans in June 1941.[178] By autumn 1942, Section V had expanded to 12 officers at headquarters and another 12 abroad, but even this modest expansion drew criticism from its main Whitehall consumers that the SIS was pursuing counter-espionage 'at the expense of… operational intelligence for the Services'.[179] Nonetheless, the section expanded rapidly and, by 1944, numbered 60 HQ staff and the same number overseas.[180] When, in March 1941, Section VIII took over RSS from MI8, the RSS's Radio Analysis Bureau was for a time under the control of Section V as Section Vw, but this arrangement proved unproductive, and Vw was eventually transferred to Section VIII as the Radio Intelligence Section (see below).[181]

As it developed, Section V became subdivided into a range of geographical and functional subsections, with the geographical subsections controlling the various Section V residents abroad, much of whose work involved running the foreign side of the Double-Cross programme. In 1941, the geographical side was divided into Vb1, which handled Germany and Scandinavia; VB, which dealt with The Netherlands, Belgium, France and North Africa; Vd, which handled the Iberian Peninsula, Spanish Morocco and the Atlantic Islands; Ve, which handled North and South America; and Va, which absorbed the

139

'rest of the non-British world'.[182] In 1943, Section V had six instead of five geographical sections and four functional subsections. The functional sections handled Double-Cross agents and deception; enemy espionage communications (Trevor-Roper's Vw); Soviet espionage and communism (possibly Vc); and, finally, a security section for what the official history describes as the 'protection of SIS itself against penetration', for which it has not been possible to identify the Section V designation.[183] At the end of 1943, a subsection was set up in conjunction with the BSC to deal with German trans-Atlantic smuggling of war materials.[184] The winding down of the European phase of the war, and the hiving-off of both the anti-Soviet counter-espionage section and protective security to Vivian's direct control after his lateral move to become a Deputy Director controlling all security and counter-intelligence functions as DD/SP (below) left Section V a very different organization from that which had probably reached its peak in 1943 on the strength of ISOS and Double-Cross. In late 1944/early 1945, Section V's geographical side consisted of Va, which handled what was left of Axis espionage in the Far East, Pacific, and North and South America and liaison with Indian Political Intelligence; Vb, which handled France, Corsica, Andorra, Belgium, The Netherlands and Luxembourg; Vd, which handled the Iberian Peninsula; VE, which handled Hungary, Romania, Bulgaria, Italy, The Balkans, the Near and Middle East, and Russia, and VF, which dealt with Germany, Poland, Czechoslovakia, Scandinavia, Iceland and Greenland. The functional side included Subsection SP/SD, which acted as a support staff for Vivian as DD/SP as well as counter-intelligence liaison with the American OSS; Vc, which handled travel documents and passes for SIS personnel and agents, such as documents exempting them from the London Receiving Centre (LRC) that processed travellers coming into the UK, information on non-communist subversion in the UK uncovered by the SIS, and Section V liaison with the LRC; Vh, which processed counter-espionage information from Section H's 'XX' information from censorship; Vx, which handled Double-Cross work and agents in coordination with the London Controlling Section and the Supreme Headquarters, Allied European Forces (SHAEF) on the Continent; and the Section V Registry Vl, as well as an assortment of minor departments dealing with photography, teleprinters, and translation.[185]

The Section V presence abroad took two forms. In the first place, the section posted resident officers to SIS stations who held ISOS decrypts and handled the foreign arm of the Double-Cross programme. Because the Section V residents were concerned with detecting and intercepting espionage, sabotage and subversive agents being infiltrated into British territory, they progressively took over the Passport Control Office cover, with SIS Heads of Station moving to more conventional diplomatic cover provided by the Foreign Office.[186] From 1944, however, a new arrangement, under SHAEF, provided for the SIS to attach Special Counter-Intelligence Units (SCIU) to the advancing Allied armies. SCIUs received information about hostile espionage and sabotage agents known to be in the area of military operations over a separate Section VIII radio link. The SCIUs would convey their ISOS and Double-Cross-derived information to the army security staffs[187] much as the SCU/SLU attachments carried and disseminated operational ULTRA.

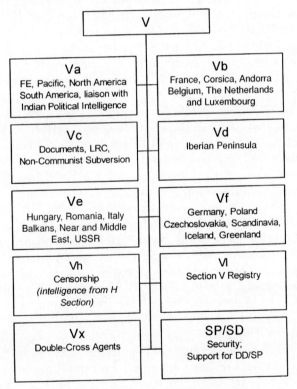

Figure 4.6: Section V in late 1944

141

Despite MI5 pressure on the SIS for more access to ISOS and greater coordination between the two counter-espionage bodies, for much of 1940 and 1941, MI5 was absorbed by its own internal crises. It was completely overwhelmed by reports generated by yet another fifth column scare (like that in 1914–15), and between June 1940 and April 1941, the Security Service underwent two changes of senior leadership. During this period of MI5's internal difficulty, Menzies extracted from Sir David Petrie, MI5's new Director-General of the Security Service (DGSS), agreement to an April 1941 memorandum, which reinforced the traditional geographical division of labour between the SIS and MI5. According to this memorandum, the geographical division of labour established by the 1931 Secret Service Committee was reiterated but Palestine and Egypt were specified as part of the MI5 remit, while the SIS was to retain control of all counter-espionage reporting abroad. However, he added: 'In order that MI5 may be able to fulfil their responsibility it is essential that they should not be flooded with extraneous matter...unless the particular paper under consideration, or connected papers, show that there is a likelihood that the case in hand will require executive action in this country, or a part of the Empire, in the fairly immediate future, it should NOT be sent to MI5.'[188] Despite this agreement, throughout 1941, the SIS/MI5 relationship continued to deteriorate. The March transfer of the RSS to Section VIII (which was, as we shall see, not merely supported but recommended by Petrie) gave SIS exclusive control not only of the operations of the RSS, but also of the interpretation and dissemination of its take. There was, to be sure, a joint committee overseeing the work of the RSS, but this became chiefly a forum for assorted mutual grievances. Section V complained that the Security Service was lax in maintaining proper security of ISOS decrypts, while MI5, noting that most espionage in the UK originated from abroad, concluded that it should have access to all SIS counter-espionage information. The fact that MI5's only input to the control of the RSS was through the joint committee was itself a matter of grievance.

By autumn 1941, MI5 had come to the conclusion that a geographical division of labour was counter-productive. In September, the head of the MI5 registry submitted a proposal to the SIS, backed by MI5's B (Investigations) Division, that his Registry should take over the recording and collating of *all* counter-intelligence while the SIS would be restricted to collection. The SIS rejected this proposal in terms which prompted Petrie to investigate the matter himself. Petrie, overall, does not appear to have been particularly willing, at first, to adopt his new agency's views. Just as he had backed the SIS's takeover of the RSS in March, Petrie rejected B division's call for increased access to foreign counter-espionage information. He did, however, meet with Menzies in November to seek a compromise, but Petrie's approach was rebuffed, and although a new joint committee was set up, it achieved little. Finally, when the Security Service learned that Section V had withheld information concerning the overseas work of two of MI5's stable of domestic Double-Cross agents (codenamed GARBO and TRICYCLE), MI5's line hardened into a claim for overarching responsibility for *all* counter-espionage operations, at home and abroad.

In April 1942, a year after supporting Menzies on the SIS/MI5 division of labour, Petrie wrote to C, proposing that Section V should be absorbed completely by B Division. This escalated the debate, and in June the matter was taken to Lord Swinton, head of the Home Defence Security Executive (HD(S)E). By now, Menzies was willing to compromise, but argued that any joint body should be housed with Section V at St Albans. A visit in August 1942 by Security Service officers to Prae Wood discovered that, contrary to their convictions, the volume of Axis espionage and sabotage against British interests outside British territory vastly exceeded that within it. They concluded, however, that Section V was underequipped to keep up with the work required, and although they backed Menzies's proposal for a joint section, they argued instead that the joint section should be based in London. MI5's senior management, however, remained unreceptive to dual control on principle, and although the matter was referred back to the HD(S)E again (now under the control of Duff Cooper) in July, no real amelioration of Section V/MI5 relations developed until the section's relocation to Ryder Street, in London, in 1943.[189]

Vital to the ISOS counter-intelligence SIGINT effort was RSS. It is often asserted that SIS acquired RSS from MI5, over the security service's objections, and that this was one of the sources of friction between the two agencies which marred their cooperation throughout the war.[190] However, as pointed out by Hinsley and the former post-war Deputy Director-General of MI5, C.A.G. Simkins, in Volume IV of the official history of British intelligence in the Second World War, nothing of this sort took place. The RSS was acquired by the SIS from the War Office signals organization, MI8, with the very explicit backing of DGSS Sir David Petrie.[191] However, the process by which this developed was nothing like as consensual as Hinsley and Simkins suggest, with considerable resistance appearing, not from MI5, but from MI8 and even the DMI.

The RSS as such did not take shape until November 1939. Before this, there was originally only a very small body staffed and equipped by the General Post Office (GPO) to intercept illicit wireless as MI1g. It consisted only of three fixed and four mobile intercepting stations, and a nascent corps of voluntary intercept operators.[192] The process which would eventually result in the transfer of the RSS from MI8 to SIS can be traced to one of the reports of Lord Hankey's review of secret service. Hankey produced in August 1939 a paper entitled 'Leakage of Information about Military and Other Movements in this Country', which examined, among other things, the risk of Axis agents using clandestine radio communications from within the UK to contact their controllers abroad. In his report, Hankey noted the existence of three related signals organizations, one handling 'the *internal problem* of the detection of illicit wireless transmission from within the UK', a second, also under War Office control, dealing with radio beacons, and finally Gambier-Parry's 'organization under the independent control of the Secret Service which deals with the *external problem* of illicit communication from our own agents in foreign countries'.[193] Hankey argued that the three bodies' work was 'in many respects complementary', that they had the disadvantage of being separate and subordinated to different departments, and therefore that the three should be hived off as a new, independent organization dealing, on the one hand, with radio beacons, and, on the other hand, with 'the interception of illicit wireless and allied methods of communicating at home and abroad'. Hankey added that 'it would be necessary to make special provision to safeguard the exceptional character of the Secret Service Branch of this organization but I see no insurmountable difficulty in this'.[194] The actual result of Hankey's inquiry was much more limited, with the small GPO unit being established as a service in its own right as the Radio Security Section (RSS), placed under the War Office interception (Y) service, MI8, as MI8c.[195]

By autumn 1940, as the official history notes, the RSS consisted of 'a headquarters staff of 20 officers and other ranks provided by the army, of about 1,000 interception and technical staff provided, not entirely to the satisfaction of MI8, by the GPO, and of another 1,000 part-time voluntary interceptors'. The RSS had grown from being a small, domestic interception service to a network of domestic and foreign stations responsible for intercepting all enemy espionage radio traffic.[196] The RSS and GC & CS were already reading two *Abwehr* ciphers, and by the end of the year had broken yet another, a highly valuable hand cipher, which provided a comprehensive order of battle for the *Abwehr* and its stations abroad.[197] Thus, it was during this period that MI8 concluded that the work being done was essentially of security interest, and not particularly relevant to the military duties of Military Intelligence. Therefore, in October, MI8 proposed that the RSS be transferred to MI5. At this time, MI5's interest in secret radio was confined to a small, newly created branch called W Division tasked with searching for possible means of enemy espionage wireless communications. W Division pursued this task through liaison with the RSS, and was headed not by a career intelligence officer but by someone seconded from the British Broadcasting Corporation (BBC), and included within it an SIS officer,[198] the latter presumably because of the potential foreign counter-espionage value of any of its findings.

The question of the RSS's status was taken up by Swinton and the HD(S)E, which had also commissioned a review of MI5 management and operations by Sir David Petrie at the time. The official history suggests that Petrie's support of the RSS being moved to the SIS may have hinged in part on the serious managerial overload problems he was finding in the Security Service, especially its bloated B Division.[199] However, in the actual minute of January 1941 to Swinton, Petrie's expressed reasoning goes rather beyond this. Although Petrie remarked therein that 'if possible, MI5 should be spared any further additions to its already heavy burdens', he seems to have been most centrally concerned with the technical expertise involved in performing and managing espionage wireless interception. As long as it was felt that the RSS could continue to function effectively under MI8, he saw no reason why it should not remain there. However, if this was not the case, he argued:

> The standard of technical efficiency it appears will inevitably be that of the administrative body. ... Spy detection and the like are a highly specialised branch of wireless. Special equipment, special technique and special experience are all needed. We cannot expect RSS to be suitably found in all these respects so long as it is run by

a branch which does not specialise on these particular lines. . . . The only organisation known to me that has knowledge in all three sides of the work is the very efficient wireless installation maintained by MI6 . . . [MI5] has no such side to it.[200]

Petrie was essentially arguing that where clandestine wireless was concerned, one should set a thief to catch a thief, much as Hankey had suggested a year previously.

The set-a-thief reasoning set forth by Hankey and Petrie was not, however, accepted by all concerned. Colonel W. Worlledge, Controller of the RSS, opposed the proposed transfer vigorously. In a 14 February minute, he argued, on the basis of a conversation with Gambier-Parry the day before: 'I am left with some doubt as to whether MI6 does actually possess the necessary powers or administrative organization to the extent Sir David Petrie appears to believe'. Worlledge's view of RSS work was very much focused still on *military* intelligence, especially the danger that 'illicit transmitters will be dropped into the country, manned by soldiers in uniform', with RSS providing strictly *military* intelligence in the event of an invasion. More critically, Worlledge argued, Gambier-Parry had only 'small knowledge of either the technical equipment or the work done by RSS, his visit yesterday being the first he has paid to this unit, and it was obvious . . . that his knowledge was very incomplete'.[201] This criticism was taken up by the head of MI8, Colonel D.A. Butler, who wrote to the DMI echoing Worlledge's sentiments that the decision to subsume the RSS under the SIS appeared to have been taken 'without full knowledge of the facts'. Unlike Worlledge, Butler hedged his bets by adding as a disclaimer: 'I know [Gambier-Parry] and though in so far as I am aware he has little or no experience of this type of work I think he will be quite capable of running the show efficiently.'[202]

Major General F.H.N. Davidson, then DMI, in turn wrote to Lord Swinton on 15 February, expressing his department's doubt about the transfer. Davidson appeared agreeable to the transfer in principle, remarking that 'if you are satisfied that the present proposal to transfer the Radio Security Section to MI6 is indeed in the best interests of efficiency, I am quite prepared to agree and ready to implement the decision'. In fact he was much less than enthusiastic, going on to write that 'I must add that I doubt if the decision has been reached with a full knowledge of all the governing facts.' Davidson also argued that Petrie had not consulted either Butler or

Worlledge, and, moreover, that 'MI6 is concerned with the transmitting of signals and not their interception or location'. Therefore, contrary to Petrie's interpretation, the necessary experience 'from the Intelligence [sic] angle and from the point of view of the special equipment and technique necessary is, I am sure, greater in MI8 than it is in MI6.[203] Davidson further voiced concern that the mixed assortment of military and GPO personnel would require a comprehensive reorganization of the RSS and expressed doubt 'whether MI6 does actually possess the necessary powers or administrative organization to equip, staff and run RSS purely as an Intelligence department'. Davidson also questioned the future status of the RSS's foreign intercept stations.

Swinton responded five days later in no uncertain terms. He countered Davidson's objections at several levels. In first place, he argued, there were no problems of divided control or interests between the SIS and the Security Service on the grounds that both the SIS and MI5 came under the control of the HD(S)E as far as operations within the UK were concerned, and were, therefore, 'virtually one' under Swinton's direction. He further pointed out also the existence of the SIS/MI5 joint committee handling ISOS materials and giving direction to the RSS, and repeated Petrie's argument about the SIS holding w/t know-how that MI5 did not. Swinton answered Davidson's concerns about the intercept work in the rest of the empire to the effect that he saw no reason why the current arrangements, in which intercept stations were run by the various service branches, could not continue. The main problem noted by Swinton was that of training RSS staff. This, he suggested would be most readily resolved by modelling RSS training on that of GC & CS in which the various service branches seconded training officers to the organization in question.[204]

On 10 March 1941, it was finally decided that the RSS would shift to SIS's Section VIII, with the financial burden of the organization shifting from the War Office to the Foreign Office.[205] The actual transfer took place in May, although it was agreed that the RSS facilities in the empire would remain under the supervision of MI8 for six months before eventual transfer to the SIS. For his trouble, Worlledge was moved out of the RSS proper and assigned as liaison to the Imperial Wireless Interception organization for the six months before its final transfer to the SIS. His offices were not at the RSS headquarters in Hanslope but in London, at MI8.[206]

Prior to its absorption by the SIS, the RSS maintained an analysis and interpretation group called the RSS Analysis Bureau. When the RSS was taken over by the SIS in May 1941, the Analysis Bureau became Section Vw. This was not a successful change in organization because Section V's passion for need-to-know conflicted with Section Vw's need to correspond with GC & CS, MI5 and the Service departments in order to interpret the arcane language of the decrypts.[207] The official historians remark tactfully that this 'running battle' was 'sustained by personal animosities', but the perceptions of Hugh Trevor-Roper, head of the Analysis Bureau, were less compromising. At one point, the conflict between Trevor-Roper and Cowgill and Vivian resulted in the latter two petitioning C to have him dismissed. Trevor-Roper recalled later

> How well I recall that 'trial' – *in camera* of course – with Colonel Vivian as prosecutor and C as judge! It was a narrow squeak. I have always felt grateful to C for his ultimate rejection, on that occasion, of the argument of DCSS, who maintained with increasing urgency, and in lamentable tones, that whatever the merits of the case it was quite impossible, after this, for me to remain in the organization. However, thanks to C, I did remain: indeed, the organization was afterwards adjusted to separate me from Section V in which I had been an indigestible particle.[208]

Although Curry's account of these events in his official history of MI5 is more prosaic, it agrees with Trevor-Roper in virtually all respects.[209] The solution involved carving the Analysis Bureau out of Section V and attaching it to Section VIII[210] (which already controlled the rest of the RSS), where it was redesignated the Radio Intelligence Section (RIS).[211]

The kind of outside intervention necessary to resolve the Section V/MI5 conflicts became increasingly prevalent in other areas where overlapping jurisdictions were inevitable, particularly the running feud between the SIS and SOE. Despite the widespread role of this conflict in the existing literature on SOE, less closely examined are the various agreements and accommodations negotiated beyond the day-to-day sphere of the main London headquarters of the two organizations. In Denmark, the secret intelligence role was completely taken on by SOE, with SIS agreement, when SOE contacts turned out to be the best available sources for pure intelligence.[212] The original reasoning behind the separation of Section D from the rest of the SIS had been essentially an argument from the economies of scale that were anticipated from bundling together the propaganda and subversion functions shared by Section D and the Foreign Office propaganda unit at Electra House and the irregular warfare functions shared by Section D and MIR. If anything, Section D stood on a middle ground, with MIR and Electra House at the two extremes of what might compose special operations. In the event, however, the combined Special Operations organization yielded virtually no advantages from vertically integrating the three agencies. Propaganda had virtually no assets or needs in common with covert political contacts and sabotage, while the latter shared a common need to maintain clandestine networks of contacts, and political opposition served as a prime mover for the members of sabotage and guerrilla cells. As a result, no advantage accrued from amalgamating the three organizations, and SO1 and SO2 went their separate ways.

The result of the rivalry between the SIS and SOE was that the coordination of secret intelligence and special operations had to be relocated to a higher level of governmental authority to act as arbiter and intermediary. In the UK, these hostilities required intervention by the JIC. Indeed, on two separate occasions, conflict between SIS and SOE was met with the suggestion, first by the Joint Planning Staff (JPS), in May 1942, at the request of the Joint Intelligence and Joint Planning Committees, and later, in 1943, by MI5, that the two organizations should be amalgamated into a single body. The JPS report stressed that the head of the combined organization should not be under the Foreign Secretary or a Service Branch Minister but an executive head sitting on the Chiefs of Staff committee (COS), with special arrangements for the Foreign Office's need for political information. This proposal was not acted upon, although the threat of a common abolition stimulated Broadway and SOE headquarters at Baker Street to make some efforts to increase mutual contact, and Petrie's suggestion was blocked personally by the Prime Minister.[213] In 1942, a working compromise over intelligence was adopted in which the SIS Circulating Sections would collate and distribute SOE intelligence to consumers in government,[214] but this was abandoned a year later on the grounds that SOE intelligence production exceeded the ability of SIS to collate and disseminate the additional material along with its own product and warranted its own direct link with consumers.[215] In April 1943, conflicts not merely between SIS and SOE but also between SIS and MI5 prompted the creation of a short-lived Secret Services Coordinating Committee chaired by Desmond Morton, although this was disbanded after its second meeting.[216]

In the Middle East, ISLD Cairo, MI9 and Special Operations Middle East (SOM) were coordinated through a Secret Activities Committee (SAC) set up in 1941.[217] This did not stop rivalries and hostilities from developing between SOM and elements of ISLD Cairo, such as that between the ISLD Cairo Greek Section and its SOM opposite number.[218] In North Africa, a paper issued by the Chiefs of Staff Committee in spring 1942 led to SOE and SIS setting up an ad hoc body, the Westmacott–Clarke Committee, under the ISLD Algiers head, Captain H.A. Westmacott, and his SOE opposite number Brian Clarke. Under this set of arrangements, the SIS would provide any intelligence it had acquired that might be relevant to SOE's work, while Clarke's SOE would provide any 'incidental information that come their way' while keeping SIS informed concerning any operational plans that might affect its intelligence networks.[219] Although the SIS proved willing to contribute by making its records available to SOE,[220] by July 1943, continued conflicts between the two units required the creation of an SAC comparable to that in Cairo, meeting every two weeks and attended by the British Resident Minister.

In the Far East, once Mountbatten's South East Asia Command (SEAC) was set up in 1943, a P (Priorities) Division had to be set up to referee relations between the SIS, Force 136 (SOE Far East), MI9 and the American OSS.[221] Here again the debate focused on SOE production of secret intelligence as well as putting ISLD (FE) networks at risk. As a result, under P Division oversight, ISLD (FE) took the role of disseminating Force 136 intelligence product through its Collating Section,[222] but not merely as a passive intermediary. An SOE report on its relations with the ISLD states: 'Before passing them on...ISLD often break up reports in order to meet the needs of recipients, so that in one case a long report from a single source may be sent out in the form of several reports, whilst in another case a number of kindred reports may be combined into one.'[223] P Division provided both a general coordinating body for operations in the Far East, as well as a forum for managing inter-agency disputes.

In West Africa, a debate about the control of SOE networks which were producing only intelligence was resolved, over Menzies's objection, by fusing the SIS and SOE organizations there into a single headquarters under the cover of the Resident Minister's Information Bureau in 1943.[224] In East Africa, the directive of June 1942 installing an SOE East African mission ordered the SOE to pass all raw intelligence to the SIS for collation and dissemination, and the SIS to provide information 'which might conceivably affect SOE's plans' to the SOE in that area.[225] These decisions reflected a more general agreement between the two agencies that intelligence produced by SOE should be passed to the SIS for dissemination to consumers.[226]

Headquarters conflicts at whatever level notwithstanding, the necessity of cooperation and coordination often forced SIS and SOE officers in the field simply to ignore the more divisive orders from their controllers and work out their own modus vivendi on the spot.[227] Only under Stephenson's BSC were SIS/SOE relations managed smoothly, and that was as diverse elements under a common integrated command, but then again BSC was never an *operational* headquarters for the SOE, so no conditions for rivalry over scarce transportation resources, line-crossing, or SOE intelligence production existed.

As already discussed reconstructing its European networks was a slow business for the SIS, beset with setbacks such as a failed initial attempt to set up a network in The Netherlands, and the penetration and collapse of the Polish-originated INTERALLIE network in France in 1942–43 (the SIS had become aware of the penetration by early 1942, but continued to play the network back on the Germans until mid-1943). The installation of a network of coast watchers, first in Norway, and later in France, progressively generated operational intelligence which could be used by RAF Coastal Command and the Navy's Home Fleet against German shipping in areas such as the North Sea, the Skagerrak and along the French Channel ports.[228] This nonetheless involved a hiatus in intelligence production of nearly a year, with only a gentle, upward slope of recovery. This produced considerable dissatisfaction among the SIS's consumers, leading to unwillingness on the part of the Navy and Air Force to provide elements for special duties in support of secret intelligence work, as opposed to special operations, and an unwillingness to use SIS reports in departmental assessments.[229]

Despite the inevitable loss of its European presence and despite the now long-established 1921 arrangement, the SIS's main customers seemed determined to interpret the organization's

151

underperformance during the early years of the war as a consequence of its failure to understand their requirements. The result was the imposition of internal organizational reform by the Service Branches in a series of changes more than passingly reminiscent of the MacDonogh scheme of late 1917. At the beginning of 1942, the Service Directors of Intelligence again pressured C for reform and reorganization. The resulting solution was that each of the three Service Branches attached a senior officer to SIS HQ, as the official history puts it, 'to ensure that the requirements of his Intelligence Branch were better understood'.[230] Menzies had apparently promised the Service Branches that the three new officers would be taken on board with the rank of Deputy Directors, with full access to information about the workings of the SIS relevant to their respective areas of concern.[231] Instead, Menzies skewed the appointment of the new Deputy Directors, DD/Air, DD/Navy and DD/Army, respectively, to work as a stop-gap solution to the chronically weak integration of the SIS highlighted by Vivian in his 1941 minute, and to a span of control problem which was of crisis proportions.

Menzies's appointment of Dansey as ACSS and Vivian as DCSS without a clear hierarchy of division of labour between them essentially neutralized the possible advantages of having deputies at all. Dansey was concerned chiefly with operations in western Europe and Switzerland, while Vivian was variously absorbed by counter-espionage, on the one hand, and more generally 'out of the loop', so to speak, on the other hand. As a result, the day-to-day management of the SIS senior staff devolved directly to Menzies, who had continued the interwar practice of encouraging senior officers, such as heads of section, to come directly to him, as had Sinclair before him.[232] However, SIS's headquarters presence in the UK had expanded massively during the first 18 months of the war, both because of general wartime pressure and the relocation of the European stations to London as the Production or 'country' sections. Therefore, the span of control under Menzies consisted roughly of: approximately one dozen Production Sections; eight nominal Circulating Sections; and a range of administrative and support sections, including AO, DOCS, technical aids, Slocum's Transport Section, the Central Registry, and administrative oversight of ISLD Cairo, ISLD (FE), and BSC, not to mention his ancillary and considerable responsibilities as the titular head of GC & CS and intercept-bearer to the Prime Minister. Menzies therefore used the appointment of the Deputy

Directors to reduce his management span on the Production side by forming them and an SIS Deputy Director into what the official history describes as 'a board responsible for directing SIS activities throughout the world, with each deputy in charge of a different theatre'.[233] Colonel John Cordeaux, RM, as DD/Navy took charge of The Netherlands and Scandinavia, or what became known as the Northern Area,[234] and the DD/Army, Brigadier Beddington, oversaw operations in the Far East,[235] and the DD/Air, Air Commodore Payne, was concerned with the western hemisphere.[236] Given that Dansey for the most part oversaw operations in western Europe and Switzerland directly,[237] this would have left Africa and the Middle East for the SIS Deputy Director. Godfrey, who, as DNI, had led the campaign against the SIS, protested against how Menzies had implemented the appointment of the Deputy Directors, but failed to find support from his colleagues on the JIC, and so Menzies's arrangements stood.[238]

In practice, however, the service Deputy Directors were only weakly integrated into the SIS chain of command, and their theatre-level responsibilities appear to have been only very loosely and informally worked out. Much as the ACSS/DCSS arrangements suffered from weak implementation, Vivian's role as DCSS being virtually unknown in some quarters, surviving accounts and interviews with wartime officers betray a general lack of awareness among SIS officers of this ad hoc operational 'board' of Deputy Directors.[239] Moreover, operational control of the Far East and Middle East lay chiefly with the theatre-level military commands, with Broadway's responsibility limited to administrative support and staffing of the two ISLD groups. Likewise, BSC at the time had, if not a monopoly, certainly a pre-eminence in the western hemisphere, so for the most part the members of the operational board proved surplus to requirements, as well as completely unable to affect the main problem, which was the unmanageably wide, flat organization of SIS in the UK. They were viewed deeply askance by both the career 'professionals' and wartime 'amateurs' of SIS headquarters, who dubbed them, rather scathingly, the 'Service Commissars'.[240] One limited impact made by the 'Service Commissars' outside what Philby calls their 'spheres of obscurity' was their suggestion that since, by 1942, the SIS had begun training its offensive intelligence-gathering agents at SOE schools, it seemed reasonable that Section V personnel should also undergo a training course. In aid of this, instructors were brought in from Metropolitan Special Branch, in a programme that one officer interviewed considered thoroughly off-topic, being concerned 'mainly with policing' and matters such as 'the advantages of the three-point surveillance system',[241] all of which had very little to do with, and betrayed a weak understanding of, the business of targeting and handling Double-Cross agents abroad.

The Foreign Office approach to criticism of the SIS took a different approach from that of the Services. The Foreign Office's terms of dealing with the SIS were threefold: as intelligence consumer, as the Department of State overseeing the SIS, and as a body operating in parallel with the SIS abroad, acting overtly, but needing to coordinate SIS actions with its own policy. The Foreign Office did not opt to have its own Deputy Director, but took advantage of its direct executive authority to appoint to C a Personal Assistant (PA/CSS), in the form of a Foreign Office official. PA/CSS was to perform a double role; on the one hand, he was to act as an intermediary between SIS and the Foreign Office at home and abroad, while, on the other hand, PA/CSS was intended to introduce to the SIS some of the administrative skills essential to the running of the Foreign Office but made distinctive by their absence in the SIS.

The initial PA/CSS was Patrick Reilly, appointed in 1942.[242] One of the recurrent criticisms of the SIS from its consumers was the vagueness of SIS reports,[243] and so one of Reilly's first tasks was to train SIS officers in the sort of drafting skills for reports that were essential to the routine in the Foreign Office and the rest of Whitehall. These skills had not really been developed in an SIS that had traditionally sought to keep itself detached from the normal Whitehall committee machinery.[244] In the summer of 1943, Reilly was promoted to First Secretary and moved back to overt work in Algiers, while a new PA/CSS was appointed in the form of Robert Cecil, who continued the work of overseeing SIS administrative effectiveness and coordinating SIS plans with the Foreign Office until summer 1945. In conjunction with Menzies's Chief Personal Assistant (CPA/CSS) and a Principal Staff Officer (PSO/CSS), PA/CSS was the third member of Menzies's C/SS Secretariat. Where PA/CSS was concerned with FO liaison, PSO/CSS stood in for C in other non-Service liaison problems, and CPA oversaw the work of Secretariat, and handled internal problems and dissent within SIS.[245]

By 1943, the Deputy Directors and their operational board were judged unsatisfactory by the SIS senior staff, and in the autumn of

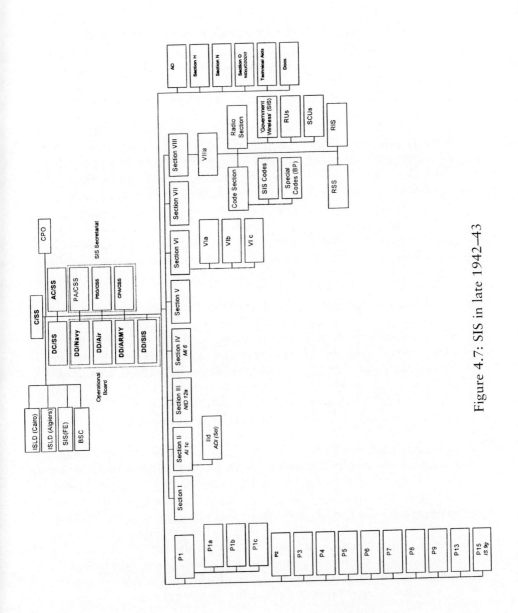

Figure 4.7: SIS in late 1942–43

that year the board was abolished. The three Service Deputy Directors remained at Broadway, taking over their respective service Circulating Sections,[246] but the model of the operational board was retained, and the 'Service Commissars' were replaced in their operational role by four regional Controllers who actually did absorb the immediate Production span of control in London: Controller Western Area, handling the France, Belgium, and Iberia P Sections (P1, P2, P7 and P15); Controller Northern Area, handling The Netherlands and Scandinavia (P8, P9); Controller Eastern Area (P3 and P6); and Controller Eastern Europe (P5, P13).[247] Menzies also expanded the Board of Deputy Directors and the system of Controllerates to include a range of other personnel and functions, further streamlining the span of control and chain of command within the service. The SIS Deputy Director became DD/Admin, overseeing Section VII and the numerous support sections, possibly including the Central Registry,[248] and Menzies also took the opportunity finally to resolve the struggle for supremacy between Dansey as AC/SS and Vivian as VC/SS.

Menzies's solution to the Dansey/Vivian feud again involved essentially another opportunistic deflection of consumer pressure. The appointment of the 'Service Commissars' coincided with the progressive recovery of the service's agent networks on the Continent; as a result, once production began to recover, complaints about comprehension of requirements abated.[249] That same period had been marred also by conflict between the SIS and SOE. Beyond the sustained efforts of Ministers and the JIC to negotiate an end of hostilities in Whitehall, and the creation of P Division to try to referee in the Far East, the War Office developed an alternative plan for the UK end of the problem. This new strategy entailed seconding one of its senior generals, James Marshall-Cornwall, first to Baker Street, and then to Broadway, his task being to 'bring about more harmonious relations between these two organizations and prevent mutual friction'.[250] Marshall-Cornwall, by his own admission, was in the unenviable position of being 'high up in the list of full generals, but there was no active command for which I could be selected, owing to my lack of experience with fighting troops'.[251] As a consolation prize, Marshall-Cornwall was given the task of learning about both agencies from the inside, and then finding a way to mediate their dealings with one another.

Marshall-Cornwall began his assignment with a six-month

posting to Baker Street in October 1942, and then moved to the SIS, where, 'during April and May, 1943, I sat at Claude Dansey's feet . . . and was inculcated into the methods and mysteries of MI6.'[252] Marshall-Cornwall was a full general while the Chief himself was only a major-general, and so to minimize any awkwardness, Marshall-Cornwall waived his senior rank while attached to Broadway. Under the new arrangements, the post of DC/SS was abolished, and the post of AC/SS given to Marshall-Cornwall; Dansey took on a newly created position of Vice-Chief of Secret Service (VC/SS) while Vivian was made a Deputy Director overseeing all security and counter-espionage functions as DD/SP.[253] While Philby has described this as being 'kicked downward and sideways' in his memoirs,[254] according to the information he provided the KGB at the time, it is apparent that under the new scheme Dansey was confined to operational matters abroad while Vivian directly controlled all counter-espionage and security functions.

Section IX, the last addition to Vivian's domain as DD/SP, was created in March, 1944, when the anti-communist sub-section of Section V was carved out and set up as a free-standing circulating section. A great deal has been written about this particular development, chiefly because the new section came to be headed by Soviet penetration agent Kim Philby, and even more so because of the contentious nature of Philby's version of his accession to the post in his *My Silent War*. Robert Cecil notes that 'Philby in his book dates the struggle to reactivate [*sic*] Section IX as early as 1943, presumably with the intention of implying that SIS, with Foreign Office connivance, was embarking on the Cold War long before the Hitler war was over'. Cecil counters that the new unit did not take shape until 'late 1944'.[255] To be precise, Philby dates his own posting as IX to the summer of 1944,[256] and describes the earlier 1943 development as 'a modest start . . . made by setting up a small section, known as Section IX, to study past records of Communist activity. An officer named Curry, approaching the retiring age, was imported from MI5 to get the section started.'[257] The creation in 1943 of an anti-Soviet subsection of Section V has since been confirmed by the official history, and Philby is almost certainly referring to that development. However, this creation of an anti-Soviet counter-espionage section would in no way indicate that the SIS was in some way making an unprovoked intelligence offensive against the USSR. Soviet intelligence cooperation had been limited at best since the USSR's entry into the war, and attempts by the Soviets to penetrate British intelligence abroad had already come to the attention of British intelligence in the same year the new section was set up. SIME had attempted to develop a collaborative relationship with the NKVD in Persia during 1943. Menzies tried to warn SIME off, on the grounds that it would be little more than 'a waste of time and an embarrassment' because the Soviets were 'more interested in penetrating our intelligence than in helping'. In the event, the Tehran Defence Security Officer (DSO) found that, as the official history puts it, 'some practical collaboration was achieved while hostilities lasted, but blatant attempts were made to recruit the DSO's staff as agents'.[258] During the following year, as Philby was installing his new Section IX, conditions continued to deteriorate, as SOE clandestine operators in Poland working with the resistance there found themselves arrested by the NKVD immediately upon the liberation in 1944/45, while the Poles' own agents were rolled up, imprisoned and as often as not executed wholesale.[259] These were the sorts of things going on in the background as thinking at Broadway returned to the pre-war Soviet opponent.

In March 1944, Section IX was formally severed from Section V, and Philby replaced Curry.[260] A year later, Philby presented his finished scheme, or 'charter' to C and PA/CSS for approval, an ambitious plan which included a field organization of counter-intelligence officers stationed abroad under diplomatic cover along much the same lines as the Section V residents,[261] and made Philby responsible for the 'collection and interpretation of information concerning Soviet and communist espionage and subversion in all parts of the world outside British territory'.[262] Under Philby, Robert Carew-Hunt, who later wrote *The Theory and Practice of Communism*,[263] and Jane Archer, formerly of MI5, studied the activities of communist political and 'national liberation' organizations, while the rest of the section was divided along geographical lines. However, secret intelligence was hard to come by on the subject, and so the new section confined itself primarily with background research on the subject, and its proposed field organization failed to materialize.[264] Section IX would not really become a major concern until after the end of the Second World War and the beginning of the Cold War.

As a result, by the end of 1944, Vivian, as DD/SP, controlled a fairly extensive domain, including Sections V, VI, and IX and the former security section eventually designated the Inspectorate of Security

(I/S).[265] Perhaps the last word on DD/SP's domain should deal with that least-discussed feature of the wartime SIS, its security section. The quality of SIS protective security has often been a point of criticism, since it allowed penetration by Philby and later Blake. But Nicholas Elliott, who would confront Philby in Beirut in the early 1960s and ended his career as Director of Requirements, has recalled that

> security in our Intelligence Service was in one way much stricter than today. Almost comically, you were not supposed to tell your wife 'the nature of your work'. This was an absurd ruling, and the officers who were in charge of administering it were often figures of fun. ... The following is an example of a conversation that I had with a security officer on my return from the Middle East in February 1945...
> Security Officer: 'Sit down. I'd like to have a frank talk with you.'
> NE: 'As you wish, Colonel.'
> SO: 'Does your wife know what you do?'
> NE: 'Yes.'
> SO: 'How did that come about?'
> NE: 'She was my secretary for two years and I think the penny must have dropped.'
> SO: 'Quite so. What about your mother?'
> NE: 'She thinks I'm in something called the SIS which she believes stands for Secret Intelligence Service.'
> SO: 'Good God! How did that come about?'
> NE: 'A member of the War Cabinet told her at a cocktail party.'
> SO: 'Who was he?'
> NE: 'I'd prefer not to say.'
> SO: 'Then what about your father?'
> NE: 'He thinks I'm a spy.'
> SO: 'Why should he think you're a spy?'
> NE: 'Because the Chief told him in the bar at White's.'[266]

By the time the war ended, there was indeed a relatively streamlined chain of command under C, consisting of a board of approximately six Deputy Directors overseeing the various aspects of consumer liaison, administration, security and counter-intelligence (DD/Army, DD/Navy, DD/Air, DD/Admin and DD/SP, respectively) on one side and six geographical and functional controllers on the operational side (Controller Northern Area, Controller Western

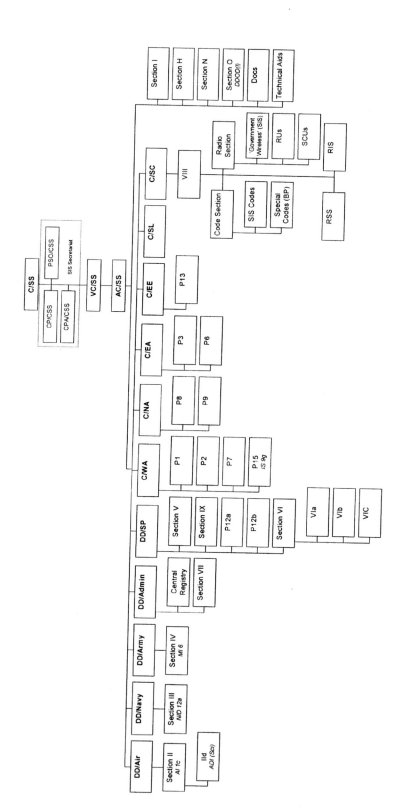

Figure 4.8: SIS in 1945

Area, Controller Eastern Area, Controller Eastern Europe, Controller Special Liaison and Controller Secret Communications), a Secretariat of three staff officers (PA/CSS, CPA/CSS and PSO/CSS), and a minor constellation of individual specialist officers dealing with relatively limited duties. This was a great improvement from the state of affairs in 1942 when the service was teetering on the brink of internal collapse regardless of any setbacks in its operations abroad. Even so, Menzies and his service still had no overall, self-aware plan for integrating the very broad range of personnel and functions required by the intelligence world of 1944-45.

The expansion in SIS infrastructure was driven by both the increased production required by the war, and by the diversification of tasks required to undertake that production. But coupled with this was an explosion in consumer demand, and that, in conjunction to the collapse of SIS's European organization, was a major factor in that agency's internal crisis in 1942. During the pre-war years, at least consumers had understood that the SIS was starved of funds and resources. By comparison, when dealing with the consequences of the German *blitzkrieg* across Europe and the comprehensive collapse of the western European networks after the Venlo incident, the consuming departments concluded that the SIS's problems lay in a failure to grasp their requirements rather than the loss of foreign assets. Naturally, once SIS production picked up again, these complaints abated; the peculiarity of the complaint is the consumers' preference for this explanation rather than the possibility that an organization with no networks on the ground could not produce any intelligence. Even with a Circulating Section right at the heart of the SIS, a Deputy Director with a hand in operations as well as representing War Office interests, close liaison links with MI5 through its Protective Security (C) and counter-sabotage (D) directorates, as well as the appointment of Defence Security Officers, the MID would still have preferred even more control over 'the selection of personnel or the disposition of [SIS and MI5] on whose efficiency military security and information depend'. It is impossible not to wonder what form or degree of War Office involvement in secret intelligence, short of simply taking the agencies over again, *would* have been satisfactory.

In the last analysis, the SIS quite literally muddled through the Second World War with its own leadership often very nearly its own worst enemy. It suffered from a weak command and control infrastructure, and a prohibitively wide span of control under

161

Menzies, who had no credible mechanism of delegation under him. It approached the emerging new tasks of a generalized national covert capability with profound inflexibility, only to find itself out-produced in its own field by separate, often competing agencies as a result. It did manage to lead the way on secure w/t, and did eventually, but belatedly, begin to take on board the ideas of systematic training and innovative technical support. Menzies proved a better Whitehall operator than SIS manager, ultimately preserving an agency beleaguered in terms of Whitehall bureaucratic politics by a combination of luck and inventive opportunism, relying on a hand strengthened more by his control (no less ineffectual) of GC & CS, which, in turn, had the good fortune to have had Polish, French and British information and ingenuity pooled to attack and break the German Enigma codes. Without an equivalent to GC & CS's Enigma successes to compensate for more general mismanagement (GC & CS was at least as badly organized for much of the war), SIS languished and struggled to prevent a complete loss of credibility. Typically, government agencies function as monopoly suppliers of their respective goods, but SIS had experienced a thorough dose of competition from the SOE and MI9. It was manifestly obvious that the SIS had to change, and however reticent or delinquent Menzies might prefer to be about review and reform, the SIS's consumers, the Service Departments, the Foreign Office and the increasingly powerful JIC, would give the agency little choice in the matter.

NOTES

1. H. Mongomery Hyde, *Secret Intelligence Agent* (London: Constable, 1982), p. 19.
2. The Venlo incident is a standard in the literature on SIS operational failures, but the central feature from the point of view in this study is the fact that it occurred under direct consumer guidance, and that at Cabinet level. The SD deception of the SIS consisted of representing one of its officers as a representative of an anti-Nazi faction within the German high command (much as Dzerzhinsky's Trust had entrapped the SIS and its aristocratic White Russians in the 1920s). As the official history stresses, the contacts between the SIS and this notional German dissident group were 'authorized and supervised' by the Foreign Office, with additional approval from Chamberlain as Prime Minister at what appeared to be key points in the negotiations. See F.H. Hinsley, E.E. Thomas, C.F.G. Ransom and R.C.

Knight, *British Intelligence in The Second World War: Its Influence on Strategy and Operations*, vol. I (London: HMSO, 1979), p. 57 (footnote).

3. David Stafford, *Churchill and Secret Service* (London: John Murray, 1997), p. 164.
4. Several accounts of Menzies's accession to C exist, the most detailed of which is that in Christopher Andrew, *Secret Service: The Making of the British Intelligence Community* (London: Sceptre, 1987), pp. 614–16. See also Anthony Read and David Fisher, *Colonel Z: The Secret Life of a Master of Spies* (London: Hodder and Stoughton, 1984), pp. 329–30, and Nigel West, *MI6: British Secret Intelligence Service Operations 1909–1945* (London: Grafton, 1988), pp. 143–4.
5. Robert Cecil '"C's" War', *Intelligence and National Security*, 1, 2 (April 1986), p. 178.
6. Ibid., pp. 177–8.
7. Hugh Trevor-Roper, *The Philby Affair: Espionage, Treason and Secret Services* (London: William Kimber, 1968), pp. 28, 71–2; Philby, *My Silent War* (New York: Ballantine, 1983), pp. 59–60; Philip Johns, *Within Two Cloaks: Missions with SIS and SOE* (London: William Kimber, 1979), p. 40.
8. Vivian to C, 6 January 1941, reproduced in Cecil, '"C's" War', p. 185.
9. Ibid., p. 186.
10. Cecil, '"C's" War', p. 178.
11. Quoted in Read and Fisher, *Colonel Z: The Secret Story of a Master of Spies*, p. 12.
12. Ibid., p. 12.
13. Philby, *My Silent War*, p. 77.
14. Johns, *Within Two Cloaks*, pp. 39–41.
15. James Langley, *Fight Another Day* (London: Collins, 1974), p. 132.
16. Philby, *My Silent War*, p. 76, Cecil '"C's" War', p. 176.
17. i-15.
18. Philby, *My Silent War*, p. 77.
19. Vivian to C, in Cecil, '"C's' War', p. 186.
20. This was the impact of surplus demand on GC & CS organization, see for example, Philip H.J. Davies, 'Organizational Politics and the Development of Britain's Intelligence Producer/Consumer Interface', *Intelligence and National Security*, 10, 4 (October 1995), pp. 121–2.
21. Philby, *My Silent War*, p. 104; Cecil, 'Five of Six at War', *Intelligence and National Security*, 9, 2 (April 1994), pp. 351.
22. i-15.
23. Hugh Trevor-Roper, *The Philby Affair: Espionage, Treason and Secret Services* (London: William Kimber, 1968), pp. 38–9.
24. Hinsley et al., *British Intelligence*, vol. I, p. 171; F.W. Winterbotham, *The Nazi Connection: The Personal Story of a Top-Level British Agent in Pre-War Germany* (London: Weidenfeld & Nicolson, 1978) p. 201; R.V. Jones, *Most Secret War* (London: Coronet, 1978) p. 182.

25. 'Air Scientific Intelligence in War', Section 4, in AIR 8/1532, PRO.
26. Hinsley et al., *British Intelligence*, vol. 1, p. 15.
27. Jones, *Most Secret War*, pp. 92–3.
28. i-03.
29. 'Air Scientific Intelligence', Section 118.
30. Hinsley et al., *British Intelligence*, vol. I, p. 284; Jones, *Most Secret War*, pp. 242–3.
31. i-03.
32. Concerning the latter, Jones recounts in particular how he was in fact 20 minutes late for his first meeting with Churchill because of his initial suspicion that his appointment was a practical joke. Jones, *Most Secret War*, pp. 144–5.
33. Ibid., p. 330.
34. Ibid., pp. 93–4.
35. Ibid., pp. 104–8; Hinsley et al., *British Intelligence*, pp. 99–100; 508–12.
36. Jones, *Most Secret War*, pp. 112–13.
37. Ibid., p. 240.
38. R.V. Jones, *Reflections on Intelligence* (London: Jonathan Cape, 1989), pp. 254–6.
39. 'Naval Intelligence Division: Staff and Distribution of Work' editions for February and December 1940, ADM 223/257, PRO.
40. 'Reorganisation Along Home and Foreign Lines', NID 0216/40, of 31 May 1940, ADM 1/10456, PRO.
41. 'Naval Intelligence Division: Staff and Distribution of Work', editions for May and October 1941, ADM 223/257, PRO.
42. 'Naval Intelligence Division: Staff and Distribution of Work', for April 1943, ADM 223/257, PRO.
43. *War Office List* for 1939, p. 97.
44. *War Office List* for 1941, p. 93.
45. 'Reorganisation of MO and MI', DMO & P 307a in WO 208/4696, PRO.
46. H.A.R. ('Kim') Philby's reports to NKGB reprinted from Soviet archives in Nigel West and Oleg Tsarev, *The Crown Jewels; The British Secrets Exposed by the KGB Archives* (London: Harper-Collins, 1999), p. 324.
47. Johns, *Within Two Cloaks*, pp. 117–18.
48. H.A.R. 'Kim' Philby's reports to NKGB, West and Tsarev, *The Crown Jewels*, p. 304.
49. Ibid., p. 302.
50. INTERALLIE is one of the most visible wartime human intelligence operations in the literature, and was highly productive prior to its November 1941 collapse after being betrayed by Mathilde-Lily Carre. See, for example, Czerniawski's own memoir of the events in his *The Big Network* (London: Ronald, 1961), and, as always, Ladslav Farago's, *Game of Foxes* (London: Hodder and Stoughton, 1971). Accounts of Interallie's failure can be found variously in Ian Colvin's translation, *Colonel Henri:*

The War Memoir of Hugo Bleicher, Former German Secret Agent (London: William Kimber, 1954), and Lauren Paine, *Mathilde Carre: Double Agent* (London: Robert Hale, 1976).

51. i-01 and i-15 estimated 10 and i-021 estimated 11 P Sections. Nigel West, *Secret War* (London: Hodder and Stoughton, 1993), p. 26, gives 14 P Sections, of which 12 were country sections, with P15 being IS9g and P19 photographic (presumably photographic services in support of HUMINT operations, since the SIS photo-reconnaissance section under Section II had been taken over by the RAF in 1940).

52. Nigel West, *Secret War*, p. 26; i-021; George Blake, *No Other Choice* (London: Jonathan Cape, 1990), p. 86.

53. West, *Secret War*, p. 26.

54. i-15. i-01 thought P3 might have been Germany, as it was in part after the 1945 reorganization. Since i-15 served for a time in the wartime SIS Swiss organization, his version is here adopted.

55. West, *Secret War*, p. 26; Blake, *No Other Choice*, p. 86. Although it has commonly been held that the SIS had no human sources inside Germany, recent evidence has shown that this was not, in fact, true. A summary of this evidence, and SIS operations into Germany out of Stockholm, can be found in Michael Smith, *New Cloak, Old Dagger: How Britain's Spies Came in from the Cold* (London: Gollancz, 1996), pp. 104–5.

56. George Blake, *No Other Choice*, pp. 86–97; West, *Secret War*, p. 26; i-01 thought P8 might have been 'Western hemisphere', but since Blake actually ran P8 near the end of the war, his version and that presented by West on the basis of his sources has been adopted.

57. West, *Secret War*, p. 26.

58. This is not entirely certain, although a War Office organization chart from 1943 clearly indicates ISLD responsibility for operations in Italy. i-12 also pointed out that the Yugoslav section fell under ISLD Italy for a time, so how these arrangements vis-à-vis the P Sections were handled remains somewhat unclear. See organization chart in HS 3/170, PRO.

59. Wesley Wark, 'Beyond Intelligence: The Study of British Strategy and the Norway Campaign, 1940', in Michael Graham Fry (ed.), *Power, Personalities and Policies: Essays in Honour of Donald Cameron Watt* (London: Frank Cass, 1982), p. 238.

60. Hinsley et al., *British Intelligence*, vol. I, pp. 91–2.

61. Ibid., p. 160.

62. Bickham Sweet-Escott, *Baker Street Irregular* (London: Methuen, 1965), p. 24. Note that in the original, Sweet-Escott could get clearance to publish his memoir only by substituting the confusing cryptonym 'Z' for 'C' throughout the volume. Sweet-Escott's observations are echoed by Philby, *My Silent War* (New York: Ballantine, 1983), p. 28.

63. Philby, *My Silent War*, pp. 27–8. Philby's description of Burgess as designating Philby D/UD rather than D/U1 because 'he wanted us to be

regarded as equals' was not wholly out of keeping with SIS organizational culture.

64. 'Section History, Section D' in HS 7/5, PRO.
65. Ibid.
66. 'History of the Research and Development Section of the Special Operations Executive', foliated as part of the larger 'History of the AD/Z Directorate' in HS 7/27, PRO.
67. 'Section History, Section D' in HS 7/5, PRO.
68. Appendix 1, memorandum on Norway, 1 September 1940 in HS 2/240, PRO. Bickham Sweet-Escott, *Baker Street Irregular*, p. 20, also notes that 'if there had been a charter [for Section D], it would have covered a wide range of activities, of which sabotage, political subversion and underground propaganda were the most important'.
69. Philby, *My Silent War*, p. 29. Some debate exists between Philby and Sweet-Escott about whose recollection placed the school originally at Aston House.
70. D/H correspondence appears in HS 3/136, PRO; note especially D/K to A/D, 19 December 1940.
71. 'Minute on D Activities' in HS 3/154, PRO.
72. For the work of D/X, see the SOE papers on the Oxelsund operation in HS 2/263, PRO
73. Memorandum on the origins of SOE's Scandinavian section D/S, 18 September 1945, in HS 2/12, PRO.
74. H. Montgomery Hyde, *Secret Intelligence Agent* (London: Constable, 1982), pp. 23–4.
75. 'Hungary', report of 22 August 1940, in HS 4/193, PRO.
76. D/XE to D/G 26 October 1939 HS / 263, PRO.
77. There existed at least five additional sections (D/Q, D/PA, D/FX, D/KX, D/O and D/C), whose functions are not apparent from papers available in the public archives. It is, however, clear from the context of much of the Section D correspondence held in SOE papers in the PRO that D/Q, D/C and probably D/O were geographical sections.
78. A discreetly written version of this operation has been recounted in David E. Walker, *Adventure in Diamonds* (London: Evans Brothers, 1955).
79. Sweet-Escott, *Baker Street Irregular*, p. 36; Foot, *SOE in France*, pp. 5, 150.
80. Charles Cruickshank, *SOE in Scandinavia* (Oxford: Oxford University Press, 1986), pp. 26–49. Documents covering the arrest of Rickman and his network can be found variously in HS 2/261, HS 2/264 and HS 2/268, PRO.
81. Sweet-Escott, *Baker Street Irregular*, p. 38.
82. Foot, *SOE: An Outline History*, p. 17. A detailed account of the AU's and Section D's stay-behinds has been published by David Lampe in his *The Last Ditch: The Secret of the Nationwide British Resistance Organization* (London: Cassell, 1968), pp. 64–5 and *passim*.
83. 'Section History, Section D' in HS 7/5, PRO.
84. Ibid.

85. Foot, *SOE: An Outline History*, pp. 19–20.
86. D/XE1 to D/G, 16 April 1940, HS 2/263, PRO.
87. Foot, *SOE: An Outline History*, p. 18.
88. Ibid., p. 19.
89. Ibid., pp. 19–21.
90. See, for example, Foot, *SOE in France*, p. 5; Foot, *SOE: An Outline History*, p. 22. David Stafford, *Britain and European Resistance 1940–1945: A Survey of The Special Operations Executive, With Documents* (Toronto: University of Toronto Press, 1983), remarks vaguely that Grand, 'whose activities as head of Section D had alienated influential figures in the Foreign Office, War Office and SIS, was quickly dismissed' (p. 36).
91. Annex II, minutes of a meeting between C and D, 15 September 1940, in HS 3/174, PRO; emphasis added.
92. Memorandum of 7 August 1940 concerning transfer of D/H and D/K organizations to SO2 in HS 3/198, PRO.
93. Hinsley et al., *British Intelligence*, p. 278.
94. Foot, *SOE: An Outline History*, p. 24.
95. Admiralty records concerning SIS requests for RAF support and the allocation of a flight of special duties aircraft of its own and RAF refusals to cooperate can be found in documents on aerial reconnaissance in the 1947 post-war review of intelligence collection methods in ADM 1/475, PRO, and also in Hinsley, *British Intelligence*, vol. I, p. 275. Accounts of RAF special duties aircraft in the European and Far East theatres can be found in Gibb McCall, *Flight Most Secret: Air Missions for the SOE and SIS* (London: William Kimber, 1981), and Terrence O'Brien, *The Moonlight War: The Story of Clandestine Special Operations in Southeast Asia 1944–1945* (London: Collins, 1987), respectively.
96. Hinsley et al., *British Intelligence*, vol. I, p. 276.
97. 'Norwegian Refugees Arriving in Norway' of 23 October 1940, in HS 2/240, PRO; see also minute sheet from D/J to DCSS of 23 October 1940, also in HS 2/240, PRO.
98. Minutes of a meeting between A1, G3, and D/Navy and D/N, from 24 October 1940, HS 2/240, PRO.
99. West and Tsarev, *The Crown Jewels*, pp. 320–1.
100. Admiralty memorandum cited in Foot, *SOE*, p. 87.
101. Identification of Slocum's unit as NID(c) appears in NID 'Staff and Division of Work' for April 1943, ADM 223/257, PRO (this file does not include any 'Staff and Distribution of Work' report for 1942) and D/Navy to CD of 17 December 1942 in HS 3/59, PRO.
102. Hinsley et al., *British Intelligence*, vol. I, p. 276; for special duties in the Far East, see O'Brien, *Moonlight War*.
103. ADM 223 257; Slocum appears in the April 1943 list for NID 17, but not the November 1944 entry for NID 12a, Naval Section, London, presumably because, as far as the Admiralty was concerned, he was now on

167

the operational rather than the intelligence side.

104. Hinsley et al., *British Intelligence*, vol. II, p. 15.

105. D/Navy to CD, 17 December 1942 in HS 3/59, PRO.

106. Memorandum on Norway, 1 September 1940 in HS 2/240; unfoliated documents referring to SIS parties trained at STS 101 in HS 4/4, PRO; David Stafford, *Camp X*, p. 201; see also Oluf Reed Olson's account of his training in the UK in his *Two Eggs on My Plate* (London: Arrow, 1952), pp. 100–1.

107. Charles Fraser-Smith, Gerald McKnight and Sandy Smith, *The Secret War of Charles Fraser-Smith* (London: Michael Joseph, 1981), p. 75 and *passim*.

108. Ibid., p. 24.

109. Ibid., p. 137.

110. FIN/FD/11339 and CDR/A/43/128, in HS 1/128, PRO.

111. 'Directive for Doctor Higgins: Joint Scientific Laboratory in Calcutta' of 9 August 1944, in HS 1/228, PRO.

112. M.R.D. Foot and J.M. Langley, *MI9: Escape and Evasion 1939–1945* (London: Futura, 1980), p. 42.

113. 'Attachment A: Historical Record of MI 9', p. 94 in WO 208 3242, PRO.

114. Ibid.

115. James Langley, *Fight Another Day*, chapter 8, 'The Resurrection of IVz', *passim*; the same designation is used in Foot and Langley, *MI9*, p. 67, but here Arabic numerals are used and IVz is rendered 4z.

116. Langley, *Fight Another Day*, p. 133.

117. Airey Neave, *Saturday at MI9* (London: Grafton, 1989), and Donald Darling, *Secret Sunday* (London: William Kimber, 1975).

118. 'Attachment A: Historical Record of MI9', pp. 93–4.

119. Organization chart for IS9g, 'Attachment A: Historical Record of MI9', p. 95.

120. 'Attachment A: Historical Record of MI9', p. 94.

121. i-12.

122. Hinsley et al., *British Intelligence*, vol. I, p. 207.

123. West, *MI6*, p. 156; i-12.

124. Hinsley et al., *British Intelligence*, vol. I, p. 207.

125. i-12.

126. i-12. Unlike other stations abroad for which the local security service was the first point of contact, links with the Egyptian government and police lay with the Security Service representative in the theatre, the Cairo Defence Security Office (DSO). See F.H. Hinsley and C.A.G. Simkins, *British Intelligence in the Second World War: Security and Counterintelligence*, vol. IV (London: HMSO, 1990), p. 150.

127. i-12.

128. Nigel Clive, *A Greek Experience 1943–1948* (Wilton: Michael Russell, 1985), p. 29. In a later meeting with Malcolm Woolcombe, head of Section I, Clive learned that *none* of his political reports had been forwarded to

London by ISLD Cairo (p. 146). However, it should be noted that British policy concerned with Greece and the Balkans was essentially a matter for the Commander-in-Chief Middle East and his Foreign Office Political Adviser in Cairo, so (without even invoking security compartmentalization), Section I did not really need to know.

129. i-11; i-12.
130. Hinsley and Simkins, *British Intelligence*, vol. IV, p. 151.
131. i-11; Hinsley and Simkins, *British Intelligence*, vol. IV, p. 152.
132. Hinsley and Simkins, *British Intelligence*, vol. IV, p. 152; i-12.
133. i-12.
134. Hinsley et al., *British Intelligence*, vol. I, pp. 13, 50.
135. i-12 suggested that SIS Algiers did not adopt the ISLD designation until after the Middle East and African forces combined, although SIS documents released with SOE papers concerning SIS at AFHQ Algiers in 1942 carry ISLD letterhead. HS 3/59, PRO.
136. i-12 identified the consolidation of ISLD Cairo and Algiers, but suggested the transfer of ISLD control to Algiers; however, an SOE organization chart outline of Allied secret organization work in Italy clearly placed ISLD Italy under the direct control of ISLD Cairo, not AFHQ. HS 3/170, PRO.
137. Organization chart in HS 3/170, PRO; i-12.
138. Hinsley and Simkins, *British Intelligence*, vol. IV, p. 269; i-12.
139. i-12, Organization chart in HS 3/170, PRO.
140. i-12.
141. Hinsley and Simkins, *British Intelligence*, vol. IV, pp. 269–70; i-12.
142. Telegram from Commander-in-Chief Far East to Air Ministry of 6 January 1941, CAB 81/900, PRO; emphasis added.
143. Ibid.
144. Richard Aldrich, 'Britain's Secret Intelligence Service in Asia During the Second World War', *Modern Asian Studies*, 32, 1 (1998), pp. 179–217.
145. Ibid.
146. Ibid.
147. Memorandum from Captain G.A. Garnons-Williams, RN, Head of P Division, to Director of Intelligence, Head of SOE in India, Advance HQ Force 136, ISLD and Chief of OSS of 2 October 1944. HS 1/303, PRO.
148. Fairly damning criticisms of the misinformation surrounding Stephenson and the BSC have been published by David Stafford, 'Intrepid: Myth and Reality', *Journal of Contemporary History*, 22, 2 (April 1987), and more recently and with access to an internal wartime BSC report as a primary source, by Timothy Naftali, 'Intrepid's Last Deception: Documenting the Career of Sir William Stephenson', *Intelligence and National Security*, 9, 3 (1993).
149. H. Montgomery Hyde, *The Quiet Canadian: The Secret Service Story of Sir William Stephenson* (London: Constable, 1989), p. 50.
150. Ibid.
151. Hinsley and Simkins, *British Intelligence*, vol. IV, p. 142.

152. Hyde, *The Quiet Canadian*, pp. 58–9.
153. Ibid., pp. 51–2.
154. Johns, *Within Two Cloaks*, p. 119; Johns's dealings with the BSC arose from his term in 1942 as Head of Station Buenos Aires.
155. Hinsley and Simkins, *British Intelligence*, vol. IV, p. 146.
156. Ibid., p. 144.
157. Hyde, *The Quiet Canadian*, p. 62
158. Stafford, 'Intrepid: Myth and Reality', p. 309; Hyde, *The Quiet Canadian*, p. 134; Hinsley and Simkins, *British Intelligence*, vol. IV, p. 144. Hyde dates the creation of the SO Division to 'early in 1941', although Stafford and Hinsley and Simkins date the Division to late 1940, on the basis of British official documents (Stafford sourced his own claim to information provided by the FCO SOE Adviser from archives still held by the FCO when his article was written).
159. Hyde, *The Quiet Canadian*, p. 191.
160. Hinsley et al., *British Intelligence*, vol. II, p. 55.
161. Hyde, *The Quiet Canadian*, pp. 181–210 and *passim*; note also Francis Macdonnell, 'The Search for the Second Zimmermann Telegram: FDR, BSC and the Latin American Front', *International Journal of Intelligence and Counterintelligence*, 4, 4 (1988) which argues that besides propaganda, the BSC engaged in a certain amount of deceptive action and circulated false information and forged Axis documents to Roosevelt and members of the US national security community of the day.
162. Hyde, *The Quiet Canadian*, pp. 170–1. Hyde remarks, somewhat plaintively, that 'the fact remains that relations between Bowes-Lyon and [the American Office of War Information] were never so close or so productive as were the previous arrangements with BSC' (p. 171).
163. Timothy Naftali, 'Intrepid's Last Deception', p. 74 and p. 89 (footnote 14). Naftali argues that Stephenson's status had been growing in the first half of 1942, but that 'he may well have believed that with the working environment becoming more hostile in the United States, he had to prove BSC's intrinsic value to be confident that support would continue' (p. 89).
164. Hinsley and Simkins, *British Intelligence*, vol. IV, p. 147.
165. F.W. Winterbotham, *The Ultra Secret* (New York: Dell, 1974), p. 31. Bletchley Park is also referred to as Station X by R.V. Jones, *Most Secret War*, p. 94.
166. Winterbotham, *Ultra Secret*, pp. 41–2.
167. Housed in buildings which still stand, roughly in the centre of the estate, and continue to be maintained (admittedly as empty shells) by the Bletchley Park Trust.
168. Benton, 'The ISOS Years: Madrid 1941–3', *Journal of Contemporary History*, 30, 3 (July 1995), p. 370.
169. Ellic Howe, *The Black Game* (London: Futura, 1982), pp. 78–9.
170. Howe, *The Black Game*, pp. 80–1.

171. Ibid., pp. 156–74; David Stafford, *Camp X: Canada's School for Secret Agents 1941–45* (Toronto: Lester & Orpen Dennys, 1986), pp. 156–8.
172. Howe, *The Black Game*, p. 77.
173. Hinsley et al., *British Intelligence*, vol. I, pp. 276–7.
174. Stafford, *Camp X*, pp. 156–68.
175. Ibid., p. 201.
176. Y 1301/069/G of 16 March 1944 in FO 850/137, PRO.
177. Y 6772/G, Foreign Office to Tehran of 18 November 1944 and Y7294/G Tehran to London of 10 December 1944 in FO 850/244, PRO.
178. Hinsley and Simkins, *British Intelligence*, vol. IV, p. 132.
179. Ibid., p. 180.
180. Ibid., p. 180 *infra*.
181. John Curry, *The Security Service 1908–1945* (London: Public Record Office, 1999), pp. 210–11.
182. KGB questionnaire to Philby, 30 October 1941, reproduced in West and Tzarev, *The Crown Jewels*, p. 310.
183. Hinsley and Simkins, *British Intelligence*. vol. IV, p. 180.
184. Ibid.
185. Information from Nigel West. It is worth noting that the documents in West's possession differ somewhat from the undated Philby information he subsequently received from ex-KGB archives in his work with Oleg Tsarev on *The Crown Jewels*, pp. 310–11. Part of the problem here is that the Philby KGB information clearly dates from at least two intervals a minimum of two years apart (in one part he outlines pre-1941 A and G Sections, and in another part post-1941 P Sections as well as post-1943 Service Deputy Directors). Although the latter Philby information is undated, internal evidence within it suggests a date in either very late 1944 or early 1945, as Cowgill and Philby have both departed the section.
186. Robert Cecil, 'The Cambridge Comintern', in Christopher Andrew and David Dilks, *The Missing Dimension: Governments and Intelligence Communities in the Twentieth Century* (Chicago: University of Chicago Press, 1984), p. 179; for specific examples, see Johns, *Within Two Cloaks*, p. 69; Benton, 'The ISOS Years', pp. 371–3.
187. Hinsley and Simkins, *British Intelligence*, vol. IV, p. 263.
188. Ibid., pp. 131–2.
189. Ibid., pp. 132–7.
190. See, for example, West, *MI6*, pp. 148, 284 (although West also – correctly – identifies the RSS as having originally been under the War Office as MI8c), and in greater detail in his earlier, *MI5: British Security Service Operations 1909–1945* (London: Triad/Granada, 1983), pp. 201–4. This version of events is also suggested in the first volume of the official history, Hinsley et al., *British Intelligence*, vol. I, p. 277, although the official history corrects its position in the fourth volume on counter-espionage and security (see below).

171

191. Hinsley and Simkins, *British Intelligence*, vol. IV, pp. 72–3.
192. Ibid., p. 43.
193. 'Leakage of Information about Military and Other Movements in this Country' in WO 208/5096, PRO; original emphasis.
194. Ibid.
195. Hinsley and Simkins, *British Intelligence*, vol. IV, p. 43; it should be noted that in internal RSS documents released in the PRO after the publication of the official history in WO 208/5105, as MI8c the RSS was referred to as the Radio Security *Section*, not *Service*.
196. Hinsley and Simkins, *British Intelligence*, vol. IV, p. 72.
197. Ibid., pp. 88–9.
198. Ibid., p. 67.
199. Ibid., p. 73.
200. Sir David Petrie to Lord Swinton, 30 January 1941, in WO 208/5096, PRO.
201. Foliated in MI8 1422 in WO 208/5105, PRO.
202. Cover note to Worlledge's minute, in MI8/1422, WO 208/5105, PRO.
203. Davidson to Swinton, in MI8/1422, WO 208/5105, PRO.
204. Swinton to Davidson, 20 February 1941, in MI8/1422, WO 208/5105, PRO.
205. Note by Alexander Cadogan, 10 March 1941, in WO 208/5095, PRO; transfer to 'Section VIII of SIS' is explicitly noted in attached papers.
206. 'RSS – Transfer to MI6', D.A. Butler, 15 May 1941, also note to Butler, probably from Gambier-Parry (name withheld under Section 3(4) of Public Records Act), dated 12 May 1941. Both in WO 208/5105, PRO.
207. Hinsley and Simkins, *British Intelligence*, vol. IV, pp. 183, 281; Hugh Trevor-Roper (Lord Dacre), *The Philby Affair*, p. 38, has described the affair somewhat more tendentiously as his having been 'secretly denounced as probably being in touch with the Germans and more openly – and more justly – accused of consorting with the immediate enemy, MI5'.
208. Trevor-Roper, *The Philby Affair*, p. 38, *infra*.
209. Curry, *The Security Service 1908–1945*, p. 211–12.
210. Robert Cecil, 'MI6', p. 744. However, the RIS was subordinated directly to C, according to Curry, *The Security Service, 1908–1945*, p. 212. It would be entirely consistent with the loose organization of the SIS for the RIS to have been subordinated to Section VIII for most day-to-day purposes but for Trevor-Roper still to have had direct access to Menzies.
211. Hinsley and Simkins, *British Intelligence*, vol. IV, p. 183; Curry, *The Security Service 1908–1945*, p. 212. Note that Curry employs the term 'Radio *Intelligence* Section', and Hinsley and Simkins refer to it as the 'Radio *Analysis* Section'. As Curry's document is the only original documentary source available, the latter usage has been adopted, but it should be kept in mind that as Curry's report is a history it is technically a *secondary* source, and not a *primary* one.
212. Hinsley et al., *British Intelligence*, vol. I, p. 278.

213. Ibid., pp. 14–17.
214. Ibid., p. 278.
215. Ibid., vol. III, Part 1, p. 463.
216. Ibid., vol. IV, pp. 174–5.
217. ISLD Memorandum No. 1272, 20 July 1943 in HS 3/59, PRO.
218. Nigel Clive, *A Greek Experience*, p. 30.
219. Unfoliated memorandum in HS 3/59, PRO.
220. 'Notes on a Meeting Held in B.M. Clarke's Office at 11 am on 3rd June 1942', in HS 3/59, PRO.
221. Charles Cruickshank, *SOE in the Far East*, p. 21.
222. HPD to Director of Intelligence, 2 October 1944, in HS 1/303, PRO.
223. 'Summary of ISLD Reports' or 8 September 1945 in HS 1/210, PRO.
224. D/CD to CD of 15 November 1941, cover note by C dated 29 November 1941, HS 3/73; W/AW/7099 of 30 February 1943 in HS 3/75, PRO.
225. 'Directive for SOE East African Mission', June, 1942, in HS 3/14, PRO.
226. Hinsley et al., *British Intelligence*, vol. I, p. 278.
227. See, for example, Nigel Clive, *A Greek Experience*, *passim*; this was also stressed by i-01 and i-15.
228. The impact of this intelligence has been examined by Christine Goulter, 'The Role of Intelligence in Coastal Command's Anti-Shipping Campaign, 1940–45', *Intelligence and National Security*, 5, 1 (January 1990), pp. 84–105.
229. Hinsley et al., *British Intelligence*, vol. I, p. 275.
230. Ibid., vol. II, p. 18; Cecil '"C's" War', p. 180; Philby, *My Silent War*, pp. 117–18.
231. Philby, *My Silent War*, p. 118.
232. Cecil, '"C's" War', p. 177.
233. Hinsley et al., *British Intelligence*, vol. II, p. 18.
234. Philby, *My Silent War*, p. 119.
235. Beddington has been identified in this capacity by Richard Aldrich, 'Britain's Secret Intelligence Service in Asia During the Second World War' (p. 24).
236. Philby, *My Silent War*, p. 119.
237. Philby, *My Silent War*, p. 123; Langley, *To Fight Another Day*, p. 131; P3 appears to have been almost a notional P Section, Dansey took such a close interest in operations there, according to i-01 and i-15.
238. Hinsley et al., *British Intelligence*, vol. II p. 18. The resulting scheme bears an uncanny resemblance to the contemporaneous SOE panel of Service deputy directors.
239. Philby refers only obliquely to Cordeaux's and Payne's regional interests, while i-01 proved entirely unaware of the board's existence.
240. Philby, *My Silent War*, p. 118. R.V. Jones has recalled how Payne was convinced by the staff at Broadway that the pigeons which infested the building's window sills 'were our main means of communications with the

French Resistance. For days, at our instigation, he solicitously provided them with saucers of water!' Jones, *Most Secret War*, pp. 404–5.

241. i-19.

242. Cecil, 'The Cambridge Comintern', p. 179.

243. See, for example, Hinsley et al., *British Intelligence*, vol. I, p. 91.

244. i-01.

245. Philby questionnaire reproduced in West and Tsarev, *The Crown Jewels*, p. 321.

246. Hinsley et al., *British Intelligence*, vol. III, Part 1, p. 462; Cecil, 'MI6', p. 745.

247. Hinsley et al., *British Intelligence*, vol. II, p. 18; vol. III, p. 462; West, *MI6*, pp. 388–9; West, *Secret War*, p. 31.

248. i-01. i-15 suggested that DD/Admin oversaw the Central Registry, although the timing on this is uncertain, and i-028 positively confirmed this for the post-war administration directorate.

249. Hinsley et al., *British Intelligence*, vol. II, p. 18.

250. James Marshall-Cornwall, *Wars and Rumours of War* (London: Leo Cooper, 1984), p. 203.

251. Ibid., p. 202.

252. Ibid., p. 205.

253. Philby, *My Silent War*, p. 119; Anthony Cave Brown, C, p. 963; KGB questionnaire to Philby reproduced in West and Tsarev, *The Crown Jewels*, pp. 323–4; i-15; i-017. Rupert Allason (Nigel West) also permitted the author to inspect copies of Section V documents in his possession which clearly indicated the existence of a security section directly answerable to DD/SP.

254. i-15, who also recalls having to submit a project at one point for I /S approval and being 'terrified' of Vivian.

255. Cecil, 'The Cambridge Comintern', p. 178.

256. Philby, *My Silent War*, p. 110.

257. Ibid., p. 101.

258. Hinsley and Simkins, *British Intelligence*, vol. IV, p. 188.

259. Peter Kemp, *Thorns of Memory* (London: Sinclair-Stevenson, 1990), pp. 259–64; Foot, *SOE: An Outline History*, pp. 198–9.

260. Hinsley and Simkins, *British Intelligence*, vol. IV, p. 180 (footnote).

261. Cecil, 'The Cambridge Comintern', p. 180.

262. Philby, *My Silent War*, p. 109.

263. Robert Carew-Hunt, *The Theory and Practice of Communism* (London: Bles, 1951).

264. Philby, *My Silent War*, p. 114.

265. I-15; I-17.

266. Nicholas Elliott, *With My Little Eye* (Wilton: Michael Russell, 1993), pp. 17–18.

5

A New Kind of War, 1946–56

By the time our final bulky report was ready for presentation to the chief, we felt we had produced the design of something like a service, with enough serious inducements to tempt able young men to regard it as a career for life.

H.A.R. (Kim) Philby
My Silent War[1]

DESIGNING A 'MODERN' SECRET SERVICE

The main thrust of organizational change during the first years of the Cold War derived from the first attempt at organizational design in the history of the SIS. Having muddled through the Second World War as what Vivian described as a 'collection of independent units' loosely associated through a network of horizontal lines of communication and coordination, there was a real determination, by 1945, that some sort of order should be imposed on the whole affair. However, one of the most interesting features in the development of most organizations is what a limited role conscious design actually plays in their formal structure. The difference between MO3's design in 1905 for a secret service in Europe and the actual form Cumming's organization was forced to take are a good indication of that. A great deal of what goes on in organizations is the ad hoc creation of offices, departments and procedure to accommodate emergent, unanticipated circumstances, or certain realities of the organization's work that organizational designers may have failed (or been unwilling) to take into account. As a result, the development of SIS in the first decade after the Second World War can be divided into two distinct intervals. The first interval, from 1945 to 1948 was that of a positive effort to 'design' a modern MI6 along the prevailing managerial principles of the day. This 'design' took roughly a year to develop and most of the next two years to implement. The second interval from 1948 until 1956 involved refining the 1946 scheme and resolving difficulties that emerged from the kind of imperfections inevitable in any organizational plan, and adapting to new functions and circumstances.

Unsurprisingly, however, the initiative for the first round of comprehensive reorganization and reform originated not so much with the SIS as with its consumers in Whitehall, and the Joint Intelligence Committee (JIC) in particular. The progressive winding down of the war meant that a series of reviews of intelligence comparable to the Secret Service Committees of 1919, 1920 and 1921 was an inevitability. Unlike the First World War, the UK government's intelligence machinery now had an increasingly central tasking and administrative body in the form of the JIC, and so the necessary infrastructure for a comprehensive and ongoing review was already in place. The JIC's powers remained limited, however, by the fact that it was a sub-committee of the Committee of Imperial Defence and not directly backed by the authority of Cabinet or the Cabinet Office. This meant that any decisions reached depended upon a consensus of the JIC's membership for execution.

Despite the constraints upon its *de jure* powers, the JIC had become de facto the Cabinet's main body for assessing intelligence, and directing and managing the intelligence producers by late 1941.[2] In mid-1943, that brief had been extended from Service Branch to national intelligence requirements through a Special Sub-Committee on Intelligence Priorities, which Hinsley *et al.* note 'was part of a process whereby the JIC gave increasing attention to the supply of information needed for the study of post-war problems in Europe'. They further argue that the JIC 'accepted these responsibilities reluctantly because the authorities who needed the information were largely civilian, but did so in order to avoid the establishment of individual and overlapping intelligence sections in civilian ministries'.[3] During 1945, the JIC undertook reviews of both SIS and SOE post-war requirements, dealing with matters of organization and management, as well as their expected post-war roles. The War Office would also mount a series of its own reviews during the same year. By mid-1945, SOE was lobbying hard for a global and permanent post-war brief. SIS was, therefore, under considerable pressure to take a long, hard look at itself and come up with reforms which would ensure its effectiveness, and possibly even its survival, after the end of the war. There was, however, a tide of reform and reorganization that would sweep over the entire British intelligence community in 1945, and a demand-driven SIS could not possibly remain untouched.

Both internal and external considerations came into play in the formulation of the 1946 scheme for SIS reorganization. Internally, SIS had become virtually unmanageable during the Second World War, its span of control under C expanding far beyond the management capacity of one man. It had been beset by internal rivalries and schisms, and vital administrative, personnel and support functions were very weakly coordinated. The Committee of SIS Reorganization of 1945 would have to address all of these concerns. However, it was also confronted with a number of changes in its operational and governmental environment. Both the SIS's Production and counter-espionage capabilities had become custom-fitted to the Axis threat, and had to be tailored to deal with Soviet communism instead. Technical methods and support had been steadily increasing in importance since the 1930s, and the SIS would have to cope with this as well. SIS's governmental environment had also changed since the inter-war period when its 'pull' architecture had evolved. The essential interests and demands which grounded the original 1921 arrangement remained in place, but the peacetime British colonial administrations were also to need secret intelligence suited to their own specific needs as much as had the wartime GHQs. In London, SOE would be wound down and its role and assets reabsorbed by the SIS. More fundamentally, changes were happening in the way intelligence tasking and assessment were structured in Whitehall, an ongoing trend away from purely separate, departmental analysis and towards central, joint assessment, a trend traceable to the 1936 creation of the JIC, and extended by the post-war creation of the Joint Intelligence Bureau (JIB, about which more is below). The first decade of the Cold War would herald the beginning of a transformation in the way requirements were organized, and in the day-to-day workings of the Requirements and Production relationship.

Ultimately, the attempted redesign of the SIS in 1945/46 can be viewed in two ways. On the one hand, it represented the first attempt to put the SIS on a 'professional' footing, with some kind of conscious attention being paid to matters of organization and methods. The approach taken was based on the prevailing managerial wisdom of the day, which sought to emulate a military hierarchy, and took the form of an attempt to impose a simple bureaucracy on the SIS. Sections were bundled together into directorates, and officers placed in strict hierarchies of seniority. On the other hand, the intrinsic pressures towards horizontal control and coordination that we have seen throughout the agency's history resulted in a series of work-arounds and improvisations that bypassed the vertical hierarchy in favour of lateral communications. As a result, while the 1946 scheme did indeed resolve many of the SIS's recurrent problems – in particular, those of span-of-control – it failed to address the fundamental features of how the SIS worked in practice.

In early 1945, a JIC sub-committee on the future of the SIS was convened under the JIC Chair, Victor Cavendish-Bentinck, consisting of the Foreign Office officials Neville Bland and Ivone Kirkpatrick (later central in the development of the Russia Committee and the IRD), with Colonel Denis Capel-Dunn as Secretary. The results of their considerations were submitted to the Chiefs of Staff (CoS) on 5 June 1945, although the conclusions of the committee regarding SIS have yet to be disclosed, apart from the suggestion that Menzies 'hoard all the money he could before the war ended because...the Treasury wouldn't give a penny if it didn't have to'.[4] The SIS responded to the pressure to reform and confront the new era by convening its own internal Committee on SIS Reorganization in September 1945.[5] Much has been written about the decisions of this committee which has been variously intensely critical, and, as often as not, intentionally or unintentionally misleading. Hugh Trevor-Roper wrote of the SIS in 1945 that 'We won the war: and SIS, at the end of it, remained totally unreformed',[6] while Anthony Verrier has described the process as nothing more than a few 'trifling administrative changes'.[7] Philby, who was a participant, goes to some length in his memoir to portray the entire process as a personal bureaucratic victory in his 'secret war' against the SIS in particular and capitalism in general. While the deliberations of the committee remain unknown, the changes made to the SIS in the wake of their deliberations amounted to far more than 'a few trifling administrative changes', and should be evaluated against not merely the proverbial 20-20 hindsight, but also what had gone before and the pressures and constraints acting upon the service during

1945–46, and, indeed, throughout the opening years of the Cold War.

The SIS Committee consisted of PSO/CSS (H. Christopher Arnold-Forster, formerly IIIa); the SIS liaison to GC & CS, Captain Edward Hastings, RN (formerly III); the Head of Section I (David Footman); the Head of Section IX (Philby), the Controller, Northern Area (Colonel John Cordeaux RM, formerly DD/Navy) and a committee secretary (Alurid Denn).[8] Teasing out the considerations of the committee as reported by Philby takes some careful appraisal. According to Philby,

> our first task was to clear up untidy survivals from the bad old days. During the war, finance and administration had gone separate ways, with inadequate coordination. The G Sections [sic] were generally messy, those concerned with Western Europe working for Dansey, the rest directly for the chief. Looking at it from the other direction, Dansey was nominally vice-chief of the service as a whole; but in fact he was only interested in the production of intelligence in Western Europe.[9]

As a summary of the state of SIS organization in 1945, this description is acutely misleading. By the time the committee was convened, the former G Sections (now P Sections) were grouped under six Area Controllers with a seventh handling communications, and Menzies had a board of five Deputy Directors dividing the various counter-intelligence, administrative and consumer liaison functions between them, as well as a three-man Secretariat to assist him in overseeing this system. Admittedly, there was a certain idiosyncrasy in how the various Circulating Sections had been divided up among the Deputy Directors, and a couple of the controllerates were survivals of earlier arrangements. Moreover, at the time, Menzies still had formal control of GCHQ (which he would not retain long after the war's end). The disastrous wartime spread of control had been eased, although there was still a lack of general ordering logic to the resulting system. But it was nothing like as chaotic in 1945 as Philby suggests.

The most fundamental matter in SIS organization discussed by Philby was the debate over vertical versus horizontal organization for the service, and this would reappear as an issue in SIS organization and management 30 years later in the 1970s.[10] The fundamental issue in question was, as he put it, 'should the primary division of the service be along vertical lines, with regional organizations responsible for the production, assessment and circulation of information relating to their respective regions? Or should it be along horizontal lines, between the production of information on the one hand, and the processing, assessment and circulation on the other?'[11] Philby confessed in 1968 that 'I still do not know the right answer to this question', and one officer interviewed noted regarding the 1974 reorganization that very often one had only a single expert with specialist technical knowledge on certain matters, making geographical subdivision of that know-how impossible.[12] The vertical/horizontal argument is probably less about right and wrong answers than it is about alternative trade-offs. In any event, Philby notes that 'the body of service opinion in favour of the vertical division was weakly represented in committee, and horizontal solution was finally adopted'.[13] But, here again, Philby is misleading, albeit with greater subtlety.

Philby presents the decision in favour of 'horizontalism' as a personal, manipulative bureaucratic victory, since under a horizontal arrangement he could anticipate greater access and influence. However, what he avoids acknowledging is that SIS *was already based on a horizontal division of labour*.[14] Apart from basic bureaucratic inertia, the evolution of the horizontal system based on the consumer-liaison C Sections had resulted from the political *force majeure* of various departments of state seeking a degree of control over the intelligence collection process. That pressure had not reduced during the war, and had been the driving force behind the appointment of the 'Service Commissars' in 1942. In 1945, the C Sections were still based on the major consumers seconding complete sections of their own intelligence branches to the SIS, and adopting the vertical solution would have come up against the very Whitehall dynamics which had resulted in their original creation. The SIS ultimately had very little choice about its organizational structure.

The end of the war brought about a number of changes in the senior leadership as well. Although Vivian lingered into the early 1950s, no longer a full Deputy Director but running a rather diminished Inspectorate of Security (I/S)[15] responsible only for SIS protective security. In practice, Vivian, who was quite elderly at this point, made far less of the position than he might have, with Philby referring to the I/S position as a 'sinecure', and one officer interviewed calling it 'a retirement consultancy'.[16] Vice-Chief Claude Dansey retired immediately after the war and his deputy, General James Marshall-

Cornwall, asked Menzies for relief on 16 October 1945.[17] Menzies was, therefore, forced to assign both a new VC/SS and a new AC/SS.

For reasons which are not entirely clear, Menzies brought in outsiders for both positions, selecting General John Sinclair, former DMI as Vice-Chief, and Air Commodore James 'Jack' Easton from Air Intelligence as Assistant Chief. This may have been in response to continued pressure from the service branches for effective post-war control. The 1921 arrangement had originally required that the Service branches should take turns providing the new C, but the first two had been Admiralty, and although Menzies was ex-army, he had been attached to the SIS since 1919. Service Branch doubts about the SIS appear to have lingered, as a 1947 report on intelligence collection methods past and future compiled by DNI John Godfrey was sternly critical of the SIS.[18] By appointing Sinclair and Easton as VC/SS and AC/SS, Menzies was continuing in the pattern of the 1921 arrangement and placing both the War Office and Air Ministry in the line of succession for the post of C. Assessments of Sinclair have not always been favourable, even by his own staff. One former officer interviewed who served as Head of Station in a European state during Sinclair's term as C recalled how he had been grilled by Sinclair on the way to the office from the airport. Sinclair enquired of the officer whether the country's premier was a 'good man or bad man?' The officer recalled trying to explain that it was more complicated than that, but Sinclair waved the man's concerns aside and repeated his demand for the assessment, 'good man or bad man'.[19]

Because the Committee of SIS Reorganization began its deliberations in late 1945, it took until well into 1946 and 1947 for the changes to take effect. The centre of those reforms was restructuring the SIS into five directorates beneath C and his Deputies: Director Finance and Administration (D/FA); Director of Production (D/P); Director of Requirements (D/R); Director of War Planning (D/WP) and Head of Training and Development (H/TD).[20] The SIS Production Side, including the P Sections, Area Controllers and 'longstop' headquarters in the Middle and Far East all came under D/P. The Circulating Sections were redesignated Requirements Sections and placed under D/R, and the administrative and financial functions were consolidated under D/FA along with a new personnel section. While these features essentially streamlined the command and control of the traditional SIS infrastructure, the two remaining Directorates, D/WP and H/TD, were the legacy of the SIS's sister organization and sometime rival, the Special Operations Executive. This reform of the SIS's senior management was also coupled with an extensive range of changes, modifications and reforms to the various sections, departments and resources beneath the new Board of Directors.

Despite the discussions and impetus to reform and modernize a variously war-battered and administratively moribund SIS, the most distinctive feature of the 1946 reforms is that the essentials of the 1921 arrangement emerged virtually unchanged. There were some alterations in the nature and character of the consumers, and these affected the structure and function of the consumer liaison sections, but SIS's objectives were still to be set explicitly by its customers in Whitehall and Downing Street via consumer liaison sections. The Requirements Directorate consolidated the old Circulating Sections together under a single senior officer responsible for overseeing the evaluation and circulating of production side's intelligence product, and the agency's overall relations with its consumers. The Circulating Sections were relabelled Requirements (R) Sections, and for the most part their numerical designations remained more or less unchanged. R1 continued to be Political Intelligence, working on behalf of the Foreign Office; R2 the Air Section; R3, Navy; and R4, the Military.[21] However, with the end of the war with Germany, Section V was abolished and Philby's anti-communist Section IX became the agency's counter-espionage unit and took on the designation R5. Section VI would outlive its original consumer, the Ministry of Economic Warfare, and continue to produce industrial and commercial intelligence for a wide range of departments as R6. R.V. Jones's IId was hived off from the Air Section to handle scientific intelligence as R7. Section VIII, now R8, was stripped of its Radio Section at Hanslope Park, the Radio Security Service and Radio Intelligence Section, and even the venerable old Cipher Section, and was reduced to a single officer handling liaison with GCHQ. Even though R2, R3, R4 and R8 were greatly reduced in peacetime, R1, R5, R6 and R7 were sizeable entities, divided mainly along geographical lines conforming to the four Chief Controllerates. R1, for example, was subdivided regionally into R1a, R1b, R1c and R1d, with similar arrangements prevailing in the other R Sections.[22]

SIS counter-espionage after the war has proven an area of some concern because of the successes of Soviet penetration in the form of Kim Philby and George Blake, exacerbated by the fact that R5 was originally headed by Philby. Anthony Verrier has argued that counter-intelligence was relegated to a very minor role after the war, in which 'counter-intelligence sections were, in practice, subordinate to regional directors, whose requirement to produce [operational intelligence] material dominated all other considerations', arguing that there prevailed a view that 'penetration of an enemy... intelligence organization was a secondary requirement, a factor which enabled Philby to be a traitor secure from detection for many years'.[23] Philby provides a foundation for this interpretation by rather disingenuously suggesting during his discussion of the Committee of SIS Reorganization that the SIS cut back on its counter-intelligence capability, and capped his nefarious bureaucratic manoeuvring when he remarked that one of the Committee's 'minor decisions' was 'the abolition of Section V'.[24] Earlier in his narrative, however, he claims that Section V and Section IX were in fact 'united' under his control apparently after a sustained back-stabbing campaign against Section V's head, Felix Cowgill.[25]

Philby's version of how he acquired responsibility for Section IX, and in due course R5, has been contested by a number of authors,[26] but all of these approaches focus on personalities and to a very real degree under-represent the structural conditions which prevailed during the transition from Section V and Section IX to R5. The abolition of Section V was less a final blow in a round of bureaucratic infighting than something of a structural inevitability. Section V's infrastructure had been tailored to the Axis target, and had been undergoing progressive attrition since 1943 as enemy-occupied territories were liberated. The anti-Soviet section had already been hived off as Section IX in 1944, as had the Security Section under Vivian's direct control in his capacity as DD/SP. The Section V geographical sub-sections oversaw residencies abroad and their agent runners whose stables of human sources were members of the Double-Cross programme and were specifically penetrations of the Axis intelligence system. Most of their assets were of little potential use against the USSR, were unlikely to spy against their own liberation governments and would, therefore, have to be paid off and deactivated with the end of the war.[27] The W Board liaison section handling deception was needed only as long as there was a W Board with which to liaise. Similarly, the ISOS-handling section had a *raison d'être* only as long as there was a flow of ISOS from Bletchley and of RSS intercepts from Hanslope Park, a flow which had slowed to a trickle and then stopped as the Allies advanced across Europe. As a result, by 1945, Section V was reduced to a bare shadow of its former self. This was the organizational context in which the remaining elements of Section V that might have a post-war utility and Philby's Section IX – just as tailored as Section V, but to the Soviet target instead – were amalgamated under Philby in April 1945.[28] To a very real degree, therefore, the demise of Section V and the rise of Section IX/R5 were less a function of machination and intrigue than of environmental pressures.

In much the same fashion, although Philby claims credit for the eventual design and structure of R5, that section's form displayed a very high degree of consistency with precedent even as far back as the 1920s. Even when it was subordinate to Section V, the anti-Soviet section had held the dual function of monitoring both Soviet espionage and the propagation of communism. As we have already seen, Desmond Morton's anti-Soviet section in the 1920s (which prompted the Zinoviev letter scandal) had exactly the same dual mandate, as did the original Section V in 1931. Nominally, communist subversion should have abated with Stalin's abolition of the Comintern at the demand of his wartime allies; however, after the war the pace of subversion rapidly picked up again to pre-war levels through the new organization Cominform. As a result, the new CE Section, R5, was divided into two main sub-sections: R5 Int, dealing with counter-intelligence and counter-espionage against Soviet bloc intelligence services, and R5 Com, which studied Soviet ideological subversion efforts, and the clandestine efforts of foreign communist parties and Cominform R5 Int was headed by Maurice Oldfield, a future C, and R5 Com by Charles Ransom, a future Director of Requirements.[29] Each of these was in turn subdivided into four regional sections conforming to the four controllerates on the Production side, with R5 Com divided into R5a, R5b, R5c and R5d, and R5 Int into R5e, R5f, R5g and R5h, with each sub-section itself subdivided to approximate the distribution and designation of the P Sections.[30] One of Philby's more ambitious proposals was a global network of Section IX residents, which never materialized.[31] It should be kept in mind that the Section V residencies were a wartime phenomenon, and, before 1941, Section V had operated via the SIS's Group Sections and their foreign stations. Thus, the absence of a separate Section IX residencies was essentially a return to established peacetime practice. Nonetheless, opportunities comparable to those

leading to Section V's wartime field organization never developed in
the case of the Soviet target. R5's operational capability remained
fairly limited, as successes against Soviet espionage during the first
decade took the form chiefly of defections such as those of Tokaev in
1947 and Kokhlov in 1955, but initially no counter-espionage
penetrations were achieved. Potentially, the most significant defection
for the SIS had been that of Konstantin Volkov in Istanbul in 1945,
foiled, of course, by Philby. Nor were there any code breaks to
provide a substitute for ISOS in support of its operations against
Soviet intelligence, for even VENONA was a retrospective exercise
decrypting NKVD/NKGB traffic from the 1930s and 1940s.[32] R5
was, therefore, something of a return to Section V's original pre-war
role as a conventional Circulating Section, confined to issuing
requirements for counter-espionage work and collating product
generated for it by the Production side.[33]

Section VI survived the Ministry of Economic Warfare which,
according to the official history of the economic blockade, had come
'quietly and quickly to an end' by 1 June 1945, when its remaining
staff were absorbed by the Foreign Office as the Economic Warfare
Department. This department oversaw the dismantling of the
remaining trade controls, the last of which (Navicert and certificate-
of-origins) were shut down on 30 September 1946.[34] Section VI,
renamed R6, now processed industrial and commercial intelligence
on behalf of the Board of Trade, the Treasury, the Joint Intelligence
Bureau's Economic Intelligence section, the Foreign Office sections
concerned with international trade, and even the Bank of England.[35]
In this sense, R6 was in the forefront of the nascent changes in the
consumer-side mechanisms of tasking and dissemination, and the
correlated changes in Requirements to adapt to those changes. As
Section VI, industrial/commercial intelligence was the first consumer
liaison section to have been staffed by SIS specialists rather than
officers seconded from the consuming department. After 1946, the
section moved even further away from partisan representation to
handling matters of common interest to multiple departments, less a
matter of 'joint control' between the SIS and a single consumer than
a point of contact and communication between the SIS and a range
of consumers.

In July 1945, the JIC issued a report entitled 'Organization of
Scientific and Technical Intelligence', which was quite critical of the
wartime arrangements for scientific and technical intelligence on the

grounds that they were not 'uniform' between the various departments who had set them up independently of one another.[36] Indeed, at least within the SIS Air Section, Section II, had had almost complete control of scientific intelligence, although IId, R.V. Jones, found during the war that the other Circulating Sections had to make use of his department's services. The JIC paper concluded regarding the SIS that 'C's Scientific Intelligence Section should include a Scientific Advisor *independent of all three services* and, as assistants to the latter, such other scientists as "C" may find necessary'.[37] Thus, IId was hived off from Section II (by then R2) to become R7.[38] Under these arrangements, like R6, R7 officers were not to be drawn from external consumer departments, but were to be career SIS scientists. The same report noted that while for the Service Branches the Scientific Intelligence personnel would ideally be 'drawn from, and after a period of years, return to their [respective service's] Scientific Research Organization', 'C's staff will probably need to have a life-long career'. Initially, separate arrangements were made for atomic intelligence being gathered for the Tube Alloys Committee, and atomic intelligence was in turn hived off from Jones's IId and set up as R9.[39] R9, however, proved short-lived and was soon absorbed back into R7.[40]

R7 was to be a far less ambitious entity than IId had been. Despite Jones's continued campaign for a central 'scientific intelligence service', potentially located within the SIS, the post-war arrangements moved back in the direction of the traditional 1921 arrangement. R7 was stripped of IId's all-source analysis role, and became simply a relatively passive R Section in the same mould as the Service liaison sections. In the first instance, it serviced the Joint Scientific Intelligence Committee (JSIC) and Joint Technical Intelligence Committee (JTIC), or rather, their combined entity, the Joint Scientific and Technical Intelligence Committee (JS/TIC). By the 1950s, the JIB had set up its own Directorate of Scientific Intelligence, which received and employed R7's information in conjunction with that provided by service intelligence branches and open sources from the JIB's Procurement Section.[41] Much as the Service Intelligence Branch liaisons possessed double identities with their own particular designations within their home departments distinct from their SIS designations (for example, R4 was MI6 in the War Office), R7 had its own double identity within Whitehall as the JIB Technical Coordinating Section (TCS).[42] R7, therefore, embodied two emerging trends in post-war tasking and assessment. While it was reduced to being a consumer liaison section, it had not merely a single consumer, but represented several, all of which were not single Departments of State, but joint assessment bodies themselves servicing a plurality of departments. As a result, R7 embodied many of the same trends as R6.

While IId acquired a new degree of independence as R7, Section VIII was cut down to a minimal role. During the war, the Communications Section had handled SIS cipher production; the Radio Section and its global wireless network based at Hanslope Park; the Radio Security Service (RSS), also based at Hanslope Park; and Hugh Trevor-Roper's Radio Intelligence Section. Under the post-war reorganization of intelligence, all SIGINT functions apart from interception were consolidated under GCHQ, including the RSS and Radio Intelligence Section, while COMSEC was now taken over by the Foreign Office through its London Communications Security Agency.[43] As noted previously Section VIII's radio and wireless work had expanded far beyond its intelligence remit carrying not only SIS and GC & CS traffic but also SOE and PWE transatlantic communications and providing clandestine transmitters for the PWE's propaganda broadcasts to Europe. By 1944, the Foreign Office was already casting a proprietary eye over Gambier-Parry's organization, referring to it less as SIS secret radio than government 'diplomatic' wireless. As a result, after the war, the resources of the Radio Section were hived off from the SIS entirely to become the Foreign Office's Diplomatic Wireless Service (DWS).[44] Gambier-Parry moved to the Foreign Office to oversee the transfer as the FO's first Director of Communications in 1947,[45] replaced at Broadway by his assistant, Colonel Maltby, who oversaw the transition from the SIS end.[46]

The transfer of the Radio Section to the Foreign Office had also, in part, been made possible by a shift in diplomatic convention concerning the use of independent radio communications by embassies, previously banned by the Madrid Convention. During the Telecommunication Conference in Atlantic City in August 1947, where post-war agreements on international telecommunications were being negotiated, the Swiss delegation raised the question of the legality of the Diplomatic Wireless Service. In response, the UK delegation was briefed by Gambier-Parry and the Communications Section of the FO to the effect that the delegation 'were to avoid discussion of the subject on the grounds that diplomatic wireless was a matter of diplomatic privilege and was not covered by the Madrid Convention which the conference had been convened to revise'.[47]

This was a somewhat disingenuous reply since, as noted above, the reason British legations abroad had not been equipped with wireless before the war was precisely that it was forbidden by international law. However, the Second World War had so disrupted communications that the use of government wireless had developed as the only available option, regardless of international law. As a result, as Gambier-Parry noted on the issue of DWS legality in September of that year:

> Diplomatic wireless has been used by a number of governments for some years now, and as far as we know, has never been challenged. It seems, therefore, to be well on the way to becoming established in international practice and eventually in international law. We are advised, however, that it would be unwise to discuss the question with foreign governments at present if this can be avoided since it might be difficult to dispose of the argument that, although the right to communicate by telegraph and in cypher is acknowledged, it cannot be said that there is any international sanction for the use of this relatively novel method of doing so.[48]

The war, therefore, had created the circumstances for secure diplomatic radio to acquire a substantial degree of legitimacy, if only through precedent and the force of circumstances. There were even debates within the Foreign Office concerning whether or not British firms abroad should be allowed use of diplomatic wireless to communicate with their head offices in London.[49] Although run primarily by the Foreign Office for communication with its missions abroad, the DWS remained nonetheless the medium for secure wireless communications with SIS stations abroad, and with human agents using clandestine transceivers. The DWS also operated a factory at Boreham Wood that manufactured radio equipment for overt and covert communications purposes. The Boreham Wood factory was managed on the same basis as the Royal Ordnance Factories; that is, although run by the Foreign Office and producing communications equipment for the Foreign Office and intelligence and security agencies, it was carried on the budget of the Ministry of Supply.[50]

Under the new arrangements, R8 was reduced to two functions: liaison with GCHQ, and overseeing the continuing work of Section N.[51] As GCHQ liaison, R8 received GCHQ intercepts required by the SIS for its operations, while passing to GCHQ cryptomaterials acquired by that agency from its human sources or local technical operations. A single officer, R8, was expected to act as 'GCHQ's man in the building', much as were the Service Branch representatives R2, R3 and R4, although, unlike these secondments, R8 was an SIS officer.[52] R8's work routine consisted of a weekly meeting on Tuesdays at GCHQ's London offices on Palmer Street, with a monthly meeting at GCHQ headquarters (in due course in Cheltenham).[53] Section N's work went on in the post-war world much as it had before and during the Second World War, although the section had also acquired the minor additional task of processing the product of MI5 taps on foreign embassies for any information of operational intelligence value rather than counter-intelligence interest.[54] However, as fewer and fewer countries felt the need to rely on the Foreign Office to transport their diplomatic bags, Section N's work progressively dwindled in the 1960s until eventually it petered out completely.[55]

The other side of the 1921 arrangement, SIS operational organization, was one of the areas most in need of streamlining and clarification. Under the 1946 reorganization, this was tidied up, and the P Sections were resorted, numbered more or less consecutively and grouped under regional Controllers, who in turn answered to a single Director of Production (D/P). D/P was Z Organization alumnus Kenneth Cohen. His task was to act as what one officer interviewed described as a 'global controller', overseeing, in the first instance, the wartime area controllerates, Controller Northern Area (C/NA), (Scandinavia and The Netherlands), Controller Western Area (C/WA), (Belgium, France, Italy, and the Iberian Peninsula), Controller Eastern Area (C/EA), (Germany, Austria, Switzerland), Controller Eastern Europe (C/EE), and new controllerates for the Middle East (C/ME) and Far East (C/FE).[56] C/EE was to prove short-lived as the Soviet occupation forces closed down access to Eastern Europe. Hence, by the end of 1945, the production side had been due for a reorganization through force of circumstance more than because of any administrative or political impetus to modernize, reform or streamline.

The country P Sections had taken shape during the war because the field stations had been forced to relocate to the Head Office in London and infiltrate agents across the English Channel and North Sea. However, with the Allied advance across Europe, the field stations were moved back abroad again, stripping SIS HQ of its wartime operational infrastructure. Initially, the P Sections began to relocate their staffs back abroad into the liberated areas, and then, as national governments were restored to formerly occupied countries, the field stations were re-established in the capitals as they had been before the war. George Blake, for example, has recalled how, as the Allied forces advanced through the Low Countries, P8 in London dwindled to three officers with the rest of the section running a new field station in the liberated part of The Netherlands. In his memoirs, he recalls how 'VE day found me alone, in charge of P8, now reduced to a mere shadow of a section. A week before, the German armies in the Netherlands had surrendered and Major Seymour... had gone to the Hague to open an SIS station there.'[57]

The SIS therefore returned to its pre-war formula of Head Office acting as a central locus for administration, tasking and dissemination, with the operational machinery reconstituted on regional rather than country lines. Under the new system P1 handled Belgium, France, Italy and Iberia under C/WA; P2 dealt with Scandinavia and The Netherlands, under C/NA; P3 dealt with Austria, Germany and Switzerland under C/EA; P4 handled the Middle East; and P5 the Balkans under C/ME.[58] C/FE oversaw an arrangement comparable to C/ME, although none of the sources available could identify the P Section numbers for the Far East.[59] Similarly, P Sections existed for Eastern Europe and the Soviet bloc, although Controller Eastern Europe was abolished soon after the war and its functions absorbed by a new Controller Production Research (C/PR) in 1947/48.[60] The allocation of countries, however, was not carved in stone, and during the following decades, when communication lines shifted or officers with specialized regional knowledge occasionally moved diagonally up the ranks into a new Area Controllerate or regional Chief Controllerate, 'their' country would move with them. As a result, according to one officer, Romania and Greece ended up at one point rather incongruously under the Western Area when a long-time Balkans hand was promoted to C/WA, taking responsibility for those two countries with him, while Bulgaria shifted from C/ME to C/EA when the Foreign Office began routing its diplomatic bags from Budapest to London via Vienna instead of Cairo.[61] Between 1944 and 1946, the Soviet Union's consolidation of its occupied territories in Eastern Europe turned that part of the world into a 'denied area' much as most of Continental Europe had been under the Germans. With little or no opportunity for residential work, and opportunities to mount operations into Soviet dominated territories coming chiefly from flanking states, the wartime Eastern Europe Controllerate was phased out.

By late 1947 or early 1948, a new controllerate took over C/EE's work alongside several other functions. This new controllerate was designated Controller Production Research (C/PR). C/PR's function was threefold. In the first instance, 'If anybody needed expert advice on some technical or commercial operation, or a particular kind of cover for an agent, which could be provided by a British firm or organization, it was the job of C/PR . . . to arrange it.'[62] C/PR was also to seek assistance from UK citizens journeying to and from the USSR, and to mount operations against foreign nationals in the UK, attacking targets legally considered foreign soil albeit lying within the three-mile limit, such as trade delegations and embassies.[63] C/PR also operated the UK Station, the first of what have since come to be termed 'natural cover' stations. It was set up under the code name BIN at Londonderry House, Victoria,[64] and the Eastern Europe and Soviet bloc P Sections were subordinated to C/PR because the difficulties of operating in the Soviet bloc forced those units to rely on Third-Country operations out of the UK, often via states bordering the Soviet bloc. The UK Station's primary function was to provide a staging point of operations deployed behind the Iron Curtain from the UK on behalf of the Soviet bloc P Sections.[65] The Head of Station UK also acted as C/PR's deputy.[66] Since BSC had been abolished in 1946, C/PR also took over responsibility for operations in the western hemisphere,[67] and the first Controller Production Research was, in fact, a former senior BSC officer.[68]

Placing the Soviet bloc and Eastern Europe P Sections under C/PR resulted in a degree of friction between C/PR and the other controllerates. This was because the Soviet bloc P Section under C/PR could credibly claim that it should be indoctrinated into any Third-Country operations into the USSR and Eastern Europe by other controllerates into his jurisdiction. The other areas viewed this as impinging on their jurisdiction and, moreover, a potential violation of compartmentalization.[69] This would remain a sore point throughout the next decade.

The SIS also continued to operate regional headquarters or 'controlling stations'[70] in the Middle and Far East. During the Second World War, the SIS had had to set up semi-autonomous 'longstop' headquarters under the various theatre GHQs in the Middle East,

North Africa and the Far East. With the end of the war, however, the need for these 'controlling stations' continued. In the Middle East, the old cover name ISLD (ME) was abandoned in favour of a new title, the Combined Research and Planning Organization, Middle East (CRPO (ME)), and ISLD (FE) in Kandy was relocated to Singapore with the re-establishment of British colonial administration, where it was referred to more directly as SIS (FE).[71] Within the SIS, the designations of CRPO (ME) and SIS (FE) were, respectively, Middle East Controller (MEC) and Far East Controller (FEC).[72] No sooner was CRPO set up in Cairo than, in December 1945, the Egyptians demanded a revision of the 1936 treaty with Britain. In 1946, British forces were withdrawn from Egypt to the Canal Zone; in 1949, faced with riots and general hostility from the populace, the British completely abandoned Cairo and Alexandria, and the MEC was relocated to Ismailia.[73] Then, with the Egyptian seizure of the Canal Zone, the MEC was relocated to Cyprus; from 1951 to 1955, it was in Nicosia, and then moved with the staff of the Political Office to Middle East Forces (POMEF) to the British Military Hospital (BMH) Compound at Episkopi.[74]

In South-East Asia, the end of the war ushered in a reassertion of British civilian government of former possessions in the region. A Governor-General for South-East Asia (concerned primarily with the Federated and Unfederated Malay States, the Straits Colonies and British Borneo), a Special Commissioner for the UK in South-East Asia and a Governor of Singapore were installed. The governmental situation in South-East Asia was somewhat confused as the region included both British-governed colonial possessions (which fell within the remit of the Colonial Office) and an assortment of independent 'native states' such as Burma and Thailand (strictly the concern of the Foreign Office). As a result, the Special Commission potentially fell between two governmental and constitutional stools, and the resulting administrative arrangements had to reflect this dual nature. The individual chosen as Special Commissioner was Lord Killearn of the Foreign Office, described by one historian as an 'old Imperialist' but also someone well familiar with regional and colonial intelligence administration problems from his wartime experience as British Minister in Cairo.[75]

Killearn remained on as Special Commissioner until 1948. After his departure, in May of that year, the posts of Governor-General of Malaya and Special Commissioner were consolidated into a new

Commissioner-General for the United Kingdom in South-East Asia (Singapore retained its own Commissioner during the 1950s). The dual nature of the Commission thus became even more pronounced, as reflected by the fact that the newly appointed Commissioner-General received two deputies, one each for his colonial and foreign affairs staff.[76] Under the Commissioner-General, the Far East intelligence arrangements, which had been mainly carried over directly from the Second World War,[77] underwent a review in which they were consciously modelled on those in the Middle East. One significant difference was that where JIC/ME was responsible directly to the Commander-in-Chief Middle East, the JIC(FE) came under the auspices of the British Defence Co-ordinating Committee (BDCC/FE) in the first instance, rather than the Far East Commander-in-Chief or Commissioner-General.[78]

A review in 1948 of intelligence arrangements in the Far East not only examined the role of the SIS and MI5 there, but also proposed upgrading their relationship with the JIC(FE) to one roughly comparable to their position on the London JIC.[79] As a result, the SIS and the Security Service were to contribute to any 'government assessments' generated by the British colonial administrations. However, on the grounds that the two covert organizations were responsible only for the gathering of information, and not its assessment, they were not 'signing members'; that is, they were not signatories to any joint assessments made by the JIC/FE. In this capacity, they were required to produce information to be contributed to the joint assessment process, and, as a result, were tasked by the regional colonial administrations, disseminating their product directly to consumers within those administrations. In order to do so, the SIS/FE headquarters in Singapore could issue JIC/FE requirements to the subordinate field stations under the FEC's control in the region. To facilitate this division of functions, the FEC had under its authority three distinct SIS stations, housed in separate offices. The FEC's immediate staff was housed with the Commissioner General's staff at Phoenix Park,[80] with a standard field station that targeted neighbouring states under the traditional Third-Country scheme, and a Singapore 'City Station' that, as one officer put it, 'talked to Lee Kwan Yew and people like that'.[81] Among the Singapore residency's successes was counted the penetration of Indonesian President Sukarno's Cabinet in the form of the Trade Minister, Dr Sumitro Djojohodikoesoemo, as well as other senior

Indonesian politicians,[82] although it would later become involved in the disastrous attempt to undermine the Sukarno government during the 1958 PERMESTA coup (in conjunction with the Special Political Action Section (SPA), as discussed below).

The functions of the 'longstop' controlling stations were much as they had been during the war: to provide regional, day-to-day control more conveniently than could London several thousand miles away and at a time when global telecommunications were still comparatively slow (a signal from either HQ would require several 'relays', that is, retransmissions, to reach London), and to task SIS resources in those theatres directly according to the needs of the Middle East and Far East colonial administrations. To this end, MEC and FEC were tasked by their respective JIC, as well as D/P in London.

The relationship between the Controllers and the P Officers appears to have been somewhat ambiguous. Some officers interviewed firmly maintained that the role of the P Officer was strictly administrative support for the area's field stations, while the Controller was responsible for operational planning and direction.[83] Another argued that the relationship was far less clearly defined; in his opinion, P Officers were involved in operations 'as much as' the Area Controller, although the Controller was ultimately in charge.[84] According to one-time P1, Desmond Bristow, 'As [P1] I was responsible for the administration of the stations in the Iberian section, and all communication to and from these stations was channeled through me. For instance, a demand from the Air Ministry for more information on a foreign air force would be requested through the [P] Section.'[85] Anthony Cavendish, although a junior officer, has provided one of the most lucid descriptions of the requirements/production relationship. In Cavendish's description, a desk officer in, for example, MI, would write a brief outlining the information required and pass it to R4. R4 would, in turn, take the matter up with the P Officer covering the geographical area in question, who would task a field station. Cavendish has suggested that 'the R4 officer would know the full details of the source', but would not reveal that to his MI consumer, providing instead a source report 'which would give some details of the source' indicating the agent's level and quality of access.[86] While this sequence of events was also indicated by other officers interviewed,[87] one argued that the R Section would not, in the ordinary course of things, be informed of the actual identity of a source, although he did note that in some cases the information acquired indicated a level and particular range of access which would only be possible for one particular person.[88]

Both Bristow and Cavendish also recall that the consumers would usually provide feedback concerning the quality of the report, Bristow adding that 'the report would be digested by its recipients and then returned to me marked with an A, B, C or D according to its importance, usually accompanied by a request for further information'.[89] For example, in 1947, the War Office practice for laying its requirements on the SIS consisted of issuing R4 (still designated MI6 within the War Office) with Standing Questionnaires, which covered permanent requirements, such as the strength and deployments of Soviet forces in the Occupied Zones and Eastern Europe; 'Special Questions' which covered specific items or details not covered by the Standing Questionnaires; and 'Special Supplementary Briefs', which covered any items not covered by the previous two procedures. At one meeting between MI6 (R4) and representatives of other MI subsections records, the consumers were reminded by their War Office colleagues of

> the necessity for careful phrasing when putting Special Questions to MI6. Where possible, a short background explanation should be given and the question related to it. Thus instead of asking point blank for, say, the whereabouts of the 5th Inf. Division, sections should preferably say something on the following lines:– 'It has been reported that the 5th Inf. Div. has left its old location at "Blacktown" and is now thought to be in the area of "Whiteberg", the move is thought to have taken place in early November. Confirmation of this move is required together with the new location of the Div. HQ.' A similar procedure would apply for questions on organization, equipment, personalities, etc.[90]

Finally, Bristow recalls, 'every six months, I and my colleagues in [P1] would evaluate each agent in collaboration with the recipient departments of his or her reports and the head of station supplying the reports'.[91] Just as before and during the war, the initiative for mounting operations could originate at any stage in the process, that is, with an officer on station, the P Officer, the Controller or an officer on the Requirements side, but the Area Controller was responsible for getting authorization from C or his deputies, and for briefing anyone 'with an angle' on the operation who might be affected.[92] However, the very ambiguities in role show that the working relationships were less a matter of narrowly defined hierarchy and division of labour than of a less formal, pooling of effort in which 'stratification' was less crucial than contribution and consultation.

Stations in the field would vary in size from Berlin, which, in the 1950s, counted over 100 officers and staff, organized into four operational sections (political intelligence and Soviet penetration; Soviet and East German armed forces; scientific intelligence; and the technical methods section),[93] to 20 officers at Horseferry Road's UK station,[94] to barely half a dozen in Tehran.[95] The cover of Passport Control Officer had long been abandoned; during the war, it had been taken over by Section V's residents abroad, and when Section V was shut down, the post was abandoned completely by the SIS. As a result, SIS officers under diplomatic cover were typically given conventional positions within embassy staffs. This was not without its problems, in this case with the Diplomatic List, in which, as one diplomat has observed, one could easily find among the 'comparatively junior First Secretaries, suddenly one festooned with CMGs and other honours sticking out like a sore thumb', a problem resolved eventually by allowing SIS officers more senior cover. Another problem was the Foreign Office seniority table from which SIS officers, listed as diplomats at the various missions, were omitted because they were not actually in the FO hierarchy. This problem was solved by abolishing the Seniority Table at the front of the Foreign Office list.[96]

Just as in the past, the station's 'first point of contact', as one SIS officer interviewed put it, was 'the local security service, on the notional grounds that we were there to help protect them against spying by their neighbors'.[97] This function, and its consequences for station cover, has also been noted by former Deputy Chief John Bruce Lockhart:

> In neutral countries professional intelligence officers from the friendly secret intelligence services usually work in embassies or missions. Everybody knows who they are. The KGB know. They are in close liaison with the local intelligence services. . . . The Head of Station might arguably have 'Intelligence Attaché' on his door. The decencies have to be observed, so he is called '1st Secretary Trade', 'Labour Attaché' or whatever is considered appropriate. The cover is just the fig leaf of convention.[98]

Former SIS Foreign Office Adviser (see below) Geoffrey McDermott has similarly argued that under such circumstances cover is of 'secondary importance'.[99] In less friendly settings, of course, considerably more concern was taken over diplomatic and non-diplomatic cover for officers in the field.

Two separate pressures came to bear on the creation of the Requirements Directorate, one of which was internal and the other external. The internal pressure for the new directorate derived from the same span of control concerns which drove the creation of the Production Directorate. In the previous decades, SIS's consumers had multiplied, its C Sections had multiplied in kind, and the matter was exacerbated by a tendency to group any non-operational section (Finance or Communications) with the C Sections. However, the external pressure was of a very different order, and represented the beginning of a very fundamental change in the structure of tasking and analysis within the British government. Between the wars, the emphasis on tasking and dissemination for the SIS had been on the basis of single departmental consumers, who then conducted their own, independent, in-house, all-source analysis on what they received from the SIS, GC & CS, and consular and published sources. Joint planning, joint operations and joint intelligence were all nascent developments, but ones forced into rapid evolution by the combined mutagenic and selective pressures of the Second World War. With the end of the war, intelligence analysis underwent much the same kind of JIC-level review as intelligence collection and special operations, with the result that the JIC proposed the creation of a new joint intelligence organization, the Joint Intelligence Bureau (JIB).

The purpose of the JIC was mainly to prepare strategic and policy-level joint assessments (since the war effectively, but not officially, at a national level[100]), but hard experience from the Second World War had taught the value of joint *tactical* intelligence dealing with economic, geographical, technological, psychological and assorted other factors. As a result, the JIB was to provide a vehicle for just such a 'contributive' pooling of information, and, besides acting as a recipient and analyst, was given its own Procurement Section to gather information from open, published sources.[101] However, from SIS's point of view, the JIB was now an additional consumer, although, instead of requiring a new consumer liaison section as had developed in the past, the breadth of the JIB's interests and requirements meant that it was treated as an additional consumer for most of the existing liaison sections, in particular economic and scientific intelligence.

The impact of the post-war JIC and JIB structure and process was that the tasking process, or *requirements*, now began to reflect not merely partisan interests but the need for balanced 'objective' inputs to a joint, all-source assessment process at both the strategic and tactical levels. The work of the tasking and dissemination officer was to increasingly become that of a detached intermediary, who ensured that the information received by consumers was, as one officer put it, 'not influenced by the imperatives of the Production side, i.e. making poor agents look good or good agents look better'. The relationship of case officer to their source, the officer further observed, being 'something of a partnership...a bond of loyalty [which] tends to make sheep out of goats, and Requirements Sections are supposed to ensure that goats remain goats'. However, he added, that the objectivity of the Requirements Sections was also required to ensure that intelligence reporting was not distorted by 'political influence from customers in Whitehall'.[102] The growth of central, inter-departmental, all-source assessment constituted a progressive pressure on SIS tasking and dissemination away from simple departmental, partisan representation to an additional role of detached and bias-neutral quality control of SIS contributions to the new joint intelligence process, a process now based on topical distinctions rather than departmental interests.

During the war, a Deputy Director for Administration had been appointed when the board of Deputy Directors (the 'Service Commissars') was abandoned in favour of area controllers drawn from the senior SIS operational staff. DD/Admin oversaw both the Administrative Section and Finance, formerly Section VII.[103] After the war, this function was combined with a new recruitment and person-nel section, creating the Directorate of Finance and Administration. John Musson, who came to the SIS after overseeing the SOE Liquidation Party at Baker Street (see below), became the first D/FA.[104] D/FA directly oversaw the Financial Section, while the role of DD/Admin continued to exist under D/FA in the form of Frank Slocum, formerly of the joint SIS/SOE 'water bus' programmes during the war.[105] DD/Admin controlled the administrative sections (possibly including the Central Registry[106]) and the new Personnel Section with two sub-sections, one for providing intelligence officers and the other, secretarial staff.[107]

Under the new personnel arrangements, the salary structure was revised and linked approximately with Civil Service grades under a doctrine of 'parallelism'[108] and a programme of systematic recruitment from the universities began 'in competition with the regular Civil Service and industry'.[109] The new staff grades created under 'parallelism' consisted of six ranks ranging from Junior Officer to Director, with the posts of Assistant Chief, Vice-Chief and C ranked above Director.[110]

The post-war Central Registry was, however, a very different creature from the understaffed Central Registry relegated to St Albans during the war. No longer was it to be the sort from which Philby could requisition and work his way through the sources books which listed SIS's stable of agents across the globe.[111] It was now organized along geographical lines, with each Area Controllerate's records housed close at hand, rather than at a single, central location. This ensured both the ready availability of records of an area interest, and the effective compartmentalization of SIS records.[112] At this point, however, administrative and support arrangements did not yet account for training, a function that was finally dealt with as part of the SIS absorption of the Special Operations Executive.

The end of the Second World War sounded the death knell for the Special Operations Executive (SOE). The most commonly held judgement on SOE's demise is that expressed by the late Robert Cecil, that 'SOE was liquidated with almost indecent haste. If relations with SIS had been more cordial, one first-class organisation might have been created by merging the best elements of the two; but the chance was missed.'[113] From this viewpoint, the absorption of SOE back into the SIS in 1946 was, at bottom, simply the final act in a conflict which had been played out since Section D had been excised in 1941. As noted above, however, the headquarters conflict was not always pursued with equal vigour in the field, and the necessary overlaps between jurisdiction and function were so great that in a number of theatres the separation of Special Operations and Secret Intelligence seemed both artificial and unnecessary. Cecil's view of events also underestimates the role of the Foreign Office and Chiefs of Staff in the process, beyond any residual hostility felt among the post-war SIS leadership.

The accepted course of events is that the remnants of SOE were absorbed into SIS as a 'Special Operations Branch',[114] and both David Stafford and Richard Aldrich have traced the demise of SOE and its

199

incorporation into SIS as its 'Special Operations Branch' in public archives in some detail.[115] In fact, some of the interviews undertaken and a number of the SOE archives recently released to the Public Record Office suggest that the process was a good deal less amicable than even Cecil suggests, with Gubbins and SOE struggling for a 'global role' to the bitter end. However, SOE's survival within Broadway was a more complex and diffuse affair than simply becoming a 'rump' organization or 'Special Operations Branch' within SIS.

By May 1945, SOE had 'no future task', as it was put in the records of the Chiefs of Staff (CoS).[116] An ad hoc Committee on the Future of SOE was set up, chaired by Victor Cavendish-Bentinck, Chair of the JIC, much as had been done for the SIS earlier that year. In the course of this committee's deliberations, Cavendish-Bentinck polled the Foreign Office's Heads of Mission abroad on their preferences for the SOE. For this process, Gubbins had formulated a global 'three-year charter' for SOE, and encouraged the CoS to set up their own 'SOE Evaluation Committee' to run in parallel with the Cavendish-Bentinck review.[117] Certainly, SOE's putative three-year charter was met with scepticism and even a note of alarm by Cavendish-Bentinck and his colleagues. Writing to Lord Killearn, then still British Minister in Cairo, and to his opposite number in Beirut, on 12 June 1945, Cavendish-Bentinck pressed the diplomats for a response to his request for his recommendations on the future status of SOE in the Middle East. He advised them that he needed a 'brief statement of what we consider should be done with SOE in the Middle East countries' before the meeting of the ad hoc Committee 'Monday next', on the grounds that Cavendish-Bentinck expected to be 'faced with all sorts of suggestions from the SOE for grandiose activities in the Middle East with allegations that they are regarded as absolutely necessary by our representatives in those countries'.[118] Killearn, at least, was unambiguously hostile to SOE, noting that he would be perfectly happy to see SOE activities in the Middle East 'wound up', and that Cairo already had perfectly adequate Secret Service arrangements.[119] Nonetheless, both the ad hoc Committee on SOE and a separate CoS SOE Evaluation Committee concluded that there existed a broad consensus that closer coordination between secret intelligence and special operations than had existed during the war was necessary.[120]

The eventual conclusions of the ad hoc JIC sub-committee

presented to the Defence Committee in September 1945 were that a 'new global secret service' should be set up, in which the SIS and SOE should be placed under 'an Executive Head of the Secret Service having separate Special Operations and Secret Intelligence branches with common services'.[121] Stephen Dorril has portrayed this as a comprehensive defeat for Gubbins,[122] but this does not appear to have been uniformly so perceived by SOE members at the time. The proposed amalgamation seems to have appeared acceptable to both agencies. An internal SOE Swedish Section communication of 15 September notes:

> We have now received the official news that the ad hoc Committee's suggestions for putting SIS and SOE as separate branches under one head have definitely been accepted as an interim measure and the merger will take place in January of next year. It is now understood that the head of the combined organisation will be 'C' himself. As you know, the putting of SIS and SOE under one combined head is only an interim step on the way to creating a much bigger reorganisation which the Powers that Be intend to carry out in due course... the global charter for SOE has now been fully approved except for certain final details and it is very satisfactory from our point of view as it definitely puts SOE well on the map for the future.[123]

At least in certain SOE quarters, plans to integrate the SIS and the SOE were seen – or at least portrayed internally – as a de facto acceptance of SOE's role and the substance of its proposed charter.

It must be clearly understood that at this point what was planned was a new organization with two branches, Secret Intelligence (SI) and Special Operations (SO), on an even footing much as the OSS Secret Intelligence (SI) and Special Operations (SO) branches had been during the war, with C's joint headship of the SIS and GCHQ as a precedent. It was in this context that Gubbins, on 12 November 1945, met the incoming new Supreme Allied Commander, South-East Asia (SACSEA), Lieutenant General F.A.M. Browning, and presented him with a document entitled 'SOE Future Tasks in the Far East'. At this meeting, Gubbins confirmed to Browning that 'both Services (SIS and SOE) would disappear as individual services on 15 January approximately and would be re-formed under one head from that date'.[124] Under these arrangements, the new 'Combined Secret Service' would consist of a

Special Operations Branch, a Special Intelligence Branch and 'common services in the form of Administration, Finance, Communications, Research and Development, etc.'[125]

According to Gubbins's ideas about SOE's future, the function of the Special Operations (SO) Branch of the Combined Secret Service (the terms actually used in Gubbins's briefing to SACSEA), and agreed to by the CoS were to be

(a) To maintain an organisation capable of rapid expansion in time of war.
(b) To undertake research and development of means of communication, special devices, weapons, etc. and to arrange for their production on a large scale if required.
(c) To train personnel required for [SO] work whether agents or service personnel.
(d) To make such clandestine contacts as may be necessary in foreign countries.
(e) To establish clandestine means of communication where required.
(f) To undertake Special Operations as may be required by a theatre commander or other Government Departments.[126]

Gubbins further noted that 'Activity under (d) (e) and (f) in any foreign country will, however, be subject to Foreign Office approval.'

By December 1945, matters had turned against SOE and Gubbins's plans for the future. The terms of the amalgamation had changed. Two factors militated very strongly against the amalgamation of the SIS and the SOE taking the form of a Combined Secret Service with equal SI and SO branches. In the first place, SOE was, by November 1945, already under Foreign Office control instead of the defunct Ministry of Economic Warfare,[127] and perhaps even more critically, the entire combined organization was to be headed by Menzies, and the final form it took would be Menzies's decision (subject, of course, to whatever pressures were put upon him by the Foreign Office). As a result, it was decided that, instead of forming a Combined Secret Service, on 15 January 1946, 'that part of SOE which was required by the Secret Service should be merged *into* the SIS'.[128] In due course, the January date for amalgamation arrived, and the CoS minutes for the 17 January 1946 meeting note almost in passing that 'The Chiefs of Staff were informed that the amalgamation of SOE and SIS had taken effect from the 15 January and that the Special Operations Branch of the Secret Service was now under the command of "C". The liquidation of SOE, which was being kept separate, was being carried out at No. 14 Kendrick Place, Baker Street...and any relevant questions should be referred to the "SOE Liquidation Party".' The note concludes, rather ominously given the history of SIS–SOE antipathy: 'The process of liquidation was estimated to take about one month.'[129]

With amalgamation, Gubbins was dismissed along with his deputy Henry Sporborg, and an SOE officer called John Musson was left in charge of the Liquidation Party,[130] a process hampered by a fire there that destroyed a large portion of the SOE's files. In the event, liquidation took rather longer than the original estimate of one month. In March 1946, the Liquidation Party submitted an interim report on manpower releases to the Chiefs of Staff, and in May the Party was given until 30 July, by which time 'the SOE should finally be wound up'.[131]

SOE's existence as the Special Operations Branch of the SIS was so brief as to be almost notional, although official correspondence continues to refer to a 'combined Secret Service' well into 1946, and perhaps the grafting of SOE components onto the SIS may have been genuinely seen as such by some of the participants. During the following year, the operational assets of the SOE, its officers, networks and agents, taken over by the SIS were absorbed into the agency's Production side,[132] while, as Claude Dansey noted in a lecture to one of the military colleges in July 1946, 'a nucleus war planning staff has already been set up inside the combined Secret Service which will study every aspect of clandestine warfare and plans for wartime expansion'.[133] That SIS 'nucleus war planning staff' itself was created to service the Joint Intelligence Committee's War Planning Committee and War Planning Staff in much the same fashion as R7 existed to service the Joint Scientific and Technical Intelligence Committee(s). The JIC War Planning Committee was envisioned by the 1945 Capell-Dunn enquiry into postwar intelligence as being 'charged with planning and making all preparations for the expansion and modification of the Intelligence machine that would be required for war.'[134] The 'nucleus war planning staff' appeared in the SIS order of battle as the Directorate of War Planning (D/WP)[135] and was placed under Brigadier John Nicholson, ex-SOE and wartime General Staff Officer Intelligence (GSOI) in the Middle East.[136] To assist him, D/WP had a former SOE officer as Staff Officer to the Directorate of War Planning (SO/DWP).[137] The D/WP essentially took Special Operations back to the 1938 role of Section D as a planning and coordinating body. As in Philby's proposals for Section IX, there was some thought of creating a limited field organization in the form of subordinate war-planning headquarters in the Middle and Far East alongside the regional 'longstop' controlling stations in Cairo and Singapore,[138] but these did not materialize.

The D/WP functioned in two ways. In the first place, War Planning was to undertake the special operations planning just as described in Gubbins's briefing to SACSEA (item a). The skeleton organization for wartime mobilization was not handled directly by the D/WP however, but through War Planning Officers attached to the area controllerates. The area War Planning Officers' tasks were to oversee the planning for sabotage and subversion operations in their respective areas, and to oversee the recruitment of stay-behind networks under the authority of the Controller (items d and e).[139] The other side of D/WP's work was a post-war doctrine being developed at the time that the natural successor to the SOE for operations in the field during the post-war area would be the Special Air Service (SAS). Therefore, one of SO/DWP's tasks was liaison with the Colonel Commandant of the SAS to coordinate plans between the SIS and the SAS for the latter to take on SOE's field role in the event of war.[140] The wartime SAS had in fact performed precisely these tasks, sending in teams to support partisans in Italy and the Balkans.[141] A review of SAS work conducted by the Director of Tactical Investigation in October 1945 at the behest of Chief of the Imperial General Staff noted on SOE/SAS relations that the 'SAS cannot successfully operate without good intelligence, guides, etc. SOE can only do a certain amount before requiring, when their operations became overt, highly trained, armed bodies in uniform to operate and set an example to the local resistance.' SOE, it further remarked 'are the "white hunters" and produce the ground organisation on which SAS operates'.[142] This description passed over the work of SAS British Liaison Officers in Italy and Albania, who *clandestinely* trained and organized partisans. Plans developed by the post-war SAS commandant and SO/DWP built upon the work of the SAS British Liaison Officers, and employed a doctrine in which SO work would be done by four-man teams consisting of a team leader, his deputy, a translator or local guide, and a w/t operator, on the basis of a ground organization laid down by the SIS.[143] As a result, unlike the proposed Combined Secret Service SO Branch, D/WP carried no operational brief whatsoever. Installing the networks would fall to the Area Controllers and the Production organization, while the actual paramilitary work during hostilities would fall to the SAS on the basis of those networks.

As well as recruiting stay-behind cells within British territories at risk in the case of a general communist offensive (such as Germany, Austria, as well as Hong Kong and Mesopotamia[144]), the Area Controllerates had begun organizing and recruiting resistance networks in neutral states, and running them into Soviet-dominated territory from neighbouring states in the classic Third-Country approach almost immediately after the war. However, for the most part, both the stay-behind groups and resistance cells were intended to lie fallow until the outbreak of a general war, a preparatory measure to avoid a desperate dash like that in 1940–41 to recruit stay-behind units behind the rapidly collapsing Allied lines in Europe.[145]

One resistance network for which a first-hand account exists in English is the Hungarian Catholic Resistance Movement, as recounted by Paul v. Gorka in his *Budapest Betrayed*.[146] The Catholic Resistance Movement was controlled by Vienna Station. The network was set up in 1947, centred on a former Hungarian naval officer, Béla Bajomi, who had slipped across the Austrian border to join his brother, who was reportedly already working for the British Secret Services. Bajomi then recruited his own son to act as his sub-agent in Hungary and 'to organize a group for resistance and intelligence activities'.[147] Just as SOE proved capable of gathering raw intelligence when it was not actually disrupting affairs behind enemy lines, in the absence of any 'hot' war, the Catholic Resistance Movement maintained caches of arms,[148] while their initial operational role was to collect intelligence. Gorka, for example, was in the government department dealing with 'new mining installations…new heavy industrial combines, and… transport relating to them', and routinely travelled around the vicinity noting the occupying Soviet forces' 'types of vehicles, armour, tanks, and the number plates on them'. His industrial and military information was communicated to SIS by secret writing, using 'white chemical carbon paper', and mailed to an accommodation address in Vienna.[149]

Gorka blames the failure of the Catholic Resistance Movement on Philby. However, as Philby was in Turkey by 1947, it seems unlikely he would have been indoctrinated into the operation. Gorka himself points to a very serious breach of operational security by the resistance group members themselves, on the same order as many of the breaches by the French wartime *réseaux*, when he reminisces on the network's last year of operation in 1950: 'It was a beautiful, hot summer... we had just a short walk home, stopping on the way at one of the most famous pub-cum-expresso houses called "Kevdes" (Sweetie) at the bottom of the Hill of Roses. There we often had some schnapps (Hungarian rum) and exchanged information about the task we had undertaken on behalf of the British Intelligence Service.'[150] Thus, it seems likely that a main cause of the network's collapse may have been somewhat closer to home. At any rate, on 13 August 1950, Michael Bajomi was arrested and in less than a week the Hungarian secret police, the AVO, had rolled up the entire organization.[151]

At least in the Baltic States, the resistance work was supposedly more active. According to Tom Bower's reconstruction of events leading to the 'Forest Brotherhood' debacle in the Baltic States, the Controller Northern Area, Harry Carr, approached C with plans for covert political support for anti-communist groups and the infiltration of clandestine operators in the area as early as late 1945. This was to consist, firstly, of attaching radio operators to act as liaison between SIS and groups of partisans still reportedly fighting against the Soviet occupying forces, and, secondly, of approaching appropriate leaders of the émigré opposition groups.[152] To this end, a Special Liaison Centre in Ryder Street (the wartime location of Section V) was set up under Northern Area to train recruits and coordinate the operations. In the event, C/NA was required to keep R5, then still under Philby, briefed on operations in the Soviet area for a counter-intelligence input to the operations, and, unsurprisingly, the operations were intercepted by the Baltic KGB offices from the very beginning. However, rather than simply arrest and try the infiltrated agents, the Soviets elected to play them back in a sustained double-cross operation. Although the Baltic networks were active groups like the French Maquis, and not lying fallow like the Hungarian Catholic Resistance, it should be kept in mind that when the programme was originally conceived in 1945, the partisans the C/NA sought to contact were believed to be already engaged in an armed campaign against Soviet authorities in the theatre. In this respect, the Baltic operations were not so much an extension of war planning and post-war SO doctrine in the SIS as a traditional SIS political operation in support of anti-communist dissidents, and did not fall under the ambit of the D/WP.

The D/WP may not have been an operational body, but its officers were liable to be tasked in support of sabotage operations conducted by the Area Controllerates. David Smiley has reported how, as SO/DWP, he 'spent time on operations in the Mediterranean', tasked by former Section D Balkan hand and wartime SOE head of Polish Section, Harold Perkins.[153] Perkins was, at this time, on the Production side, although it is not clear whether as a P Officer or a Controller.[154] These operations were, in all likelihood, the SIS campaign of sabotage actions against illegal immigration into Palestine and the traffic of arms to paramilitary groups like Haganah prior to the end of the British mandate.[155] Smiley notes of these operations: 'I had not only been under the orders of Perks [Perkins] for certain operations but he insisted on joining me for the more hazardous and exciting missions.'[156] In this case again, the SO operations were not D/WP projects, but Mediterranean area projects in which SO/DWP was brought in mainly as an experienced clandestine operator. What is most peculiar about these actions was that headquarters officers, holding important managerial responsibilities and indoctrinated into all manner of highly secret projects outside the operational theatre were deployed into the field in roles more appropriate to junior officers, a serious risk not only to security but to the administrative effectiveness of the SIS London HQ. D/WP would also play a central role in the ill-fated paramilitary programme in Albania.

The post-war brief for SOE was also to have included training officers in special operations, and the development of special equipment (items b and c of the SACSEA briefing). Here, SOE's plans for the future converged with those of SIS, as the latter had been moving increasingly throughout the war towards SOE-style training of its agents and the use of special equipment along the lines of the so-called 'Q devices' pioneered by SOE and MI9. This even involved sharing some of its technical development work with SOE and having its own agents trained at SOE Special Training Schools.[157] Thus, a major aspect of SOE's post-war survival as a part of the SIS took the form of the Training and Development Directorate, which brought SOE and SIS technical and training facilities together. After the war, John Munn, SOE's head of training, became a junior director, as Head of Training and Development (H/TD; he was probably later promoted to full director as D/TD).[158]

With the end of the war, one officer interviewed recalled, that there was a sense in Broadway that all of the operational experience accumulated by SOE should not be lost.[159] With this as well as the wartime lesson of the need for comprehensive training, SOE's training assets were used to form the basis of a new Training Section, which would be based chiefly at Fort Monkton, near Gosport. There has been a considerable amount of criticism of the training programme at Fort Monkton during the first years after the war. Experienced officers were recalled from stations abroad to undergo a sort of educational retrofit, leading to some rather bemused recollections. Verrier has noted how 'Post-war entrants into SIS... found themselves trained, rather haphazardly, for tasks ranging from agent running on classic intelligence lines to planning "an opposed river crossing" as so many had done in the war.'[160] One officer interviewed recalled 'crawling through the Hampshire countryside, blowing up trains on a length of disused railway track', and another officer with SIS from before the war complained that the training that the new section was providing was ill-suited to the needs of SIS officers, being concentrated on special operations rather than agent-running.[161] Likewise, the post-war P1 Desmond Bristow recounts how, in March 1950, at a 'turreted mansion in Hampshire', he and other officers 'carried out night landings in rubber boats, learned how to use explosives, and the destructive power of two gallons of petrol. We were receiving lessons on wartime special operations'.[162] This seems to indicate that the course which experienced officers were called back to take was specifically designed to augment their practical intelligence-gathering experience with special operations capabilities.

SIS training was not, however, confined to wartime SO techniques and from spring 1946 experienced SIS and SOE agent runners were being called back to the Training Section to train new recruits in handling human sources.[163] Anthony Cavendish has provided the only published account[164] of those early years of the conventional espionage side of SIS training:

> I was sent on an intelligence course, known as the General Trade Craft Course, which lasted eight weeks. It was held in an old building in Palace Street. ... Our course director... explained that we were divided into syndicates and that in the various coming exercises the syndicates would be pitted against each other. ... Some of our exercises involved shadowing or being shadowed through the streets of the West End... There were also exercises in making contact with an 'agent' at a given rendezvous and at a given

time with necessary recognition signals and passwords. . . . We had long lectures on famous examples of agent handling and innumerable discussion sessions in which problems were raised and we were invited to solve them.[165]

Cavendish adds that most of the techniques employed 'had not changed much since they were used for wartime SOE meetings'. Both Fort Monkton and the General Trade Craft course were used to train officers from allied services, and agents due for infiltration such as the C/NA's Latvians.[166]

At the end of the war, SOE had possessed sizeable stocks of portable transceivers, weapons and so forth, all of which passed to SIS.[167] SOE had also convened a Scientific Advisory Committee, composed of Sir Edward Appleton and the Scientific Advisers from the Admiralty, Ministry of Aircraft Production, and Ministry of Supply, to 'concentrate on research for special operations equipment, dealing primarily with wireless, sabotage equipment and weapons'.[168] Gubbins proposed to C that the Scientific Advisory Committee 'should continue as the scientific advisors to the Combined Secret Service, and that the Research Establishment for peace-time (two scientific superintendents, three assistant superintendents and suitable staff plus laboratories, etc.) could also cover all the requirements of the SI [Secret Intelligence] Branch'.[169] This it might have done, but not as Gubbins envisaged, for after the 1946 amalgamation, SOE's technical facilities were to be asset-stripped just as its operational resources had been, and then combined with the SIS's remaining technical support departments, such as Technical Aids and Docs,[170] into a single Technical Section, its head designated H/Tech[171] and answering to H/TD. H/Tech's staff was headquartered in Artillery Mansions (near Westminster Hall), where technicians and craftsmen manufactured such items as 'false passports, identity cards and ration books; secret compartments built into suitcases, torches and cigarette lighters; and places for cameras and microphones in boxes and cases which the enemy might never suspect'.[172]

During this first decade of the Cold War, the SIS also consulted regularly with scientists outside the intelligence community, one such example being the annual Colemore Committee meetings in which 'once a year MI6 invited a dozen top scientists from outside the secret world into a safe conference room in Carlton House Terrace' where the Security Service also participated.[173] However, even though the SIS possessed its own specialist technical facilities, it was often forced to

209

bring in outside support, on certain large-scale technical jobs, such as the tunnelling operations in Vienna and Berlin, which were mounted on the basis of technical skills provided by the GPO's Experimental Unit at Dollis Hill.

IMPROVISATION AND ADAPTATION FOR A NEW KIND OF WAR

Military planning tends to be based on the war most recently fought, and the SIS's programme of reform and reorganization was likewise geared towards repairing the failings of the Second World War.

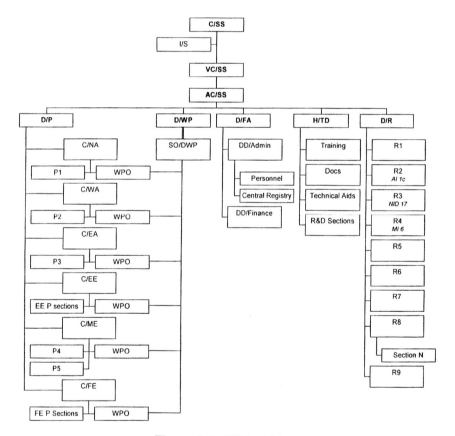

Figure 5.1: SIS in 1946

However, the Cold War was to prove a very different kind of conflict. It was an increasingly technology-intensive conflict, and one where the participants were locked into a balance of terror that had no parallel in the previous experience of international relations. Even the sabre-rattling years and the naval arms race prior to the First World War and the pandemic fear and certainty of an imminent and devastating general war in Europe pales in comparison with the geopolitical stand-off, nuclear arms race and fear (and in all too many people's minds, an almost pathological certainty) of a global thermonuclear holocaust. Today, more than a decade later, half a generation of adults have matured without the ambient and pervasive daily fear of nuclear war, between six and twenty minutes away, with no recourse, no protection and no hope. It is at least as impossible for those who lived through the Cold War to express to the young adults of today the miasma of dread that overhung two generations of humanity as it is for those who lived through the privations of the Second World War to impart their experience to the Cold War youth who lived out their years of dread in the lap of unprecedented luxury. When examining the development of the SIS during these years, therefore, it is important to keep in mind that the intelligence agencies of this era were in many respects front-line combatants in a conflict frozen by the danger of escalation and catastrophe. SIS structural changes tended to reflect a number of factors from fine-tuning the 1946 reforms through Foreign Office demands for increased control to finding new ways to spy across the raked minefields, barbed wire and ranked, poised armies along the Iron Curtain.

By 1948, what one SIS officer described as the 'experiment' of having a 'global controller' in the form of D/P was 'deemed a failure'.[174] Certainly, Menzies had repeated his ill-fated wartime pattern of assigning two deputies beneath him, improved, on the one hand by establishing a clear seniority of VC/SS over AC/SS, while worsening it, on the other hand, by bringing in two outsiders. He had also interposed three levels of hierarchy between himself and the Controllers seeking to clear operations, while retaining the ethos of informality and direct access to C for senior officers. On the basis of interviews, Tom Bower has suggested that the Area Controllers were routinely bypassing AC/SS Easton in getting their operations authorized; instead, they 'preferred to obtain approval for their activities directly from "C" or occasionally from his Vice-Chief, Sir

John Sinclair. ... [their] refusal to consult Easton was not sinister but merely a habit of confining secrets to the family circle.'[175] Bower may even be overestimating the role of secrecy in the process; a request for clearance taken up with D/P or AC/SS would still require C's ultimate approval. Just as the layers of controllers and P sections seemed unnecessary duplication to some officers, so the additional strata of senior direction must have seemed even more so. In another quarter, just as the layers of hierarchy were multiplying, so also was the number of Controllers answering to D/P. By 1948, there were eight: C/NA, C/WA, C/EA, C/ME, MEC, C/FE, FEC and C/PR; of these, MEC and C/ME had overlapping jurisdictions, as did C/FE and FEC. As a result, by 1948, the posts of D/P and D/R were both abolished, Production was subordinated to VC/SS and Requirements to AC/SS, and Production was reorganized on a regional level above the Area Controllers through a small number of Chief Controllers.

Under the new arrangements, there were three Chief Controllers who oversaw seven of the eight Area Controllerates, with C/PR continuing to deal with the UK, Soviet bloc and the western hemisphere on an equivalent footing to the three Chief Controllers. Kenneth Cohen, who had been Director Production, was 'promoted sideways' to become Chief Controller Europe, overseeing C/NA, C/WA and C/EA; C/ME and MEC were both subordinated to a single Chief Controller Mediterranean, John Teague; and C/FE and FEC were placed under the Chief Controller Pacific, James Fulton.[176] In the absence of a single Director of Production, the practice was for the Chief Controllers to attend the weekly Directors' Meeting.[177] Even the VC/SS-AC/SS arrangement proved relatively short-lived: when Menzies finally retired in 1952, Sinclair became C and Easton became his deputy as VC/SS but was not replaced as AC/SS. Instead, the post of Director of Requirements was reinstituted and, by the beginning of 1954, it was held by George Kennedy Young, formerly MEC in Cyprus.[178]

In the field, the problem of running agents in the very hard target of the Soviet bloc states meant that alternative methods had to be investigated, and chief among those proved to be tapping telephone landlines in hostile territory. The prospect of the SIS mounting local technical operations, particularly intercepting landline communications, was not a phenomenon only of the increasingly high-tech Cold War. Just prior to the outbreak of the Second World War, the agency had received a requirement to tap into telephone communications

Major General Sir John 'Sinbad' Sinclair
(right, with General Mark Clark)

between Molotov and von Ribbentrop during the negotiation of the Non-Aggression Pact.[179] Typically, such operations were mounted under a version of the Third-Country System where the target's line would be attacked where it passed through a neutral or allied country, and even then the station would employ its role as liaison to secure the cooperation of the host country's security services.[180] No such contact with foreign local authorities was required in the British Zone of Vienna and the Western zones of Berlin where the largest scale landline intercept operations of the early Cold War took place.

In 1949, Peter Lunn, at the Vienna Station, is reported to have noticed from one of a 'pile of reports from a source in the Austrian Post, Telegraphs and Telephone Administration ...that a number of telephone cables, requisitioned by the Soviet Army and linking their HQ with several units, airfields and establishments in their zone of occupation, ran through the British and French sectors of Vienna.'[181] The resulting scheme involved running a six-metre-long tunnel from a nearby British military police post to the cable. An engineer was brought in from the GPO Experimental Station at Dollis Hill to develop the technical specifics of tapping the cable, and a commercial mining consultant was brought in to dig the tunnel and the chamber at the end where the actual tap would be attached. Lunn approached his seniors at Broadway for, and received, clearance and funding for this first tunnelling operation, code-named CONFLICT.[182] However, the operation was viewed as being so potentially contentious that, while the British Head of Mission, Sir Harold Caccia was informally briefed (and gave his equally informal approval) no formal request for Foreign Office approval was made either by the station or the embassy.[183] CONFLICT was so successful that two subsequent taps, SUGAR and LORD were undertaken, the former from underneath a British-run jewellery store and the latter from a villa in Vienna's suburbs occupied by a British Army major and his wife.[184] The Service Branch consumers were extremely pleased by the volume of intelligence taken from the three taps,[185] and so, by the time the Foreign Office became aware of CONFLICT, SUGAR and LORD not only were they *fait accompli* but they also had powerful political support from SIS's consumers in the Service Branches.

CONFLICT produced such a huge volume of raw product, *en claire* for the most part but also mainly in Russian, that it completely overwhelmed the capacity of the Vienna Station and SIS HQ to process it. The initial thought was to have Section N, already processing MI5 embassy wiretaps for anything of SIS interest, take on

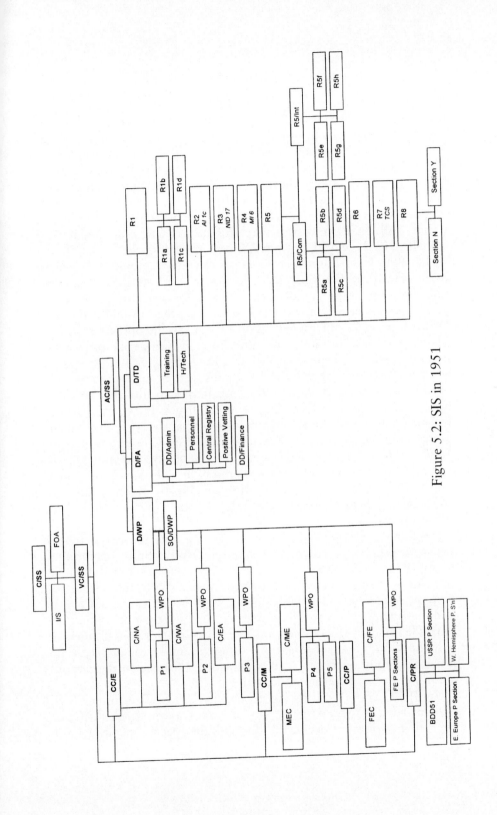

Figure 5.2: SIS in 1951

the task of translating and collating the product. Section N was, however, judged too small, and was at the time located in quarters at the head office which would not permit ready expansion.[186] As a result, a new unit, Section Y, was set up in more extensive facilities at 2 Carlton Gardens.[187] Section Y consisted of several sub-sections dealing with transcription, translation and interpretation, respectively, and in the latter capacity Y Section officers liaised directly with the R Sections receiving the product. Section Y eventually came to process virtually all of the clandestine wiretap product being generated by SIS anywhere in the world, not just Vienna's three tunnels.[188]

In 1953, Peter Lunn was posted to Olympic Stadium as the new Berlin Head of Station, and once there decided that a similar tunnelling operation could be undertaken to attack telephone lines under the Soviet Sector. By 1953, of course, the SIS had a Foreign Office Adviser (see below) at Broadway and so the operation had to be cleared at that level by the Foreign Office before being implemented.[189] The new operation, STOPWATCH-GOLD, was so sizeable and expensive that the Americans were brought in to provide resources and to carry some of the cost. It appears also that cost was not the only factor. According to John Bruce Lockhart, another reason for bringing the Americans in was that the most convenient point from which to run the new tunnel was in the American Sector.[190] However, although George Blake may have blown the Berlin operation to the Soviets from its inception, he did not join Section Y until 1953 (after his incarceration in North Korea), and so CONFLICT, SUGAR and LORD had nearly four years to run uncompromised in Vienna.

Section Y, although quite sizeable by the time the Berlin tunnel began to generate product, was, like the D/WP, not an operational entity. It existed purely to process the product of the tunnelling operations while operational control rested with the Heads of Station, Area Controller (both operations were under P3 and C/EA) and the Anglo-American committee coordinating the operation. Like War Planning, it functioned on the basis of horizontal lines of communication and coordination, although, unlike the D/WP, it did not originate projects but merely provided a service to the various controllerates and consumer departments.

In 1949, War Planning was to change hands. The former SOE Balkans hand, C.M. ('Monty') Woodhouse, was approached to take over the position but declined.[191] Instead, the special operations arm was passed to Harold Perkins, formerly head of the SOE Polish Section, and apparently involved in Mediterranean operations against Jewish terrorist groups during the closing years of the British mandate in Palestine.[192] Under Perkins, War Planning became directly involved in paramilitary operations intended to destabilize, and, if possible, cause the collapse of, Enver Hoxha's regime in Albania in close cooperation with the American Office of Policy Coordination. The matter of the origin and political clearance of the paramilitary operations in Albania has been a debatable question for years. In the perceptions of SIS personnel at the time, the programme had the personal blessing of the Labour Foreign Secretary, Ernest Bevin.[193] However, Richard Aldrich has located documents suggesting that Foreign Office enthusiasm was limited and short-lived, and while Bevin shared the US conviction that it might be desirable to 'make trouble for the Albanian regime', he also suspected that the situation lacked plausible candidates for a substitute government.[194] Nonetheless, Ivone Kirkpatrick on the Foreign Office Russia Committee was favourable towards what he described as creating in Albania much the same conditions as those achieved by the Soviets in Greece.[195]

In the event, the actual operational phase of the Albanian programme, code-named VALUABLE by the SIS, amounted to little more than a reconnaissance by native Albanians to assess the prospects for a more thoroughgoing campaign of destabilization.[196] To this end, War Planning brought David Smiley back, an experienced Balkans and Far East SOE operator, to set up a training school in Malta for the recruits.[197] According to Smiley, 'the course consisted in weapon training with pistols and submachine guns, wireless and PT [physical training]', the wireless procedures using a version of the SOE wartime B2 portable transceivers.[198] After infiltration of the agents by motor fishing vessel, Smiley set up a wireless base on Corfu, while relocating to Athens to supervise the operation and the return of the agents across the border.[199] Once the 20 agents surviving of the original 24 had been accounted for, the Athens and Corfu facilities were shut down and Smiley returned to his regiment.

The events and subsequent collapse of VALUABLE have been told at length in several places,[200] but the *organizational* aspects of the operation require closer inspection. Specifically, the operation was unusual in that it was mounted directly under the auspices of War Planning rather than under the direction of the relevant Area

217

Controller. To be sure, the Athens station was indoctrinated and provided facilities in Greece as staging points from which the motor fishing vessels (MFVs) could operate and finance for the MFVs and their crews, as well as serving as the local headquarters for controlling the debriefing of the agents once exfiltrated.[201] However, this work was conducted under the authority of the D/WP, rather than the Middle East Controller. This was a significant shift away from the D/WP's intended function as a body to lay down and coordinate stay-behind and resistance programmes implemented by Production or the SAS.

By 1951/52, as one officer interviewed recalled, the failures of VALUABLE had left the D/WP in very bad odour.[202] The American side of the operation, which had continued long after the British reconnaissance had established the firm foothold held by the Hoxha government and the Albanian secret police, the Sigurimi, resulted in an embarrassing and public failure.[203] While the Korean War had brought expectations of an imminent general war with the USSR and war-planning work to a fever pitch, by the end of that conflict the threat of immediate war had receded considerably, and the D/WP was seen as surplus to requirements and was quietly phased out.[204] This does not mean that war-planning work was discontinued; in a pattern which would be reflected in other specialist fields such as local technical operations and covert action, the locus of war planning shifted to the Area Controllers, and the work was planned and implemented on a strictly geographical basis.[205] Indeed, so much of the bulk of war planning and special operations work in general was conducted on a controllerate basis that the ultimate demise of the D/WP in the wake of the Korean War seems to have made very little impression on the officers dealing with it.[206]

Why D/WP became directly involved in VALUABLE is far from clear. The operation was confined to a single theatre, and so would not have required operational coordination above the level of Area Controller, let alone regional Chief Controller. Thus, it remains something of a mystery why things happened the way they did. It may be something of a social scientific conceit to look too deeply for a structural cause; personality may here be explanation enough. It could simply have been Perkins's nature to want to be directly involved in the operational side of things, rather than delegating and awaiting telegrams. Certainly, the very flat personnel hierarchy and the informal arrangements which still prevailed at Broadway would have permitted his participation, and the Foreign Office would not begin tightening its control of SIS operational details until three years after the Russia Committee instigated VALUABLE.[207] There is no reason to conclude that Perkins's and War Planning's direct involvement in VALUABLE was a factor in its downfall, and the downfall of the D/WP. Rather, the chief difficulty with VALUABLE was that it had been penetrated so extensively at all levels from the training camps to the joint US–UK committee coordinating the affair.[208] While such a public failure may have contributed to the political vulnerability of the D/WP within Whitehall, the main reasons for the D/WP's quiet disappearance more probably lay in a waning enthusiasm in British foreign policy circles for paramilitary special operations in peacetime. No doubt, this was partly because of a diminished sense of immediate threat, as suggested by a number of the officers interviewed,[209] but, perhaps more crucially, as Richard Aldrich has argued,[210] because the detonation in 1949 of the first Soviet atomic bomb had raised the stakes of armed confrontation, clandestine or otherwise, above what the Foreign Office considered an acceptable level of risk.

Although Philby would not come under suspicion for some time, the progressive discovery and exposure of Soviet agents following the detonation of Russia's first atomic bomb in 1949 set into motion a succession of reforms within the SIS security and counter-intelligence system, in concert with a broader concern about security in the British government. The 1949 bomb test may have put paid to schemes such as VALUABLE and the Directorate of War Planning, but it also sowed the seeds for the creation of a full Directorate of Counter-Intelligence and Security (today's Directorate of Security and Public Affairs). The first step was the adoption of a more rigorous system for positively vetting applicants, and monitoring serving SIS personnel. As we have already seen, SIS had set up a security section within Section V in 1943, which, by late 1944, had been carved out and placed directly under the auspices of Valentine Vivian, formerly Deputy Chief of Service, and now 'promoted sideways' to head the section as Inspector of Security (I/S).[211] Despite these improvements, one of the most devastating penetrations of the SIS was already in place in the form of Philby, with his colleagues Donald Maclean and Guy Burgess in the Foreign Office, John Cairncross at the Treasury and (although he was cycled out after the war) Anthony Blunt in MI5 making up the rest of the 'Cambridge spy ring'. The net was already closing in on the 'Ring of Five' because of information provided by the GRU cipher clerk Igor Gouzenko, who had defected in Ottawa in September 1945, and on the progress made on the VENONA breaks. Gouzenko had given evidence during his debriefing that a colleague in the Ottawa *rezidentura* had told him that there was a Soviet source code-named 'Elli' in 'Five of MI'. According to Jack Easton, then AC/SS, in an interview with Anthony Cave Brown:

> 'C' kept at it. He told me about it [Elli] at our first meeting and raised it with me regularly afterwards. Since Colonel Vivian was the chief of internal security I raised 'Elli' with him and Vivian responded that 'he had his best man on it'. When I asked who that best man was I was given the name of Philby. I then called Philby to my office and asked what he was doing about 'Elli'. Philby then replied that *he* had *his* best man on the job. This proved to be Philby's closest friend and deputy in counter-espionage, Tim Milne. I saw Milne and he was fairly consistent in the view that the suspect was not in SIS at all but in the Security Service. 'C' shared that suspicion.[212]

Also in September 1945, Philby managed to foil the defection of Konstantin Volkov, who had indicated in his contact with the Istanbul Station before Philby's arrival that there was an NKVD source 'fulfilling the duties of a Head of Department in British Counterintelligence'.[213] As head of counter-espionage, Philby promptly flew down to deal with the situation, having also tipped off his Soviet controllers about Volkov's approach to the SIS. Meanwhile, the pursuit of the other sources identified by Gouzenko continued, in particular 'Homer', a senior Foreign Office official. Robert Cecil notes that 'By April, 1951, all other candidates for the unenviable role of "Homer" had been eliminated and the finger was pointing unmissably to Maclean',[214] and, consequently, both Maclean and his 'evil genius', Guy Burgess, disappeared on or around 26 May 1951.

The Americans had already been pressuring a resistant UK government to adopt positive vetting in the wake of Klaus Fuchs's exposure, and the Burgess and Maclean defection prompted the Americans to press for a new tripartite conference on security, at which they again pressed for the Attlee government to adopt the practice. Shortly before it was voted out of office, in October 1951, the Attlee Cabinet accepted positive vetting 'in principle', but it was not until the second Churchill government that positive vetting was introduced in January 1952.[215] By this time, the suspicions raised by Philby's connections with the absconded Burgess and Maclean had led to his dismissal from the SIS.

The adoption of general positive vetting by the UK government was reflected in the SIS in the form of a new Positive Vetting (PV) section. PV consisted of a small staff, probably no more than four or five officers, whose task was to positively vet the SIS staff list, each member of the agency as well as new recruits. It would proceed down the staff list 'until they reached the end, and then they would start again'.[216] This constituted a significant change from the previous tradition of the much simpler 'negative vet' in which the SIS and the Security Service consulted their records to make sure the prospective employee had never been investigated or fallen under suspicion in the past. It took the shock of the Burgess and Maclean defection, however, to force not merely the SIS but the UK government at large to pay the monitoring costs necessary to ensure security.

Despite the progressive tightening of security and vetting procedures, SIS managed to make a blunder in 1953 which completely dwarfed the recruitment of Kim Philby: the re-employment of George Blake after his internment by the Communist North during the Korean War. According to Blake, it was during his imprisonment that he was converted to communism (although he suggests that his first exposure to its ideas had actually been Carew-Hunt's R5 booklet on communism). Once returned to the UK, Blake was interrogated by SIS officers in Room 070 at the War Office to assess whether he could safely be returned to duty at Head Office. Blake notes that the interrogation was of a 'purely formal character and directed towards our identities and official functions', and by the second day of questioning turned away from security issues to become an intelligence debriefing of Blake and his colleague from the Seoul Station who had also been taken captive, Norman Owen. At the end of the second day of questioning, Blake was invited to return to Broadway buildings to report to 'the Far East Section', which had controlled the Seoul station. Blake remarks that he even found himself 'for a short while, a bit of a celebrity'.[217] 'Brainwashing' may have been little known in those days, and the 'Stockholm syndrome' would not enter common parlance for nearly 20 years, yet the willingness to return Blake to operational duty – on as sensitive a post as Section Y to boot – after nearly two years in enemy hands seems at best ill-considered. There was, perhaps, a precedent for such things in the posting of wartime escapers such as James Langley, Airey Neave and Donald Darling to posts within the SIS. As a result, posting Blake back to secret work may not have been quite as acutely naive as it may appear in retrospect. Nonetheless, during the next seven years, Blake would come to compromise whole areas of the SIS's efforts against the Soviet bloc.

A developing issue during the 1950s was that of the Foreign Office's desire for increased control, or at least oversight, of SIS operations abroad. Under the 1946 reforms, the SIS's operational work remained intimately tied to the demands of its consumers through what was still essentially a version of the 1921 arrangement, but the Foreign Office was still concerned that military or naval requirements could run counter to or endanger diplomatic relations with both target and host countries. Beyond the consumer liaison machinery, the Foreign Office had been without a supervisory presence at Broadway since the end of the war. In August 1946, Robert Cecil, the SIS's second PA/CSS was reassigned without replacement at the same time as SIS was implementing its reorganization, Section IX under Philby was poised to absorb Section V as R5, and as the first resistance organizations were being recruited and installed behind what would become the Iron Curtain. It was, as Cecil himself has observed, 'a bad moment at which to relax FO supervision over the SIS'.[218] Moreover, with David Footman's departure to Oxford, R1 came to be headed by a succession of career SIS officers, loosening Foreign Office influence still further. As a result, when Sir Patrick Reilly, the first PA/CSS, returned to the intelligence community as Chairman of the JIC in 1950, he took the measure of reinstituting a Foreign Office attachment to Broadway, this time in the form of a Foreign Office Adviser (FOA).[219]

Geoffrey McDermott, who served as FOA from 1956 to 1958, has described the role of the FOA in considerable detail. Writing in 1971, he recalled: 'The chain of command in [SIS] head office has always gone up through the ranks of the SIS via the Foreign and Commonwealth Office adviser, who will consult FCO departments as necessary, to C, who with the agreement of his adviser will submit his plans and ideas to the deputy undersecretary responsible for all intelligence and strategic matters in the FCO.' Subsequently, the FOA could 'either approve the project, or consult yet higher authority in the shape of the Permanent Under-Secretary or the Secretary of State'.[220] In practice this would mean referral up through the Deputy

Under-Secretary who served as head chairman of the Permanent Under-Secretary's Department (PUSD) and chairman of the JIC in the first instance. The PUSD was a department created *circa* 1948 to coordinate intelligence and covert political action under FO supervision, although given the SIS's role in providing covert capability in support of most such operations it is not surprising that as Richard Aldrich has recently observed, 'The term PUSD itself was considered secret and was often used as a cover-name for SIS.'[221]

McDermott, however, proved to be sanguine about SIS stations occasionally indulging in unauthorized operations on the grounds that although SIS officers in the field 'have direct contact with their head office in London...they would be saints rather than human beings if, in the occasional burst of inspiration or exasperation with officials, they did not employ a little private enterprise'.[222] In any event, Foreign Office clearance was necessary only at a relatively general level. McDermott notes that SIS operational methods 'should...have the broad approval of the FCO as regards their political implications, though obviously details are left to the experts of the SIS'.[223] For example, while the Foreign Office would have to clear a programme of clandestine border-crossings, clearance would not have to be sought for each individual infiltration.[224] Thus, while the FOA provided a general mechanism to restrain SIS actions, its primary concern was avoiding unnecessary risk and keeping operations in conformity with national policy. Naturally, Foreign Office intervention in SIS activities was not universally welcomed, and one SIS officer complained bitterly that the FOA had once flatly refused to clear a proposed *coup d'état* in one particularly ruthless Third World dictatorship when the opportunity had presented itself during the 1960s.[225]

Within a year after establishing the FOA, SIS would become embroiled in the largest political action in its history. Ironically, this would occur under circumstances that rendered the system all but academic. This is because in late 1951 the agency would find itself tasked to overthrow a foreign government – by the Foreign Office itself.

While wartime special operations may have fallen by the wayside during the late 1940s and in the wake of VALUABLE and with a Russian nuclear capability raising the stakes of armed confrontation above acceptable levels, SIS had throughout this period been involved in political actions which did not require a paramilitary dimension.

223

The convening of the Russia Committee in the Foreign Office in 1948 had from the very beginning taken propaganda as being one of the primary tools of any political conflict with the Soviet Union.[226] The Information Research Department (IRD) had been set up in the Foreign Office to produce white and grey propaganda, but black work was not within the IRD brief.[227] Black propaganda and clandestine contacts with dissident and opposition groups fell within the SIS ambit, just as during the war when Gambier-Parry's 'Research Unit' transmitters carried the PWE's notionally German *Soldatensender Calais*[228] and Section D aided Contentinental dissidents. The role of political action was, however, far more deeply interwoven into SIS operational practice than simply overseeing the sort of vehicles of influence and deceptive action that the IRD preferred to remain above.

After the absorption of the SOE, the SIS had developed a new doctrine in which networks could, in principle, serve double or triple duty as intelligence networks, agents of political influence, and, in some cases, potential stay-behinds or resistance cells.[229] More generally, SIS agents and networks were viewed simultaneously as intelligence and political assets. Any agent well enough placed to provide high-grade information would, almost by definition, be so placed as to exert a high degree of personal and institutional influence, and vice versa. As one officer interviewed put it: 'You have to understand, if we had a resource we would not hesitate to use it *operationally.*'[230] Similarly, the origins of the coup in Iran, operation BOOT, lay in a human intelligence and influence network which had been inherited by the SIS from the wartime PWE.

After the Iranian seizure of the Anglo-Iranian Oil Company (AIOC) refinery at Abadan in 1951, under National Front Prime Minister Mohammed Mossadeq, the initial response by the Foreign Secretary, Herbert Morrison, in September of that year was to propose direct use of force. Fearing a negative US response to such an action, the Attlee Cabinet rejected this route, and instead the British withdrew from the oil fields.[231] As an alternative to the traditions of gunboat diplomacy, the Foreign Office elected to galvanize opposition to Mossadeq through a campaign of political influence spearheaded by Robin Zaehner, late of the PWE, who had retained contact with a family of wealthy merchants, the Rashidian brothers, known collectively within the SIS simply as 'the Brothers'.

The Rashidians had been Zaehner's contacts during the war, but while most wartime anti-Nazi networks had been stood down after the war, the Rashidians had kept theirs intact.[232] In practice, the Rashidians were treated as a network supported by the SIS Tehran Station. C.M. ('Monty') Woodhouse, who took over as Head of Station in August 1951, describes his Station's resources as 'considerable', although they were on a far smaller scale than the 100-man Berlin Station or even Horseferry Road's 20 officers. In August, the Tehran Station included 'three or four able young men in the Embassy who specialized in intelligence on Iran and the Communists', one who 'cultivated contacts with leading Iranians who were hostile to Mossadeq', and one more who fulfilled the traditional SIS station liaison duty 'approved by the Shah, with the Chief of the Security Police, who was well informed about the Tudeh [Communist] Party'.[233]

Having started the machinery of subversion under a Labour government, which had begun assembling a force for military intervention,[234] the Foreign Office, by the end of 1951, found itself under a new Foreign Secretary, Anthony Eden, and a newly returned Conservative government under Churchill. The Foreign Office solution, according to Woodhouse, was to pass the requirement to the SIS. The process by which this happened is far from clear; certainly, there were serious second thoughts about any effort at subversion in the Foreign Office, and Woodhouse creates the impression that he actively campaigned to have the requirement issued to the SIS rather than see the project liquidated. Among the arguments that Woodhouse recalls making was that of the danger that the British diplomatic presence might also be expelled, in which case contact would have to be maintained from abroad, the SIS's particular strength.[235] SIS capabilities and Foreign Office caution converged on this occasion, and the SIS was officially tasked with the operation.

The SIS's strategy was twofold. On the one hand, the Rashidian brothers acted to mobilize urban support, while, on the other hand, the SIS also had contacts with the weakly governed tribes in the north. The northern tribes lacked arms; therefore, in mid-1952, Tehran Station arranged with the Service attachés to secure weapons and a light aircraft to fly them to RAF Habbaniyah. Of these weapons, Woodhouse remarks, 'In the event [they] were never needed. Only one man in Iran knew where they were, and probably they were never seen again.'[236] Apart from this outbreak of SOE-style activity, BOOT remained directed at the urban political scene. As feared, a year after the subversion campaign began, on 17 October

1952, Mossadeq did indeed expel the British, including the embassy and its SIS presence, and control devolved to the Middle East Controller in Cyprus, at that time George Kennedy Young.[237] These difficulties, as well as the cost of mounting the coup, prompted the British to approach the CIA for operational back-up. The name BOOT has been described as 'unsubtle',[238] and 'rather too obvious' even by Woodhouse. However, it should be kept in mind that officers no longer assigned cryptonyms according to their fancy, but instead the cryptonyms were allocated from a random list held by the Central Registry.[239] As has been often recounted, the British sold BOOT to the Americans (who code-named it AJAX for their own purposes) on the basis of forestalling the communist Tudeh party who held rather too much sway over Mossadeq's premiership. As Foreign Secretary, Anthony Eden, proved much less enthusiastic about BOOT than his Labour predecessor, and the operation temporarily stalled in February 1953, leading the Foreign Office to propose that the brothers be strictly limited to intelligence collection.[240] Eden, however, fell ill in June, and Churchill took on the Foreign Office portfolio during his brief convalescence. Christopher Andrew has noted Churchill's persistent fascination for, and often exaggerated faith in, special operations,[241] and Woodhouse also recalls that he 'enjoyed dramatic operations', and so, during Eden's short absence, Churchill gave the final authorization for BOOT to proceed.[242]

The specifics of BOOT are a standard in the literature on post-war SIS operations, and several very thorough accounts exist of the blow-by-blow operational work of getting it done.[243] Anthony Verrier has argued in his account that BOOT represented 'the influence of the SOE and its collective penchant for political theory', which, he argues, 'was still strong in SIS'.[244] However, as is apparent from the ultimate demise of the SOE described above, and the dispersal of SOE personnel to the four corners of the Production directorate, and to peripheral directorates such as Training and Development and the (by 1953) defunct War Planning, SOE influence in the corridors of the SIS was at best tenuous. To be sure, Woodhouse was a former SOE officer, but the operation originated, not with a cabal of ex-SOE plotters, but with the post-war Labour government and the Foreign Office. Indeed, the ultimate authority which saw Mossadeq under house arrest by December 1953, and the Shah restored with bolstered, even autocratic, powers lay with the personal authority of the Prime Minister.

Woodhouse ends his 'peremptory account' of BOOT and its consequences with an account of a conversation with Macmillan, then Minister of Defence, in November 1952.

> [Macmillan] said he had heard 'vague rumours about [BOOT] before', but he did not question me on the facts. He was clearly looking to the future possibilities, and he mused aloud 'Of course, what you want is one man in charge of this sort of thing, but who is it to be? I can't see the solution yet, but I have only had three or four weeks to look around, and I'm sure there must be a solution. It's just the same whether you're building houses or whatever it is. If you want a thing done, you must make one man responsible for it and let him pull it together. You can't do it by committees.'[245]

Thinking was already going in this direction at 54 Broadway, where a series of discussions and meetings between senior officers was leading to the creation of a new section to do just that. BOOT had demonstrated what SIS could do in terms of political actions, and paved the way for SIS thinking and Macmillan's search for a 'solution' to converge on the creation of a new Special Political Action Section (SPA) in late 1953/early 1954. Since its operations were essentially *political* and concerned with foreign policy, SPA was placed under the authority of R1, and the head of R1 thereafter doubled as head of SPA as R1 *and* SPA.[246]

SPA's functions included coordinating operations originated by the Controllers, as well as originating operations itself and then approaching Controllers for assets to use operationally. Either R1/SPA or the relevant Controller could then go to the FOA to seek clearance for the operation.[247] The types of operations which fell into the SPA's ambit included those like BOOT (such as the 1958–59 failed PERMESTA rebellion in Indonesia, and the successful overthrow of the Congo's Prime Minister Patrice Lumumba in 1961), influencing elections, deceptive actions, black propaganda, and any other such uses of SIS agents 'operationally'. SPA was also the SIS's liaison with the Foreign Office's Information Research Department (IRD), which very pointedly confined itself to the tidier worlds of white and grey propaganda.[248] Thus, SPA, again, was not an operational entity, any more than Section Y or D/WP was originally, and through its direct links with the Foreign Office, firstly as an arm of R1 and secondly as the link between the SIS and the IRD, it

227

reflected once again the practice of direct tasking of SIS by its consumers. SPA was also fundamentally an organic entity, coordinating effort in diverse areas, and working on a peer-to-peer basis with the Controllerates in mounting and running political actions.

The Soviet Union's testing of an atomic bomb in 1949 also prompted a chain of events that ultimately affected R6, the Economic Intelligence Requirements section. In that year, the states of the Washington Treaty agreed upon a series of controls on the export of strategic materials to the Soviet bloc under a regime which would come to be known as the Coordinating Committee on Multilateral Export Controls (COCOM). The items covered included electrical and electronic goods, nuclear technology, metals such as copper and aluminium, and rare earths. It was in the interests of enforcing these controls that successive UK governments elected to keep the emergency wartime export control legislation, the Import, Export and Customs Powers (Defence) Act of 1939, in force.[249] In 1953, the new Director of Requirements, George Young, proposed that the SIS should develop a systematic programme of intelligence collection in support of COCOM enforcement, a project which received the codename SCRUM HALF.[250] Since 1938, Section VI, now R6, had been tasking SIS's operational side against contraband and blockade violations, and so the new Strategic Trade section was set up under R6.[251] According to Desmond Bristow, weaknesses in the Bill of Lading as a means of monitoring shipments led to an arrangement in which 'the Office [SIS] and the CIA set up agents in jobs that would enable us to monitor sea traffic as closely as possible. Once goods arrived in the country, customs officers would carry out random investigations on the receiving companies.'[252]

While having HM Customs and Excise make spot inspections on the basis of intelligence was a relatively straightforward affair, trying to halt violating shipments to the USSR from other countries was a very different matter. It was under these circumstances that the SIS station's role as liaison with the host country's security and police agencies would come into play. Provided with information from the ST section, and possibly also its own sources (duly sanitized), the station would then have to approach the local agencies and convince them to make the necessary inspection. One officer interviewed recalled that there was a very real risk of diplomatic incidents resulting when SIS stations abroad would approach the local police to intercept shipments crossing the host-nation's borders, especially when the shippers were nationals of the host country, and not the UK.[253]

1956: THE YEAR OF THE FLAP AND THE END OF AN ERA

1956 represents one of the worst single years for operational setbacks in the SIS's history; its disasters were perhaps not quite as comprehensive as the wholesale loss of foreign stations during 1940–41, but, in many respects, they were politically far more consequential. In April 1956, the C/NA's 'Forest Brotherhood' were finally exposed for what they really were, a Soviet deception;[254] the Soviets officially 'discovered' the Berlin tunnel before the world's press; and finally, and most devastatingly, came the so-called 'Frogman incident' in Portsmouth harbour. In autumn 1956, the SIS and the CIA would manifestly fail to repeat their earlier joint success of BOOT, in the ill-fated attempted coup in Syria code-named STRAGGLE[255] while still later in the year the same British foreign policies which had given rise to STRAGGLE would lead to the Suez crisis, in which it would turn out that those SIS networks and sources not interdicted by Egyptian security had been providing misleading information.[256] However, by the time momentum carried the SIS forward into the latter two crises, the April debacles had taken their toll, and in July there had been a changing of the guard at the SIS, with Sinclair dismissed and a new, external appointment to C made in the form of MI5's Director-General, Sir Dick White, supposedly to whip the SIS back into shape. A wide range of factors contributed to this succession of all too public failures, many of which have been attributed to poor SIS management and lack of accountability, but these assertions require closer inspection. It is particularly important to examine what role the 1921 arrangement had in these events, as well as the intrinsic risks of these operational failures.

Of these operational failures, the Frogman incident is of central interest not merely because it had such dire consequences for the service, but also because it intimately involved both the SIS's Requirements/Production system and its procedures for Foreign Office clearance. The operation was mounted by SIS's UK division, Controller Production Research, but it entirely bypassed BDD 51 and the UK Station.[257] According to Nicholas Elliott, who was C/PR at the time,[258] the initiative for the operation against the Soviet cruiser

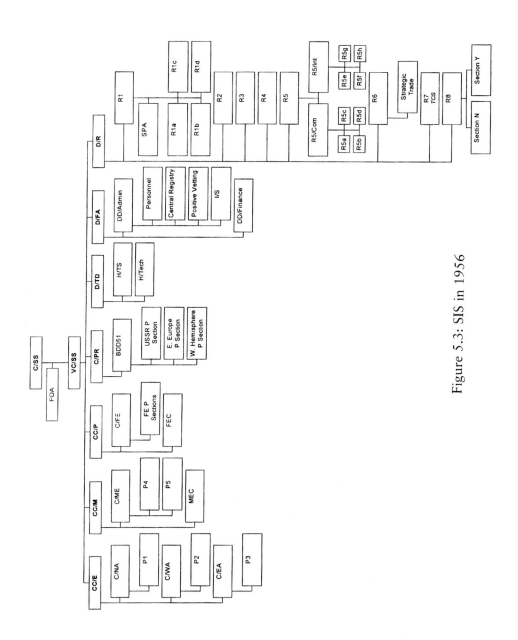

Figure 5.3: SIS in 1956

Ordzhonkidze during Khrushchev and Bulganin's state visit came in the first instance from the Navy, who issued a requirement for the dive to the SIS. Elliott asserts not only that the Navy specifically requested a dive on the grounds that they 'were anxious to find out, as a matter of high intelligence priority, about certain equipment under the stern of the ship', but also that he further sought and received 'a written assurance of the Navy's interest'.[259] It is from this point that things began to go wrong.

SIS was for the most part geared towards recruiting and running agents and mounting local technical operations (and even then it tended to have to bring in outside expertise). Putting divers in the water was more the kind of thing done by the Special Boat Service and the Royal Marine Commandos. It therefore had to bring in a diver from outside, and chose the ageing, albeit heroic, Lionel Crabb. According to Crabb's biographer, Marshall Pugh, Crabb had already undertaken a similar dive the year before under the *Ordzhonikidze*'s sister ship, the *Sverdlov*,[260] and, if so, the *Ordzhonikidze* dive could quite reasonably have been viewed as entirely feasible. However, Crabb was in late middle age, and, as is often noted, not in the best physical condition. The second problem occurred in securing clearance from the Foreign Office Adviser (FOA), Michael Williams. According to Williams's close personal friend and successor to the post of FOA, Geoffrey McDermott, on the day that he was approached to clear the dive, Williams had, 'at the end of an exceptionally hard day', just learned that his father had died. Williams is described by McDermott as being 'distraught' when he inspected the proposed operation, and approved it instead of seeking advice from the Deputy Under-Secretary as he should have done in such a circumstance.[261] In the event, something did go very wrong, as Crabb was detected beneath the *Ordzhonikidze*, leading to a serious diplomatic incident and an Exchange of Notes between the UK and Soviet governments. Crabb disappeared after his detection by the Soviets and was generally believed to have died, possibly from a heart attack, during the arduous swim around the headland. However, although the body of a decapitated frogman did indeed wash up on the British coast a year later, it was never definitively identified as Crabb.[262] During the public scandal that followed, Eden asserted that the dive had been undertaken without the knowledge of Ministers, an assertion which was true as far as it went, although technically, of course, the dive was not conducted without the knowledge of *government*, at least at the levels of the Admiralty and Foreign Office. Indeed, as McDermott noted above in his discussion of clearance procedures, Ministers would not ordinarily have needed to know about operations unless the Permanent Under-Secretary felt it necessary to refer to the Foreign Secretary after himself having been consulted by the Deputy Under-Secretary and the FOA.

In 1993, however, Nicholas Elliott himself added a surprising footnote to the Crabb affair. In his second volume of memoirs, *With My Little Eye*, he recalls that a second, unofficial dive took place under the *Ordzhonikidze*. This dive proved successful, the Royal Navy diver returning undetected, with the required pictures. The problem with the unauthorized second dive, recalls Elliott, 'was to explain how the pictures had been obtained – or not explain. And that will remain a secret.'[263]

Ultimately, if any single, specific conclusion is to be reached at this point, it is that Trevor-Roper and Verrier are in error. The reform and reorganization of SIS in 1945/46 was indeed a thoroughgoing one, albeit not without its flaws. The structure under the 1946 scheme represented both continuity and change. In the first place, the agency underwent a very real change in terms of *professionalization*, both in the ordinary and sociological terms of that word. The haphazard recruitment practices of the past were abandoned, and new recruits had to undergo training in a wide range of skills – agent running, clandestine communications and special operations – in order to gain membership of the service. The agency was also becoming far more sophisticated about technical methods, which both aided and could be aided by human sources. It did not simply abolish SOE, but absorbed that organization's collective experience to a very real degree, through officer experience in dealing with the sort of 'denied areas' that the Continent had been and Eastern Europe was to become, through the adoption of SOE training practices and infrastructure, and through SOE's openness to new technologies and the use of special equipment. The agency also developed a new operational doctrine in which human 'resources' could serve both as sources of intelligence and agents of covert action. The organization's management structure was also extensively reformed and streamlined, and, by 1948, it had resolved both the span-of-control problems which had plagued the wartime service, and dispensed with the redundant, intervening layers of upper-middle management that Menzies had repeatedly inserted between himself and his Directors and Controllers.

However, there were very real, essential, areas of continuity. The organization retained its fundamentally demand-driven 'pull' architecture, sometimes to its detriment as well as its benefit (both BOOT and the *Ordzhonikidze* dive were consumer-originated operations). The service retained the informal, horizontal lines of communication between its Production and Requirements sides which had marked the traditional relationship between the G and Circulating Sections under the 1921 arrangement. Indeed, the appointment from 1952 of the FOA to the service furthered the close link between the SIS and its consumers, and, perhaps more importantly, overall British foreign policy.

Changes to SIS's counter-espionage (CE) arrangements also represented a degree of continuity from the structures and practices of the inter-war and wartime precedent. Unfortunately, the operational conditions for CE were not as favourable as those of the Second World War, and R5 remained limited in purview and activities throughout the first decade of the Cold War. Verrier has, of course, argued that the post-war SIS viewed CE as a side-issue, subordinate to the 'robber barons' and their geographical 'fiefs', but this would hardly describe the aggressive machinery visualized by Philby, or the track records of officers holding senior positions in R5, such as Charles Ransom, Maurice Oldfield, and, the vigorous anti-communist in overt and covert life alike, Robert Carew-Hunt. The weaknesses of R5 during this first decade of the Cold War reflected more than anything else the strengths of the Soviet intelligence and security systems, as well as a pervasive slowness in the uptake of anti-communist security endemic to wartime and post-war UK government and politics. One officer interviewed observed that SIS's new generation of wartime recruits had 'cut their teeth and learned their stuff on the relatively soft target of their German equivalent',[264] the *Abwehr* being a very different calibre of adversary from the NKVD. In Philby's case, by the Cold War, he was already well in place and respected by his contemporaries and trusted by Vivian, while Blake's treason required more than a year in a North Korean prison camp to take root. Beyond strict CE effectiveness, Blake's cursory debriefing and prompt re-employment represent a failure to grasp the possible extent of brainwashing undertaken in the North Korean camps, as well as the subtler tendency of captives to identify with the captors upon whom they are dependent after a long period of confinement.

Nonetheless, the nature of the 1946 scheme proceeded, in some respects, from false assumptions. While it did indeed resolve many of the more persistent management problems, the attempt to impose a conventional bureaucratic hierarchy was ill-conceived. The need for organic management repeatedly asserted itself throughout the following decade. This need was not confined to the Production/ Requirements relationship either, but also became increasingly manifest in areas such as War Planning, Special Political Action, COCOM enforcement (ST) and CE. In the cases of War Planning, the SPA and the ST, there were economies of scale which favoured a single, central office to coordinate all the threads of stay-behind recruitment and provisioning, covert political measures or the transnational flow of information and goods generated by COCOM violations. However, in all three cases, the specialist section worked *with* Controllers and consumer sections on a virtually equal footing. Special Political Action was a particularly decentralized activity, with initiatives potentially coming from consumer departments, Controllers or the SPA itself. Within this organic arrangement, either a Controller or SPA could approach the FOA for political clearance. The demise of War Planning was more likely a consequence of the fact that a receding threat of immediate war with the USSR undercut the need for central control than a result of the failures in Albania. Stay-behind recruitment and provisioning could be devolved to the Area Controllers without loss of efficiency. The emphasis on 'horizontalism' also proved both an advantage and a disadvantage, as the reliance on a central Soviet counter-intelligence input on most operations into the Soviet bloc provided 'Kim' Philby with an overview of anti-Soviet operations, at least until 1947, a perspective he would regain as Washington liaison in 1949. Nonetheless, the emerging trend in SIS organization was the implementation of formal organic structures through the Area War Planning Officers or informal, collegial relations of coordination such as those employed by SPA and ST, all of which short-circuited the nominal hierarchy created by the 1946 scheme.

The catastrophes of April 1956 were not, for the most part, any direct consequence of SIS malorganization or malpractice. The failure of the 'Forest Brotherhood' project might, perhaps, be traced to poor inspection and oversight within the production machinery, and the FOA in 1952 had no brief for retrospective evaluation and reauthorization of operations already in play. However, to a very real degree the difficulties encountered in the Baltic States were much the same as those encountered by the SOE in The Netherlands or by the *Abwehr* everywhere during the war, that is, that a well-run double cross is a very hard thing to detect. The failure of STOPWATCH-GOLD in Berlin resulted mainly from Blake's betrayal of the SIS. Moreover, a penetration agent, once in place and supported by consistent and competent clandestine communication, like a double-cross agent, is another very hard thing to detect. Finally, the chain of errors leading to the Crabb disaster was not caused by bad procedures, or even the intrinsic unsoundness of the operation. On the contrary, similar dives had apparently worked before; just such a dive also worked subsequently, and there were strict clearance mechanisms to ensure proper political authorization for the operation that had worked in the past and yet that failed completely, for entirely unique reasons, on 7 April 1956. Nonetheless, the system *had* broken down, the government *had* been embarrassed, and someone to blame *had* to be found. Therefore, a new broom was brought in, and changes were, of course, to be expected.

NOTES

1. H.A.R. ('Kim') Philby, *My Silent War* (New York: Ballantine, 1983), p. 124.
2. For a detailed discussion of this transition in the context of the evolution of a general consumer-driven intelligence architecture in the UK government, see Philip H.J. Davies, 'Organizational Politics and the Development of Britain's Intelligence Producer/Consumer Interface', in David A. Charters, Stuart Farson, and Glenn P. Hastedt, *Intelligence Analysis and Assessment* (London: Frank Cass, 1996), p. 124.
3. Hinsley et al., *British Intelligence in the Second World War*, vol. III, part. 1 (London: HMSO, 1984), p. 472, attributed to JIC (43) 27th (o) Meeting, 25 May, 35th Meeting, 9 July, 36th (o) Meeting, 13 July, 37th (o) Meeting, 20 July.
4. Cavendish-Bentinck, quoted in Patrick Howarth, *Intelligence Chief Extraordinary: The Life of the Ninth Duke of Portland* (London: Bodley Head, 1986), p. 199. Some of the Committee's results have since been released in CAB 163/3. The author is indebted to Christopher Murphy at the University of Reading for bringing the recently released Capell-Dunn papers in CAB 163/3 to my attention.
5. This is the date suggested by Philby, *My Silent War*, p. 121.
6. Hugh Trevor-Roper, *The Philby Affair: Espionage, Treason and Secret Services* (London: William Kimber, 1968), p. 73.
7. Anthony Verrier, *Through the Looking-Glass: British Foreign Policy in an*

Age of Illusions (London: Jonathan Cape, 1983), p. 62.

8. Philby, *My Silent War*, pp. 123; Nigel West, *The Friends* (London: Weidenfeld & Nicolson, 1988), pp. 12–13; the existence and results of the Committee were confirmed by several interviewees, most significantly i-11 and i-15, although none knew any great detail about the inner workings of the committee. Documents in private possession.

9. Philby, *My Silent War*, p. 123.

10. i-20.

11. Philby, *My Silent War*, p. 123.

12. i-20. The example cited by i-020 was that of the movement of terrorist funds and related money-laundering.

13. Philby, *My Silent War*, p. 124.

14. To be quite accurate, Philby does in fact give the horizontal organization of the wartime SIS on p. 54 of his memoir, but avoids making the connection during his later discussion. Thus, as will be seen below in his discussion of the demise of Section V, the actual information is provided, thereby avoiding actual falsehood, while narrative technique and rhetorical style are employed to create a *false impression*.

15. i-15; i-17; Anthony Cave Brown, *C: The Secret Life of Stewart Graham Menzies, Spymaster to Winston Churchill* (New York: Macmillan, 1987), p. 702.

16. Philby, *My Silent War*, p. 119; i-017.

17. James Marshall-Cornwall, *Wars and Rumours of Wars* (London: Leo Cooper, 1984), p. 208.

18. 1947 Report on Intelligence Methods, pp. 7–8, ADM 223/475, PRO.

19. i-09.

20. Philby, *My Silent War*, p. 124. This description of SIS post-war organization by Philby was confirmed by virtually all of the officers interviewed, in particular and in most detail, i-08, i-10, i-15, i-09, i-11, i-19 and i-22 all confirmed specific aspects of the Philby description, i-11 noting that, in general, Philby was accurate 'as far as he goes'. Note that the existence of war planning is confirmed in David Smiley, *Irregular Regular* (London: Chatto and Windus, 1988), p. 188. Among the primary sources of his which Nigel West (Rupert Allason) made available for inspection was a US intelligence memorandum recounting a meeting between a US intelligence official code-named Saint and Valentine Vivian, in which Vivian briefs Saint on the 1946 reorganization. In this document, the Requirements Directorate is referred to as the Directorate of Requirements *and Intelligence*.

21. i-08; i-20.

22. i-09.

23. Verrier, *Through the Looking-Glass*, pp. 62–3.

24. Philby, *My Silent War*, p. 124.

25. Ibid., p. 108.

26. Robert Cecil, '"C's" War', *Intelligence and National Security*, 1, 2 (April

1986), pp. 176–7; Cecil, 'Five of Six at War', *Intelligence and National Security*, 9 , 2 (April 1994), pp. 350–2; E.D.R. Harrison, 'Some Reflections on Kim Philby's *My Silent War* as a Historical Resource', in Richard Aldrich (ed.), *Intelligence, Defence and Diplomacy: British Policy in the Post-War World* (London: Frank Cass, 1994).

27. Agent motivation is the critical matter in recruiting networks, and agents who might be committed operators against fascism and Axis occupation might feel no great desire to spy against communism or their post-occupation governments. See, for example, Hans Nutt's *Escape to Honour* (London: Hale, 1985), which is the memoir of a German recruited by SIS during the war who turned down the agency's request that he remain an informant after the war.

28. Philby, *My Silent War*, pp. 108–9; Desmond Bristow, *A Game of Moles: The Deceptions of an MI6 Officer* (London: Little Brown, 1993), p. 171.

29. Anthony Cavendish, *Inside Intelligence* (London: Collins, 1991), p. 41; i-010.

30. i-17.

31. Robert Cecil, 'The Cambridge Comintern', in D. Dilks and C.M. Andrew (eds), *The Missing Dimension* (London: Macmillan, 1984), p. 180.

32. The United States Government has made VENONA materials available on-line at *http://www.nsa.gov*; for a (contested) British version of the VENONA story, see Peter Wright, *Spycatcher* (Toronto: Hodder & Stoughton, 1987), ch. 13 *passim*.

33. i-10; i-20. i-10 described R5 as mainly a 'research section' during this period, while i-20 described it bluntly as 'moribund'.

34. W.N. Medlicott, *The Economic Blockade*, vol. II (London: HMSO, 1959), pp. 628–9.

35. i-10; i-12; i-15; i-17.

36. JIC (45) 229 of 26 July 1945, in ADM 1/20088, PRO.

37. 'Organization of Scientific and Technical Intelligence'. JIC (45) 229 of 26 July 1945, ADM1/20088, PRO.

38. i-03; i-15; i-08; see also Cavendish, *Inside Intelligence*, p. 41.

39. i-15; R.V. Jones, *Most Secret War: British Scientific Intelligence 1939–1945* (London: Coronet, 1978), p. 623 (although Jones is rather vague, remarking that atomic intelligence 'would have a foothold in MI6 denied to the rest of Scientific Intelligence'); Richard Aldrich, 'Secret Intelligence for a Post-War World', in Aldrich (ed.), *British Intelligence, Strategy and the Cold War* (London: Routledge, 1993), p. 30 and footnote 74, pp. 45–6.

40. i-15 recalled R9's being 'very short-lived', and Anthony Cavendish claims that in 1948 the tube alloys function was already the role of R7; i-03 expressed a similar sentiment, but suggested a slightly later date for the absorption of R9, possibly as late as the beginning of the 1950s.

41. R.V. Jones, *Reflections on Intelligence* (London: Jonathan Cape, 1989), pp. 8–11.

42. Memorandum from Alan Lang-Brown to Chairman, JS/TIC, of 6

September 1949, TCS/441. DEFE 40/26, PRO; DSTI 101/51 of 4 March 1965. DEFE 31/45, PRO.

43. James Bamford, *The Puzzle Palace* (London: Sidgwick & Jackson), p. 335, notes that the GCHQ did not acquire its COMSEC function until absorbing the LCSA from the FCO; however, it should be noted that, according to A.G. Denniston, 'The Government Codes and Cipher School between the Wars', *Intelligence and National Security*, 1, 1 (January 1986), pp. 48–70, the CSA was, at least during the inter-war and wartime periods, under Lt.-Cdr. Travis, future Director of the GCHQ, within GC & CS.

44. i-10; i-15.

45. See Gambier-Parry's entry in *Who Was Who* (London: A & C Black, 1972), p. 410.

46. i-15.

47. 'Note on the Legality of Diplomatic Wireless', 25 September 1947, FO 850 236, PRO.

48. Ibid.

49. See, for example, Y 6772/G of 18 November 1944, and Y 7294/G of 10 December 1944, both in FO 850/244, PRO.

50. For details of the role and budgetary arrangements for the Boreham Wood factory, see unfoliated papers in T 220/120, PRO. Concerning its intelligence and security functions, see D/7999 of 22 October 1956 from Major General Scott to the Foreign Office, noting that the factory had recently acquired a development and production contract for the London Communications Security Agency (also under the Foreign Office), and that 'the factory has been kept fully occupied because...it has had many short term demands made on it arising out of the political Crisis in the Middle East'; also in T 220/120. Peter Wright, *Spycatcher*, p. 47, also says the Boreham Wood factory produced equipment for MI5, asserting erroneously that Boreham Wood was run by the SIS.

51. i-10; i-15.

52. i-15; i-10; i-20.

53. i-15.

54. George Blake, *No Other Choice* (London: Jonathan Cape, 1990), p. 10.

55. i-15.

56. Documents in possession of i-03; i-10; i-15; i-17. The Netherlands is identified as falling under C/NA from 1943 on by George Blake, *No Other Choice*, pp. 85–6.

57. Blake, *No Other Choice*, pp. 91, 96.

58. P sections identified by i-10, i-15 and i-17; i-17 seemed uncertain concerning the distinction in titles between the controllers and the P Sections, at one point claiming that P2 under C/WA was actually called PWA.

59. i-10; i-15; i-17; i-20.

60. i-10 noted that for a brief period in 1947 there were only five controllers, C/WA, C/NA, C/EA, C/ME and C/FE.

61. i-10.
62. Blake, *No Other Choice*, p. 184.
63. Ibid.; Tom Bower, *A Perfect English Spy: Sir Dick White and Secret War 1935–90* (London: Heinemann, 1995), p.159; i-09; i-11; i-15. A later example of this cross-jurisdictional work can be found in Bill Graham, *Break-In: Inside the Soviet Trade Delegation* (London: Bodley Head, 1987).
64. Bower, *A Perfect English Spy*, p. 159. Bower's material on BIN is drawn from his interviews with Nicholas Elliott, and can therefore be considered reasonably accurate on this subject.
65. i-10; i-011; i-15; i-20.
66. i-15.
67. See Cavendish, *Inside Intelligence*, p. 41; i-15.
68. i-15.
69. i-20.
70. i-10.
71. For CRPO (ME), JIC (48) 60 'Review of Intelligence Organization in the Middle East' in L/WS/1/1051; for SIS(FE) WS/7065 'Appendix A: Draft Charter for JIC(FE)' of 7 January 1948, L/WS/1/1050, both IOLR. The existence of both documents was first published by Richard Aldrich, 'Secret Intelligence for a Post-War World', in Richard Aldrich (ed.), *British Intelligence, Strategy and the Cold War* (London: Routledge, 1992), pp. 15–41.
72. i-10; i-15; i-17.
73. For the withdrawal of British forces from the 'Delta cities', to the Canal Zone, see Keith Kyle, *Suez* (London: Wiedenfeld & Nicolson, 1991), p. 21; i-010.
74. i-10; for documents concerning the redesignation of the British Middle East Officer (BMEO) to POMEF, see 'New Directive for POMEF to replace BMEO' Draft, V1052/48 of 20 September 1955, FO 371/115478.
75. For a detailed account of the development and complication surrounding the Special Commission and Commissioner-General for the UK in South-East Asia, see Tilman Remme, *Britain and Regional Cooperation in South-East Asia, 1945–49* (London: Routledge, 1995), esp. pp. 116–19.
76. Remme, *Britain and Regional Cooperation in South-East Asia*, p. 117.
77. Plus or minus the somewhat piecemeal 1945–46 demise of Force 136, the Special Operations Executive's Far East presence was primarily absorbed by the SIS (although not completely, as demonstrated compellingly by Richard Aldrich, 'Unquiet in Death: The Post-War Survival of the Special Operations Executive 1945–1951', in Anthony Gorst, L. Johnman and W. Scott Lucas (eds), *Contemporary British History 1931–1961: Policy and the Limits of Policy* (London: Pinter, 1991), pp. 193–210.
78. WS/7065 'Appendix A: Draft Charter for JIC(FE)' of 7 January 1948, L/WS/1/1050, IOLR.
79. Ibid.

239

80. Bower, *The Perfect English Spy*, p. 228; i-31; i-32.
81. I-31; i-32.
82. Bower, *The Perfect English Spy*, p. 228.
83. i-10; i-19; i-20.
84. i-15.
85. Bristow, *A Game of Moles*, p. 175; Bristow uses the early Second World War terms 'G Officer' and 'G Section' rather than P Officer/Section throughout his volume.
86. Cavendish, *Inside Intelligence*, pp. 40–1.
87. i-15 and i-09 were both very specific on the bureaucratic procedures involved. i-15 described the process of receiving an intelligence report from the station via the Central Registry, which would keep one copy in records, circulate another copy to the P Section controlling the source or operation, and send the top or action copy to the main indicated recipient, that is, to the R Officer in the case of an intelligence report, or to the controller in case of an operational matter. i-09 indicated a similar arrangement from the field station's point of view, in formulating and sending a 'source report' which summarized the product and indicated which consumer at HQ was most likely to be interested in its content.
88. i-20.
89. Bristow, *A Game of Moles*, p. 176.
90. War Office. 1947. 'Minutes of MI6 Liaison Meeting No. 22 Held at the War Office Room 218 at 1500 hrs, 4 Dec 1947', MI6/203/1353. WO 208/4749, PRO. Published in Aldrich, *Espionage, Security and Intelligence in Britain*, pp. 27–9.
91. Bristow, *A Game of Moles*, p. 176 *infra*.
92. i-15.
93. Blake, *No Other Choice*, pp. 168–9. It should be noted that the Berlin Station verged on a status comparable to the controlling stations in the Middle and Far East (CRPO and SIS/FE) as it also directly served the Germany regional JIC.
94. Bower, *A Perfect English Spy*.
95. C.M. Woodhouse, *Something Ventured* (London: Granada, 1983), pp. 110–11.
96. Geoffrey McDermott, *The Eden Legacy* (London: Leslie Frewin, 1969), p. 213; McDermott adds that one cost of this was that it 'deprived a number of keeny-beaks of one of their principal pleasures, that of counting the months till probable promotion always of course on the optimistic assumption that dear old Francis would get caught in the wrong bed once too often or lovable Ronald would drop dead'.
97. i-20; this 'first point of contact' doctrine can also be seen in the close relationship between the heads of station and local security services/secret police agencies noted by Philby, *My Silent War*, pp. 139–41 (although Philby stresses that the direct connection in Istanbul in 1946 was via

passport control); Blake, *No Other Choice*, p. 162; and Woodhouse, *Something Ventured*, p. 111.

98. John Bruce Lockhart, 'Intelligence: A British View', in K.G. Robertson (ed.), *British and American Approaches to Intelligence* (London: Macmillan, 1987), p. 44.

99. Geoffrey McDermott, *The New Diplomacy and Its Apparatus* (London: Plume, 1973), p. 142.

100. The JIC's move towards central assessment body for the War Cabinet is covered by the official history in Hinsley et al., *British Intelligence*, vol. I, p. 160.

101. Kenneth Strong, *Intelligence at the Top: The Recollections of an Intelligence Officer* (London: Giniger, 1968), p. 223; documents covering the creation, organization and work of the JIB can be found in L/WS/1/1088, IOLR.

102. i-28.

103. i-01.

104. Musson was identified as D/FA by i-10, i-15 and i-17; Cavendish refers to D/FA as the Establishments Department in his *Inside Intelligence* (p. 39).

105. i-15.

106. i-15; i-28.

107. i-11; i-15; i-17.

108. i-10.

109. Philby, *My Silent War*, p. 124; i-11 remarked that the new staffing procedures and 'handsome terms' of remuneration were major considerations in his decision to remain with the SIS after the war.

110. Cavendish, *Inside Intelligence*, p. 78.

111. Philby, *My Silent War*, pp. 71–2.

112. Wright, *Spycatcher*, p. 277; i-028. Wright's take on the SIS registry is somewhat different from that of SIS officers; he describes the resulting arrangement as a poorly collated 'mess'.

113. Cecil, '"C's" War', *Intelligence and National Security*, 1, 2 (April 1986), p. 182.

114. See, for example, Verrier, *Through the Looking-Glass*, pp. 62–3; Verrier appears rather muddled about the various 'Special' bodies, and muddles Special Operations with Special Political Action, two very different functions and departments.

115. David Stafford, *Britain and European Resistance 1940–1945: A Survey of the Special Operations Executive with Documents* (Toronto: University of Toronto Press, 1983), pp. 202–3 and Aldrich 'Secret Intelligence for a Post-War World', pp. 26–7, and 'Unquiet in Death: The Post-War Survival of the "Special Operations Executive", 1945–51', in A. Gorst, L. Johnman and W. Scott Lucas (eds), *Contemporary British History 1931–1961: Politics and the Limitations of Policy* (London: Pinter, 1991), pp. 196–9.

116. Stafford, *Britain and European Resistance*, p. 202.

117. Aldrich, 'Unquiet in Death', p. 198.
118. Cavendish-Bentinck to Lord Killearn (Cairo) and Mr Shone (Beirut), 12 June 1945, in E4569/G, FO 371/45272, PRO.
119. Killearn to Cavendish-Bentinck in E4569/G.
120. Aldrich, 'Unquiet in Death', p.198, with specific reference to the CoS study in WO 106/6024, PRO.
121. Minutes of Defence Committee DO(45) 4th Meeting of 1 September 1945, CAB 69/7 PRO, cited in Stafford, *Britain and European Resistance*, p. 203. By comparison, Richard Aldrich's work on this transitional period stresses the role of decisions taken by the CoS in January 1946 (cited below), and extracts from the diaries of Lord Alenbrooke indicate that it was 'agreed by all' that 'by amalgamating the Secret Intelligence Service with the SOE, we could provide a combined organisation which would function automatically in Peace and War' in that month. See Aldrich, 'Unquiet in Death', p. 198, and 'Secret Intelligence for a Post-War World', p. 26. Alanbrooke's interpretation of the events of January appears somewhat idiosyncratic given the evident 'paper trail' pointing to a much earlier decision at the CoS level, as well as the JIC and the Cabinet Defence Committee. Aldrich's interpretation is particularly odd since Stafford's work predates his own, and Aldrich's refers explicitly to Stafford's work and sources in his own work.
122. Stephen Dorril, *MI6: Fifty Years of Special Operations* (London: Fourth Estate, 2000), pp. 27–8, 31–3.
123. Message between two SOE officers using cryptonyms only, '6206' to 'RWX', G/170 of 15 September 1945, HS 2/269, PRO.
124. 'Minutes of the Meeting Held at "Seaspray" Bungalow at 1130 on 12 November 1945', Copy No. 3, 13 November 1945, not foliated, in HS 1/226, PRO; emphasis added.
125. 'Appendix A: Future Tasks of the SOE in South East Asia', appended to the "Seaspray" minutes.
126. Ibid.
127. 'Seaspray' minutes.
128. CoS (45) 289th meeting (not 389th, as given in Stafford, *Britain and European Resistance*, p. 277), of 27 December, 1945. CAB 79/42, PRO; emphasis added.
129. Extract from the minutes of CoS (46) 9th Meeting, which can be found, and was originally found and its existence published by Aldrich, 'Secret Intelligence for a Post-War World', p. 26, on a torn-out strip of paper eight inches wide by about two inches deep, attached to a one-inch square cover note signed by L.C. Hollis, assistant to General Sir Morley Mayne, buried in the middle of a folio with little or no bearing on SOE or SIS, located L/WS/1/970, IOLR.
130. i-20.
131. CoS (46) 58th meeting of 11 April 1946, CAB 79/47, PRO.

132. i-11.
133. 'SOE in the Far East', notes for a series of lectures by VC/SS in July 1946 in HS 7/1, PRO. The records do not indicate at which staff college Dansey gave his lectures.
134. 'The Joint Intelligence Machine: Report to the Joint Intelligence Sub-Committee' January 10, 1945, p. 18. See also JIC organisation chart given as Annex B to the report CAB 163/3, PRO.
135. Philby, *My Silent War*, p. 124; i-022.
136. Dorril, *MI6: Fifty Years of Special Operations*, pp. 32–3.
137. Smiley, *Irregular Regular*, p. 188.
138. 'SOE in the Far East' HS 7/1, PRO.
139. i-15.
140. Smiley, *Irregular Regular*, p. 188.
141. For accounts of SAS operations in support of partisans in Italy, see Charles F. Delzell, *Mussolini's Enemies: The Italian Anti-Fascist Resistance* (New York: Columbia University Press, 1988); for the Balkans, British Liaison Officer (the SAS designation for a clandestine operator aiding partisans) William Jones's memoir, *Twelve Months with Tito's Partisans* (Bedford: Bedford Books, 1946); and for operations in France, M.R.D. Foot, *Resistance: An Analysis of European Resistance to Nazism 1940–1945* (London: Methuen, 1976). A summary of SAS 'Jedburgh teams' in support of Resistance groups can also be found in the undated War Office report 'Control of Special Units and Organizations', Appendix A in WO 106/6024, PRO. Note, however, the limited reference to the Liaison Officer role in John Strawson, *History of the SAS Regiment* (London: Grafton, 1986), except for Appendix 5 which reproduces the document 'Future of SAS Troops'.
142. Memorandum by J.M. Calvert, Brigadier, Commander, SAS Troops, 12 October 1945, reproduced in Strawson, *History of the SAS Regiment*, p. 396.
143. i-22.
144. i-09; i-15.
145. A good discussion of war-planning work during this period appears in Smith, *New Cloak, Old Dagger*, pp. 117–18.
146. Paul v. Gorka, *Budapest Betrayed* (Wembley: Oak Tree, 1986). Gorka consulted with former SIS Deputy Chief George Kennedy Young in the preparation of his memoir of the Catholic Resistance (see p. x).
147. Ibid., pp. 4, 41.
148. Ibid., p. 50; during the collapse of the network, Gorka notes that the group 'had enough weapons to shoot our way across the border'.
149. Ibid., p. 48.
150. Ibid., p.47.
151. Ibid., pp. 50–1; by Gorka's estimates, the collapse of his organization resulted in 45 executions by 1955; see pp. 152–3.

152. Tom Bower, *The Red Web: MI6 and the KGB Master Coup* (London: Mandarin, 1993), p. 67.
153. Smiley, *Irregular Regular*, p. 188; *Albanian Assignment* (London: Chatto & Windus, 1984), p. 158.
154. i-22.
155. This has been suggested by West, *The Friends*, p. 33.
156. Smiley, *Albanian Assignment*, p. 158.
157. Both SIS in London and BSC sent agents to be trained at STS 101 or 'Camp X'. David Stafford, *Camp X: Canada's School for Secret Agents 1941–1945* (Toronto: Lester & Orpen Dennys, 1986), p. 201; see also Hans Nutt's account of his training by SIS in his *Escape to Honour* (London: Hale, 1985), and a similar account by Oluf Reed Olsen, *Two Eggs on My Plate: The Famous True Story of Espionage in Wartime Norway* (London: Arrow, 1966).
158. Both terms were invoked by interviewees, although H/TD appears to be the title held immediately after the war. John Munn was identified as H/TD by i-015 and i-019.
159. i-10.
160. Verrier, *Through the Looking-Glass*, p. 63,
161. i-20.
162. Desmond Bristow, *A Game of Moles*, p. 215.
163. i-15.
164. More recently, however, disaffected SIS officer Richard Tomlinson has provided a blow-by-blow account of the contemporary Intelligence Officers New Entry Course (IONEC) in his *The Big Breach* (Edinburgh: Cutting Edge, 2001), pp. 45–79.
165. Cavendish, *Inside Intelligence*, pp. 42–3; note that Cavendish then refers to it as the 'General Field Craft' course on p. 44, so it is not clear which is the correct designation.
166. i-15; Bower, *The Red Web*, pp. 143–4.
167. i-10.
168. 'Seaspray' minutes.
169. Ibid.
170. This is evidenced by the production by the 'Technical Services Division' of a forged brandy label for a bottle prepared as a gift for Oleg Penkovsky to present to his superior, General Ivan Serov, in 1962, Peter Deriabin and Jerrold Schechter, *The Spy Who Saved the World: How a Soviet Colonel Changed the Course of the Cold War* (New York: Charles Scribner, 1992), p. 228, and by Bower, *The Perfect English Spy*, p. 178.
171. According to the recollections of Peter Wright, *Spycatcher* (Toronto: Hodder & Stoughton, 1987), p. 115, the Technical Section was run by an officer designated H Tech 1, but the term 'H/Tech' is more consistent with the SIS conventions and is employed herein.
172. Bower, *The Perfect English Spy*, pp. 178–9.

173. Wright, *Spycatcher*, p. 115.
174. i-15.
175. Bower, *The Red Web*, p. 65.
176. Cavendish, *Inside Intelligence*, p. 39; i-008; i-009; i-010; 0-015. i-017 claimed that C/ME in London was actually designated DCCM, Deputy Chief Controller Mediterranean, but i-010 was certain that for the most part the title was MEC, although he did think that for a time it may have been CEM, Controller Eastern Mediterranean, responsible for the workings of P5.
177. i-08; i-015; i-017. i-17 claimed that R5 and R1 attended the director's meetings as well, but i-08 denied this, from first-hand experience. i-017 may have been thinking in terms of the Foreign Office Adviser's participation after 1952, and R5's promotion as a junior director under White; see Chapter 6.
178. This change proved one of the most difficult to ascertain. Most officers interviewed agreed that D/R had been reinstituted, but could not recall when. Many could even name former D/Rs from the 1950s and 1960s (one even held the post). George Blake, *No Other Choice*, p. 21, identifies Young as D/R during the deliberations on the Berlin tunnel in February 1954.
179. John Whitwell, *British Agent* (London: William Kimber, 1966), p. 95,
180. Blake, *No Other Choice*, pp. 13, 162.
181. Ibid., p. 8.
182. Ibid., p. 9.
183. i-15.
184. Blake, *No Other Choice*, p. 9.
185. i-15. David Stafford, in his recent *Spies Under Berlin* (London: John Murray 2002) has argued that while the FO was out of the loop, Caccia was informally briefed and approved of the operation, p. 26.
186. Blake, *No Other Choice*, p. 10.
187. Ibid., p. 12; Blake's description of Y Section was confirmed in virtually all details by i-15, a former Section Y officer. For a detailed account of life and work at Carlton Gardens, see David Stafford, *Spies Under Berlin*, pp. 58–66.
188. Ibid., pp. 13–14.
189. Ibid., p. 21.
190. Dorril, *MI6: Fifty Years of Special Operations*, p. 523.
191. Woodhouse, *Something Ventured*, p. 104.
192. Three SIS officers, i-10, i-15 and i-19, all identified Perkins as running the 'Special Operations Section' at the time of Valuable. i-10 referred to D/WP as the 'SO Section', describing its *raison d'être* as being to preserve SOE expertise. Perkins's assignment to D/WP cannot have been much earlier, as the post was occupied by Nicholson and, as noted above, it had been offered to Woodhouse in 1949. Source i-22 was queried specifically on the possibility that there existed a second section doing SO, but he rejected this

possibility because, by the nature of his position at the time, had there been such a section he is convinced he would have known.

193. See, for example, Anthony Verrier's description of events in *Through the Looking-Glass*, pp. 53–7; i-11.
194. Record of a conversation between Schuman, Dean Acheson and Ernest Bevin, cited in Aldrich, 'Unquiet in Death', p. 206 and footnote 60.
195. FO 371/71687, FO 371/77623.
196. i-22.
197. Smiley, *Albanian Assignment*, p. 159.
198. Ibid., p. 161.
199. Smiley, *Irregular Regular*, p. 192.
200. See, for example, Bethell, *The Great Betrayal*, and, of course, Philby's own account of his role in betraying VALUABLE from Washington in his *My Silent War*, pp. 159–62, Verrier's account in his *Through the Looking-Glass*, pp. 57–77, and West's account in *The Friends*, pp. 51–68. Bethell's account, like Bower's of the Baltic operations, is thoroughly researched but geared chiefly to the 'sharp end' of the operation, recounting the stories of the personnel operating in the field, with little or no detail on the SIS HQ end of things.
201. Bethell, *The Great Betrayal*, pp. 44–8; Smiley, *Irregular Regular*, p. 192.
202. i-10.
203. Bethell, *The Great Betrayal*, pp. 171–92.
204. i-10; i-15; i-19; i-20.
205. i-15; on one occasion, I was touring the Imperial War Museum's 'Secret Wars' display with one of the former SIS officers interviewed when we came upon an SIS stay-behind kit, consisting of an airtight perspex case holding (dummy) explosives, capped and sealed with aluminium. 'Oh my', he remarked, all but salivating, 'we never had anything like *that* in my day.'
206. Several officers interviewed had served on station abroad during War Planning's existence, and even served as controllers dealing with their respective War Planning officer. However, despite the day-to-day presence of D/WP's influence at both field and HQ levels of the production side's work, every single officer interviewed was singularly vague about the section's disappearance. One (i-15) was firm that it had been phased out because of the reduced risk of an immediate general war with the USSR after Korea, while i-10 remarked on its 'bad odour', and expressed a vague sense that the 'Special Operations Section', as he called it, had petered out in the early 1950s.
207. The main vehicle of this tightening was the creation of the central post of Foreign Office Adviser, responsible for reviewing and authorizing all SIS operations for political risk and consistency with UK foreign policy. For the implementation of the FOA's post, see Cecil, 'The Cambridge Comintern', p. 182, and West, *The Friends*, p. 83. To date, the most detailed published version of the FOA's job description has been provided by a former incumbent of the office, Geoffrey McDermott, in his *The New Diplomacy*

and its Apparatus (London: Plume, 973), pp. 138–42.

208. See Bethell, *The Great Betrayal, passim*, and Philby, *My Secret War*, p. 162.
209. i-15.
210. Richard J. Aldrich, 'British Intelligence and the Anglo-American "Special Relationship" During the Cold War', *Review of International Studies*, 34, 3 (July, 1998), pp. 338–40.
211. Philby, *My Silent War*, p. 118; Brown, C, p. 693; i-15; i-17; both interviewees used the title 'Inspector of Security'.
212. Quoted by Brown, C, p. 693.
213. Wright, *Spycatcher*, p. 280; similar phrasing appears in Philby, *My Silent War*, p. 126.
214. Cecil, 'The Cambridge Comintern', p. 192.
215. Peter Hennessy and Gail Brownfield, 'Britain's Cold War Security Purge', *Historical Journal*, 25, 4 (1982), p. 970.
216. i-15; the existence of PV was confirmed by i-10 and i-11.
217. Blake, *No Other Choice*, pp. 154–6. One officer during an interview commented on Blake's brief term as an in-house celebrity, 'He sat right there where you are right now. That very chair.' The author studiously remained seated, and carried on regardless.
218. Cecil, 'The Cambridge Comintern', p. 182.
219. West, *The Friends*, p. 83.
220. McDermott, *The New Diplomacy and Its Apparatus*, p. 141. This conforms to the description of the FOA's role provided by i-08, i-15 and i-19. Note that McDermott, writing in 1973, refers to the Foreign Office as the Foreign *and Commonwealth* Office (FCO), the designation applied after the FO absorbed the Commonwealth Relations Office in the mid-1960s.
221. For the development of the PUSD in detail, please see Richard Aldrich, *The Hidden Hand: Britain, America and Cold War Secret Intelligence* (London: John Murray, 2002), p. 157.
222. McDermott, *The New Diplomacy*, p. 142.
223. Ibid., p. 138.
224. i-15; i-20.
225. i-19. In this case (and the date and identity of the nation in question cannot be revealed for obvious reasons), the coup had been proposed by the area controller responsible, rather than SPA.
226. For a general study of the origins, policy and methods of the Information Research Department, see W. Scott Lucas and C.J. Morris, 'A Very British Crusade: The Information Warfare Department and the Beginning of the Cold War' in Aldrich (ed.), *British Intelligence, Strategy and the Cold War* (London: Routledge, 1993), pp. 85–107; by comparison, Lucas and Morris, Lyn Smith, 'Covert British Propaganda: The Information Research Department 1947–1977', *Millennium*, 9, 1 (Spring, 1981), pp. 67–82, is very vague on the distinctions between white, grey and black propaganda, on what is covert and what is not, and upon IRD's relationship with

Britain's intelligence machinery.

227. Propaganda can be divided broadly into three types. 'White' propaganda is information that makes no attempt to conceal or downplay its source; 'grey' propaganda is information planted with friendly but nominally independent media; and 'black' propaganda purports to be information from a source other than that from which it genuinely derives.

228. Sefton Delmer, *Black Boomerang* (London: Secker & Warburg, 1962).

229. See, for example, the discussion of the Hungarian Catholic Resistance above.

230. i-08.

231. Discussion of this Cabinet session, in particular expressions of concern that allowing Iran to escape unscathed might encourage Nasser, appears in Keith Kyle, *Suez* (London: Weidenfeld and Nicolson, 1991), pp. 8–9.

232. Woodhouse, *Something Ventured*, p. 105; Woodhouse was the Tehran Head of Station during Boot and so his version of events is a first-hand account of some value.

233. Ibid., pp. 110–11; note that the direct link with the Shah's Security Police reflects the 'first point of contact' doctrine for SIS stations abroad.

234. Ibid., p. 111.

235. Ibid., p. 112.

236. Ibid., p. 116.

237. Cavendish, *Inside Intelligence*, p. 140. Although Cavendish writes second-hand of BOOT, his portrayal of the operation evidently derived from George Young, who wrote the book's preface.

238. For example, and most recently, Christopher Andrew, *For the President's Eyes Only* (London: HarperCollins, 1995), pp. 203–7.

239. i-15.

240. Woodhouse, *Something Ventured*, p. 123.

241. Christopher Andrew, 'Churchill and Intelligence', *Intelligence and National Security*, 3, 3 (April 1988) *passim*.

242. Woodhouse, *Something Ventured*, p. 125.

243. Of these, the most thorough and informative is that given by West, *The Friends*, ch. 8, *passim*. A brief but generally accurate description appears in Verrier, *Through the Looking-Glass*, pp. 107–8. The American version of events is provided by the CIA officer involved, Kermit Roosevelt, in his *Countercoup: The Struggle for Control of Iran* (New York: McGraw-Hill, 1979). A somewhat idiosyncratic account, probably derived from Young's perceptions, appears in Cavendish, *Inside Intelligence*, pp. 139–41.

244. Verrier, *Through the Looking-Glass*, p. 107.

245. Woodhouse, *Something Ventured*, p. 133.

246. i-08; i-11. i-08 noted the relevance of BOOT in creating SPA. i-10, i-19 and i-20 all confirmed the existence and overall functions of SPA. i-19 even suggested that SPA had, during the 1960s, cultivated contacts with the British National Union of Students in order to forestall Soviet-backed operations. For an

account of Soviet-backed operations and front organizations directed at student organizations in the west see, for example, Roy Godson and Richard H. Shultz, *Dezinformatsia: The Strategy of Soviet Disinformation* (New York: Berkeley, 1986), pp. 26, 124 and *passim*.

247. i-08.
248. i-08; i-11; i-19; i-20.
249. Sir Richard Scott, *Report of the Inquiry into the Export of Defence Equipment and Dual Use Goods and Related Prosecutions* (London: HMSO, 1996), Section C 1.28.
250. i-015.
251. Bristow, *A Game of Moles*, pp. 234–9; ST's location under R6 was identified by i-15 and i-20.
252. Bristow, *A Game of Moles*, p. 236; Bristow's use of 'random' seems peculiar since the investigations were evidently intelligence-led.
253. i-15.
254. According to Bower's interview-derived account, *The Red Web*, pp. 220–39.
255. For accounts of Straggle see Anthony Gorst and W. Scott Lucas 'The Other Collusion: Operation Straggle and the Anglo-American Intervention in Syria 1955–56', *Intelligence and National Security*, 4, 3 (April 1989), pp. 576–93, and Andrew Rathmell, *Secret War in the Middle East: The Covert Struggle for Syria, 1949–1961* (London: Tauris, 1995). These two pieces link together nicely, since Gorst and Lucas detail the London/Washington end of STRAGGLE while Rathmell concentrates on Arab political participation.
256. i-15; Bower, *The Perfect English Spy*, p. 160. Judging from what could be gleaned in interviews and from McDermott's recollection of events in *The Eden Legacy and the Decline of British Diplomacy* (London: Leslie Frewin, 1969), pp. 12–30, the versions of this incident provided by both West, *The Friends*, pp. 79–86, and Bower, pp. 159–61 can be judged to be overall highly accurate.
257. Bower, *The Perfect English Spy*, p. 160; i-15.
258. i-11; i-15. Elliott refers obliquely to his posting as C/PR in his *Never Judge a Man by His Umbrella* (Wilby, Wiltshire: Michael Russell 1991), remarking on p. 171, 'On return to England in 1951 I had been given a highly interesting job but it was conditional on my living in London in circumstances in which I could entertain.'
259. Nicholas Elliott, *With My Little Eye* (Wilby, Wiltshire: Michael Russell, 1993), p. 24.
260. Marshall Pugh, *Commander Crabb* (London: Macmillan, 1956).
261. McDermott, *The Eden Legacy*, p. 129.
262. The disappearance of Crabb's body led to a succession of 'Buster' Crabb didn't-die-he-defected hypotheses, most notably in three books by J. Bernard Hutton, *Frogman Spy* (London: Neville Spearman, 1960), *Commander Crabb is Alive* (Edinburgh: Mainstream, 1968) and *The Fake Defector* (London: Howard Baker, 1970). All three books rely in common on a 'secret dossier' of

a notional interrogation of Crabb after his discovery, in which, among other things, Crabb's name is consistently misspelled, there is a photograph of a young Soviet naval officer considerably Crabb's junior but with a passing resemblance to the older man, and three very different hypotheses are proposed as to why Crabb defected. A marginally less plausible version of events is provided by W.J. and A.J. Welham in their *Frogman Spy* (London: W.H. Allen, 1990), in which they suggest that Crabb allowed himself to be captured so that he could infiltrate the Soviet navy's diving programme. Elliott, *With My Little Eye*, pp. 23–4, describes these stories as 'doubtlessly' reflecting a persistent Soviet disinformation effort, although he does not indicate whether this assertion is based on suspicion or intelligence.

263. Elliott, *With My Little Eye*, pp. 26–7. Elliott maintains, not entirely plausibly, that this second dive was undertaken by the Royal Navy diver on his own initiative, with an unidentified individual acquiring the pictures for '30/– and a large scotch', subsequently passing the results to the SIS. It is reasonable to conclude that Elliott's account represents far less than half of the complete story. Certainly, certain members of the intelligence community recall the second dive as having been properly authorized by ICHR.

264. Elliott, *With My Little Eye*, p. 12.

6

To the End of the Cold War and After, 1956–95

Above all, White was determined that a professional SIS would not be expected by Prime Ministers and Foreign Secretaries to believe, let alone do, six impossible things before breakfast.

Anthony Verrier
Through the Looking-Glass[1]

THE WHITE REFORMS

That Sir Dick White's arrival at SIS from the Security Service ushered in a period of organizational change is all but a truism in the literature on SIS. However, the form which that change took is often less than clear. He is reported to have introduced 'line management', and 'a simplified and more straightforward chain of command',[2] and Richard Norton-Taylor in his obituary of White and Anthony Verrier in his *Through the Looking-Glass* assure us that, by 1959, an SIS system of 'directors who had almost absolute control over their fiefdoms'[3] was replaced by 'controllers with regional responsibilities related to functions'.[4] In fact, the reverse was true. The SIS Board of Directors in 1956 consisted of Directors for Requirements, Training and Development and Finance and Administration, but the regional responsibilities were divided between the three Chief Controllers and C/PR. To be sure, there were changes in SIS structure under White, and these came in two phases; one of progressive, relatively limited changes, and one of comprehensive redesign near the end of his term as C. However, many of the changes which the SIS experienced during C's term hinged less upon a conscious campaign of reform, than upon environmental changes, in both the international arena and the workings of tasking and assessment within Whitehall. These

Sir Dick White who became 'C' after serving as Director General of the Security Service (photo courtesy of Anthony Glees)

Sir Maurice Oldfield

environmental trends continued to act on SIS, prompting subsequent changes under Maurice Oldfield and Arthur 'Dickie' Franks that would change the *form* of the SIS's 'pull architecture', and, in many respects, its content as well. It would, however, create a template for SIS organization that would adapt to the post-Cold War transformation more easily than changing gears from the Second World War to the Cold War had been.

If there is a fundamental change in the way the SIS was organized under White and his successors, it was that the approach to organizational design increasingly began to take into account the horizontal, organic pressures, intrinsic to how the agency worked and its relationship with its environment. The notion of 'collegiality' would not become explicit until Franks's accession as C, but the essence of organic and collegial thinking informed the changes under White and Oldfield, even if it was not described as such. Most of the changes which streamlined the chain of command had less to do with White than with changes in the operational environment. The two most important trends at this level were Britain's withdrawal from its colonial possessions in the Middle and Far East, which removed the need for 'longstop controlling stations' while shifting former colonies to 'foreign' SIS targets instead of 'domestic' Security Service concerns, and the steadily increasing pace and pressure of the Cold War with the Soviet bloc. However, it was under White that one began to see real attempts to create cross-controllerate operational arrangements, and an effective, horizontally organized system for tighter internal and operational security and counter-intelligence. It was also under White that effective collegial, joint SIS/MI5 arrangements were developed to resolve the long-running problems of jurisdictional overlap and ambiguity.

Besides changes in the operational environment, the SIS's governmental environment was also undergoing alterations in what has since become known as Britain's 'central' or 'national intelligence machinery'. Indeed, it was during White's term that the JIC moved from the Ministry of Defence to the Cabinet Secretariat, becoming genuinely *central* at last. The JIC now became the overseer, arbitrator and nominal formulator of the country's *national* intelligence requirements and priorities. Intelligence analysis for Ministers and the Cabinet moved in the first instance through the JIC. This represented the first fundamental change in tasking and analysis since the '1921 arrangement' was imposed on MI1c. The centrality of the JIC in the intelligence process both for consumers, and as a consumer of SIS product, provided a very firm impetus away from the old C Section/R Section system of simple, partisan departmental representation. This shift away from narrow partisan requirements was further emphasized by the 1964 consolidation of the Service Departments under the Ministry of Defence and the amalgamation of the three Service Intelligence Branches with the JIB. Progressively, Requirements was less a matter of departmental demand than common areas of interest shared by two or more departments. The structure and process of the Requirements/Production relationship would have to change to adapt to its new governmental environment, and this was the central concern of the organizational changes which occurred under Oldfield and Franks.

White's move to the SIS came shortly after his own campaign of modernization and reform within the Security Service. Once in harness at Broadway, he began a series of reforms there as well. One of the first features to which he turned his attention was the Directorate of Finance and Administration, particularly the question of recruitment and staffing. This had been a theme during his term as DG/SS, when upon being promoted he had restructured the operational support and administrative functions in MI5 originally combined in A Branch, dividing them into A and B Branches respectively, with Counter-Intelligence becoming D Branch.[5] In SIS, the administrative side was in at least a comparable state of disrepair. As one officer interviewed put it, personnel management in the post-war SIS had become something of a 'pendulum between two attitudes of mind', the traditional view being that the personnel section existed to serve the needs and demands of the Controllers, and the other being that there should be a measure of 'career management' under which an officer should not be given a posting which would be counterproductive to his or her career path.[6] The two points of view were manifestly visible among the officers interviewed, the same officer called the traditional arrangements a 'Director's slave market',[7] while another officer of a much earlier generation blithely described the same role of personnel as 'horses for courses'.[8] One of White's long-term, progressive reform efforts was the shift of emphasis from 'horses for courses' to 'career management'. A first, early step in this direction was the creation of a separate Recruitment Section under the Head of Personnel, which was tasked with scouting for potential new officers throughout

Britain's universities,[9] instead of through the 'old boy' networks at Boodle's and, White's and narrow post-war personal connections with Oxford and Cambridge dons. At this time, D/FA was relabelled the Directorate of Personnel and Administration (D/PA), to emphasize the change in priorities.[10]

The same process seems to have involved carving Training Section out of D/TD and shifting it to D/FA under a Head of Training Section (H/TS) while the technical development and support side of D/TD now became simply the Directorate of Support Services (D/SS).[11] Under D/PA, training apparently languished until the late 1960s when a new H/TS 'pulled things together', relocating most of the section's work to Fort Monkton, a move which led eventually to a six-month training course for new recruits[12] and to the contemporary Intelligence Officers' New Entry Course (IONEC).

Unsurprisingly, the other direction towards which White – as a counter-intelligence (CI) practitioner – turned his attention was the SIS's CI and counter-espionage machinery. SIS had, for the most part, proved unwilling to pay the price of the kinds of monitoring costs engendered by the Cold War. While it did set up a fairly sizeable CI system in the form of R5, CI remained relatively low in the chain of command, only one Requirements Section out of eight, subordinate to the Director of Requirements. To be sure, Area Controllers dealt with R5 directly to seek a CI input to operations (which had cost the service dear when Philby was R5), and unlike the other relatively small R Sections, it possessed two sub-divisions, each composed of four geographical sub-sections. Nonetheless, it was still relatively junior in the chain of command. Positive vetting had fared the same or worse, as a small, undermanned and very subordinate subsection of the Directorate of Finance and Administration. Finally, the Inspectorate of Security had probably been the most ill-equipped element, being run for the first years of its existence by an elderly and fading Valentine Vivian. Thus, the CI and security efforts of the SIS were relatively subordinate and completely fragmented. With his own experiences of the atom bomb spies investigation and the Burgess and Maclean affair under his belt, White began a sustained campaign to strengthen the CI and security aspects of the SIS. The first step was to carve R5 out of the Requirements Directorate and put it on a footing comparable with the other directorates. As a result, the officer holding the position of R5 was made a junior Director with the title Head of Counter-Intelligence (H/CI), and made a member of the SIS Board of Directors, sitting in on the weekly Directors' meeting.[13]

The sort of aggressive CI attitude that White sought to develop was also essential to the creation of 'Targeting Sections',[14] which functioned at the same hierarchical level as the R and P Sections. As one officer observed during interviews, 'at some points, R functions melded with Production'.[15] However much Requirements might, since the war, have been intended to be a detached and objective perspective on operations and their product, the need for Production to target the right people in the right places, and Requirements' need to know as much as possible about a source in order to evaluate that source, created a very real overlap. This was especially the case in attempting to spy on 'hard targets', or what analyst John Dziak has since termed 'counter-intelligence states',[16] such as the USSR, other Eastern Europe countries and China. In these cases, the Third-Country approach was of critical importance not merely for security and safety reasons, but also because agent recruitment inside those states was almost prohibitively difficult. One officer interviewed remarked of station officers working inside 'hard target' states that 'it was too much to ask officers there to recruit agents while running agents as well'.[17] Effective recruitments had to take place *outside* those countries, with an eye to running any agents suborned in their native country after they returned home. This was, of course, an essential rationale for C/PR and the UK Station, but this was an imperfect fix and led to internal turf wars over Third-Country operations launched by other controllerates from the Soviet flanks. Moreover, C/PR and the UK Station were not a solution to the issue of recruiting 'hard-target' nationals when they travelled abroad, a type of operation which lay more strictly within the particular geographical spheres of the individual controllerates.

The functions of the T Sections were to monitor the movements of 'hard-target' nationals abroad, maintain files on potential targets, and provide the necessary information for operations against these individuals on a cross-controllerate basis. As one officer interviewed described it, station officers abroad had a great many tasks to perform in the first place, most of which would not ordinarily bring them into contact with Soviet bloc nationals; therefore, 'the Targeting Sections provided the motivation, knowledge and encouragement for officers to make the effort to work on the hard targets'.[18] There were originally three T Sections: Soviet Union, Eastern Europe and China.

They came under the immediate authority of their respective area controllers, but could work across regional boundaries and acted as intermediaries between the Production and Requirements sides. The T Sections kept records on all the various potential targets living abroad, and undertook liaison with their area opposite number sections in MI5's D Branch, and with allied services. It was also often an officer from the relevant T Section, rather than a resident officer from the station, who would make the final approach to a Soviet bloc or Chinese official being targeted for recruitment. Such officers deployed from SIS HQ from the T Sections or UK sections came to be known as 'Visiting Case Officers' (VCO).[19] As the same officer put it, the 'Targeting Sections served as the "operational spearhead" against the main world's hard-target states'.[20]

The T Sections provided the first step towards resolving the overlapping geographical jurisdictions of the Soviet and Eastern Europe P Sections under C/PR, and the other controllerates mounting operations into the USSR from along its flanks. It did so by creating an organic, cross-jurisdictional system which was aimed at increased joint-working arrangements between controllerates.

In 1957, the external processes of tasking, dissemination and analysis in Whitehall and Downing Street underwent another change which had fairly profound implications for the process on the work of Requirements side of the SIS, and the Requirements/Production relationship. In 1946, the increased post-war centrality of the JIC as an assessment as well as administrative entity, and the creation of the JIB, shifted the emphasis in requirements from strictly partisan representation to a concern for disinterested 'objective' evaluation (a shift further emphasized by the fact the R1, R6 and R7 all served multiple consumers). However, at this point, the JIC was still essentially one consumer among many, albeit *primus inter pares*, and so the majority of intelligence requirements issued to the SIS were matters of departmental demand. In 1957, according to the official account, 'as a reflection of the broadened scope and role of intelligence, the JIC was brought within the Cabinet as part of the interdepartmental committee structure under the authority of the Secretary of the Cabinet'.[21] Percy Cradock, chairman of the Joint Intelligence Committee during the late 1980s, has elaborated this move in greater detail. He notes that 'by the 1950s it was becoming clear that intelligence was now covering a variety of fields outside those purely military'. What he has described as the 'old constitutional limitation' of having the CoS as its chief reporting conduit was far too limiting, and anyway, 'in practice JIC papers commonly had a wider audience'.[22] In other words, subordination to the CoS was not only a limitation, it was an artificial one observed chiefly in the breach. Much as SIS had to by-pass its own 1946 hierarchy to improvise collegial mechanisms of 'joint control', so the JIC had also 'outgrown its old framework'. It received a new charter to this effect – although its administrative role overseeing the wider machinery of intelligence headed that new mandate as it had the earlier one. This change to the JIC's role and mandate represented a profound change in the role of the JIC as the body formulating *national* intelligence requirements in support of a *national* assessments process, that is, one working at the level of the Cabinet Office on behalf of Ministers and Departmental Permanent Secretaries and Under-Secretaries. The JIC was also now responsible for coordinating all the requirements and priorities which could be laid upon the 'Security and Intelligence Agencies' by their consumers in Whitehall. The result was an annual review of intelligence requirements, leading to an annual National Intelligence Requirements Paper (NIRP), through a process consisting of 'rigorous analysis of the requirements for secret intelligence with extensive consultation with consumer departments and consideration of the financial and other resources required'. Apart from the establishment of the Cabinet Intelligence Coordinator in 1968, this system has remained substantially the same ever since.[23] The annual NIRP therefore involved not only a shopping list for intelligence, but one which assigned priorities to potentially competing demands; in other words, it put individual *departmental* demands in the context of both *national* requirements and limited operational resources.

The portion of the national intelligence requirements list allocated to SIS came to be formulated in the SIS 'Red Book',[24] distributed to stations abroad by SIS HQ, and in terms of which any proposed operation had to be justified.[25] To be sure, the R Sections continued to be the direct conduit for specific requests from, and the circulating of reports to, individual customers in Whitehall, but the national requirements list and the Red Book meant that even those departmental requests had to be within the bounds of national parameters and priorities. The creation in 1957 of a genuinely *central* intelligence machinery provided a permanent check on the dangers of surplus demand created by the 1921 arrangement. To employ a metaphor, if the national intelligence requirements list was the Torah, the Red Book was the Talmud, and it was now the place of the Requirements Section officers to interpret these Holy Scriptures unto the people actually mounting and running the operations. Requirements as a whole had moved even further away from the inter-war doctrine of partisan representation; besides being disinterested evaluators, the R Sections had become the in-house arbiters of a single, interdepartmentally agreed set of intelligence priorities and needs as they were applied to SIS operations. The move in 1957 of the JIC from the MoD to the Cabinet Secretariat, and the development of a national intelligence requirements system, therefore constituted something of an environmental *force majeure*, altering not only the relationship between the SIS and its customers, but also the internal relationship between Requirements and Production. SIS was forced over time to change its inner workings to conform to the changed structure and process in what was now Britain's genuinely central intelligence machinery.[26]

The most extensive internal change under White's initial programme of progressive reform was the abolition of the area and regional controllerates and chief controllerates, and their replacement with four regional Directorships of Production (D/Ps). The abandonment of the Area Controllerates in favour of regional Directorates arose out of two completely different sets of considerations. On the one hand, the 'longstop' controlling stations in Cyprus and Singapore were phased out as a result of Britain's steady withdrawal from empire, a withdrawal which accelerated after Suez. This was again a matter of environmental *force majeure*, in which the colonial administrations and the regional JICs they served were shut down, removing the regional consumers who provided the main *raison d'être* for the 'longstop' controllerates. Intercontinental telecommunications had also improved by the end of the 1950s, so that the communication difficulties which had been an additional factor in 1946 were increasingly a thing of the past. However, the abolition of the junior Area Controllers in London, and the promotion of the Chief Controllers to full Director arose out of a conscious attempt to streamline the structure of the SIS headquarters Production machinery.

The first controllerates to go were the 'longstop' stations in the Middle and Far East. In Cyprus, the MEC was part of the FO's Political Office to Middle East Forces (POMEF) in Episkopi. Between 1958 and 1960, negotiations were undertaken between the Middle East High Command and the government of Archbishop Makarios to

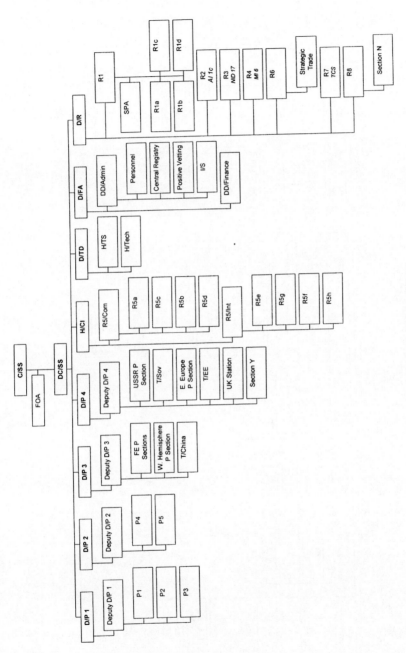

Figure 6.1: SIS in 1959

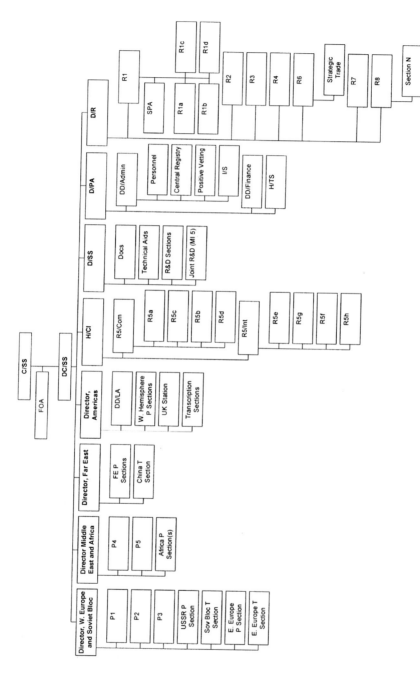

Figure 6.2: SIS in 1962

secure Cypriot independence, the termination of British administration, and the confinement of British strategic interests to the British Sovereign Base Areas. The FO's Political Representative (and head of POMEF) on the High Command involved in these negotiations was the former SIS Foreign Office Adviser, Geoffrey McDermott, who recounts the fate of MEC (not referred to as such) in his *The Eden Legacy*. Far from being abolished to increase direct control from London, the MEC fell prey to what McDermott, in retrospect, views as 'a ridiculous bit of Whitehall warfare'. Cyprus elected to become a member of the British Commonwealth, and, as a result, it fell not within Foreign Office and SIS jurisdiction but instead under that of the Commonwealth Relations Office (CRO). Therefore, in 1958, 'the MI6 man, who had provided much useful intelligence, was immediately removed because gentlemen of the Commonwealth do not spy on one another. According to CRO custom an MI5 man was substituted to work in liaison with the Cyprus government.'[27] The Middle East Controller was replaced with a Middle East Liaison Officer, who was to act simply as a conduit for intelligence of 'area interest' to British Middle East forces in Cyprus, and, as one officer interviewed put it, 'MEC became MELO'. Operations were thereafter overseen directly by P4 under CC/M (by 1959 redesignated D/P2) in London.[28]

The Far East Controller in Singapore suffered much the same fate. In 1957, Malaysia had gained independence, including Singapore, but the UK government retained its Colonial Commission, armed forces, the British Defence Coordinating Committee (FE) and JIC (FE) machinery in Singapore. In 1964 the government of Singapore declared independence with little or no warning given to either London or Kuala Lumpur, and Britain's colonial machinery there was subsequently dismantled. As a result, the Singapore station's controlling function was discontinued with the shutting down of the JIC (FE) and the BDCC (FE). During the transition, however, stations in the Far East continued to copy reports on an 'area interest' to Singapore, but operational control was direct from what had been CC/P, but was by then called D/P3 in London.[29] The Singapore station continued to operate, however, but just as a conventional field station.

Under the SIS command and control arrangements with which White found himself confronted in 1956, the regional Chief Controllers and C/PR had been acting essentially as a Board of Directors since the abolition of a global Director of Production around 1948.[30] The Chief Controllers were, for the most part, very

263

senior SIS officers who had been with the agency since the Second World War, and had built up their regional specializations over 20 or more years.[31] One officer rather cynically compared it with a corrupt local government where the Chief Controllers were all promoted because they had put in their years and it was felt that they were entitled to the status and benefits of full directorships.[32] A less bleak interpretation is simply that the Chief Controllers had been acting as de facto members of the Board of Directors alongside D/TD, D/FA, D/R and (the defunct) D/WP since 1948, and the creation of the regional Directorates of Production simply acknowledged this fact. As a result, Chief Controller Europe was redesignated D/P1, Chief Controller Middle East was D/P2, Chief Controller Far East became D/P3 and Controller Production Research was D/P4.[33] A more substantial change was the abolition of the intervening spread of Area Controllers, all of which were abolished and replaced with a single Deputy under each D/P (DD/P).[34]

The Americas, which from 1946 had been under C/PR, were transferred from D/P4 to D/P3, on the grounds of their proximity on the Pacific Rim.[35] However, D/P4, by 1958, had acquired Section Y. Even though the Berlin tunnel had been blown nearly two years before, the Y transcription sections were still processing the massive backlog of intercepted traffic.[36] Y Section was placed under the control of Deputy D/P4 (D/DP4), where it was progressively wound down. Without a small number of very large-scale intercept operations to create a significant scale economy of Y work, the initiative for and control of intercept operations devolved to the regional D/Ps, and their P Sections and field stations abroad, and Y Section was broken up into a brace of separate transcription sections answering administratively to DD/P4 but handling take generated by the regional D/Ps and circulating the resulting product to the relevant R Sections.[37]

In 1962, there was an additional series of minor reorganizations affecting both Production and Support Services. The Penkovsky case (about which more below) may have been a factor in changes to the Production side. Oleg Penkovsky, as a Soviet source, came under the operational control of DP4. As long as this meant running Penkovsky in the USSR and during his visits to the UK as a member of the State Committee for the Coordination of Scientific Research (GKKNR), there was no difficulty. However, Penkovsky's debriefing in Paris created a dilemma in terms of compartmentalization, since D/P1 had not been indoctrinated into the Penkovsky case. As a result, the Paris debriefings had to be handled by the Paris station *without* informing D/P1.[38] As noted above, placing the Soviet bloc and Eastern Europe P Sections under CPR-D/P 4 while also employing on Third-Country operations along the USSR's flanks to penetrate the Soviet Union created internal SIS 'turf wars' between C/PR-DP4 and the other controllerates/directorates. Therefore, in 1962, the Soviet bloc and Eastern Europe P Sections and the staff handling third-country operations against the Soviet bloc from the UK and under UK or 'natural' cover (later called Soviet Operations (Sov/Ops)) were excised from D/P4 and transferred to D/P1, which now became Director Western Europe and Soviet bloc. Although the western hemisphere P Sections had gone to DP3 in the late 1950s, these were now returned to D/P4, which became Director, Americas. As a result, the new Production side organizational consisted of Director, Western Europe and Soviet Bloc; Director, Middle East and Africa; Director, Far East; and Director, Americas. Director, Americas also included at least one area Deputy Director, overseeing Latin America, as well as the UK Station.[39]

The SIS and the Security Service had been in limited contact over research and development since the 1950s, sharing some resources and techniques such as the GPO 'Special Investigations Unit Research' section at Dollis Hill, and various technical intelligence-gathering methods developed by the two agencies.[40] Since both SIS and the Security Service had essentially similar requirements for research and development, and both were prevented by considerations of security and specialised needs from acquiring the bulk of their technology on the open market, there existed both administrative and productive economies of scale in pooling their research and development programmes. James Adams has asserted that basically the SIS needs these developments to perform espionage and that MI5 is developing counter-measures should the same techniques be employed against the UK by an adversary,[41] but this really oversimplifies the situation. Since the SIS is responsible for counter-intelligence and security abroad, while the Security Service collects intelligence in the UK, both services have a percentage in developing both offensive techniques and counter-measures for use in their respective jurisdictions. Therefore, in 1961/62, a joint SIS/MI5 research and development section was set up, pooling their common interests, and bringing the SIS and MI5 research scientific staff together under a joint head.[42]

265

In 1964, White's long-running campaign to strengthen the counter-intelligence and security mechanisms of SIS culminated in the creation of a Directorate of Counter-Intelligence and Security (D/CIS), which subsumed all of these functions under a single head. H/CI, formerly R5, had been steadily increasing in importance, mainly through a series of Eastern European counter-espionage successes such as NODDY, a walk-in from the Polish intelligence service.[43] The period between 1961 and 1963 also represented a watershed for SIS counter-espionage and security. The year 1961 saw both the discovery of a second penetration agent in the SIS, George Blake,[44] and the first successful penetration of the Soviet (as opposed to Eastern European) intelligence system in the form of GRU Colonel Oleg Vladimirovich Penkovsky.[45] The Penkovsky case ran until 1962, the same year in which Philby was finally confronted by Nicholas Elliott in Beirut, provided both a limited (and highly deceptive) confession, and then promptly escaped to the USSR. Any lingering doubts about Philby's treason disappeared, and the weaknesses in SIS security were manifestly apparent. The Soviet penetrations and Philby's defection also helped prompt the creation of the joint SIS/MI5 FLUENCY committee to investigate Soviet penetration of the intelligence and security agencies, creating additional pressure on the SIS to make a firmer security and counter-intelligence effort. Nonetheless, the ability to run Penkovsky, in the heart of Moscow, from 1961 to late 1962, and to have him available as a high-grade human source during both the Berlin and Cuban missile crises demonstrated two things. In the first place, it demonstrated that the SIS could operate effectively against the USSR despite the setbacks of Philby and Blake. In the second place, it demonstrated that the Soviet agencies *could* be penetrated, and at a reasonably high level. But Blake's exposure demonstrated that the risk of penetration had not abated, and a great many targeting operations against Soviet nationals had been compromised by Blake during his term with D/P4. For a sustained counter-espionage effort against the Soviets to succeed, security would itself have to be that much tighter.

Just as BOOT had provided the evidence needed to justify creating the SPA, so the combination of Penkovsky, Blake, Philby and FLUENCY reinforced both the increased need for, and scale economies of, a strengthened and unified counter-intelligence and security architecture. The result was that a new Directorate was set up to combine and coordinate these tasks, in the form of a new

Directorate of Counter-Intelligence and Security (D/CIS).[46] In 1964, Maurice Oldfield was brought back from Washington, where he had been heading the SIS liaison office, to head the new directorate and become the first D/CIS.[47]

D/CIS absorbed the old Inspectorate of Security and PV sections, as well as R5. The I/S's operational security role was taken over by a Security Branch, Operations (SBO) and its staff of Security Branch Officers (also SBOs) who, like the War Planning Officers in the late 1940s, were attached to the various controllerates but were ultimately subordinate to D/CIS.[48] The disgruntled former SIS officer, Richard Tomlinson, has described SBOs as senior SIS officers who 'are past the normal MI6 retirement age of 55 and have been rehired because of their rich operational experience'. Although he notes that they are informally (and a little unkindly) referred to as 'retreads', he adds that 'their role is advisory and they have no control over operations, but only a foolish officer would ignore them'.[49] The personnel security side of I/S was taken over by a new Security Branch, Personnel (SBP), which operated in close cooperation with the Head of Personnel.[50] The Positive Vetting Section now became Security Branch, Vetting (SBV).[51] Within D/CIS, counter-intelligence operations were overseen by a number of area Counter-Intelligence (CI) Sections, including CI3 (China), CI4 (Soviet Union) and CI7 (Eastern Europe).[52] At one point, the possibility was mooted that D/CIS should have specialist CI residencies abroad, much as Section V had during the Second World War.[53] However, this was not acted upon. Partly it was prevented by resistance from the Production side, but, more significantly, it was prevented because attaching the SBOs to the controllerates and CI Section participation in the headquarters control of counter-espionage operations mounted by the controllerates provided the necessary area involvement required by D/CIS.[54] In the process of absorbing R5, R5 Com was shut down, on the grounds that monitoring the activities of foreign communist parties was, as one officer interviewed put it 'not frightfully exciting', and its responsibilities were assumed by the various controllerates.[55]

Organic 'jointery' was essential to the working of D/CIS. Under the new system, in the case of developing a counter-espionage operation, the Area Controller would maintain control of the operation on the ground, while the planning and management of the operation would jointly involve the Controller, the SBO and the relevant CI section.[56] Moreover, attaching the SBOs provided Area

Controllers with both a CI input to operations and someone other than the Area Controller with a comprehensive view of operations in that area while retaining Compartmentalization. The SBP and the SBV both had to work 'hand in glove' with Personnel, and in the case of the SBV, with MI5's C (Protective Security) Branch. In general, D/CIS dealt closely with MI5 and, as one officer put it, 'in the event of a "happening" the Security Service would be called in at a very early stage'.[57] After a few years, the degree of internal 'jointery' on targeting and counter-intelligence was increased again by amalgamating the Soviet Union, Eastern Europe and China CI Sections with their equivalent Targeting Sections into three Targeting *and* Counter-Intelligence Sections (TCI), which functioned under the 'dual control' of D/CIS and their respective Area Controllers.[58]

The resulting new organization for counter-intelligence and security resolved one of the fundamental difficulties of counter-espionage management that had plagued the early Cold War SIS. In the mid-1940s, the bulk of the SIS's Third-Country operations into the Soviet bloc had been compromised because the area controllers had to consult with Philby, as R5, for a counter-intelligence input to their operational security arrangements. The alternative, of course, would have been to set up separate counter-intelligence arrangements under each area controllerate, but given the reliance on Third-Country operations and the global targeting of Chinese and Soviet bloc nationals abroad, this would have involved a great deal of duplicate labour and record keeping in the controllerates, and introduced new problems of interdepartmental governance in coordinating duplicate and potentially overlapping efforts between the various controllerates' CI efforts. Thus, for a small organization such as the SIS, there have always been strong productive and administrative economies of scale in favour of a single, centralized CI/CE effort conducted on the basis of organic interdepartmental working relations with the area controllerates. SIS was not in a position to abandon a central CI/CE and security apparatus. The geographical subdivisions and their collegial working arrangements with the controllerate, however, meant that even interdepartmental consultation and coordination could remain strictly compartmentalized along geographical lines. Even if another Philby were to come up the ranks in D/CIS, his impact would be severely limited by its geographical compartmentalization.

In January 1966, nearly a decade after becoming C, White finally initiated a programme of organizational redesign. Unlike the previous reforms during his tenure, the 1966 reorganization was a comprehensive review of the SIS's internal management. Partly this was because of a demographic shift within the SIS. By the mid-1960s, the senior officers who had served as Chief Controllers under Sinclair and under White as the four D/Ps were finally retiring, and a new generation of officers were finding their way into the senior directorships. The agency's internal review also coincided with the deliberations of the Fulton Committee on the Civil Service, which had begun its deliberations in February of that year. The scale and extent of the SIS review remains an incompletely appreciated stage in its history. For example, a standard item in the literature on the SIS concerning the 1966 reorganization is the creation of a Controllerate for Africa during the 1966 review.[59] However, the fact that this was a *controllerate* and not a *directorate* clearly indicates that this was only the tip of the iceberg in SIS reorganization. Indeed, the 1966 reorganization was far more comprehensive than is generally indicated, and was the exercise in organizational redesign in which the regional directorates were indeed abolished at last.

One officer interviewed described the succession of organizational changes as a lot of 'cutting and changing' that 'depended on the personal preferences of the prevailing C; there was always a debate over whether it was preferable to have controllers over small areas or directors over big areas'.[60] As we have seen, however, there were real and persistent problems of how to manage a global programme of work, especially one where departmental remits and operational details tended to overlap. Under a comprehensive review of the SIS's organization by White and his new senior staff, the single post of Director of Production (D/P) was reinstituted, alongside Requirements (D/R), Counter-Intelligence and Security (D/CIS), Support Services (D/SS) and finally Personnel and Administration (D/PA). Why this specific change was made is not clear. One possibility suggested by both Verrier and a different officer interviewed is that the regional directors were simply too powerful.[61] Alternatively, one could look to the 'corrupt local government' hypothesis suggested earlier for the creation of the regional directorates; that is, officers of directorial seniority were in the process of retiring (as Tom Bower had put it, they were 'invited to retire'),[62] and a more junior grade of officer was coming up the hierarchy. Finally, it has to be considered that decolonization was increasing the SIS's range of activities globally, and regional directorates such as D/P2 (Middle East) and D/P3 (Far East) were covering a rapidly multiplying number of targets, stretching the span of control under the P Sections, the D/Ps and their deputies. Whichever individual or combination of these reasons may have been the case, the central feature which has to be recognized is that the 1966 reorganization was essentially a return to the 1945 scheme developed by the Committee for SIS Reorganization.

Under the new DP, there was a span of seven Area Controllers, much as there had been just after the war. The Western Europe and Soviet bloc directorate was broken up, into Controller Europe (C/EUR) and Controller Soviet bloc (C/SOV). The Soviet bloc and Eastern Europe T Sections were placed under C/Sov. Western Hemisphere was hived off from what had been D/P4 again, now under a Controller Western Hemisphere (C/WH). D/P3 became the Far East Controllerate (C/FE), while D/P2 was split up between Controller, Middle East (C/ME) and Controller Africa (C/AF). What had been D/P4 and Director Americas was now reduced more or less to its original C/PR dimensions as Controller UK (C/UK), overseeing the UK Station which provided operational support in the UK, and the Transcription Sections which had been inherited from Section Y.[63] Under the new arrangements, the P Section organization was: P1 (France), P2 (Scandinavia), P3 (Germany and Austria) and P6 (Greece, Turkey and Cyprus) under Controller Europe; P4 (Eastern Europe) and P5 (Soviet Union) under C/Sov; P7 (USA, Canada), P8 (Latin America) and P10 (Caribbean) under C/WH; P9 (China), P11 (South East Asia, Australasia), P12 (Japan) and P13 (India and Pakistan) under C/FE; P16 and P17 (both different Middle East areas) under C/ME; four different African P Sections P14, P15, P18 and P19 under C/AF; and P20 (UK) under C/UK. These controllerates and P Sections would characterize the SIS throughout the 1960s and 1970s.[64]

The Requirements side had recently experienced a limited reorganization, but confined to its armed service consumers rather than within the SIS. In 1963/64, on the basis of a government White Paper, the three armed services were amalgamated under the Ministry of Defence, chiefly on the grounds that there were administrative economies scale to be had combining the civilian Civil Service machineries of the War Office, Admiralty and the Air Ministry. In the process, the three Service Intelligence Branches were consolidated with the JIB. The initial change was fairly chaotic. Despite being under a common command, many of the various NID, MID, AI and JIB sections retained their original designations or a joint DIS/service branch designation, as in DI(MI), DI(NI) or DI(AI) followed by the Section number, such as DI(AI)7. Moreover, almost as soon as the amalgamation took place, the DIS was required to cut back staffing by 8 per cent, or 78 posts.[65] Among the areas affected by the 1964 cutbacks was the size of Service Branch secondments to the SIS. A summary of the reductions, however, sought to minimize these consequences, stating that 'Cuts proposed … include a number of officers serving with MI6 and the JIS, and minor reductions in various supporting sections. No task will be given up completely, and general efficiency should not suffer, although there may be some slowing down of work.'[66] It would appear that it was at this point that the Service R sections finally found themselves once again reduced to a single representative officer at SIS's new headquarters, Century House.[67]

In the course of the reorganization, not merely of departments but of the alphabet soup of abbreviations by which defence and intelligence officialdom navigated, some duplication arose, in one instance to the concern of the SIS. In early March 1965, an SIS officer called H.T. Carlisle (Office G.01, Century House) complained to the Director of Scientific and Technological Intelligence at the DIS that the Defence Telephone Book for 1965 included two entries with the designation TCS. The first was the DSTI's own Technical Coordinating Section, otherwise known as R7, while the other was the RAF's Training Combat Survival Branch. Perhaps with the early post-war fiasco of the Combined Regimental Pay Office (CRPO) receiving truck loads of top-secret documents intended for the SIS cover organization in the Middle East, the Combined Research and Planning Organization (CRPO) in mind, Carlisle asked that something be done. The DSTI duly minuted Major General Sir Kenneth Strong, formerly head of the JIB and now head of DIS as Director General of Intelligence (DGI): 'I understand that new instructions regarding the transmission of documents will soon be issued to Century House. However I feel strongly that serious consideration should be given to changing the titles of one or the other of the TCS branches.'[68] Carlisle also lobbied the Security Officer at the DIS Metropole Building headquarters, who also wrote to the DGI eight days after the DSTI: 'I have today received strong representations from Century House that the title of the Technical Coordinating Section should remain unchanged. They therefore hope that the Air Force Department can be persuaded in some way to redesignate their Training Combat Survival Branch.'[69] The DGI's

271

The Broadway Buildings

response was blunt, and delivered by one of his assistants rather than Strong himself: 'The DGI cannot accept responsibility for negotiating the removal of any duplication which may exist between the short titles of branches in two separate Departments.' Instead, it was suggested that any material for the Technical Coordinating Section 'should include Century House or a Box address'[70] (the SIS occasionally being known euphemistically as Box 850, Ministry of Defence).[71]

Apart from any confusion arising from duplication, the DIS was badly in need of a reorganization which would resolve its internal structure. It took until 1966, but a scheme was adopted in which the DIS adopted a structure in which analogous or related service bodies were combined into single DI sections with Army, (A), Navy (N) or Air (Air) sub-designations; for example, the Soviet geographical section of the Directorate of Service Intelligence (DS Int) became DI3, subdivided into DI3(A), DI3(N) and DI3(Air).[72] Under the consolidation of the Service Intelligence branches, the Service Branch liaisons with the Security and Secret Intelligence Services were consolidated under DI5 and DI6 respectively. Within DI6, therefore, the designations of R2 (Air Intelligence liaison), R3 (NID 17) and R4 (MI6) would have become DI6(Air), DI6(N) and DI6(A), respectively.[73]

Personnel also underwent a limited change during 1966, essentially the final blow to area controllers treating personnel (as well as operations) in their jurisdictions as local 'fiefdoms'.[74] In 1966, the Head of Personnel (H/PS), who held the same level of seniority under D/PA as the controllers did under the reinstituted Director of Production, was made the voting secretary of the SIS appointments board.[75]

Since the inter-war period, relations between SIS and the Security Service had often been fraught with turf wars. In principle, the two agencies' spheres of operations were both geographically and constitutionally quite distinct. However, the nature of the threats with which they dealt forced an overlap between domestic counter-intelligence and foreign counter-espionage. Operations by foreign governments against the UK tended to cross the demarcation line between the two agencies. As actions originating abroad they fell into the SIS's sphere of competence, but being conducted on the ground within the British and colonial territory placed them within that or MI5. During the Second World War, the problem also arose of SIS agents and MI5 agents geographically relocating into the other service's jurisdiction, as in the case of TRICYCLE's (agent Dusko

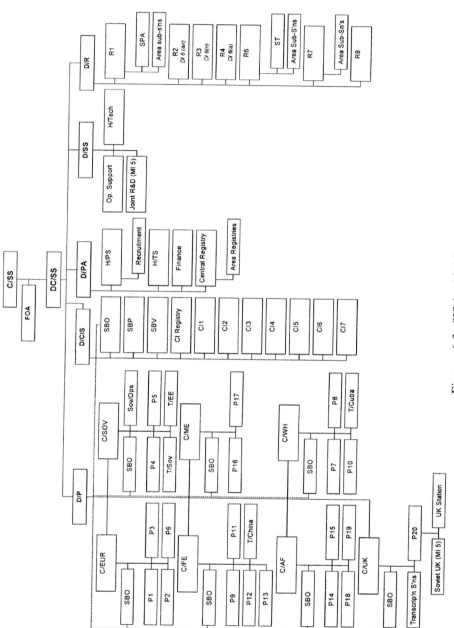

Figure 6.3: SIS in 1966

Popov) journey to the United States. This problem was exacerbated when the only country available to mount a Third-Country operation against a hard target was the UK itself. During the late 1950s, C/PR-DP4 had gone in for targeting and recruiting Soviet and Eastern European nationals in the UK with an eye to subsequently running them abroad in their home country, a strategy that Blake (who participated in such operations) accused of being a flagrant and wilful flouting of MI5 jurisdiction.[76] However, as pointed out above, such operations were an almost inevitable result of the need to operate against hard-target nationals while they were travelling outside their home 'counter-intelligence' states. Domestic Third-Country operations also bring to light a second ambiguity in the domestic/foreign distinction. A foreign embassy, consulate or trade mission is *legally* foreign soil, although it lies within British territory, meaning, in principle, that foreign soil is under SIS jurisdiction even though it lies within the three-mile limit, and such institutions were prime sources for third-country recruitments in the UK. Similarly, the *Ordzhonikidze* was legally foreign territory even while moored in Portsmouth harbour.

Various solutions had been proposed and rejected, usually involving integrating all or part of one agency into the hierarchy of the other. This, of course, invariably met with intense resistance, and neither the amalgamation of MI5 into SIS nor of Section V of the SIS into B Division of MI5 ever came to fruition. Indeed, in the case of the wartime Section V/B Division conflict, differences were very adequately resolved when Section V returned to London from St Albans, and the two staffs were physically close enough to permit regular contact and consultation. SIS Cold War domestic operations were necessarily a potential source of friction between the two agencies, which had already been in conflict over counter-intelligence and security considerations since the initial indications that Philby was a penetration agent in 1951/52. Proposals involving the cutting and pasting of lateral integration from one agency into the hierarchy of another were no more likely to succeed in the 1960s than in the 1920s or the 1940s, but the Section V/B Division relationship *after* 1943 pointed to the possibility of effective collegial *jointery* between the two agencies, and this was the direction proposed by C/SOV, Harold Shergold, in consultation with MI5.[77]

Instead of working independently and potentially crossing juris-dictions, the new approach proposed by Shergold would involve creating a joint section bringing SIS officers into a working relationship

Century House as it appears today, refitted as luxury apartments
(to the incredulity of its former occupants)

with MI5 counter-intelligence personnel from MI5's K Branch, targeting and operating together against cross-jurisdictional targets such as accredited foreign nationals and installations within the operational jurisdiction of the Security Service.[78] Within the SIS, the joint section came under the control of C/UK. The original joint domestic station was targeted primarily against the Soviet and Eastern European presence in the UK.[79] One of its earliest and most dramatic successes was the recruitment in 1971 of Oleg Lyalin, a KGB officer working under cover as a member of the Soviet Trade Delegation. Accounts of Lyalin's defection generally attribute the honeytrap targeting him, and his voluntary continuation as a penetration agent within the trade delegation, to MI5.[80] Nigel West, however, refers to the Lyalin recruitment rather elliptically as the product of 'a new period of [SIS] co-operation with the Security Service, targeting the numerous Soviet "legal" facilities in London for joint attention', and he describes the Lyalin operation as...[o]ne of the first such operations'.[81] As recalled by Peter Wright, Lyalin 'was recruited by two of the best officers in MI5, a bluff Yorkshireman named Harry Wharton and a former SIS undercover officer of conspicuous courage, Tony Brookes [sic]'.[82] In fact, Brooks, one of the SOE clandestine operators who took the post-war career path into the SIS, never worked for MI5 as such but instead was head of the joint Soviet UK section.[83] The consequence of this successful implementation of SIS–MI5 jointery came to an abrupt end when Lyalin was arrested for drunken driving in London, and forced to seek asylum and defect once and for all. The Lyalin case also had a longer-term legacy than just demonstrating the success of SIS–MI5 collaboration and providing the first successful penetration of Soviet intelligence since Penkovsky. Lyalin's information was a vital part of the evidence[84] that led to the expulsion in 1971 of 90 Soviet 'diplomats' from the UK and 15 more being barred from re-entry, after which, the SIS penetration agent in the KGB, Oleg Gordievsky, has observed, 'the London residency never recovered from the expulsions ... during the next fourteen years ... the KGB found it more difficult to collect high-grade intelligence in London than in almost any other Western capital'.[85]

The joint Soviet UK section would prove a long-running success. A decade after the Lyalin success, Bill Graham, a glazier recruited by the anti-Soviet joint section for a bugging operation directed against the Soviet Trade Delegation (again) in the early 1980s, would later recall how his case officer 'told me openly that he was with MI6 and he explained briefly that his service normally operated outside the United Kingdom while MI5 dealt with threats to the internal security of the country, but as the Soviet Trade Delegation, like an embassy, was technically foreign territory, it came within his jurisdiction'.[86] Operating the joint section provided two benefits: in the first place, it provided a way around cross-jurisdictional problems, while at the same time it allowed foreign intelligence and counter-intelligence to approach the same target in terms of what one officer interviewed described as their 'different optics'.[87] Likewise, former MI5 Director General Stella Rimmington has recalled of the joint section that it was 'a valuable place for the two cultures [SIS and MI5] to meet and learn to understand each other.' There was an additional value in sharing skills between security service and secret service personnel, and Rimmington adds that 'it was of great value for a young MI6 officer to learn how a sophisticated security service worked so that he would understand what he was up against when he went out undercover on his foreign postings. For the MI5 officers. there was much to be learned from their MI6 colleagues about the techniques of agent-running, and the behaviour of intelligence officers under cover.'[88] The original joint section set an important precedent and was evidently viewed by the two agencies as a success: by 1972, there was an additional joint section targeting China's facilities and personnel in the UK, and, as both domestic and foreign-originated terrorism became an increasingly central intelligence issue during the decade, two additional counter-terrorist joint sections were subsequently added to C/UK's growing empire (about which more below).[89]

RETRENCHMENT AND RESTORATION

Within two years of his campaign of comprehensive reorganization, White, in 1968, retired to serve as the first Intelligence Coordinator. Although, among the many professional intelligence officers, Maurice Oldfield, ex-D/CIS and subsequently DC/SS since Bruce Lockhart's 1967 departure, seemed the obvious candidate to succeed White, this was not to be the case. The replacement for White was not Oldfield or any other career SIS officer, but the Foreign Office Deputy Under-Secretary with responsibility for defence matters, Sir John Rennie. Despite White's extensive reforms of the agency, and successes such as the Congo and Penkovsky affairs, the 1960s had been a bad decade for the SIS. It began in the spring of 1961 with the discovery that George Blake was a Soviet penetration agent. Two years later, after being confronted by Nicholas Elliott in Beirut, 'Kim' Philby disappeared, defecting at long last to the USSR in the new year of 1963. Both of these events were almost certainly crucial factors in the creation of D/CIS, but that was at best bolting the barn door after the horse's theft. More telling from a foreign policy point of view was the political surprise and intelligence failure to provide warning of the Rhodesian Unilateral Declaration of Independence in the mid-1960s. As a consequence, the Foreign Office evidently concluded that the SIS needed to be brought under closer supervision, and Rennie was appointed C, notionally on the grounds that 'No suitable candidate was at that time available from within the Service.'[90]

In all fairness, Rennie was no newcomer to the world of intelligence and national covert capability. He had served as head of the IRD in the early 1950s, and, prior to his appointment as C, his posting as Deputy Undersecretary (DUS) with responsibility for strategic and defence matters meant that his tasks included chairmanship of the JIC, and oversight of the SIS and GCHQ, and he was the FOA's immediate senior. Nonetheless, many within the SIS had expected Oldfield to be appointed, and Rennie's appointment was greeted, and is usually recalled, with scepticism and hostility. The former DC/SS, George Young, wrote later of Rennie's term that 'intelligence collection ground to a halt, morale sank to zero and security suffered'.[91] A more measured but no less critical note was sounded at the time by former Foreign Office Adviser, Geoffrey McDermott, who warned during Rennie's tenure that: 'employing a diplomat as C can only be an inhibiting and restraining influence, turning the SIS into a sort of second-rate diplomatic service, whereas previous chiefs were in a position to pick up the phone and speak direct to the Prime Minister or his Cabinet colleagues.'[92] One SIS officer interviewed took a completely different view of the matter, observing that, 'under Rennie, Oldfield really ran the Service; which was unfortunate. I had a good opinion of Rennie, but he was not tough enough to command Oldfield.'[93] Whatever the truth of Rennie's term as C, he was subject to unenviable pressures coming from an increasingly financially and politically beleaguered UK government that had to cope with the loss of empire and the concomitant loss of international status, chronic contraction of an economy that would eventually become mired in the 'stagflation' of the 1970s, and a disintegration of public order tied to the deterioration of the situation in Northern Ireland and the almost pandemic crisis in popular political consensus that swept the West

279

between the 1960s and mid-1970s. It would be nearly impossible to retire bathed in glory in such circumstances no matter what one did. In the event, Rennie was forced to retire abruptly in early 1973 when his son and daughter-in-law were arrested and tried at the Old Bailey for possession of Chinese heroin, and the press became increasingly interested in the case given that the youth's father was not merely a senior FCO official, but Chief of the SIS to boot.[94] It was in such inauspicious circumstances that Oldfield was finally appointed as C after six years as DC/SS.

Oldfield inherited an agency in which political restraint driven by a diminished global role was compounded by financial restraint driven by a succession of economic setbacks leading to both operational caution on the part of the SIS's overlords in the overt government and extensive staff reductions across the entire organization.[95] The SIS experienced considerable staff reductions, on both the Production and Requirements sides of the organization.[96] Twenty- and 100-man field stations were a thing of the past by the early 1970s, as the average SIS station numbered no more than two or three officers. These small resident staffs were dependent upon Operational Support, a section of D/SS in London, to dispatch officers with specialized, technical skills to stations abroad rather than maintaining on-station technical collection capabilities like those of the Berlin station in the 1950s.[97] The SIS's operational brief also became progressively less ambitious, and would lead eventually to the discontinuation of the SPA section in the mid-1970s by Oldfield as well as extensive and ultimately disastrous cutbacks in the Production side's overseas presence.

The combination of restraint and disorder that prevailed during Rennie's and Oldfield's terms as C/SS also meant that the UK Controllerate would first grow to a minor empire in the first half of the decade and then be pared back to a minimal role by the end of the 1970s. Out of the various reforms and transitions during the 1960s, C/UK had retained what had originally been Section Y's Transcription Sections (which it had originally acquired as D/P4 in 1959). Besides its own Soviet Operations section, it also oversaw additional UK-based stations or 'natural cover' sections, including the joint SIS–MI5 Soviet section, the joint China section, joint counter-terrorist sections operating against Middle East and Irish terrorism, and a section, as one officer put it during interviews, 'handling people who do work for SIS for love, running safe houses and so forth'.[98] This last section has since been publicly identified by Richard Tomlinson in the 1980s as designated UKN and described as consisting of surveillance operatives that can 'blend into foreign streets' as well as professionals as diverse (during his term with the agency) as an air taxi pilot and a yacht master.[99]

A great deal has been made of the 1971 appointment of an SIS officer to the Northern Ireland brief. This appointment is often portrayed as evidence of a lack of satisfaction with MI5's performance on the part of Edward Heath's government, and later a positive distrust of the Security Service by the subsequent Wilson government, and finally a source of friction between the SIS and the Security Service.[100] Less generally understood is the joint nature of the SIS's Northern Ireland presence, which was modelled on the SIS/MI5 collaborative structure for targeting Soviet assets within the UK. If the SIS had indeed been playing a lone hand, MI5 might well have felt marginalized. Of all of the commentators on British intelligence, only Rupert Allason, writing as Nigel West, has come close to the actual working arrangements for dealing with Irish terrorism, observing: 'From its headquarters in the Vauxhall Bridge road, SIS mounted routine operations in support of the Belfast station, exercised clandestine technical surveillance of target diplomatic missions [see above] and liaised more closely with MI5.'[101] Likewise, Anthony Verrier argues that the function of the Belfast station was to achieve joint coordination: 'there was no co-ordination of intelligence in Northern Ireland. The establishment of an SIS station within the Representative structure would ensure that there would be.'[102]

To be precise, of course, the Northern Ireland terrorism section under the SIS was a *joint section with* MI5, and under these circumstances the persistent tales of interservice friction in the Province seem less plausible. One example that might be indicative of the Northern Ireland joint section's work appears in Nigel West's account of the Casuro travel agency affair. According to West, a notional travel agency was set up that awarded free holidays in Torremolinos to members of the Republican movement. There they were approached by SIS officers to act as informers. The operation was blown to the press by a Dublin couple who declined the SIS invitation. West concludes his account of the affair with the dry observation that the 'SIS's hidden involvement in the affair was revealed when it was learned that Casuro's single telephone line terminated inside the building occupied by SIS' London [UK]

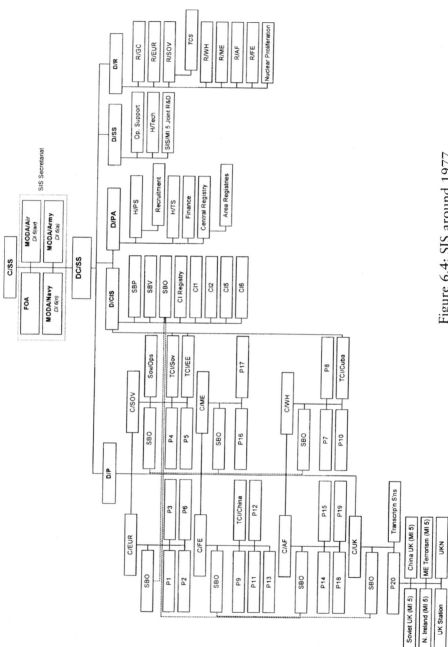

Figure 6.4: SIS around 1977

Station.'[103] The Casuro operation is, of course, highly reminiscent of Bill Graham's account of his work for the SIS/MI5 joint section. Similar arrangements also took shape during the 1970s to attack Middle Eastern terrorism which crossed the two agencies' jurisdictions.[104] Unfortunately, the SIS failed to set up comparable arrangements dealing with 'nihilist' Marxist groups such as the Red Army Faction, *Action Directe* and November 17. Despite warnings in the mid-1970s from the Western Europe Requirements Section (R/EUR, see below) and at least one station in the theatre, opportunities to penetrate these groups were passed up because they were not included in the JIC's National Intelligence Requirements Paper and hence 'did not appear in the Red Book'.[105]

In the late 1970s, however, most of the UK sections for domestic Third-Country operations were transferred to the relevant Area Controllers while the Transcription Sections moved to Administration. This meant that the joint Soviet UK section moved to C/SOV, the China UK joint section moved to C/FE and the Middle East terrorism joint section moved to C/ME. This left C/UK responsible only for P20 and its UK Station, the joint SIS/MI5 Northern Ireland section, UKN and 'other UK support operations'.[106]

Changes in the SIS's institutional setting within the UK national intelligence machinery and comprehensive financial retrenchment meant that even the reformed SIS created by White no longer fitted its governmental environment particularly well, and some degree of general reorganization was virtually an inevitability. As we have already seen, Philby recalled of the 1945 Committee of Reorganization that one of the central issues in the question of how to organize the SIS was the choice between geographical and functional organization. This issue arose again when, shortly after becoming C, Maurice Oldfield undertook his own programme of organizational redesign to meet the needs of the new austerity and Britain's reduced international role. This time, however, Oldfield and his board of Directors opted for the 'vertical' division of labour, and it was decided to reorganize the Requirements Directorate along geographical lines.[107] Historically, the SIS had always been subject to a very real environmental *force majeure* in favour of the 'horizontal', functional structure for its Requirements side. In 1945, most of the R Sections existed for the purpose of partisan consumer representation at a time and in a system in which departmental interests were pre-eminent. But during the 1960s, the structure and organizational politics of

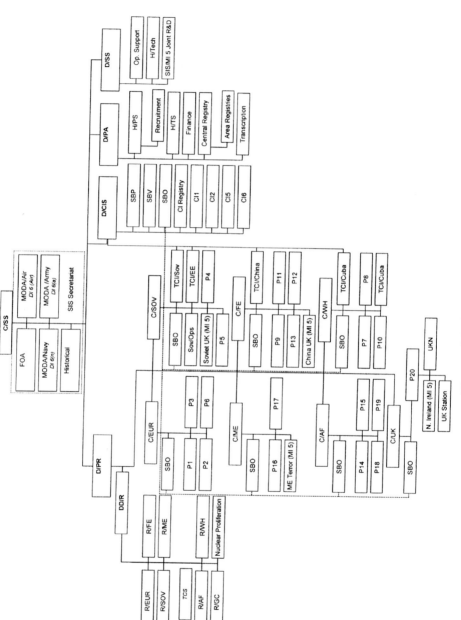

Figure 6.5: SIS in 1981

intelligence tasking, dissemination and analysis had changed completely.

The roles of partisan representation had been steadily decreased throughout the 1950s and 1960s, while joint- rather than single-service all-source analysis had been increased both by the increased centrality and power of the JIC and the 1964 consolidation of the Service Departments under the Ministry of Defence. Consolidation of the armed Services had also involved placing the individual armed Services under separate, junior Defence Ministers who were without seats in Cabinet. Therefore, the Service customers were politically weaker, as well as subject to strengthened pressures towards inter-service and interdepartmental jointery. The combined effect was to weaken very considerably any partisan pressure which served as a justification for a functional organization of Requirements.

The trend towards a geographical reorganization of Requirements was also given a push in the second half of the 1960s by the replacement of the JIC's Joint Intelligence Staff (JIS) with the Joint Assessments Staff (JAS). The Rhodesian intelligence failure had been at least as much the JIC's analytical failure as it had been an operational one for SIS, and this prompted a general review and reform effort under the Wilson government of the day, spearheaded by the Cabinet Secretary, Sir Burke Trend.[108] The JIS had traditionally been composed of a constellation of ad hoc interdepartmental groups, but, by mid-1967,[109] these had been reorganized or replaced with the more formal, but still essentially collegial, Current Intelligence Groups (CIGs) making up the JAS. Some of the CIGs were functional, but the bulk were geographical, consisting, in 1967, of Latin America, West Europe, East Europe, Middle East, Far East, Africa and Rhodesia.[110] While the SIS's area controllerates conformed closely to the CIGs, the Requirements Directorate did not. Requirements Directorate was the first point of contact with the JIC and, more significantly, the JAS. Its R Section officers represented the agency on the various CIGs.[111] But a functional Requirements Directorate could hardly be said to dovetail easily with a geographical JAS, and, as the central arbiter of national and departmental intelligence requirements, the JIC and its assessments staff were the main political powerhouse in the UK intelligence system. With such profound changes in the governmental side aspect, SIS's environment made adaptation of the Requirements Directorate to suit the new tasking and dissemination conditions all but inevitable. Perhaps one of the main indications of the reportedly moribund state of Rennie's SIS was the delay of nearly five years before that adaptation took place under his successor.

Environmental changes in the UK government's intelligence machinery converged with reductions in staff size in the specialist R Sections such as R6 (Economic/Industrial) and R7 (Scientific), which had resulted in a large part from financial pressure upon the SIS. The SIS experienced sizeable staff cuts across the board, but this was felt particularly keenly in Requirements, which, despite its centrality in SIS structure and process, was a relatively small directorate. Although R2, R3, and R4 had been reduced to single officers by the DIS staff cuts in 1964, and R8 had always been only a single officer, technically specialized sections such as R6 and R7 were still relatively small compared with R1, which had at least four geographical sub-sections as well as SPA under its ambit. The Service Department and GCHQ liaison sections *could not* get any smaller and still exist independently, and they still individually served four powerful outside consumers with very particular requirements. R6 and R7, however, did dwindle to a point where their independent existence could be challenged. As one officer put it, there were very few economic intelligence requirements at all. One did not, he noted, send officers abroad to study the economy of the country to which they were stationed. Moreover, 'there was a matter of inclination: very few SIS officers are economists while the typical SIS officer is a political animal'. There were, moreover, 'relatively few economic requirements that were not political-economic'.[112] It was, therefore, a relatively minor change to absorb R6's regional functions under the political requirements section, R1.[113]

R7's fate was more complex. R7 had evolved out of both R.V. Jones's original IId as R7 or the Technical Coordinating Section, established to service the Joint Technical and Scientific Intelligence Committee, and the short-lived nuclear intelligence or 'tube alloys' section, R9. Under the reforms of the mid-1970s, technical and nuclear intelligence were again divorced. Scientific and technical intelligence was absorbed by R/SOV, the area most concerned with technical intelligence developments.[114] Nuclear intelligence went its own separate way once again as a one-man (later two-man) section concerned with nuclear proliferation.[115]

In principle, all that would have been left from the diminution and demise of R6 and R7 would have been the Service liaison sections, R8, and a considerably expanded R1. As a result, when Oldfield undertook his 'streamlining' of the SIS after 1973, the predominantly *political* requirements sections were reorganized along geographical lines as follows: Requirements, Soviet Bloc (R/SOV); Requirements, Far East (R/FE); Requirements, Middle East (R/ME); Requirements, Europe (R/EUR); Requirements Western Hemisphere (R/WH, including the Americas and the Caribbean); and Requirements, Africa (R/AF), more closely approximating the JIC's CIGs, while R8, the GCHQ liaison, remained as R/GC (Requirements, Government Communications).[116] As the political and surviving economic aspects of Requirements Directorate were being broken up along geographical lines, the Service Branch liaisons, formerly R2 (Air), R3 (Navy) and R4 (Army), were carved out of the Directorate to become a Defence Liaison Staff. In this capacity, they were retitled 'MODA', standing for Ministry of Defence Adviser, with R4 redesignated as MODA/Army, R3 as MODA/Navy and R2 as MODA/Air.[117] Later, in the 1980s, the FOA, MODA/Army, MODA/Navy, MODA/Air and a historical section were grouped together as the SIS Secretariat under C, headed by H/SECT (recently, Alan Petty, better known as the novelist and Cumming's biographer, Alan Judd).[118]

The reductions in Requirements Directorate size and its geographical reorganization converged in turn with the increasingly close relationship between production and requirements which had been developing since the introduction of the Targeting Sections. During the mid-1970s, the practice developed of what one officer termed 'collocating R and P sections', in other words, housing the now geographical requirements sections with their relevant area controllerates. Requirements Officers were encouraged to participate in operational meetings on the grounds that greater familiarity with operational specifics made it easier for the R Sections to evaluate the information they were circulating to consumers or contributing to the deliberations of their respective CIGs, while at the same time making them more alert to the possible indicators of fabrication or deception. Area Controllers further adopted the practice of contributing to the intelligence reports issued by the R Sections.[119]

When Franks took over as C in late 1978, reportedly his first instruction to his board of directors at his first staff meeting was as follows: '*I want the Directors' Board to be a collegiate body. I will be listening to you, you will not be listening to me.*'[120] Thus, perhaps even for the first time, the collegiality of SIS working arrangements was acknowledged by SIS's own leadership. The explicit emphasis on collegial working relations coincided with the already collegial working

287

relationship between Production and Requirements, both of which were now geographically structured, and both of which came under the day-to-day geographical oversight of the Area Controllers. As a result, in 1978/79, the Requirements Directorate, 'already felt in some quarters to be too small to warrant a full Director',[121] ceased to be an independent Directorate, and Production and Requirements were merged under a combined Director of Requirements and Production, who also doubled as Deputy Chief.[122] The Requirements process, however, retained a measure of independence under a Deputy Director, Requirements (DD/R), who carried on the responsibilities that D/R had had, but in a junior capacity in SIS.[123] Although the separate Director of Requirements was a thing of the past, the functions of the R Sections continued to be overseen by DD/R, who was responsible overall for the quality of the reports produced by the R Sections, and the day-to-day relations between the SIS and its consumers in Whitehall.

One card that disappeared in the reshuffle of Requirements was SPA. During the late 1960s, under White and Rennie, the SIS had been moving away from special political actions. Such actions were both dangerous and expensive, and under Oldfield, who was concerned with shifting the emphasis of the SIS firmly back onto pure intelligence gathering, SPA was shut down shortly after his accession as C.[124] This did not abolish such actions any more than abolishing D/WP discontinued war-planning work. Ultimately, the end of the SPA involved moving responsibility for covert actions to the controllerates, and further emphasizing interdepartmental and interservice joint operations where a political or paramilitary dimension might prove necessary.

As Michael Smith has argued in his *New Cloak, Old Dagger* (1996), this shift towards 'jointery' in operations can in part be traced to a 1968 report issued by SAS Colonel John Waddy, which, according to John Strawson's *A History of the SAS Regiment*,

> called for close cooperation, even joint action, between the secret services and the military. 'The army organization', Waddy concluded, 'to do this task is the SAS.' The SAS would therefore have to be capable of carrying out not only reconnaissance and offensive operations, but also special tasks in support of MI6 or Special Branch.[125]

In many respects, just as the 1966 reorganization resurrected the 1945 scheme, special operations thinking was moving back towards the 1945–6 war-planning doctrine in which the SIS gathered the intelligence and recruited the contacts, but the SAS would actually handle any special operations in the field. However, before the new jointery between the SIS and the MoD came to full fruition, certain key events took place that would force the British government to re-evaluate the emphasis it gave intelligence and national covert capability.

The end of the 1970s and the early 1980s proved a period that would give intelligence – and defence matters in general – a new priority in government thinking and expenditure. To start with, new and hawkish, right-wing, 'neo-liberal' political administrations were elected on both sides of the Atlantic, with the Conservative government of Margaret Thatcher finding a like-minded Presidency in the Republican administration of Ronald Reagan. But hawkish rhetoric notwithstanding, there were two intelligence failures during this period that pushed intelligence in general and the SIS in particular further up the list of national priorities. The first was the Soviet invasion of Afghanistan in 1979 and the second was the Argentine invasion of the Falkland Islands in 1982. But while the invasion of Afghanistan predated the Falklands, it was the Falklands that had immediate consequences for the intelligence community, while the impact of Afghanistan accumulated over a longer period.

The Falkland Islands disaster constituted virtually definitive evidence that the UK intelligence community, and the SIS in particular, had been run down to such a level that they could no longer defend the realm from Third World dictatorships, let alone the USSR and its satellites. Among the SIS's overseas controllerates, the western hemisphere had suffered more heavily from the operational cuts than the Far East mother lode of Third-Country operations against Soviet bloc nationals and Africa and the Middle East with their historical, colonial carry-over of British economic and politico-military interests. In his account of the Falklands intelligence campaign, Nigel West claims that the SIS's 'South American stations had borne the brunt of the cost imposed by successive short-sighted governments anxious to save cash, leaving a single officer, Mark Heathcote, to cover Argentina and report to...the Regional Controller in London. All other stations on the continent had been closed as part of the SIS's programme of austerity, a far cry from the days when SIS ran fully manned stations in Santiago, Caracas, Rio de Janeiro and Lima.'[126] The reductions had been progressive over several years, the SIS maintaining for a time two stations in Latin America, for the Spanish- and Portuguese-speaking territories, respectively, but these had in turn been consolidated into a single, unsurpringly, overworked, station at Buenos Aires.[127] The official inquiry conducted into the causes of the war by Lord Franks also noted that Argentina had been accorded a low priority in the national intelligence requirements of the day.[128] Cutbacks combined with Argentina's low priority and a prevailing Foreign Office orthodoxy or 'groupthink' that war with Argentina was unlikely. As a result, no sooner had Arthur Franks been relieved by his successor, Colin Figures, than the new C found his agency embroiled in a major national intelligence failure, and a major intelligence effort on a war footing with little or no warning.[129] If anything good can be said of the war, however, it must be that the Falklands crisis brought badly needed Prime Ministerial attention to the intelligence community, along with badly needed additional funding and resourcing (including the expansion of the Latin American presence to three fully staffed stations).[130] According to her Private Secretary, Sir Charles Powell, Thatcher 'increased their funding and supported them in ways no Prime Minister since the Second World War had done'.[131] Once funding returned to the intelligence community under Prime Ministerial interest, the improved investment in the SIS paid off rapidly in many areas, not least with a successful disruption of the Lebanese paramilitary factions[132] and the attraction of defectors such as the KGB officers Vladimir Kuzichkin, who defected in Tehran,[133] and Oleg Gordievsky, who ran successfully inside the KGB for nearly 11 years.[134] Operations like these raised the agency's stock with consumers and allies alike, and improved a previously beleaguered service's morale. When Sir Christopher Curwen replaced Sir Colin Figures as Chief of Service in 1985, he took charge of an SIS that was on the mend after a decade and a half of neglect.

By contrast, the impact of first the Soviet-backed coup and the subsequent Soviet invasion of Afghanistan was less that of surprise and intelligence failure than the Falklands. Rather, it gave impetus to a new demand in foreign and defence policy circles for covert special operations – special operations in the old wartime paramilitary sense. Both the recently elected Thatcher and Reagan governments were eager to engage the Soviet Union and her allies as vigorously as possible and on as many fronts as possible. As a result, their respective intelligence services and special operations forces (SOF) became actively involved in providing advice, training and weapons, and installing clandestine supply routes to aid what grew into a multinational and increasingly radically fundamentalist Islamic resistance known collectively as the *mujahedin*. To do so, SIS needed the appropriate resources and MoD collaboration as stated in Brigadier General John Waddy's proposals, and finally a return to the old special operations doctrine methods of the long-defunct Directorate of War Planning. The SIS's involvement was necessarily on a smaller scale than that of the CIA, reportedly consisting of an annual mission to one particular faction (that of Ahmed Shah Massoud) composed of a couple of SIS officers and a handful of 'freelance' military or ex-military instructors. The former were there partly to provide what they could in terms of support and resources to Massoud, given Britain's financial limitations, and to take advantage of the extensive intelligence of Soviet movements and assets that Massoud's organization was able to collect. The latter, of course, were to provide organizational and operational training to Massoud's commanders.[135] With the availability of the *mujahedin* as a weapon to be wielded against Soviet hegemony and a tool of diversion and disruption against Soviet foreign policy,[136] aiding and equipping *la Résistance* had come back into fashion after a succession of Labour governments utterly averse to anything that their more radical backbenchers might construe as 'dirty tricks'.

On of the key areas where enhanced resourcing and support for SIS became visible during the 1980s was the renewed provision of 'Special Duties' elements made available from the Ministry of Defence for SIS operations. This took the form of 'contract labourers', serving and retired members of special operations forces such as the SAS and the SBS seconded or 'sheep-dipped' for SIS duties[137] and the allocation of a range of SOF and transport elements known colloquially as the 'increment'. It was 'contract labourers' who contributed military instruction to the annual SIS missions to Afghanistan, and it was 'contract labourers' that handled the more hazardous border-crossing operations from Pakistan, most notable among which was the acquisition of a downed Soviet Mil-24 HIND helicopter gunship, transported piece by piece across the frontier.[138] The Service 'increment' at the turn of the 1990s reportedly included an SD detachment from the RAF flying a Puma and a C-130 Hercules, while the SAS and the SBS both provided small detachments.[139] Since its establishment, coordination and tasking of the 'increment' have been routed through a fourth Ministry of Defence Adviser, typically an SAS officer with the rank of lieutenant

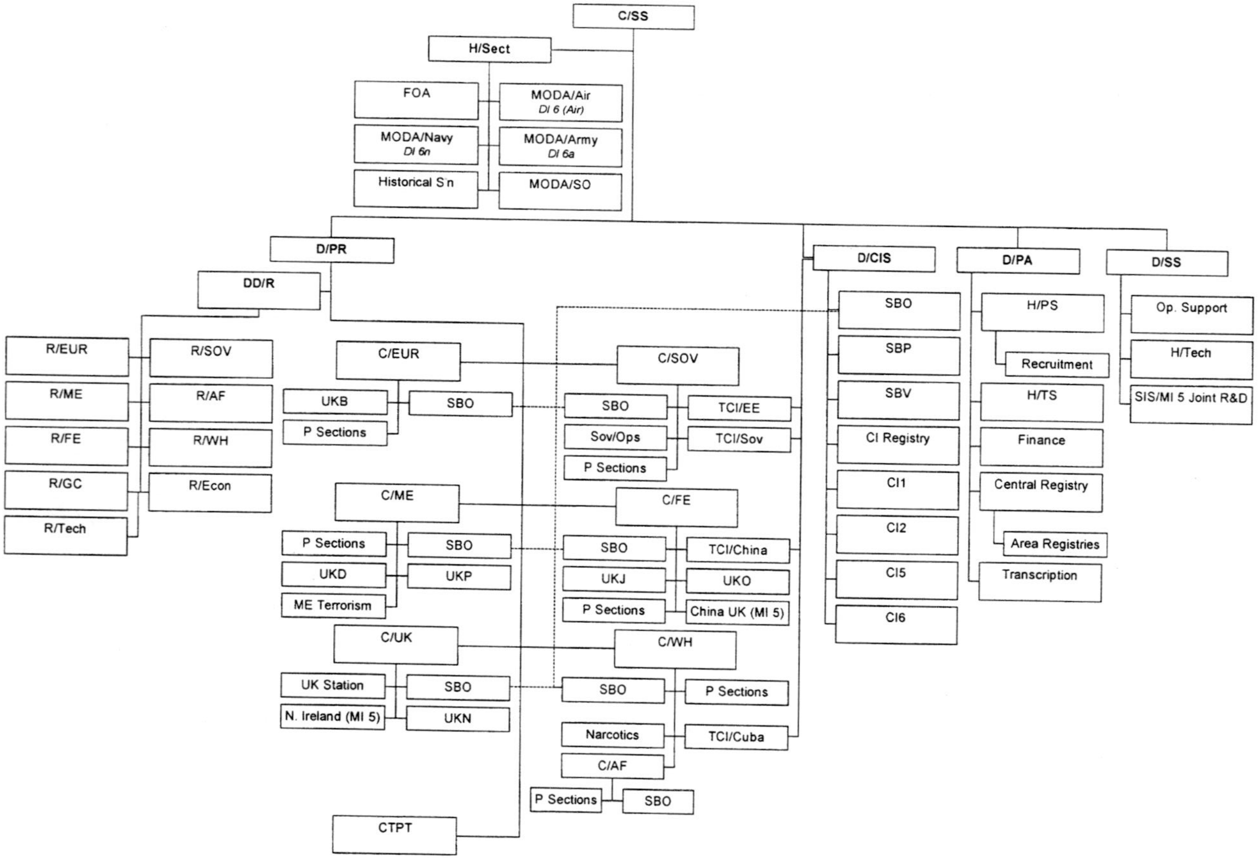

Figure 6.6: SIS in 1989

colonel[140] designated MODA/SO,[141] who joined the other Ministry of Defence Advisers in the Secretariat.

SIS intelligence collection can also be seen to have been increasingly aggressive during this period. For example, although C/UK had been cut back to a minimal role at the end of the 1970s, reliance on 'natural cover' operations increased during the 1980s. This led to a range of UK-based sections besides the self-explanatory Sov/Ops that C/SOV's precursor, Director Western Europe and Soviet Bloc, had acquired from D/P4 in the early 1960s. The other 'natural cover' sections included UKB (Western Europe), UKC (Africa), UKD (Middle East, excluding Iran), UKJ (Japan), UKO (India and Pakistan) and UKP (Iran) under their respective Area Controllers. It was ironic, however, that after dismantling C/UK's domain it was then necessary to create a 'natural cover committee' to coordinate the various 'natural cover' stations and permit them to 'share their ideas and expertise on natural cover operation'[142] – essentially shifting from a bureaucratic hierarchy to a collegial board for UK-based Third-Country operations.

During this interval, SIS also found itself forced to reverse its earlier abolition of scientific and technical intelligence on the one hand and economic intelligence on the other hand. Economic intelligence was reinstituted because of the creation of an Economic Unit within the Joint Assessments Staff during the late 1980s. In order to service what amounted to an economic CIG made up of members of the Treasury and Bank of England, SIS had to re-establish an economic Requirements Section (R/ECON).[143] Similarly, an increased traffic in technical information prompted a revivified R7, now termed R/TECH,[144] although nuclear proliferation remained separate from technical and scientific intelligence.

In 1988 and 1989, there were already changes in the national intelligence priorities that would become increasingly central in the post-Cold War intelligence refocusing and restructuring of the SIS. The two most significant, or rather increasingly significant, priorities were narcotics and counter-proliferation. Britain has never had an equivalent of the American Drug Enforcement Agency; as a result, narcotics intelligence has generally been subsumed under the remits of the regional police services and HM Customs and Excise. Neither of these two areas was yet particularly intelligence oriented in the late 1980s. Given the intelligence community's traditional involvement in intercepting contraband under its wartime strategic trade role (the original 1939 legislation for which remained in force until the early 1990s[145]) and the 1949 COCOM brief, it was not inappropriate to task foreign investigation of these problems to national intelligence services that were permitted to function abroad where the police and Customs were not. There are also economies of scale in tasking the existing intelligence services, as the alternative would be to pay for duplicate foreign operations capabilities for the police or Customs, and those costs become increasingly daunting when one considers the investment needed to give them a SIGINT capability parallel to GCHQ. Indeed, an intelligence link between SIS and the police was hardly a new idea, as we have already seen that the Special Branch had maintained its own equivalent to a circulating section to handle SIS product called SS1 during the inter-war years (but housed at Scotland Yard rather than Broadway, it was only weakly integrated into the 1921 arrangement). As a consequence, in 1988, and in response to the appearance of these requirements in the annual National Intelligence Requirements Paper, the SIS set up a Counter-Narcotics Section,[146] originally under the auspices of the Controller, Western Hemisphere (C/WH) because of the Latin American dimension of the narcotics trade.[147] However, Counter-Narcotics soon began to expand beyond the horizons of C/WH, SIS finding itself pursuing narcotics routes from South America through Poland and Czechoslovakia (the latter in collaboration with the Czech security service)[148] and then routes from and via Pakistan, Afghanistan and Iran.[149]

During the 1994 Commons debate on the Intelligence Services Bill (discussed in greater length below), Secretary of State Douglas Hurd regaled the Commons with tales of SIS derring-do, one of which involved counter-narcotics work. According to Hurd,

> A British law enforcement agency recently asked the SIS to help monitor a large consignment of drugs from a developed country believed to be destined for the UK. The Service could not rely on the cooperation of the authorities in the country concerned, so it sent an officer under an assumed identity. Soon after his arrival, in difficult and dangerous circumstances, the officer was able to identify and enlist the support of an employee of the transport organization which was innocently handling the movement of the consignment . . . the consignment was monitored to a point outside the country, where it was seized by international action.[150]

Visible in this account is the long-established SIS doctrine that the first point of contact for its resident officers is the local security authorities, which in this case was not feasible. Central also is the fact that the agency was *tasked* by a branch of the UK government, specifically an unidentified law-enforcement agency. The capacity to send a Visiting Case Officer (VCO) out in a hurry to find a human source to monitor the shipment also captures the changing pace of work in intelligence when dealing with counter-narcotics rather than the more steady progress of Cold War balance of power manoeuvring. This problem of 'operations tempo' would prove increasingly challenging as the post-Cold War requirements for criminal, terrorist and peacekeeping intelligence increased and took centre stage.

During the following year, counter-proliferation began to experience increased demand and expanded in turn. The initial impetus came from a paper prepared by the head of the FCO Nuclear Energy Department, John Gordon, highlighting the danger of British technology being acquired by foreign states for clandestine nuclear programmes. The nuclear proliferation section had expanded from one to two officers since the restructuring of requirements in the 1970s, but was still inadequate to the newly expanded demand for information on this subject.[151] It has often been pointed out that counter-proliferation, like counter-narcotics and terrorism, is generally more amenable to human intelligence than SIGINT and IMINT,[152] and SIS's limited input in this area was already seen by Gordon as 'absolutely crucial'.[153] In due course, during 1989–1990, the counter-proliferation staff was expanded, taking the form of an expanded section called Production and Targeting, Counter-Proliferation (PTCP).[154] After the Cold War's end, and especially after revelations about the clandestine weapons acquisition programmes of Qaddafi's Libya and Saddam Hussein's Iraq, the PTCP found its functions extended to include both nuclear and non-nuclear weapons of mass destruction (biological and chemical), and in due course the acquisition of advanced conventional weapons.[155]

ALL CHANGE

In 1990–91, the Cold War ended not with a bang but with the proverbial whimper. It ended, much to the surprise and relief of the world, peacefully, at times almost amiably, as the new Soviet premier,

Mikhail Sergeievich Gorbachev, took the initiative in arms reductions, in political reform through openness, or *glasnost*, through (unsuccessful) economic reform, or *perestroika*, and, finally, by allowing the states of Eastern Europe to go their own way, first East Germany, and later throughout the region in what became known, after the Czech precedent, as the Velvet Revolution. For the most part, the Eastern European Communist regimes fell relatively calmly and through peaceful and even constitutional processes (only in Ceauçescu's Romania was the change hard fought, some times building by building and street by street, with Ceauçescu and his wife suffering fates eerily similar to those of Mussolini and his mistress). In truth, the real driving force of the Cold War tensions had eased enough by October 1989 that, at a conference held in Ottawa by the Canadian Association for Security and Intelligence Studies, it was possible for the main theme of the event to be the putative role of the intelligence services in the absence of the 'traditional' Cold War polarity.[156] The old Cold War intelligence agenda was already on its last legs well before the dramatic, televised 1989 fall of the Berlin Wall.

Despite the fact that for those with eyes to see and ears to hear the Cold War was effectively over at least two years before the Velvet Revolution, the final disengagement was followed by the usual cycle of intelligence and defence introspection, reform, reorganization and retasking which we have already seen follow the Boer War, the First World War and the Second World War. The most crucial of these during the interval of rethinking and refocusing after the fall of the Berlin Wall was Sir Michael Quinlan's 1993 review. Quinlan, formerly PUS at the Ministry of Defence, concentrated partly on financial management and partly on foreign intelligence operations and requirements.[157] It was in response to this atmosphere of revision that the SIS Chief at the end of the Cold War, Sir Collin McColl, mounted a series of reforms which culminated in the so-called 'Christmas massacre' of 1993.

To appreciate the impact and scale of the SIS changes during the 1990s, it is necessary to keep in mind the wider rethinking of the role of intelligence. Most national intelligence systems underwent some degree of review and reform, although most were naturally less radical than those experienced by the former Soviet bloc agencies.[158] The main shift, from the Western perspective, was, of course, the end of the Soviet threat. The so-called 'new intelligence agenda' consisted roughly of five main items: counter-terrorism, counter-proliferation, transnational serious crime, economic security and peacekeeping.[159] On the whole, these conformed to former Director of Central Intelligence James Woolsey's now famous metaphor that having slain the Soviet dragon, the intelligence community now found itself in a jungle full of snakes.[160]

It is tempting, in view of all of the verbiage about the 'new world order' and disorder, globalization, information revolution and so forth to imagine that some fundamental break had occurred in the doing of spying, and that somehow intelligence as an activity was liable to profound change. In fact, compared to the post-1946 reforms, the changes to intelligence and especially to the SIS were marginal matters of detail, and that was all that was required. The only change in the intelligence agenda after the fall of the Berlin Wall was the absence of the bottomless financial well of anti-Soviet intelligence require-ments.[161] Because, in the last analysis, *there is nothing new in the new intelligence agenda.*

SIS's adaptation to the post-Cold War arena proceeded in two main stages. In the first place, there were minor adaptations to suit the shift to small-scale, low-intensity threats between 1990 and 1993. Secondly, under McColl's successor as C, Sir David Spedding, the organization experienced a comprehensive review and programme of adaptation to new conditions over 1993–94. During the 1990–93 interval, McColl cultivated a more visible public profile for the agency, even changing the designation of Director, Counter-Intelligence and Security, to Director, Security and Public Affairs.[162] However, the three main developments of interest were the creation of the Global Issues section, the reinstitution of an equivalent to the SPA under the designation of Information Operations (I/Ops), and the appearance of a small section tasked with acquiring intelligence through the clandestine penetration of computer systems (presumably under the auspices of Operational Support).

The function of Global Issues was to consolidate PTCP, counter-narcotics, transnational serious crime and emerging issues, such as the environment, into a single section.[163] On one side, I/Ops is the practical implementation of the former D/SPA's 'public affairs' brief, while, on the other side, it is in many respects a replacement for the long departed SPA, much as MODA/SO and the 'Increment' resurrected D/WP. It reflects both an increased willingness to cultivate a public image and an increasingly robust attitude within SIS (and the UK government) towards covert action, and, in particular, disruptive actions wherein one sets adversaries against one another. Its origins appear to lie in the aftermath of the Gulf War, in which the UK intelligence and defence communities found themselves going to war with a gravely reduced psyops capability[164] – and in a campaign where psyops and propaganda were to prove useful in encouraging Iraqi soldiers to desert rather than fight.

I/Ops is relatively sizeable by SIS standards, reportedly having as many as 20 offices,[165] and has as its primary role media and public relations, although it is also responsible for psychological operations in the relatively aggressive sense of black propaganda, and deceptive and disruptive actions.[166] Former SIS Area Controller, Baroness Daphne Park, has remarked of disruptive action:

> Once you get really good inside intelligence about any group you are able to learn where the levers of power are, and what one man fears of another... you set people discreetly against one another. ...They destroy each other, we don't destroy them.[167]

Despite her assurances that SIS does not 'destroy' people directly, SO training has remained a central feature of training at Fort Monkton in the enhanced, six-month Intelligence Officers' New Entry Course (IONEC) run there. Unarmed combat and firearms training as well as training with the 'increment'[168] are featured in classic SOE style, and, according to military personnel interviewed by Michael Smith, new officers train in the 'killing houses' used by the SAS and the SBS, conducting counter-terrorist assault exercises, and have adopted a de facto uniform of black coveralls when doing so.[169] The notion of disruptive action has become an increasingly central one in the SIS covert action repertoire, one of the classic examples cited being the creation of a sustained struggle between rival militia factions in the Lebanon during the 1980s to distract them from targeting UK and allied nationals.[170] Indeed, it has to be said that disruptive actions and their like do have the potential to undermine small and especially fractious groups that résistance-style campaigns, propaganda and supporting dissident movements against strongly established communist police states never had during the Cold War.

The sub-section for clandestine computer penetration – or what has recently been termed HACKINT in opposition to SIGINT or HUMINT[171] – took shape in the typically inauspicious SIS fashion. Strictly speaking, the notion was not a new one, and intelligence with the potential for the clandestine penetration of mainframe computers had originally been attempted by the Canadian RCMP Security Service (an agency traditionally closely affiliated with and modelled on MI5[172]) in an operation code-named HAM in 1973, while attacking networked computer systems was originally highlighted, at least publicly, in the early 1980s in the so-called 'Hannover Hacker' affair. Operation HAM involved the clandestine entry into the premises of the Quebec Separatist political party, the *Parti Québecois*, to secure and copy its membership list, which was handled on a mainframe computer. Once inside, the Security Service team removed the relevant computer tapes, duplicated them at an indoctrinated computer firm nearby run by a former Security Service officer, and promptly returned them before the start of the business day.[173] In the 'Hannover Hacker' case, a group of German computer adepts calling themselves the Chaos Computer Club, and led by one Markus Hess, made a concerted, but ultimately relatively unsuccessful attempt to penetrate US Department of Defense networked systems to find information about the Strategic Defense Initiative, also known as the 'Star Wars' antiballistic missile programme.[174] HAM and the Hannover Hacker were *causes célèbres* in their day. HAM featured in the press revelations about the Royal Canadian Mounted Police Security Service (RCMP/SS) that led to the MacDonald Commission and the agency's abolition and replacement with the civilian (non-police) Canadian Security Intelligence Service (CSIS). The activities of Hess and his associates were widely publicized by the astronomer-turned system operator who described their cybernetic transgressions in a best-selling book and a succession of professional articles about computer security. Despite the relatively visible profile of clandestine physical and network computer penetration for information technology professionals in the private sector (and evidently, the Canadian and Russian services), the idea was not seriously picked up by SIS until around 1992, at which point a single officer was invited to make a trial run of this kind of collection. He was provided with a room in Century House, a single computer and no additional budget, and challenged to see what he could do.[175] The results were sufficiently compelling that a permanent and increasingly well-equipped section was established to pursue this kind of intelligence.[176]

Along with these essentially ad hoc structural changes, McColl's SIS began to develop a revision of its existing operational doctrine for recruiting and running agents abroad. One of the early trends visible after the end of the Cold War, and the unexpected if short-lived Gulf War, followed rapidly by the collapse of Yugoslavia into the proverbial internecine Balkan quagmire, was the tendency of crises and requirements to appear in unexpected parts of the world with relatively little precedent or warning. As a result, the SIS let it be known that there was a shift in emphasis developing from its traditional and geographically relatively stable 'presence' or global range of large, fixed stations to 'capability' that would emphasize flexibility and adaptability over continuous coverage. Much has been made of this in journalistic discussions, but with relatively little examination or consideration of its substance.[177] In practical terms, SIS operational doctrine was already geared in this direction through its reliance on Targeting Sections, 'natural cover' and Visiting Case Officers,[1778] who travel to wherever a likely agent has been identified by the Targeting Sections and make the necessary approach (rather than resident station staff, whose main task in such an arrangement is agent support and communications).[179] In the post-Cold War context, an increased shift in operational doctrine involved exploiting new information and communications technologies such as the satellite telephones which figured so prominently in the press reporting of the 1991 Gulf War. McColl reportedly developed an extension of existing methods in the form of 'shoebox stations' based on a single officer operating independently of any resident station (such as one under diplomatic cover) to provide quick, on-the-ground capability in late-breaking theatres of operation such as the Balkans. According to the former SIS officer, Richard Tomlinson, these consisted of 'one officer armed with a laptop computer, encryption software and a briefcase-sized portable satellite facsimile machine'. He further adds that 'the shoe-box officer would not have the usual benefits of comfortable, free housing, car allowance or home leave of normal postings, so they would serve only six months and be paid a generous hardship allowance.'[180]

As a consequence of Quinlan's review in 1993, it was inevitable that the SIS should conduct a systematic internal review of its own. That internal review climaxed in what has since become known as the 'Christmas massacre' at the end of that year.[181] This transformation involved the comprehensive retirement of the agency's Cold War-vintage Board of Directors and their replacement with a new, younger generation of senior officers who boasted a broader range of geographical experience. McColl himself retired at the time and was replaced by Sir David Spedding, who had served as Director, Production and Requirements, under him, and before that as C/ME during the Gulf War.[182] Spedding then spent much of 1994 in a further review of the SIS that led to a comprehensive overhaul in 1995.[183]

During the same period, the UK government finally passed legislation placing the SIS and GCHQ on a statutory footing comparable to the Security Service. It is not the intent here to discuss the motivations, legal details and wider consequences of the 1994 Intelligence Services Act (ISA),[184] as most of its features served either as enabling items for activities already under way[185] or alterations and additions to the existing mechanisms of public accountability, most notably in the creation of the Parliamentary Intelligence and Security Committee (ISC). From a structure and process point of view, the changes incorporated into the Act have little relevance to the internal operation of SIS or the machinery of the 1921 arrangement. This is particularly so as the ISC's ambit – although it has changed and, indeed, expanded over the years – is confined to a right to examine vaguely defined matters of 'expenditure, administration and policy' of the agencies (as opposed to operations).[186]

The only significant alteration in functional terms is the articulation in the Act of formal procedures for authorization and warranting. However, even the legally significant step of formalizing authorizations and warrants ('issued by the Secretary of State', unlike the judicial warrants required for police activities) constituted a relatively minimal substantive change to the process of spying. Under the ISA of 1994, 'no entry or interference with property or with wireless telegraphy shall be unlawful if it is authorized by a warrant issued by the Secretary of State'.[187] Such a warrant 'shall not be issued except (a) under the hand of the Secretary of State; or (b) in an urgent case where the Secretary of State has authorized its issue and a statement of the fact is endorsed on it, under the hand of a senior official of his department'.[188] Such provisions, of course, really refer only to the abrogation of British law, and the SIS operates primarily abroad. Hence the Act also incorporates a provision for 'Authorization of acts outside the British Islands'. Under this section, 'if...a person would be liable in the United Kingdom for any act which is done outside the British Islands, he shall not be so liable if the act is one which is authorized to be done by virtue of an authorization given by the Secretary of State'.[189] Naturally, of course, the Act stipulates that warrants and authorization may be issued

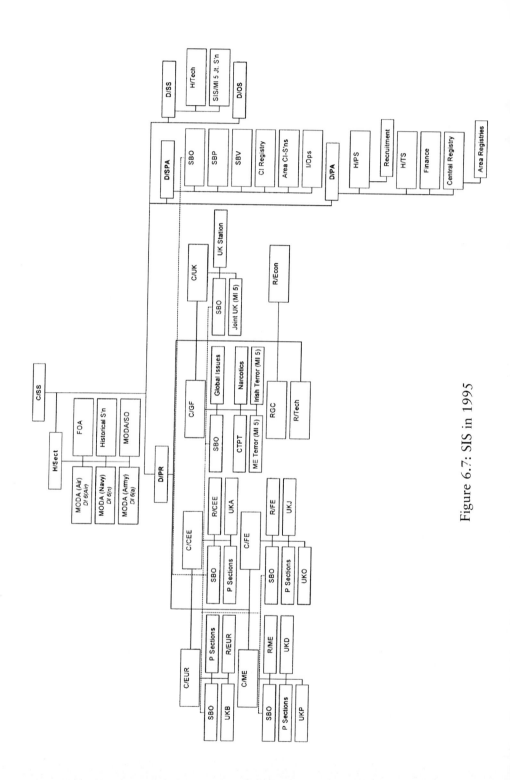

Figure 6.7: SIS in 1995

only where they are consistent with the conditions of the Act and limitations on task and jurisdiction of the agencies in question.

In practical terms, however, the addition of warrants and authorizations has changed the agency's authorization procedures minimally. As we have already seen, a rigorous (but not infallible) mechanism of operational oversight and authorization has existed at SIS HQ since the 1950s. Any operation or programme of operations proposed by the agency must first cross the desk of the Foreign Office Adviser (FOA). In his/her original capacity, the FOA was empowered to authorize operations when convinced of their viability and acceptability. However, when in doubt, the FOA could refer to his or her immediate senior in the Permanent Under-Secretary's Department, who could in turn take the matter up with the PUS/FCO, and, if necessary, refer thence to a Minister or the Secretary of State.

During the debate in 1994 over the Intelligence Services Bill, the question of authorizing was brought up by David Trimble, MP. The Foreign Secretary of the day, Douglas Hurd, responded the provision for warrants and authorization was 'a novelty in comparison with previous arrangements'. He added: 'I am already consulted if either [the SIS or GCHQ] wishes to authorize particularly sensitive operations, but that is not a statutory arrangement; it just happens.' Although Hurd initially described the 'novel' arrangements as constituting 'quite an apparatus of control', he further claimed, a little inconsistently, that all they really did was to have 'elaborated, refined, extended and put on the statute books' the existing arrangements. Indeed, he observed, that during his own tenure as Foreign Secretary he had noted 'increasing consultation of the Secretary of State when operations are proposed that are sensitive – that could cause difficulty'.[190] In practice, the use of such a 'mechanism of control' has amounted to only a tiny alteration in procedure. When the Foreign Secretary was consulted under the previous arrangements that 'just happened', he or she would receive a briefing document outlining the details of the operations, the risks, and the causes for concern over its sensitivity. All the new Act has meant is appending the warrant or authorization to the briefing document for the Foreign Secretary to sign or not once he or she has taken a decision on the operation.[191]

In the last analysis, most of the changes to the SIS's infrastructure and procedures between 1993 and 1995 were relatively minimal. The system that had emerged from the Cold War included Directors for Personnel and Administration, Support Services, Security and Counter-Intelligence and Requirements and Production. Under Requirements and Production were seven Area Controllerates for, respectively, the Soviet Bloc, Western Europe, the Western Hemisphere, the Middle East, Africa, the Far East and the UK,[192] as well as a Deputy Director for Requirements overseeing a Requirements Section for each Controllerate (except the UK), R/ECON, R/TECH and R/GC. There was also the Secretariat composed of the Foreign Office and assorted Ministry of Defence Advisers, in addition to the Historical Section. Under the 1993 review, an anticipated reduction in staff size and overseas presence resulting from general defence and security expenditure cutbacks – the 'peace dividend' – meant a reduction in staff size across the service's operational side. As a result, Africa and the Middle East were reamalgamated under C/ME, as were the Western Hemisphere and the Far East under C/FE (returning to the pre-1966 division of work in those areas). There was, of course, no longer a Soviet bloc to target; hence, C/SOV became Controller Central and Eastern Europe (C/CEE) and R/SOV became Requirements Central and Eastern Europe (R/CEE).[193] SOV/OPS became simply another natural cover station under C/CEE as UKA.[194] In light of the increased relative importance of counter-proliferation, counter-terrorism, transnational serious crime and similar 'motherhood issues' in the national intelligence priorities,[195] and the multiplication of functional rather than geographical sections to handle them, Global Issues absorbed the various counter-terrorism sections and was promoted to full controllerate status as Controller, Global and Functional (C/GF).[196] And, of course, D/CIS became D/SPA.

The most significant change was arguably the final abolition of Deputy Director Requirements, and the subordination of the R Sections to their respective controllers.[197] One officer interviewed attributed this change primarily to the use of information technology within the agency to the effect that, since the 1993 reorganization, 'Controllers have more formal responsibility for requirements; modern communications technology and computers have made it easier for everyone to know the same thing at the same time.'[198] This is not necessarily as glib an explanation as it might appear at first glance, but it does require some reflection on the impact of information technology on the intelligence process.

During the early 1980s, the SIS had moved to an electronic data storage and retrieval and electronic mail system called the Automated Telegram Handling System (ATHS). This was installed at Century House, where its supposedly TEMPESTed (electromagnetically secure)

Wang terminal proved less secure than advertised.[199] Although this initial trouble was overcome, the system has since received a less than favourable press, the generally embittered Tomlinson complaining, 'Unfortunately the word processing system was so cumbersome that only computer-literate junior officers used it, and the message handling system so slow and unreliable that it was often quicker to resort to old-fashioned pen and paper.'[200] Such difficulties are quite imaginable for anyone who had to do work under public and commercial text editors of the same vintage, such as Gnu or Emacs (or the early incarnations of the Unix email software, Pine). Indeed many senior people in government and industry spent the second half of the 1980s and the first half of the 1990s trying to cope with the 'information revolution'. The implication of an information and communications technology, such as ATHS, is that the rapid and simultaneously selective and extensive dissemination of intelligence product through Information and Communications Technologies (ICTs) has very real effects on the intelligence producer–consumer relationship. Commenting on the potential of ICTs for intelligence production and dissemination in the United States, Peter Scharfman has noted that the close communication and ready availability of intelligence information to consumers makes it easier for consumers to drive the production process.[201] Scharfman, of course, was referring to the more producer-driven US intelligence community. To apply such a technology to the UK system can only serve to intensify the existing consumer-driven relationship. Moreover, it allows a degree of direct communication between producer and consumer that potentially does away with the need for middlemen to act as intermediaries between producer and consumer.

The ATHS has since been superseded by more contemporary systems since the SIS's move to more modern quarters at Vauxhall Cross, and by the government-wide implementation of the UK Intelligence Messaging System (UKIMS). These can only have strengthened the trend already described. As a result, far from indicating a weakening of the consumer-driven UK 'pull architecture' created by the 1921 arrangement, *the abolition of DD/R points to an intensification of it*. At the beginning of the twenty-first century, the SIS remains as it was conceived at the beginning of the twentieth century: a screen between the UK government and foreign spies who may have information they wish to sell it, an intermediary between that government and the agents it employs in foreign countries, no more and no less than the covert armature of the overt British government.

NOTES

1. Anthony Verrier, *Through the Looking-Glass: British Foreign Policy in an Age of Illusions* (London: Jonathan Cape, 1983), p. 168.
2. Nigel West, *The Friends* (London: Grafton, 1988), p. 118; Peter Wright, *Spycatcher: The Candid Autobiography of a Senior Intelligence Officer* (Toronto: Hodder & Stoughton, 1987), p. 207.
3. Richard Norton-Taylor, obituary of Sir Dick White, the *Guardian*, 23 February 1993.
4. Verrier, *Through the Looking-Glass*, p. 174; unlike both Verrier and Norton-Taylor, West does not distinguish between the regional chief controllers and the eventual four directors of production, listing the titles side by side in his, *The Friends*, p. 14.
5. Tom Bower, *The Perfect English Spy: Sir Dick White and the Secret War 1935–90* (London: Heinemann, 1995), pp. 142–4; Wright, *Spycatcher*, pp. 32, 120; West, *A Matter of Trust*, pp. 62–4.
6. i-20.
7. i-20. A similar, but less intensely worded opinion was expressed by i-28.
8. i-11.
9. i-19.
10. i-19 firmly maintained that he had answered to a Director of Personnel, although he could not recall the director's two- or three-letter designation; however, the organization chart for SIS around 1981 published by Duncan Campbell gives the administrative directorate as 'Personnel and Administration', 'Friends and Others', *The New Statesman*, 26 November 1982.
11. i-19 suggested the move tentatively, while i-28 was absolutely sure about it, as was i-20 who provided the designation H/TS.
12. i-28.
13. i-10; i-11. Note that when Training and Development was originally set up in 1946, its director held a comparable title as H/TD. Nigel West refers in passing to Geoffrey Hinton's being promoted to head of counter-intelligence in *The Friends*, p. 149, without noting the significance of the position, or that the post of H/CI did not fit in at all with the organization chart he included at the beginning of the book, or at least without explaining what this new post was.
14. i-28. Targeting Sections also appear in Richard Tomlinson, *The Big Breach: From Top Secret to Maximum Security* (Edinburgh: Cutting Edge, 2001), pp. 95, 176.
15. i-20.
16. John Dziak, *Chekisty: A History of the KGB* (New York: Ivy, 1988) pp. 1–2.
17. i-28.
18. i-28.

19. For usage of the term, see Tomlinson, *The Big Breach*, p. 107.
20. i-28. See also Tomlinson, *The Big Breach*, pp. 95, 176.
21. Cabinet Office, *Central Intelligence Machinery* (London: HMSO, 1993), p. 11; the same language was used in the updated *Central Intelligence Machinery*, available on-line through the open government World Wide Web pages at http://www.open.gov.uk/co/cim/cimrep1a.htm, 30 April 1997.
22. Percy Cradock, *Know Your Enemy: How the Joint Intelligence Committee Saw the World* (London: John Murray, 2002), p. 264.
23. Cabinet Office, *Central Intelligence Machinery*, p. 13; http:www.open.gov.uk/co/cim/cimrep2.htm, 30 April 1997.
24. Verrier, *Through the Looking-Glass*, p. 4; i-28.
25. i-28.
26. For a period of around two or three years, during the Cold War, the JIC and Security and Intelligence Agencies went without a National Intelligence Requirements Document, according to Michael Herman, *Intelligence Power in Peace and War* (Cambridge: Cambridge University Press, 1996), p. 292. Although Herman uses this to suggest that a requirements list is not really very necessary, it should be noted that the situation to which Herman refers was relatively short-lived, and not adopted as permanent practice.
27. Geoffrey McDermott, *The Eden Legacy and the Decline of British Diplomacy* (London: Leslie Frewin, 1969), p. 175.
28. i-10.
29. i-15.
30. i-11; i-15.
31. Consider, for example, that John Teague, CC/M, had originally served as a Head of Station in the Middle East before the Second World War, and CC/P, James Fulton, had been with SIS(FE) since it had been CRPO(FE). C/PR, Nicholas Elliott, has been with Section B of ISLD Cairo in 1941, and had served with the SIS ever since.
32. i-10.
33. This development is traced fairly explicitly in Blake, *No Other Choice* (London: Jonathan Cape, 1990), pp. 182–4. The remaining D/Ps are identified, in parallel with the CC titles, by West, *The Friends*, pp. 13–15, a scheme also cited by Richard Norton-Taylor in his *In Defence of the Realm?* (London: Civil Liberties Trust, 1990), p. 50, although this completely contradicts the organization chart of area controllers which Norton-Taylor provides on p. 62 of the same volume. The D/P designations were confirmed, approximately dated (to around 1958/59) during interviews by i-008, i-10, i-15, i-19, i-20 and i-28.
34. i-15; i-11 (with regard to a slightly later version of the D/P scheme, see below).
35. i-15; i-28.
36. Wright, *Spycatcher*, pp. 46–7; i-15.
37. i-15; i-28.

38. i-10.
39. i-11; i-012 (he suggested this as one of two production organizations he could recall); i-19; i-28. I-011 referred to the Western Hemisphere Directorate as 'Director Americas'.
40. Wright, *Spycatcher*, p. 46; note also the apparent joint nature of the so-called SIS 'Technics Document' on technical methods, p. 117.
41. James Adams, *The New Spies* (London: Hutchinson, 1993), p. 99.
42. Wright, *Spycatcher*, pp. 168–9. The continued existence of the joint technical section is also referred to in Adams, *The New Spies*, p. 99, p. 109.
43. For NODDY, see Bower, *Perfect English Spy*, pp. 355–7.
44. Like Philby, there exists a fairly extensive literature on George Blake, although without the peculiar anti-hero worship directed at the former. Journalistic versions of Blake's story by former intelligence officers were written by E.H. Cookridge, *George Blake: Double Agent* (New York: Ballantine, 1970), and (more recently retired and far better informed) H. Montgomery Hyde, *George Blake: Superspy* (London: Futura, 1987). Blake's own account in his *No Other Choice* is, for the most part, a far more understated and far less self-serving account than Philby's memoir, and perhaps a less arcane exercise in disinformation, relying less upon unflattering caricature than upon the vague pathos of the outsider never really brought inside, who betrayed for ideological reasons and out of personal resentments but on a far less grandiose scale.
45. Apart from the public trial, the Penkovsky case has received extensive treatment in the literature. The original account, and one subject to much criticism and doubt about its authenticity, was *The Penkovsky Papers* (New York: Avon, 1965) notionally authored by Penkovsky himself but a definitive treatment – and perhaps one of the most thorough and informative treatments of any single HUMINT case ever published – appears in Peter (Petya Sergeyevich) Deriabin and Jerrold Schechter, *The Spy Who Saved the World: How a Soviet Colonel Changed the Course of the Cold War* (New York: Scribner, 1992). Assorted implausible Angletonesque hypotheses have been mooted to suggest that Penkovsky was a put-up job by Khrushchev's opponents in the intelligence and security apparatus in order to discredit his bluff and bluster over Berlin in 1961 and Cuba in 1962 (see, for example, Wright, *Spycatcher*, pp. 204–12).
46. i-10, i-11, i-15, i-20 and i-28 all identified this section by name, and agreed on the date of creation in 1964. D/CIS is also referred to in Campbell's chart in his 'Friends and Others'.
47. Oldfield is identified as head of counter-intelligence in Bower, *The Perfect English Spy*, p. 335, and was similarly identified by i-10, i-11 and i-20. Although Oldfield's unofficial biographer Richard Deacon (Donald McCormick) has asserted in his *C: A Biography of Sir Maurice Oldfield, Head of MI6* (London: Futura, 1985) that in 1964 Oldfield returned to Century House to become the deputy chief, Oldfield was identified as

D/CIS by i-11, i-15 and i-20. Moreover, according to Bower, *The Perfect English Spy*, p. 239, the officer replacing Young as D/SS in 1961 was, in fact, John Bruce Lockhart; Oldfield did not become DCSS until after Lockhart's retirement in 1965, p. 347.

48. i-10; i-11; i-20; i-28.
49. Tomlinson, *The Big Breach*, p. 104.
50. i-28.
51. i-10; i-11; i-20; i-28.
52. i-28.
53. i-20.
54. i-20; i-28.
55. i-28.
56. i-28.
57. i-28.
58. i-28.
59. Verrier, *Through the Looking-Glass*, p. 266; Bower, *The Perfect English Spy*, p. 347.
60. i-11.
61. Verrier, *Through the Looking-Glass*, pp. 62, 174; i–28.
62. Bower, *The Perfect English Spy*, p. 347.
63. i-10; i-28.
64. i-28; The 'controllerates' given in Campbell's 1982 chart consist of UK, Europe, the Soviet bloc, Africa, Middle East and the Far East, omitting the Western Hemisphere, 'Friends and Others', p. 6.
65. Documents covering the Service Intelligence Branch amalgamation were released in 1997 in DEFE 31/45 PRO.
66. 'Reduction in Defence Intelligence Staff' of 19 November 1964, DEFE 31/45, PRO. In an entertaining example of the current state of 'weeding' under 'open government', there exist in DEFE 31/45 several draft copies of the report on reductions, in all of which the cited item on the SIS and JIS has been excised. It remains, however, undeleted in the copy of the final report held in the file.
67. i-15 noted that R4 'was always the soldier' (singular), and i-20 clearly indicated that the Service liaison sections were single officers also.
68. DSTI/101/5/1 of 4 March 1965, DEFE 31/45, PRO.
69. DS 19/610 of 12 March 1965, DEFE 31/45, PRO.
70. D/DIS/1/2 of 22 March 1965, DEFE 31/45, PRO.
71. This box number made its way most noticeably in the literature surrounding the Matrix Churchill trial, and was officially acknowledged in Richard Scott, *Report of the Inquiry into the Export of Defence Equipment and Dual Use Goods to Iraq and Related Prosecutions* (London: HMSO, 1996), p. xvii.
72. See 'DS Int Reorganization on an Area Concept' of 3 August 1966 and D/DIS/1/2 of 25 July 1966 in DEFE 31/45, PRO.

73. These terms appear abruptly in literature on British intelligence during the 1970s; see, for example, Tony Bunyan, *The History and Practice of Political Police in Britain* (London: Quartet, 1977), p. 3; more compellingly, the term 'DI6' is also cited by Geoffrey McDermott, *The New Diplomacy and Its Apparatus* (London: Plume, 1973), p. 137. Both sources refer to these designations as representing the two agencies directly, but, as argued in Chapter 5, the MI5 and MI6 designations, *strictly* interpreted, referred to the War Office liaison with the Security Service (the DSO network) and the SIS (Section IV R4). This is also indirectly supported by omissions in DIS organization and distribution lists in DEFE 31/45, in which the DI section numbers hop over 5 and 6, running DI3, DI4, DI7, DI8..., much as the 1945 *War Office List* held in the PRO had MI5 and MI6 struck off by hand in blue pencil. Had DI5 or DI6 not been omitted, the numbering sequence would, of course, have run smoothly with DI5 being what was called DI7 and so forth.
74. A phrase used by both i-20 and i-28.
75. i-28.
76. Blake, *No Other Choice*, pp. 184–6.
77. Bower, *The Perfect English Spy*, p. 350.
78. Ibid.; i-10; i-20; i-28.
79. The original joint arrangements make a cameo appearance in Wright, *Spycatcher*, pp. 342–3; a detailed description of an agent's perspective of the joint section's work can be found in Bill Graham, *Break-In: Inside the Soviet Trade Delegation* (London: Bodley Head, 1987), *passim*.
80. See, for example, Gordon Brook-Shepherd, *The Storm Birds: Soviet Post-War Defectors* (London: Wiedenfeld & Nicolson, 1988), pp. 197–8, Tom Bower, *The Perfect English Spy*, p. 364. Bower goes as far as to describe MI5's recruitment of Lyalin as 'draconian'.
81. West, *The Friends*, p. 160.
82. Wright, *Spycatcher*, p. 342.
83. i-10.
84. The partial role of Lyalin's information has been compellingly argued by Brooke-Shepherd, *The Storm Birds*, pp. 198–9.
85. Quoted in Smith, *New Cloak, Old Dagger*, p. 63.
86. Graham, *Break-In*, p. 16.
87. i-10.
88. Stella Rimmington *Open Secret: The Autobiography of the Former Director-General of MI5* (London: Hutchinson, 2001) p. 143.
89. i-28. i-10 remarked 'By 1972 the "jointness" was fully developed.' See James Adams, *The New Spies*, p. 99; Tomlinson, *The Big Breach*, p. 95.
90. The oft-cited phrase comes from Sir John Ogilvy Rennie's obituary in *The Times*, 2 October 1981. See, variously, Cavendish, *Inside Intelligence*, p. 150; West, *The Friends*, p. 158.
91. George Young, 'Foreword' to Anthony Cavendish, *Inside Intelligence*

(London: Collins, 1990), p. vii.
92. McDermott, *The New Diplomacy*, p. 141.
93. i-28.
94. The account of Rennie's departure has been told and retold with almost malicious glee by a succession of commentators on intelligence. See, variously, Donald McCormick (writing as Richard Deacon), *C: A Biography of Maurice Oldfield*, p. 161; Cavendish, *Inside Intelligence*, p. 150; West, *The Friends*, p. 165.
95. West, *The Friends*, pp. 166–8; i-28.
96. West refers to the progressive run-down of overseas presence in *The Friends*, p. 167; i-28 noted that the cutbacks affected both the operational and requirements sides of the service.
97. i-28.
98. i-28.
99. Tomlinson, *The Big Breach*, pp. 77–8.
100. See, variously, Deacon, *C: A Biography of Maurice Oldfield*, pp. 157–9; J. Bloch and P. Fitzgerald, *British Intelligence and Covert Action* (London: Junction, 1983), pp. 37, 54, 217–25, 228 (Bloch and Fitzgerald are, in particular, typical of 'Green propaganda' attempts to smear British intelligence in Northern Ireland); James Rusbridger, *The Intelligence Game: Illusions and Delusions of International Espionage* (London: Bodley Head, 1989), p. 18.
101. West, *The Friends*, p. 160.
102. Verrier, *Through the Looking-Glass*, p. 301.
103. West, *The Friends*, p. 159.
104. i-28. The existence of the ME terrorism joint section is also referred to in Tomlinson, *The Big Breach*, p. 95.
105. ICHR (two sources).
106. Adams notes in his *The New Spies* that the SIS at the end of the Cold War still retained what he described as a 'small outstation in South London which is used by some of their clandestine operators' (p. 109), a far cry from C/UK's heyday in the late 1970s. i-28.
107. i-20
108. In particular, see documents published by John W. Young in his research note, 'The Wilson Government's Reform of Intelligence Coordination, 1967–68', *Intelligence and National Security*, 16, 2 (Summer 2001).
109. The general orthodoxy has previously been that the geographical CIGs appeared as part of the 1968 reform of the JIS into the JAS, driven chiefly by the UK government's account of itself (Cabinet Office, *Central Intelligence Machinery*, p. 11); see also Michael Herman, *Intelligence Power in Peace and War*, p. 262. However, the documents published by Young clearly indicate that the geographical CIGs were already in place by July 1967, that Trend's chief concerns were those of scientific/technical and economic intelligence rather than geographical representation, and,

moreover, that the JIC support apparatus was *already* called the JAS (Young, 'The Wilson Government's Reform of Intelligence', pp. 141–6). Moreover, Richard Aldrich has also uncovered documents concerning a proposed counter-terrorism CIG as early as 1966; see his *Espionage, Security and Intelligence in Britain 1945–1970* (Manchester: Manchester University Press, 1998), pp. 128–9.

110. Trend to Wilson, 'Intelligence; Interdepartmental Committee Structure', 20 July 1967, in Young, 'The Wilson Government's Reform of Intelligence', p. 146. The CIG layout has not generally varied greatly. According to Mark Urban, the organization of the CIGs in 1986 consisted of CIGs for the Soviet bloc, Middle East, Far East, Western Europe, South and Central America, sub-Saharan Africa and Northern Ireland, and functional groups for Counter-Terrorism, Counter-Proliferation and Economic Intelligence. Mark Urban, *UK Eyes Alpha: The Inside Story of British Intelligence* (London: Faber & Faber, 1986), p. 29. Urban, however, argued that the primary SIS representative on the Sovbloc CIG would be C/SOV, but this may be the result of changes to the Requirements/Production relationship in 1979/80 described below.

111. i-15 referred specifically to R1 staff working on JIS regional sub-committees; i-28; the exact quotation from the Franks report is as follows: 'Their [CIG's] membership is drawn from those in the relevant Departments [of all JIC members] with special area knowledge.' *Falkland Islands Review* (London: HMSO, 1983), p. 95.

112. i-28.

113. i-28.

114. i-28.

115. Urban, *UK Eyes Alpha* notes that there were two officers working on counter-proliferation prior to 1989; i-28 detailed the dismantling of R7 and indicated that one officer held the nuclear proliferation brief after the mid-1970s reform of the Requirements Directorate.

116. i-20; i-28.

117. See the organization chart for the SIS published by Duncan Campbell, 'Friends and Others', *The New Statesman*, 26 November 1982; i-20, with reference to documents. Tomlinson also refers to a MODA/SO responsible for the special forces contingent the MOD makes available in support of SIS operations in his *The Big Breach*, p. 142, but no alternative verification of this post was available at the time of writing, and special operations liaison is among the functions of the MODA/Army, Navy and Air.

118. Campbell, 'Friends and Others', p. 6; Smith, *New Cloak, Old Dagger*, p. 155; Tomlinson, *The Big Breach*, p. 141. During interview, i-20 suggested that the Historical Section had originally been set up to service the needs of the Hinsley official history during the 1970s and 1980s.

119. i-28.

120. Attributed by i-28.

121. i-28.
122. The combined Directorate of Requirements and Production appears in Campbell's organization chart in his 'Friends and Others', although Campbell acknowledges only the requirements role, and that vaguely, dismissing R Sections as 'salesmen'; the convergence is also vaguely noted by Jonathan Bloch and Patrick Fitzgerald, *British Intelligence and Covert Action* (London: Junction, 1983), p. 34. Michael Smith's own sources confirmed the existence of a combined directorate, and the double role of D/RP and DC/SS (*New Cloak, Old Dagger*, p. 155). i-20 and i-28 both discussed the geographical reorganization of Requirements and its consolidation with Production in considerable detail, i-20 making the matter a central one in the material he volunteered in the interview, and which formed much of the basis for questions directed to i-28, in order to clarify i-20's recollections.
123. i-20; i-28.
124. David Charters notes in his 'Sir Maurice Oldfield: Some Lessons for Canada', *Conflict Quarterly*, 2, 2 (Winter 1982) that Oldfield 'discourages initiatives of the "Special Operations" type', p. 48; i-20 remarked that SPA had 'faded out', but could not recall when, while i-28 was firm that SPA was dismantled *before* the 1977 abolition of the FCO's Information Research Department.
125. John Strawson, *A History of The SAS Regiment* (London: Grafton, 1984), p. 305.
126. Nigel West, *The Secret War for the Falklands: The SAS, MI6 and the War Whitehall Nearly Lost* (London: Warner, 1998), p. 38; Peter Urban also notes the reduction of the Latin America field presence to a single officer in his *UK Eyes Alpha*, p. 10.
127. Lawrence Freedman, 'Intelligence Operations in the Falklands', *Intelligence and National Security*, 1, 3 (September 1986), p. 312.
128. Lord Franks, *Falklands Islands Review* (London: HMSO, 1983).
129. West, *Secret War for the Falklands*, p. 45.
130. Urban, *UK Eyes Alpha*, p. 10.
131. Quoted in Urban, *UK Eyes Alpha*, p. 10.
132. British Broadcasting Corporation (BBC), 'On Her Majesty's Secret Service', *Panorama*, 22 November 1993.
133. See, for example, Vladimir Kuzichkin, *Inside the KGB: Myth and Reality* (London: André Deutsch, 1990).
134. See, variously, Oleg Gordievsky, *Next Stop Execution* (London: Macmillan, 1995); West, *The Friends*, pp. 161–5; Gordon Brooke-Shepherd, *The Storm Birds*, pp. 266–80. Strictly speaking, Gordievsky was recruited during the austerity years of the mid-1970s. However, his product as part of the total output of SIS which proved particularly influential during the 1980s.
135. Urban, *UK Eyes Alpha*, pp. 35–6.

136. At the turn of the twenty-first century, allied support of the *mujahedin* has blown back catastrophically. The result has been a decade of escalating attacks on US targets by alumni of the war in Afghanistan, from the attempted truck-bombing of the World Trade Center (WTC) twin towers in 1993, the utter destruction of the US embassies in Kenya and Tanzania in 1995, and the 1999 suicide bombing of the USS *Cole* in Yemen to the horrific climax in the devastating attacks of 11 September 2001, in which hijacked domestic airliners were used as guided incendiary missiles by teams of suicide terrorists to destroy simultaneously and completely both twin towers of the WTC and devastate one wing of the Pentagon, a fourth attack on either the White House or the Capitol being narrowly averted. The danger of these groups was not news, and a detailed discussion of the magnitude and origins of the transnational fundamentalist militant threat appears in Adams, *The New Spies*, ch. 13 *passim*.

137. Smith, *New Cloak, Old Dagger*, pp. 162–3.

138. Ibid.

139. Tomlinson, *The Big Breach*, pp. 73–4.

140. Smith, *New Cloak, Old Dagger*, p. 162.

141. Tomlinson, *The Big Breach*, p. 141.

142. Ibid., pp. 100, 128. Subordination to area controllerates is evident from the fact that Sov/Ops (later UKA) is explicitly subordinate to Controller Eastern Europe (that is, Controller Soviet Bloc pre-1993). A peculiarity in Tomlinson's account is the absence of a China UK section, but whether this indicates an omission by Tomlinson or a decision in SIS that natural cover operations were not particularly useful against as hard a target as China is impossible to say from the evidence to hand.

143. Urban, *UK Eyes Alpha*, p. 233; i-28.

144. i-28.

145. Richard Scott, *Report of the Inquiry into the Export of Defence Equipment and Dual Use Goods to Iraq and Related Prosecutions* (London: HMSO, 1996), pp. 1760, 1764–5.

146. Urban, *UK Eyes Alpha*, p. 98; interview with i-28.

147. i-28.

148. Smith, *New Cloak, Old Dagger*, pp. 159–60.

149. i-28.

150. *Weekly Hansard*, 238, 52 (22 February 1994), p. 157.

151. Urban, *UK Eyes Alpha*, pp. 98–9.

152. See, variously, Alvin and Heidi Toffler, *War and Anti-War* (New York: Warner, 1995), pp. 185–6; Adams, *The New Spies*, pp. 311–15; David L. Boren, 'The Intelligence Community: How Crucial?', *Foreign Affairs*, 71, 3 (1992) pp. 55–6.

153. Quoted in Urban, *UK Eyes Alpha*, p. 99.

154. The designation is provided in Tomlinson, *The Big Breach*, p. 176. There is some uncertainty in the literature concerning when the section was set up

as PTCP, whether before or after the Gulf War. Urban dates the section to 1989 in *UK Eyes Alpha*, pp. 99, 117, while James Adams argues it was created after the Gulf War, *The New Spies*, p. 268. In the last analysis, however, the section originated in the 1970s, and the appearance of PTCP was simply an expansion of existing arrangements.

155. Adams, *The New Spies*, pp. 268–9; Tomlinson, *The Big Breach*, p. 176.
156. Proceedings of the conference were published by A. Stuart Farson, David Stafford and Wesley K., *War, Security and Intelligence in a Changing World: New Perspectives for the 1990s* (London: Frank Cass, 1991) in which the future role of the intelligence community without the traditional Soviet threat (albeit, there is still a sizeable Soviet presence in the international arena) is a recurring theme in several of the included papers.
157. Urban, *UK Eyes Alpha*, p. 260.
158. The Soviet system, of course, underwent a radical series of transformations, as recounted in detail in Michael Waller, *The Secret Empire: The KGB in Russia Today* (Boulder, CO: Westview, 1994). By comparison, the reforms under the American Aspin-Brown Commission were surprisingly limited, and the Quinlan review was almost cursory.
159. See, for example, Carl Peter Runde and Greg Voss, *Intelligence and the New World Order: Former Cold War Adversaries Look Towards the Future* (Buxtehude: International Freedom Foundation, 1992).
160. Statement of James Woolsey, Director of Central Intelligence, Before the Permanent Select Committee on Intelligence, US House of Representatives, 9 March 1993.
161. Some SIS officers have argued that the absence of the USSR has meant that the agency could concentrate more on the 'useful' areas of terrorism and so forth, allowing intelligence to make a difference today where it could not in the Cold War, even though the Cold War is viewed in some quarters as the intelligence war par excellence.
162. Smith, *New Cloak, Old Dagger*, p. 154; Urban, *UK Eyes Alpha*, p. 267; i-028; ICHR.
163. BBC, 'On Her Majesty's Secret Service', *Panorama*; Urban, *UK Eyes Alpha*, p. 229; i-28.
164. Urban, *UK Eyes Alpha*, p. 163, suggests that the psyops presence was reduced to a single officer at the Ministry of Defence.
165. Ibid., pp. 266-7; note that Urban erroneously refers to the section as 'Operational Information'.
166. Ibid., pp. 266-7; Tomlinson, *The Big Breach*, pp. 106–7.
167. BBC, 'On Her Majesty's Secret Service', *Panorama*.
168. Tomlinson, *The Big Breach*, pp. 57, 73–8.
169. Smith, *New Cloak, Old Dagger*, p. 163.
170. BBC, 'On Her Majesty's Secret Service', *Panorama*.
171. Philip H.J. Davies 'Information Warfare and the Future of the Spy', *Information, Communication and Society*, 2, 2 (Spring 1999), p. 116; also

'Intelligence, Information Technology and Information Warfare', *Annual Review of Information Science and Technology*, 36 (2002), p. 321.

172. For the historically close relationship between RCMP/SS and the Security Service, see John Sawatsky, *Men in the Shadows* (Toronto, Doubleday, 1980); the RCMP/SS even mimicked MI5's management structure, dividing itself into lettered branches closely aligned with the pre-1953 Security Service order of battle (pp. 21–8).

173. For a reliable and informative account of HAM, see Sawatsky, *Men in the Shadows*, pp. 238–51.

174. See, in particular, Clifford Stoll, *The Cuckoo's Egg* (London: Bodley Head, 1991), *passim*.

175. ICHR.

176. ICHR; BBC, 'On Her Majesty's Secret Service', *Panorama*.

177. See, for example, Adams, *The New Spies*, p. 100, who mentions the principle but passes on after no more than a single sentence.

178. VCOs are identified as such by Tomlinson, *The Big Breach*, p. 107.

179. A natural comparison exists here with the Mossad's *Katsa* system of visiting targeting/case officers used to recruit sources abroad, as described in Victor Ostrovsky and Claire Hoy, *By Way of Deception: A Devastating Insider's Portrait of the Mossad* (Toronto: Stoddart, 1990), *passim*, although there is no direct evidence that the SIS and Mossad schemes are in any way cognate.

180. Tomlinson, *The Big Breach*, p. 143.

181. Adams, *The New Spies*, p. 106.

182. Ibid., p. 106; Urban, *UK Eyes Alpha*, p. 260; Smith, *New Cloak, Old Dagger*, p. 163.

183. Urban, *UK Eyes Alpha*, p. 262.

184. A considerable body of discussion on the ISA already exists. See, for example, the coda on the 1994 ISA in Ian Leigh and Lawrence Lusgarten, *In From the Cold: National Security and Parliamentary Democracy* (Oxford: Clarendon, 1994); Ken (K.G.) Robertson, 'Recent Reform of Intelligence in the United Kingdom: Democratization or Risk Management?', *Intelligence and National Security*, 13, 2, *passim*, and Peter Gill 'Reasserting Control: Recent Changes in the Oversight of the UK Intelligence Community', *Intelligence and National Security*, 11, 2 (April 1996), *passim*.

185. See, for example, sections 1(1), which states that 'There shall continue to be a Secret Intelligence Service'; 1:1(a), which provides for its traditional intelligence role as being 'to obtain and provide information relating to the actions or intentions of persons outside the British Islands'; and 1:1(b), which embodies SIS's on-again-off-again covert action function as being 'to perform other tasks relating to the actions and intentions of such persons'.

186. ISA (1994) 10.

187. ISA (1994) 5:1.

188. ISA (1994) 6.
189. ISA 7(1).
190. *Weekly Hansard*, 238, 52 (22 February 1994), p. 158.
191. ICHR.
192. Counts here vary in the literature; Urban, *UK Eyes Alpha*, identifies only six but omits the Western Europe Controllerate, while Smith points to seven and includes C/WH. i-28 firmly maintained that the controllerate structure that emerged in the 1970s remained more or less unchanged beyond the relative contraction of C/UK until the end of the Cold War. Hence, seven controllerates are described herein.
193. Urban, *UK Eyes Alpha*, p. 262; Tomlinson, *The Big Breach*, pp. 97, 100, 103.
194. Tomlinson, *The Big Breach*, p. 106.
195. By 'relative importance', I mean relative to alternative priorities, specifically the waning importance of the Soviet bloc and subsequently the Confederation of Independent States and the Russian Federation.
196. Urban, *UK Eyes Alpha*, p. 262; Smith, *New Cloak, Old Dagger*, p. 154. The title 'Global and Functional' was provided by i-28.
197. i-20; i-28. This development is supported by Tomlinson, *The Big Breach*, p. 60, who notes of the SIS order of battle during his term that 'P and R officers are organized in pyramidal structures into "controllerates" which have either a regional or functional focus'.
198. i-28.
199. Urban, *UK Eyes Alpha*, p. 256.
200. Tomlinson, *The Big Breach*, p. 99.
201. Peter Scharfman, 'Intelligence Analysis in an Age of Electronic Dissemination', *Intelligence and National Security*, 10, 4 (October 1995) pp. 201–11.

7

Machineries of Government and Intelligence

I have always kicked against the bureaucratic pricks – sometimes
with success, often with failure.

Nicholas Elliott
Never Judge a Man by His Umbrella[1]

THE MACHINERY OF GOVERNMENT AND THE INTELLIGENCE INTERFACE

In the last analysis, one cannot examine or understand the structural
development of the Secret Intelligence Service (SIS) without seeing it
in terms of its environment, or rather, *environments*. It is not merely
the history of an independent organization, free-standing and
independent of outside influences. Rather, the SIS's internal evolution
is intimately bound up with the development of its relationship with
its intelligence consumers, and even the evolution of the intelligence-
handling mechanisms of those consumers. It is impossible to divorce
the structural evolution of a government organization from its larger
context within and as a part of the machinery of government,
particularly one with interdepartmental responsibilities such as SIS.
From the standpoint of organization theory, an organization such as
SIS has two environments which act upon its internal structure, its
extragovernmental, operational environment, and its intragovern-
mental political and administrative environment. Developments in
either will affect its internal structure, and in the case of the SIS, it has
been possible herein to trace many – not all, but perhaps most – of
the major structural changes to SIS and their relationship with the
twin environments of international politics and the machinery of
British government. Against these pervasive, persistent and intransi-
gent institutional pressures, any would-be cultural explanation of SIS

318

management structure appears relatively weak (but not, perhaps, entirely irrelevant).

Of course, any analysis such as this cannot claim to be an *exhaustive* study of SIS organization and administration. Many minor offices, sections and subsections will undoubtedly have slipped through the historical net, and the various ad hoc committees and working groups which make up so much of the day-to-day routine in any organization have not, for the most part, been examined in great detail. Moreover, departmental designations may have varied in ways it has not always been possible to identify, and so approximate designations are occasionally used, such as that for the Joint Middle East Terrorism section and those who work for SIS 'for love' – UKN (a designation that almost certainly dates from the 1980s even though the section is much older than that). However, even if some of the fine detail has escaped scrutiny, it can be confidently said that the major features, the essentials and fundamentals of chain of command, division of labour and working arrangements, and their development, have proven amenable to inspection and analysis.

Of all the possible trends one might examine in the history of SIS, the one most pervasive and perhaps most distinctive is the interpenetration and interweaving of the overt and covert realms in the machinery of British government. Contrary to the suspicions of conspiracy theorists, the SIS does not exist in some isolated shadow land, detached and dissociated from the daylight workings of government and politics. Rather, it is intimately bound up with the less secretive Ministries and Departments of State that task the agency and receive its product, or in concert with whom it plans and mounts its operations, jointly or alone.

Originally, under the 1921 arrangement, the interpenetration was a mutual one, in which the consuming departments seconded representatives to SIS headquarters, to set requirements and evaluate the product received before disseminating the information to their masters in Whitehall. Theirs was a divided loyalty, however. While the officers of the Circulating Sections were attached from customer departments – originally, the scheme was to attach a section of each Service Intelligence Branch to the SIS – they also found themselves within the SIS chain of command, answerable to C and his appointed deputies, as well as to their respective Directors of Intelligence. While the SIS may have had Admiralty, War Office, Foreign Office and Air Ministry advocates within its walls, those self-same personnel acted as SIS representatives within their home departments, although their ultimate responsibility was to their home departments. C Section personnel divided their time and effort between both SIS and their home department. In effect, the interface between overt government and covert capability lay not between department and agency but within the boundaries of each. This interpenetration of the overt and the covert made formal the traditional collegial familiarity of the higher reaches of British public service, but, in doing so, it emphasized and strengthened that quality. Within SIS, it created a division of operational control between two different chains of command, with the operational ('G' or, later, Production), side answerable on the one hand to C in terms of agency hierarchy, but to a spread of Circulating Sections in terms of the quantity and quality of the product, on the other hand.

Despite attempts by Admiral Sinclair and Menzies to dissociate SIS from the conventional workings of the Civil Service during the inter-war period and early in the Second World War, the need to participate in overt processes such as the Committee for Imperial Defence and the Joint Intelligence Committee created another level of interpenetration between Secret Service and Civil Service. This need derived in part from the twin consequences of splendid covert isolation: neglect and starvation of resources, on the one hand, and overwhelming demand from a wide range of independent consumer departments, on the other. From the 1920 and 1921 Secret Service Committees to the 1935 Defence Requirements Sub-Committee of the CID, SIS *needed* to have its powerful customer departments lobbying the Treasury on its behalf if it was to receive anything more than the most minimal funding. The wartime and post-war machinery of the Joint Intelligence Organization provided an additional fluid medium for the security and intelligence agencies and their overt departmental consumers to interact, pool resources, and discuss, debate and negotiate problems and grievances. JIC sub-committees and their Cold War successors, the Current Intelligence Groups (CIG), extended this fluid interface still further down the chain of command, so that collegial interaction between agencies existed not merely at the level of Chief, Director or Deputy Under-Secretary, but also on a section-by-section level, making the interface of the overt and covert far more pervasive than a simple meeting place of chief executive officers ever could. As Michael Herman has recently argued, the JIC and CIG system is 'partly a meeting of intelligence professionals, but partly also a means of "gathering the voices" within government as a whole...what they produce is not strictly "*intelligence* assessment" but "government assessment".[2] The 1921 arrangement and its legacy combined with the JIC/CIG workings to make this particularly true of the SIS, generating the fundamentally collegial and organic organization structure and ethos that have increasingly characterized the agency since its inception.

This pattern of interpenetration is not unique to intelligence, but the fundamental manner in which British public administration is conducted is at the core of British central government, in areas such as the Cabinet and Defence Secretariats, foreign policy, and public finance. Collegial and organic working arrangements are not a peculiar survival of some bygone imperial and aristocratic age, but, rather are intrinsically rational ways of handling change- and information-intensive areas of government. But they are, perhaps, somewhat more pronounced in the intelligence community, partly because of its need for jointery and partly because of the contrast between that jointery and the equally vital security-driven need for compartmentalization.

COLLEGIAL AND ORGANIC TRENDS IN BRITISH CENTRAL GOVERNMENT

The organization of British government proved something of a problem in Max Weber's attempt to apply his notions of modernization and bureaucratization to the major powers of his day. It deviated from his scheme because of the very lack of state bureaucratization and therefore the failure of modernization and modern capitalism to correlate with bureaucratization. Weber had argued that it was the scale and complexity of the modern capitalist economy which forced the state to bureaucratize. Instead, Weber found the British system to be at some points an honorific and amateur system and at others collegial in structure. Weber was, therefore, forced to make a number of relatively weak and unconvincing manoeuvres to try to argue that the British system was either an atavism or a product of peculiar circumstances and political preferences.

Weber argued: 'The fact that the later British state did not participate in the Continental development towards bureaucratisation, but remained an administration of notables can be attributed...to the relative absence of a continental geography.'[3] Britain's geographical position, he argued, reduced the need for large standing armies and the bureaucratic superstructure needed to administer them. Weber resorted to attributing the lack of bureaucracy to a particular set of political *values*, somehow overriding the more sociologically profound pressures of modernization and rationalization. The lack of a large-scale bureaucratic architecture, he argued, derived from the fact that 'the state authorities increasingly "minimized" the scope of their functions at home, restricting them to what was absolutely demanded for direct "reasons of state"'.[4] On the other hand, the British Cabinet and Prime Minister constitute a variation on Weber's rationally specialized collegiality, what Weber terms (and cites the British system as an example of) 'functional collegiality with a preeminent head'.[5] Weber's view of the British system of government was embodied in his explanation of British civil law. According to him, such survivals have occurred because Britain, with 'centralised justice and rule by notables...in modern times was the first and most highly developed capitalist country, thereby retain[ing] a less rational and less bureaucratic judicature'.[6] Weber's ultimate explanation of why the British system is so far removed from the bureaucratic type is that it is a vestigial form of administration, a sort of sociological living fossil – or rather, Piltdown man.

Apart from casting the British administration as a sort of socio-logical coelacanth, part of Weber's underlying difficulty was almost certainly that the British system of government and administration was undergoing profound changes even as Weber was studying and writing. This change reflected a trend of change in organizational structure in government which went back to the early middle of the nineteenth Century. The Cabinet itself was a relatively recent development when Weber began writing in the 1890s, while in the Civil Service the recommendations of the Northcote-Trevelyan report of 1854 were still finding their way into practice. The status of 'notables' was steadily declining, a decline steepened by the Constitutional Act of 1911, which permanently weakened the House of Lords (although Peers would not completely disappear from the British Cabinet, they were relegated to junior portfolios, by the first Wilson government of the 1960s). A study in 1957 of the organization of British central government from 1914 to 1956 by the Royal Institute of Public Administration notes that, in 1914, 'The administrative duties of the central government were, in fact, sufficiently circumscribed to be carried out by small departments whose jurisdictions seldom overlapped or needed to overlap.'[7] This administrative circumscription, to which Weber referred but found difficult to reconcile with his notions of rationalization and ever-increasing administrative control of day-to-day life, meant that bureaucratization both *within* specific departments and of the *overall machinery* of government remained minimal.

Ironically, Weber developed the intellectual device needed to resolve his difficulties about British civil administration alongside his concepts of bureaucracy – that is, his concept of *collegiality*. He even applied it in a limited fashion to the emergence of Cabinet government in the UK, and yet he never seemed to see its more general applicability and utility in deciphering British political institutions.

Although Weber argued at length that collegial arrangements are less rational than bureaucracies, and must therefore be superseded by bureaucracies, this position leads to two logical inconsistencies in his work. At the very fundamental level of Weber's own ideas of rationality, the argument for the greater rationality of bureaucratic forms over collegial involves shifting the basis of assessing the rationality of the two forms. As a result, if one follows his logic through to its natural conclusion, a contradiction results. At a less abstract level, Weber's own writing on collegiality also makes it clear that there is, in fact, a form of 'modern' collegiality, which he calls 'rationally specialised collegiality'. He also develops an analysis which demonstrates a high degree of symbiosis between bureaucratic and collegial forms, in which collegial institutions provide the essential social and political context of bureaucratic organization, and, as necessary, limits to the extension of bureaucratic forms of organization. As a result, Weber's own sociology cannot sustain a hypothesis of linear, evolutionary succession from the collegial to the bureaucratic, but rather, needs both existing and developing in parallel to complete its picture of the modernization and rationalization of organization.

Weber provides a taxonomy of nine different collegial types that, as limiting factors *upon* bureaucracy, prevent the highest level of the administrative pyramid from being reduced to a single monocratic individual, issuing and supervising the rules and regulations implemented by the bureaucracy, and holding ultimate sovereignty over the means and powers of administration which are delegated to officialdom.[8] This typology is as follows: (1) 'veto collegiality', in which a number of nominally subordinate monocratic authorities must all agree upon the 'first authority' in order to implement a decision; (2) 'functional collegiality', in which essentially non-monocratic institutional arrangements require unanimous or majority votes of the membership to act; (3) a variant on 'veto collegiality', in which a body of monocratic but equal officials *without functional distinctions* must reach consensus over decisions; (4) 'functional collegiality with a pre-eminent head', in which the collegial body has what Weber calls a 'monocratic *primus inter pares*' (cited as noted as an example the British Cabinet and its Prime Minister); (5) a variation on (4), in which the collegial entity is confined to an advisory role in support of monocratic authority; (6) a variant on 'functional collegiality', in which the collegial body is made up of functionally distinct specialists with expert knowledge; (7) a variant on (6) which, like (5), is only an advisory body to the 'first authority'; (8) traditional collegial entities such as councils of 'elders'; (9) and, finally, by 'applying the collegial principle to the highest authority', that is, dividing the position of first official among a council of post-holders.[9]

Of these, variants (6) and (7), in which 'functional collegiality' is composed of a committee of experts either with executive powers or acting as an advisory body to the 'first authority', are of central interest to the problem of rational administration. Weber refers to these variants as 'rationally specialized collegiality'.[10] Under rationally specialized collegiality with executive powers, 'the preparation and presentation of a subject is assigned to the individual technical expert who is competent in that field or possibly to several experts, each in a different aspect of that field. Decisions, however, are taken by a vote of the body as a whole.'[11] The arrangements of an advisory rationally specialized collegial body are much the same, except that 'it is open to the chief to accept or reject their recommendations, according to his own free decision'.[12]

Despite his arguments that bureaucracy is the *most* rationalized, *most* efficient form of administration, Weber readily admits that 'collegiality favours greater thoroughness in the weighing of administrative decisions', and he even admits that 'where this is more important than precision and rapidity, collegiality tends to be resorted to even to-day'.[13] Weber is evidently applying the term 'precision' in a somewhat idiosyncratic form – how can something assessed with 'greater thoroughness' be less 'precise' than that assessed without as much thoroughness? The sense of the word 'precision' as used by Weber must be taken as meaning the precision of *control* over a process rather than precision of *reasoning*, and his

324

discussion of collegiality makes it quite apparent that collegial administration is very genuinely *rational* administration. Unlike the relationship between bureaucracy and honorific administration, in which the distinction is really that between *definitely* getting the job done and *possibly* getting the job done, there is no compelling evidence given that bureaucracy is *more rational than* collegiality. In fact, what appears, and what Weber works very hard to avoid conceding, is that collegiality and bureaucracy are equivalent but alternative forms of rationalization.

Where, then, does this leave Weber's theory of bureaucracy? Monocracy and bureaucracy are beasts of 'large scale tasks which require quick and consistent solutions',[14] and there is no reason to contest Weber's conclusion. But it is impossible to accept his claim that bureaucracy is intrinsically more rational than collegiality; the consequence of such a position is a contradiction. The crucial question in whether consistency, predictability and routine are the prevailing rule in human affairs. Weber, in directing his analysis towards a teleology of bureaucratic capitalism, throws his lot in with human affairs being increasingly predictable. However, there is no reason to assume that society is increasingly routine; quite the opposite, as social, political and economic affairs in the Twentieth Century have proven to be highly volatile. In part, the limitation of Weber's vision is embodied in his image of the 'iron cage' of bureaucratic capitalism running on unchecked 'until the last ton of fossilised coal is burned'.[15] Weber's bureaucratic capitalism is, therefore, also a creature of Victorian and Edwardian technology. Even as he writes of modernization and change, Weber underestimates the capacity of science, technology, and industry not merely to change themselves and society, but to do so at an increasing rate. He also underestimates the persistence of a need for rationally specialized, functional collegiality, in both government and business. He underestimates, or even ignores, the intrinsic collegiality of the board of directors and the joint-stock firm. He underestimates the continued need for 'thoroughly weighed' administrative decision making.[16]

Organizational research after Weber, and especially since the 1950s, has increasingly emphasized the importance of collegial mechanisms in management structure, especially as technological change has accelerated. The notion of 'organic' management developed by Tom Burns and G.M. Stalker at the end of the 1960s is a profoundly collegial one. It is characterized by 'the contributive

325

nature of special knowledge and experience to the common task of the concern', a 'network' system of communications based on lateral communications 'resembling consultation rather than command', and 'a content of communication which consists of information and advice rather than instructions and decisions'.[17] This they place in opposition to a bureaucratic, or, as they term it, *mechanistic* form of management. Nonetheless, Burns and Stalker are firm that both organic and mechanistic management structures are equally viable alternative modes of rationalization, the former suited best to complex and highly variable environments, the latter to simpler and less radically changeable settings and industries.[18]

Burns and Stalker even illustrate organic arrangements with explicitly collegial bodies. In one electronics firm, they describe a management committee, composed of 'two executives, the works manager, the production controller, and occasionally one or other specialist executives who might be particularly concerned'. In this system, 'although certain decisions, like the purchase of machines, were for the committee as a whole to make, the function of the meetings was to enable each member of the senior management group to arrive at decisions respecting his own part of the firm's task in the light of information derived from the others and in the light of the implications of his decisions for the rest of the firm's activities.'[19] The firm also maintained a similar Research and Development Committee.[20] These were, of course, rationally specialized, functionally collegial bodies. Later work in the field noted that there were problems in implementing organic structures in large organizations. Researchers concluded, therefore, that what was required were systems that hybridized bureaucratic and organic/collegial forms, employing a hierarchical and specialized bureaucracy for day-to-day administration but also operating (often ad hoc) organic project teams assembled across bureaucratic demarcation lines. These systems were termed *matrix* organizations.[21]

It is, therefore both possible and necessary to argue that any concept of organizational evolution in the so-called 'modern' world must incorporate both bureaucratic and collegial (or mechanistic and organic) forms of rationalization. If so, one would expect to find both forms presenting themselves in governments during the twentieth century – moreover, given the findings of the matrix theorists, one would expect collegial arrangements to be easier to operate and therefore more pronounced in smaller governments than in larger ones. Accordingly, governments, like the British state (and indeed, Great Britain and her population in general) have typically been smaller in numbers than the governments of larger, contemporaneous states such as France, Germany or the United States of America. With this in mind, it is easier to understand why Weber had such difficulty in modelling the British state.

To be sure, the British government had experienced a major move away from collegial arrangements to ministerial monocracy during the mid-nineteenth century in the shift away from appointed boards to Ministers holding a seat in Parliament. This might in the first instance appear to be an unproblematic application of the Weberian scheme, but there are dissenting interpretations. Henry Parris, in particular, has argued that the transformation from Boards appointed by the Crown to Ministers drawn from Parliament reflected the progressive transfer of sovereignty from the monarchy to Parliament in the Eighteenth and Nineteenth Centuries.[22] Parris's argument essentially reverses Weber's doctrine that bureaucracy arises from increasing monocratic control and as a reaction to the growing power of Parliamentary bodies; the evolution of Parliamentary (eventually Cabinet) ministers therefore reflected, in Parris's formulation, the expanding interests not of the monarch but of the *collegial* Parliament, making public administration accountable to individual Members of Parliament who in turn would be responsible to Parliament as a whole in the first instance, and in the second instance through the Prime Minister to the Crown. Parris's version of the process is still very much one of rationalization, but it is a rationalization centred not on the monocratic Crown, but upon the collegial institution of Parliament.

Parris's emphasis on the shift of sovereignty away from the Crown is, in fact, crucial to understanding subsequent developments in the Twentieth Century because what in fact happens to British public administration is an evolutionary *bifurcation*, with certain sectors developing along classic Weberian lines, while others move increasingly towards collegiality. In terms of orthodox bureaucratization, the parts of central government which have moved in that direction are easy to identify. The large standing armed services (whose existence Weber seems to underestimate, particularly with regard to the Navy) under the War Office and the Admiralty developed throughout the Eighteenth, Nineteenth and Twentieth Centuries as large, rigidly bureaucratic organizations.[23] After the Second World War, the growth of the British 'welfare state' involved the development of large bureaucratic departments such as Health and Social Services. Indeed, their very scale and degree of bureaucratization has been the subject of on-going concern quite literally for decades. Proposed solutions have varied from the Conservative notion of 'managerialism' to the recent Labour administration's fundamentally collegial concept of 'joined-up government'.[24] However, in three sectors in particular, increasing collegiality and organicism developed throughout the Twentieth Century. As the RIPA study of 1957 states,

> There were [in 1914], however, three institutions concerned in large degree with coordination. The first, obviously enough, was the Cabinet. ... The second was in the form of an advisory body attached to the Cabinet – the Committee of Imperial Defence (CID) – in which most of the later institutional developments in Cabinet organisation and high-level interdepartmental cooperation have their origin. The third was the Treasury, whose unique position *vis-à-vis* the other departments had evolved mainly in response to parliamentary demands for tighter control of expenditure.[25]

It has been the need for interdepartmental consultation and coordination over both policy and specific operations that has driven the need for institutional arrangements based on horizontal lines of communication and more or less consensual decision-making processes. This has led in turn to collegial and organic modes of organization.

At the Cabinet level, the Cabinet Secretariat is composed of both a small administrative staff and a system of interdepartmental committees of officials reflecting and supporting interdepartmental ministerial committees, such as the contemporary Permanent Secretaries Committee on Intelligence Services (PSIS), the JIC,[26] and the Defence and Overseas Policy Committee (DOPC). The Ministry of Defence, which evolved out of the CID, is generally considered one of the larger bureaucratic departments since it currently oversees the three armed Services as well as the civilian administration of defence. However, in its original 1946 configuration, the MoD was a much smaller entity, overseeing its own network of interdepartmental defence committees of officials, a network which has survived in the form of the Defence Secretariat. Finally, the Treasury Department, because it administers central finances for the entire government apparatus, embodies the single most forceful pressure towards interdepartmental coordination and consultation, that of financial allocation. Indeed, it is the existence of a single, central financial institution which makes a vague 'cluster' notion of government untenable. Bound together by a single financial centre, on the one hand, and a powerful Board of Directors in the Cabinet on the other, the UK government (and, indeed, virtually all national governments) organizationally resemble nothing so much as a divisionalized firm.[27] Although the RIPA study does not mention it, however, inter- departmental and consultative processes similar to those acting on the Treasury and the Central Organization for Defence have also acted upon the Foreign Office, with comparably collegial and organic results.

It is the study of Treasury structure and process which has given rise to the most forceful and influential expression of the collegial architecture in British central government as a whole, or rather, of the *detection* of that architecture in Hugh Heclo and Aaron Wildavsky's notion of the 'Whitehall village'.[28] In their study of 'village life in Civil Service society', they argue that the formal organization and flow charts of public administration are particularly potentially misleading when trying to understand the working of the British government. Instead, they argue that beyond the simple network of senior officials who 'facilitate and commiserate', of which the strongest 'web of familiarity is the Cabinet Office network' of Permanent and Deputy Under-Secretaries,[29] and amidst which 'The shadowy personal networks merge into more formal but still blurry structures. Whitehall and its vast departmental fortresses are honeycombed with joint groups, working parties, and interdepartmental officials – some ad hoc and some formal, some meeting only once or twice, some for several years ... an organization chartist's nightmare perhaps, but this flux of working arrangements does allow officials to meet when, where and in the manner they deem necessary, usually with a minimum of formality.'[30] It would be tempting to view the various networks which bind the 'Whitehall village' together as simply yet another example of informal organization.[31] However, this would underestimate the degree to which the members of associations such as the Cabinet Office network deal with each other informally but *in terms of their official capacities*, that is, as Permanent Secretary of this Department or that, however informal the terms on which they communicate with one another. Burns and Stalker, of course, point out that the distinction between formal and informal aspects of organization are less clearly defined in organic organizations, although the essential skeleton of organicism remains a formal structure.[32] Thus, what we see in Heclo and Wildavsky's 'Whitehall village' is that their 'shadowy personal networks' embed the collegial system of interdepartmental committees in a fundamental and pervasive organic system of semi-formal horizontal communication and administration.

Besides developing the 'village' view of Whitehall, Heclo and Wildavsky provide a clear description of structure and process in the Treasury that is unambiguously organic. Departmental costings are negotiated on a peer-to-peer footing and the national budget formulated on a combination of bilateral and all-channel communications routes. Heclo and Wildavsky express some surprise at the organizational workings of the Treasury:

> To those who have heard of the Treasury only by reputation, it will be surprising to discover that informal, non-hierarchical arrangements predominate within the organization. The Treasury is probably the most internally fluid of all government departments. ... Although every division man has difficulty in keeping track of his own sector, he avidly seeks information about what is happening elsewhere. ... There is simply not enough time to give orders about everything or direct others how to adjust to rapidly changing circumstances. Thus coordination is fostered by a functional redundancy, as it were, of overlapping, criss-crossing and repetitive channels of communication.[33]

From the point of view of organization theory, what one sees in the Treasury is an organization in a highly changeable, information-intensive environment, but one also subject to the additional horizontal pressures of interdepartmental consultation and coordination.

Similar tangential forces have helped shape the Foreign Office into an organic form of organization. Since the end of the Nineteenth Century, the Foreign Office has evolved from being a simple hierarchy to a more organic and collegial form, chiefly because of the increasing load placed upon the Foreign Secretary. In his summary of this structural change, Lord Strang has noted that 'the Foreign Office itself might seem to afford a depressing illustration of the depressing dictum that liaison breeds liaison'.[34] Strang argues that the Foreign Office has evolved from a simple hierarchy in which 'the threads of foreign affairs radiated outwards from the external side of the machine, but within the machine very little happened except canalisation; almost all the threads passed straight through it to the Foreign Secretary himself', but since then the Foreign Office has moved into an advisory capacity for the Foreign Secretary, because, 'as things are now, he needs the help of many brains – and tongues – as well as the labour of many hands'. In a turn of phrase almost identical to Weber's notion of advisory functional collegiality, Strang adds of officials' advisory role: 'Their advice need not be followed, and sometimes it is not: it is merely a thing available and of some intrinsic value, representing a body of some weight, hence in practice an influence on those who create policy.'[35] This advisory role of the Foreign Office has therefore combined with the interdepartmental concerns of its work to draw it into an adaptable, flat and wide structure reliant on horizontal consultation and coordination as well as vertical responsibility.[36]

This collegiality of central administration is neither a throwback to earlier forms, nor some living fossil which has survived by a combination of evolutionary fortune and political and geographical insularity, but represents a trend towards organicism which actually increased between the beginning of the Twentieth Century and its middle decades. The origins of the Cabinet Office, whose 'network' is so central to Heclo and Wildavsky's view of Whitehall, and which currently houses most of the interdepartmental coordinating machinery at the Permanent Secretary level including the 'central intelligence machinery' of the Joint Intelligence Organization (JIO), shares its origins with the Central Organization of Defence, which oversaw the JIO prior to its 1957 relocation to the Cabinet Secretariat. The common line of origin leads to the CID Secretariat of 1904. The CID was, in Weberian terms, a functionally specialized collegial body acting in an advisory role to another collegial body with executive power, the Cabinet. The original CID was chaired by the Prime Minister, but its membership was, as the RIPA study puts it, 'elastic', consisting variously of 'Cabinet Ministers, representatives of Dominion Governments, elder statesmen, prominent members of the Opposition...military and Civil Service experts attended from time to time, and a network of subcommittees was created to consider a wide range of topics.'[37] Essentially, it was a collegiate body overseeing a pinwheel arrangement of subordinate collegiate bodies. With the outbreak of the First World War, the CID changed somewhat to become the War Council and subsequently the War

331

Cabinet, with the Secretariat and network of subcommittees now handling the administration of both the military and civilian sides of the war effort. After the war, the CID was re-established, and the War Cabinet Secretariat split along civilian and military lines, but it remained under the control of Sir Maurice Hankey, who held the post of Secretary to both the Cabinet and the CID until 1938.[38]

Within the machinery of the CID, the constellation of sub-committees continued to multiply, including subcommittees on Coordination, Manpower, Air Raid Precautions and a Principal Supply Officers Committee. In 1924, the heads of the various armed Services were formed into the Chiefs of Staff (CoS) Committee. The same arrangement was expanded in 1927 with another committee, that of the service branches' respective Directors of Plans, the Joint Planning Committee, itself duly supported by its own administrative secretariat, the Joint Planning Staff, from 1936 on.[39] In 1935, the Joint Planners concluded that joint operational planning required a capacity to pool intelligence generated by the three armed services, giving rise to the notion of an additional CID Secretariat committee of the various Service Directors of Intelligence. This originally took the form of a short-lived and ineffectual Interservice Intelligence Committee, replaced in 1936 with the Joint Intelligence Committee (JIC).[40] During the Second World War, the JIC would develop its own permanent Secretariat in the form of the Joint Intelligence Staff, as well as developing a network of specialist subcommittees providing specialist appraisals which would be issued to consumers in the senior civil service and at CID and Cabinet levels under the authority of the JIC.[41] In 1957, the entire Joint Intelligence Organization (the JIC, the JIS and its various JIC subcommittees) was transferred to the network of committees under the Cabinet Secretariat.[42]

Thus, the 'Central Organization of Defence' was composed of a pinwheel hierarchy of collegial bodies, themselves answering to a hierarchy of collegial bodies leading through the CID to the Cabinet. This, like the Treasury, exhibited both the need for 'well-considered', information-impacted decision making through all-channel peer groups, amplified by the horizontal pressures of organizational politics, the various peer group members being highly autonomous and powerful Departments of State in their own right. Only a collegial arrangement would permit adequate information to be amalgamated, and ensure the degree of consensus necessary for fully committed contributions to the joint operational process. This doctrine of 'jointery' has developed as the standard way of undertaking coordinated activity in the Central Organization for Defence.[43]

It has been said that the history of Britain's Central Organization for Defence is one of 'Committee into Ministry',[44] but this perhaps oversimplifies the matter by suggesting that the trajectory is one simply from functional collegiality to monocratic bureaucracy. This would be an inaccurate description of the actual process, and even of the resulting post-Second World War Ministry of Defence. There was a short-lived Minister for the Coordination of Defence during the 1930s tasked with the 'day to day supervision and control of Committee of Imperial Defence'.[45] Churchill took on this portfolio during the Second World War, and in 1946 a new Ministry of Defence was set up on a statutory basis, absorbing the military functions previously held by the CID. In so doing, the Ministry of Defence absorbed the Chiefs of Staff Committee, the Joint Planning Committee and Staff, and the Joint Intelligence Committee and Staff.[46] The Ministry of Defence also absorbed the interservice Joint Intelligence Bureau, which pooled Service intelligence assets dealing with areas such as economic, scientific and technical intelligence.[47] The RIPA study asserts that the MoD 'was designed as a complete but small department – some might call it a large Private Office – organised functionally to assist the Minister in carrying out his detailed responsibilities, which include dealing with the increasing number of problems associated with this country's participation in international defence organizations'.[48] In this initial phase of its statutory existence, then, the Ministry of Defence really consisted of a Cabinet Minister as monocratic first official overseeing not a bureaucratic architecture but a small administrative staff plus an extensive network of collegial, interservice committees.

In 1963, the MoD underwent a second phase of development which moved it in the direction of a sizeable bureaucracy under the Minister of Defence, through the consolidation of the three armed Services under MoD jurisdiction. Through the absorption of the three relatively bureaucratic armed Services, the MoD changed from being a 'large Private Office' to one of the very large, bureaucratic Departments of State. This did not, of course, change the collegial nature of the highest-level interservice coordination bodies, although the JIO had moved to the Cabinet Office in 1957. Indeed, at least at one level, the amalgamation of the services actually led to a new area of collegial organization in the field of Defence intelligence.

The MoD had already been responsible for the JIB, and under the amalgamation it also acquired ultimate authority for the Service Intelligence Branches. It was, therefore, decided that the Service Intelligence Branches should be consolidated with the JIB in a new Defence Intelligence Staff, to be headed by the chief of the JIB, who would be designated Director-General of Intelligence (DGI). This union resulted initially in a broad and weakly integrated bureaucratic span of control under the DGI's four subordinates: the Director of Service Intelligence (DS Int), who oversaw the three former service intelligence branch area sections; the Directors of Scientific and Technical Intelligence (DSTI) and Economic Intelligence (DEI), both carried over from the JIB; and the Director of Management and Support Intelligence, who took over the former service intelligence branch sections dealing with intelligence on logistical matters.[49] The span of control and consolidation problems were particularly severe under DS Int, under whom the various duplicate geographical organizations spread out like the tentacles of an octopus. The problems of duplication and integration were not resolved until 1966, when DS Int was reorganized on geographical lines, with the trios of equivalent departments grouped together in collegial bodies functioning a little like miniature JICs. For example, the three Service Soviet sections were consolidated in DI3 as DI3 (Air), DI3(N) and DI3(A), pooling their information as a combined section.[50]

Hence, the need to pool information in an architecture of all-channel peer-group bodies is as compelling as in the Central Organization of Defence, with each participant possessing different intelligence-gathering resources, all of which need to be pooled to form a comprehensive and coherent assessment. Human sources provide part of the picture, as do communication intercepts, photographic reconnaissance and information from overt sources such as diplomatic contacts and official policy statements. Michael Herman, in his recent *Intelligence Power in Peace and War*,[51] has explicitly examined and advocated the essential *collegiality* of British central intelligence machinery. Beyond considerations of information-impactedness, Herman has stressed also the need for consensus to help prevent any assessment and subsequent decisions from foundering on the rocks of internecine rivalry and dissent.

> Departmental participation also ensures the output's acceptability; without it there will be no agreed intelligence for decision-taking. *National assessment needs some institutionalised collegiality.* The

greatest British contribution to modern intelligence is the idea that it needs committees.[52]

As has been argued throughout this discussion of organization theory, collegiality, committees and all-channel architectures are not a panacea. They, like bureaucratic hierarchy, represent a range of trade-offs. Herman also admits the drawbacks of collegiality and peer-groups as developed by Weber and Williamson, admitting that the costs of Britain's 'greatest contribution to modern intelligence' include 'the propensity towards blandness and the lowest common denominator of agreement; the search for drafting solutions that obscure real differences; stitching departmental segments together instead of looking at subjects as a whole. ... They are expensive in participants' time, and there are practical problems of getting them together. ... Some sensitive information cannot be shared by a complete group [and] there is a heavy premium on chairmanship. Getting the best out of a committee is an art in itself, and distracts from a single-minded concentration on quality and impact.'[53] Perhaps, however, the most telling aspect of Herman's examination of collegiality in Britain's central intelligence machinery, as well as its overall governmental context, is his observation that 'the JIC as a whole is *symptomatic of British interdepartmentalism*'.[54]

Herman's comment on the symptomatic nature of the collegiality of 'jointery' in defence and intelligence says more than the words seem to imply. The tendency towards committees, collegiality and organic arrangements derive not only from the environmental and operational conditions of variability, information-impactedness and the very smallness of British central administration. They derive also from very institutional and constitutional arrangements of Parliamentary Cabinet government, with executive power dispersed among powerful Cabinet Ministers and their Departments of State. Despite the *primus inter pares* role of the Prime Minister, the very absence of a ruling monocrat of the Executive Branch, be it Continental dictator or Jeffersonian president, make for an enormously powerful horizontal force dragging central government away from a simple hierarchy and into peer-group arrangements. The effect is a sort of centrifugal balance of power, as the centripetal need for interdepartmental consultation and coordination exists in a tension with the tangential forces of departmental autonomy and self-interest. In areas where policy and operations must be formulated and implemented on an interdepartmental basis, this centrifuge tends to amplify any environmental pressures towards collegial or organic organizational forms that might be experienced by any office or agency of Department of State.

In general terms, the structural evolution of the SIS after 1919 has been from a weakly rationalized functional 'pre-modern' collegiality under Cumming to an overall organic structure characterized by a high degree of modern, rationally specialized collegiality. The transition was, of course, prompted by the addition of the consumer liaison Circulating/Requirements Sections under the 1921 arrangement that created the basis for a formally constituted system of horizontal communications between producers and consumers, rather than consumer needs being expressed in top-down directives. Under the '1921 arrangement', the SIS's operational or Production side was tasked and provided with continuous feedback by the Requirements side. In their original form, of course, the liaison sections were Service Intelligence Branch sections attached to SIS HQ and incorporated into its chain of command in an early form of the 'dual control' doctrine. Over time, the R Sections evolved into intermediary bodies staffed by career SIS officers, but still serving the purpose of representing national and departmental intelligence requirements, albeit on a geographical rather than a departmental basis, and with the JIC and its national intelligence requirements as the central focus of the process. The Production/Requirements relationship provided a foundation for a collegial and organic system of management, necessitated by the information-intensive nature of intelligence gathering in a highly variable operational environment, one in which intelligence requirements change with the ebb and flow of international politics, and this has required the SIS to reorient its priorities completely on three separate occasions.[55]

Although unusual, the SIS 'Requirements side' has a rough approximation in the development of the Treasury's Principal Financial Officers (PFOs). They were originally Treasury officials appointed to spending departments to monitor expenditure on behalf of the Treasury. Since the 1920s, however, the PFOs have developed as intermediaries between the Treasury and spending departments, although they are usually career members of the spending departments.[56] Effectively, the PFO arrangement reverses the design logic of the Requirements section. If the development of Requirements within the centrifuge of inter-departmentalism was driven chiefly by the tangential forces of departmental self-interest, that of the Treasury's PFOs has resulted from the centripetal force of Treasury control over expenditure. In the former case, R Sections exist to represent the needs of consumer Departments of State 'inwards' to the SIS, and to evaluate, collate and circulate intelligence information 'outwards' to the consumers. By contrast, the PFOs exist to represent Treasury spending concerns 'outwards' to the spending departments while circulating information about depart-mental spending and expenditure needs 'inwards' to the Treasury. Both arrangements are, however, bilateral channels necessitated by extremely information-intensive and change-intensive areas of activity, embodying the need for face-to-face, collegial and organic working arrangements created by those activities.

Michael Herman, discussing in general the applicability of organic forms to intelligence organization, has summarized the case for and against intelligence service and intelligence community organicism thus:

> Intelligence's environment has its large element of change; coping with constant modifications in the target's defences is rather like dealing with competition and market changes in a volatile private sector. The need for flexibility, opportunism and entrepreneurial drive would seem to point towards 'open', 'informal' organization and the features that go with it. But there is the security require-ment for limiting, not encouraging, the spread of information inside the organization; and there are also operational pulls in the formal, hierarchical direction.[57]

To be sure, both security considerations and 'operational pulls' towards hierarchy – as well as administrative pulls in that direction – have had their impact on the organization of the SIS. The need for hierarchy is particularly visible in the pyramidal structure of the SIS Production side, with its span of Controllers, each overseeing a span of P and TCI Sections, each of which, in turn, oversees a span of field stations abroad. However, even here the relative smallness of the SIS shows through in its 'small gobbets of bureaucracy', as one officer recalled that even the largest single 'gobbet', DP3, when it combined both the Far East and the Americas, barely exceeded 80 persons all told.[58]

Perhaps the single most persistent pressure towards any degree of hierarchy, or as Burns and Stalker more carefully phrase it, 'stratification', in the SIS derived precisely from the organization's organicism. The combination of horizontal lines of communication and an organizational culture that encouraged close working relations between senior officers and their immediate juniors existed at various points in SIS history alongside multiplying functional components to create an overly wide span of control and severe managerial bottlenecks. This kind of problem peaked in 1942. SIS at that time included: five genuine Circulating sections; roughly a dozen country-based Production Sections; Communications, Counter-Espionage and Financial Sections masquerading as Circulating Sections; plus Technical Aids, Docs, the Central Registry and Sections H, N and O all competing for C's attention past his two feuding deputies. The SIS had achieved an organizational span of control which was completely unmanageable. This difficulty could be resolved only by introducing intervening layers of manage-ment, such as the 1945/46 creation of the five Directors between C, the VC/SS and AC/SS and the broad range of operational, consumer liaison, administrative and technical support sections which had proliferated over the preceding decade. Apart from these pressures towards 'stratifi-cation', the workings of each Directorate, and of each Controllerate, were nonetheless organic and highly collegial in their organicism.

The SIS also developed a strategy to deal with the centralizing, hierarchical pressures of security that retained organic management by developing internal arrangements of dual- or multidepartmental joint control of specific areas of activity. This approach is most fully illustrated by the post-1974 workings of Production under the various controllers. Any given operational concern would not merely involve the Area Controller and his immediate subordinates down to the case officer in the field. Rather, operational control was a collegial process involving the Controller, the P Section concerned with a specific operation, the area R Section for whom any product was destined (answerable to Director or later Deputy Director, of Requirements), the area Security Branch Officer (answerable to DCIS), and possibly the relevant TCI section (under the joint authority of Controllers and DCIS, and possibly an entirely different area Controller at that), and, in the case of a counter-espionage operation against a hostile intelligence service, the participation of the relevant CI section (again answerable to DCIS). As a result, by the 1970s, operational control involved representatives of three separate Directorates, Production, Requirements and Counter-Intelligence and Security. However, this system resolved security concerns by drawing a geographical boundary around the all-channel network controlling the operation. *Only* the area R Section would be indoctrinated, *only* the area SBO would be involved, and *only* the immediately relevant geographical CI or TCI section would participate. Philby's capacity to compromise the complete range of SIS operations into the USSR during his term as R5 resulted from the practice of the time of consultation being at the level of controllers and section heads rather than a geographically circumscribed collegiality at lower levels of organizational stratification. However, this form of bounded collegiality did not begin to develop in any strict form until 1964, 17 years after Philby's term as R5. Nonetheless, even confronted with its two devastating Soviet penetrations, the SIS did not simply attack the problem through rigid, secretive bureaucratization. There are no indications that the organization actively sought to avoid this alternative; rather, the prevailing operational, administrative and environmental conditions in which the SIS was situated appear to have militated against such a solution. Organic and collegial administration in the SIS has always been less a question of *organizational design* than environmental *force majeure*. Until Franks, organicism and collegiality were a result, but not a goal.

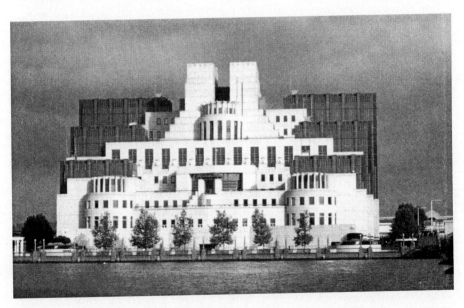

Vauxhall Cross, SIS Headquarters since 1994

CONSUMER DEMAND AND THE CONSEQUENCES OF A PULL ARCHITECTURE

If the Whitehall village may be said to have its bazaar of public goods and services, and if that bazaar may in turn be said to have a particular corner where the Security and Intelligence Agencies set up a stall and market their wares, then that Whitehall village market for intelligence is a *buyer's market*. Beyond Cumming's aversion to formal hierarchy during his term as C, the very beginning of a rationally specialized collegiality in the SIS began with the appointment of the original consumer liaison sections to the SIS under the 1921 arrangement. Nearly six decades later, the post-1974 operational collegiality described above embodied more than simply the need for 'contributive' working arrangements and variable environmental concerns pushing SIS towards organic and collegial administration. Despite changes in structure, from departmental partisan representatives to geographical intermedaries of the JIC as well as Departmental intelligence needs, and in changes in composition from external staff secondments to career SIS specialists, the basic function and effect of Requirements Directorate has remained essentially the same. The central role of the R Sections in the Production process has continued to embody the Whitehall organizational politics of intelligence demand, and the centrality and prevalence of that demand in the SIS Production process. The demand-side forces have had a fundamental impact on the development of SIS structure and process throughout its existence, and the combination of intelligence demand and collegial, Whitehall interdepartmental 'jointery' has given rise to a genuine 'pull architecture'. However, despite the enthusiasm of figures such as Peter Scharfman for a 'pull' architecture, such a system of tasking and dissemination is no intelligence management panacea. 'Pull' arrangements have their critics, and a number of the costs and consequences of a 'pull' system can be seen in the history and development of SIS.

Walter Laqueur, for example, has noted that 'in the first instance consumers may not know what they want', and even when they do, what they want may not be feasible; therefore, much of the initiative must come from the intelligence agencies themselves.[59] Similarly, Michael Herman has recently argued that, for 'large-scale intelligence production', the process, in practice, is actually a blend of 'push' and 'pull' processes, but that 'the "push" factor has to be emphasized, together with the importance of seeking [consumer] reactions rather than "pulls"'.[60] Against relying on consumer interests to drive the production process, Herman argues that 'requirements' can fall down on a number of points, some of which parallel those of Laqueur. According to Herman, consumers vary in the interest that they take in intelligence and what it may do for them; the consumers themselves do not generally 'think in broad terms about the information needs of their whole department'. Even when consumers do think about those needs, 'there is the genuine problem of defining what he [the consumer] does not know'. When they attempt this, they tend to work from short-term assumptions while 'intelligence needs to take longer views, especially in collection'.[61] When requirements are formulated, 'few of them tell intelligence anything it does not know'. Both Herman and Laqueur note that where the current American system has sought to impose strict requirements on operations, the result has been a 'bureaucratic nightmare' of additional and redundant administrative steps in the process.[62] The initiative, he argues, lies ultimately with the producers, who must act as entrepreneurs, 'selling' their 'product' to consumers who would not otherwise know what intelligence can do for them.

Unlike Scharfman, whose argument is essentially polemical and verging on the utopian, Herman does note the potential drawbacks of a 'push' architecture. Herman's concerns about the drawbacks of a 'push' system follow the precedent of William Niskanen's criticism of government agencies and their tendency towards 'overproduction'. Bureaucrats' careers are driven by their success in doing well for their respective departments, securing larger budgets and better facilities, and with a superior access to information about their production process than their consumers, the inevitable result is a surplus production of whatever good the 'bureau' provides. Likewise, suggests Herman, large-scale intelligence production through a 'push' architecture runs the risk of producing a surplus supply of product, overwhelming consumers and resulting in information overload.[63] Herman's argument is built on a very important qualifier; that is, he is referring to 'large-scale' intelligence production, and therefore the entire argument is skewed towards *technical intelligence* agencies and their product. Indeed, the bulk of Herman's illustrations are drawn from SIGINT and IMINT.[64]

Of course, the SIS is neither a large agency, nor is it predominantly geared towards arcane technical methods. As a result, the difficulties confronting the SIS have often been of a very different order from the problems with the 'pull' relationship suggested by either Walter

341

Laqueur or Michael Herman. The problems experienced by the SIS could be divided into essentially two categories: surplus demand, on the one hand, and political expendability, or what might be termed the 'Muggins syndrome', on the other hand.

If the main potential economic risk of a large-scale, technology-intensive 'push' architecture is, as Michael Herman has suggested, Niskanen's problem of surplus production, it should be no surprise that the economic risks of a pull architecture for a small, HUMINT agency are those of *surplus demand*, or what Garrett Hardin has called 'the tragedy of the commons' (also known as the 'commons paradox'). In the 'tragedy of the commons', a depletable shared or collective good is so overtaxed by a multiplicity of users, each trying to maximize individual benefits, that the common source actually gives less benefit to each consumer than if they had individually restrained their demand, allowing the source to yield its benefits with greater per capita efficiency.[65] In other words, self-interested utility-maximizing strategies yield a suboptimal outcome. It is a major implication of the commons paradox that without the restraint of a pricing system[66] and if the consumers of the common good do not voluntarily restrain their consumption, some restraint must be applied by an outside authority.

Under the 1921 arrangement, the official history notes, 'the SIS was not a strong enough organization to settle priorities between the requests that were made of it, or even able to resist demands for assistance which went beyond its resources'.[67] As a result, the SIS was so overtaxed by surplus demand that insufficient resources could be allocated to any one task to perform even a subset of its requirements effectively. Indeed, the consumers were constantly disappointed by the volume of product the SIS produced, and the low grade of source the agency was confined to recruiting. Consistent with the 'commons' model, the SIS's consumers found themselves dissatisfied with both quantity and quality of yield, the War Office complaining in 1938 that the SIS was failing to meet the 'increasingly urgent need for factual information about Germany's military capabilities, equipment, preparations, and movements', while the Air Ministry likewise complained that what nominally factual information it did receive was '80% inaccurate'.[68] Moreover, during the war, in the first two years after the collapse of its European networks, consumers mistook underproduction resulting in a loss of basic inputs for a failure to grasp their requirements adequately.[69] *The benefits to SIS consumers, therefore, were actually less than if they had voluntarily limited their own demands upon the service.*

Although the official history goes on to say in defence of the 1921 arrangement that the resulting difficulties were 'less serious than those which would have followed had it been feasible to adopt other solutions',[70] it was not until there existed a central arbiter of intelligence requirements and priorities that the problems of surplus demand began to abate. That central arbiter was the JIC. It had been set up in 1936 as the Joint Intelligence Sub-Committee of the CID, but the JIC was a relatively weak body until it became the de facto War Cabinet intelligence tasking and assessment body under Churchill's premiership.[71] Moreover, the JIC was confined to dealing with Service Branch intelligence requirements until 1944, when, by default and to avoid adding an extra layer of civilian tasking machinery, it began formulating *national* intelligence requirements through its Special Sub-Committee on Intelligence Requirements.[72] The JIC's position as national intelligence requirements arbiter was further strengthened after the war by its shift in 1957 to the Cabinet Office.[73] Today, the JIC sets national requirements through a comprehensive annual review process in which senior civil servants, Ministers and the intelligence agencies are consulted, and priorities are 'ordered according to their importance to the national security and economic well-being of the United Kingdom',[74] and then issued in the form of the National Intelligence Requirements Paper.[75] In the day-to-day relationship between the SIS and its consumers, the R Sections are as central to the process as they have ever been.[76]

The 'Muggins syndrome' has involved SIS's being tasked with operations which were simply too difficult or dangerous for the originating consumer departments to undertake themselves. Essentially, the 'Muggins syndrome' results from using the agency as a 'cut-out' to protect Ministers and senior Civil Servants. This use of the agency tempts senior decision-makers into giving it tasks which are of dubious soundness or excessively risky. If the operation goes wrong, the agency will catch the blame and not its political masters. The classic failures here would be the clandestine negotiations leading to the catastrophic Venlo incident in late 1939, and the 'frogman incident' in 1956. In each case, SIS was designated the operational body, acting, supposedly deniably, on behalf of the Cabinet in the former case and the Admiralty in the latter. Both of these cases illustrate the fundamental unsoundness in the thinking behind using the SIS, or any intelligence service, simply as deniable cut-out. When British Passport Control officials or an ex-Navy diver are captured, denial is essentially futile. The Venlo incident resulted from an error in judgement at political levels far above the SIS. In the case of the frogman incident, even if earlier and subsequent dives had proven successful and productive, the entire approach was unduly operationally and politically fraught, especially within British territorial waters (and even more especially during a high-profile state visit). Like surplus demand and its commons paradox, the 'Muggins syndrome' is fundamentally tied to the demand-driven nature of SIS structure and process. Since these events, however, the British tasking and dissemination process under the JIC has changed so that the SIS can refuse to undertake tasks it views as intrinsically unsound,[77] but this has been possible only since the 1957 move of the JIC to the Cabinet Office, making that entity powerful enough to check the demands made by individual intelligence consumers.

It should not be concluded, however, that the SIS/consumer relationship is entirely without its 'push' components. Although SIS is in no position to propose *requirements*, it must act as what Michael Herman has described as an intelligence 'entrepreneur' in order to develop operational methods and opportunities. The recruitment of the Northern Area's ill-fated post-war Baltic networks were evidently an SIS initiative, but one consistent with the strategic interests and requirements of British foreign policy (by comparison, VALUABLE in Albania was based on explicit Foreign Office and Russia Committee requirements). As argued by Laqueur, consumers are not always in a position to know what intelligence can *potentially* do for them, and this is particularly true of technical methods. The classic case of an SIS 'push' initiative was the development and implementation of the Vienna tunnels in 1948, and likewise the joint SIS/CIA tunnelling operation in Berlin in 1953. The Vienna station took the initiative so thoroughly it did not even bother getting clearance for the first of its tunnels from the Foreign Office at the time. Nonetheless, both the Vienna and Berlin landline taps were mounted in order to fulfil Service Branch requirements concerning Soviet and East German military deployments, operations and order of battle. Thus, even where the SIS might take the operational initiative in developing a source or planning a political action, it does so in order to fulfil explicit intelligence or operational requirements. The nature of the SIS's relationship with its consumers and masters in Whitehall and Downing Street is that *even when the SIS pushes, it does so in response to a pull*.

It must be stressed that to say that the SIS is *structurally* demand-driven is not the same as the reassuring government assertions that all of the various security and intelligence agencies operate only in terms of intelligence requirements laid upon them by the JIC. The Cabinet Office explains to us that

> The JIC lays detailed tasking and requirements upon the SIS and GCHQ. These are reviewed annually in a process headed by the Intelligence Co-ordinator. This combines a rigorous analysis of the requirements for secret intelligence with extensive consultation with customer Departments and consideration of financial and other resources required. The resulting list of requirements is submitted to Ministers for approval.[78]

But the process to which the Cabinet Office is referring could very reasonably be seen as an *overlay*, an administrative afterthought and retrofit. The National Intelligence Requirements Paper could arguably be portrayed as a veneer of tasking and constraint, issued by one executive department to another one, and sketch maps from the Cabinet Office and assurances from Ministers really give no indication of how that edict is viewed and implemented by the recipients of the edict. as noted, in the United States, attempts to attach explicit consumer requirements to the collection process have been criticized for adding an 'extra layer of bureaucracy', and adding to delays and inefficiencies all round.[79] However, for the tasking machinery to be as central, as fundamental and as *essential*, to the workings of an organization such as the SIS, as it has been shown to be, is a very different matter.

To be sure, even where requirements are issued directly to the inner machinery of the SIS there are limits to how far consumer control and Foreign Office approval can penetrate. As the former SIS Foreign Office Adviser, Geoffrey McDermott, has argued, while the FCO issues requirements to the SIS and then issues 'broad approval' for the means proposed by SIS to fulfil those requirements, 'obviously the details are left to the experts of the SIS'.[80] But where the consumers cannot reach, the Requirements Officers act on their behalf. The role of Requirements has, to be sure, changed, from simple partisan representatives to intermediaries who interpret and ensure conformity to the SIS Red Book of requirements, its Talmud, and to the JIC's Annual National Intelligence Requirements

Document as Torah. Nonetheless, the fact that there exists within SIS a mechanism to interpret and implement those requirements prevents the formulation and 'laying on' of national requirements from simply becoming a 'veneer', or unwieldy bureaucratic extension. Requiring operational officers to formulate their proposed actions in terms of explicit requirements, and requiring the SIS to seek FCO clearance for those actions, on the basis of those requirements, provides what one officer called 'good discipline'. It helps ensure that any action taken is taken for clearly articulated and well-considered reasons,[81] and ensures that any actions taken by the SIS are strictly circumscribed by the demands of national policy formulated by the overt side of British politics and government.

Writing in 1983, Anthony Verrier tried to suggest that the SIS was somehow inadequately restrained by the machinery of British government: 'Neither a Foreign Office chairman nor the technical subordination of the JIC to Cabinet implies complete control of the SIS ... [t]he SIS is an *independent* service, deriving from the fact that neither Act of Parliament nor known administrative *fiat* governs its roles and responsibilities.'[82] Of course, legislation is no guarantee that an agency will be effectively controlled or properly observe the rule of law or national foreign policy priorities. One need only examine the recurrent concerns about CIA accountability since its creation in 1947 by the National Security Act,[83] or the dismissal of the Canadian Security Intelligence Service's first Director-General, Ted Finn immediately after that agency's legislative creation[84] to be aware of this. Therefore, effective control must lie, as Ken Robertson has argued, in no small degree in effective day-to-day administrative and bureaucratic direction and control.[85] In 1994, the Intelligence Services Act finally did place the SIS and GCHQ on a statutory footing. In the Commons debate over the third and final reading of the Bill, Foreign Secretary Douglas Hurd assured the House that 'The SIS and GCHQ do not work to their own agenda, invent their own requirements for information or act independently without the prior knowledge and clearance of Ministers. ... They do not invent activities of their own; they carry out tasks in support of specific policies.'[86] This assertion would have carried far more force had the government and the SIS been willing to make public the specific machinery within SIS whereby SIS operations are formulated in terms of, and circumscribed by, requirements; in other words, if they had been more willing to describe and to explain how the SIS *really* works.

NOTES

1. Nicholas Elliott, *Never Judge a Man by His Umbrella* (Wilby, Wiltshire: Michael Russell, 1991), p. 179.
2. Michael Herman, *Intelligence Power in Peace and War* (Cambridge: Cambridge University Press, 1996), p. 275.
3. Max Weber, *Society and Economy* (London: University of California Press, 1978), p. 970.
4. Ibid., p. 971.
5. Ibid., p. 273.
6. Ibid., p. 977.
7. F.M.G. Wilson, *The Organisation of British Central Government* (London: Allen and Unwin, 1957), p. 282.
8. Weber, *Society and Economy*, pp. 271–2.
9. Ibid., pp. 272–4.
10. Ibid., p. 274.
11. Ibid., p. 273.
12. Ibid., p. 274.
13. Ibid., p. 277.
14. Ibid., p. 278.
15. Max Weber, *The Protestant Ethic and the Spirit of Capitalism* (London: Unwin University Books, 1967), p. 181.
16. The idea that collegiality can be rational, even as rational as bureaucracy, naturally invites the question, 'can honorific administration also be rational?' Indeed, it may be, as the appointment of especially qualified experts as consultants, investigators and advisers would seem to suggest. However, Weber makes even less provision for this possibility than he does for a 'modern' and rational collegiality.
17. T. Burns and G.M. Stalker, *Management of Innovation* (London: Tavistock, 1961), pp. 121–2.
18. An important qualification and clarification of the notion of 'change' as used throughout this discussion has to be made here. It is, of course, arguable that, under certain conditions of extreme variation, or *crisis*, the collegial option has to be abandoned once again in favour of monocracy, and a bureaucratically disciplined infrastructure capable of turning on an operational ha'penny. This is indeed so, but it should be clearly understood that the concept of 'change' *qua* crisis is fundamentally different from rapid technological evolution and the relatively volatile market conditions which go with it. The difference between *crisis* and *volatility* can be expressed in a somewhat heuristic algebraic manner. The sense of change in which it is developed by Burns and Stalker is essentially the rate of environmental change relative to the ability of a firm to adapt to new conditions. In this sense, we can speak of a ratio C of change in the environment, ΔE, to rate or pace at which new conditions or technologies can be institutionalized ΔI;

347

that is, $C = \Delta E / \Delta I$. ΔI may be said to be the infrastructural *retooling time* needed to incorporate new technology or requirements into a production process. As long as ΔE is small relative to ΔI (that is, C is small), a routine, bureaucratic structure is feasible. As C approaches 1, however, the speed of change approaches the speed at which the organization can 'retool' its production process, and this is probably a more or less fixed value governed by the speed at which new equipment can be produced and new staff trained, or existing staff retrained and deployed. The fundamental argument put forward by Burns and Stalker, and in this discussion, is essentially that as C increases and approaches unity, organic arrangements are increasingly necessary in order for an organization to get its adaptation speed as close as possible to the theoretical limit described above. However, if at any point the rate of change is such that $C > 1$, not even organic management can save the firm since it has simply been outstripped by conditions. At this point, collective decision making goes out the window, and someone has to be in the hot seat making the snap decisions required for crisis management. Organizational *crisis* would, therefore, be defined as conditions under which $C > 1$. Of course, even here, there is no reason to reject collegiality; on the contrary, either the collegial entity is essentially an advisory body, as suggested by Weber, or it can vote to cede its executive powers for the duration, much as does a parliament voting for an Emergency Powers or War Measures Act. However, this discussion is concerned with a changeable, information-impacted environment, not crisis conditions, and it can therefore reasonably be assumed that for all cases discussed herein $C \leq 1$.

19. Burns and Stalker, *Management of Innovation*, pp. 85–6.
20. Ibid., p. 88.
21. See, for example, Kenneth Knight 'Introduction: The Compromise Organization', in Kenneth Knight (ed.), *Matrix Management* (Farnborough, Hants: Gower, 1977), p. 4.
22. Henry Parris, *Constitutional Bureaucracy: The Development of British Central Administration Since the Eighteenth Century* (London: Allen and Unwin, 1969), pp. 80–105 and *passim*.
23. See, for example, the work of Christopher Dandeker on British army bureaucratization in his *Power, Surveillance and Modernity* (Cambridge: Polity, 1990), *passim*.
24. See, for example, Spencer Zifcak, *New Managerialism: Administrative Reform in Whitehall and Canberra* (Buckingham: Open University Press, 1984).
25. Wilson, *The Organisation of British Central Government*, p. 282.
26. Cabinet Office, *Central Intelligence Machinery* (London: HMSO, 1993), p. 17.
27. There are arguably two ways of envisioning this arrangement. On the one hand, it might be argued that the fact that cabinet-oriented governments

centralize finance in the treasury but decentralize executive authority among ministers and their relatively independent operating divisions would locate them in O.E. Williamson's typology as X-form or hybrid organizations with both U- and M-form features, leaning towards the M-form arrangements. On the other hand, if drawing an analogy between firm and state, it might be pointed out that each department of state has its own budget allocated by the treasury but administered internally, in which case the treasury would be serving as a substitute for the market place, acting as a single monopsony buyer, and, arguably acting in a principal-agent relationship on behalf of the electorate. It should also be noted that the mainly M-form nature of government organization would tend to reinforce P.M. Jackson's proposed application of Williamson's governance costs hypothesis to public-sector organization see P.M. Jackson, *The Political Economy of Bureaucracy* (Totowa NJ: Barnes & Noble, 1983).

As regards other national governments, the M-form architecture permits some flexibility in how the various divisions are overseen and ultimately controlled. For example, the appointed cabinet of the Jeffersonian scheme is still essentially a board of division heads, but under a stronger chief executive than the British Prime Minister, and, more amorphously, politically weaker than the British form, since, under the separation of powers, pre-eminent legislative power does not devolve to US secretaries as it does under a parliamentary arrangement.

28. Hugh Heclo and Aaron Wildavsky, *The Private Government of Public Money* (London: Macmillan, 1974).

29. Ibid., p. 6.

30. Ibid., p. 85.

31. Something like this approach has been taken in the recently fashionable 'policy network' literature in public administration. See, for example, R.A.W. Rhodes and David Marsh, 'Policy Networks in British Politics: A Critique of Existing Approaches' in Rhodes and March (eds), *Policy Networks in British Government* (Oxford: Clarendon, 1992), *passim*; or more recently, Martin Burch and Ian Holliday, *The British Cabinet System* (London: Prentice Hall/Harvester Wheatsheaf, 1996), pp. 81–105.

32. Burns and Stalker, *Management of Innovation*, p. 122.

33. Heclo and Wildavsky, *The Private Government of Public Money*, pp. 68–9.

34. Lord Strang, *The Foreign Office* (London: Allen and Unwin, 1955), p. 146.

35. Ibid., pp. 146–7.

36. For a summary of Foreign Office departmental structure and inter-departmental and 'cross-national-cross-departmental' organization and work, see Michael Clarke, 'The Policymaking Process', in Michael Smith, Steve Smith and Brian White (eds), *British Foreign Policy: Tradition, Change, Transformation* (London: Unwin Hyman, 1988), pp. 88–90.

37. Wilson, *The Organisation of British Central Government*, pp. 283–4.

38. Ibid., pp. 285–91.

39. Ibid., pp. 297–8.
40. Ibid., p. 298; F.H. Hinsley, C.F.G. Ransom, E.E. Thomas and R.C. Knight, *British Intelligence in the Second World War: Its Influence on Strategy and Operations*, vol. I (London: HMSO, 1979), p. 36; note that Wilson's volume contains a number of detailed references to the development of the JIC, the JIB and 'central economic intelligence' and their current status in 1956, 23 years before the official history began to appear in print and nearly 40 years before a comparable statement by the UK government under its 'open government' initiatives.
41. Hinsley et al., *British Intelligence*, vol. IV, p. 143.
42. Cabinet Office, *Central Intelligence Machinery*, p. 11.
43. This balance between divergent departmental interests and the pressure for defence jointery has, perhaps, been most effectively illustrated by Barry Posen, *Sources of Military Doctrine* (London: Cornell University Press, 1984), which seeks to apply Cyert and March's 'organizational politics' approach to the formulation of defence policy in the UK, France and Germany. In opposition to the divergent pressures of departmental self-interest, Posen places what he calls the 'balance of power', strategic exigencies which force departments to work together against a common foe. However, Posen does not deal with 'balance of power' and organizational politics as two forces continuously present, with each shifting to the ascendency at different times, even though his study finds that prior to the escalating tensions of the 1930s, the three service branches were planning for three entirely different kinds of war in three different global theatres. Instead, Posen tries to treat the balance of power and organizational politics as two mutually exclusive empirical hypotheses, which, of course, they are not. Nonetheless, the shift from independent, self-referential defence planning by the service branches to a more whole-hearted 'jointery' is characteristic of the interdepartmental machinery of British central government.
44. Wilson, *The Organization of British Central Government*, p. 283.
45. Ibid., p. 305.
46. Ibid., pp. 319–20.
47. Major General Sir Kenneth Strong, *Intelligence at the Top: the Recollections of an Intelligence Officer* (London: Giniger, 1968), pp. 221–26; see also documents concerned with the establishment and organization of the JIB in L/WS/1/1088, IOLR.
48. Wilson, *The Organization of British Central Government*, pp. 320–1.
49. Documents on the creation of the DIS were released into the PRO in 1997, and can be found in DEFE 31/45.
50. Strong to the Secretary of State, 3 August 1966; D/DIS/1/2 or 25 July 1966 and MO 20/1 (B), all in DEFE 31/45, PRO.
51. Herman, *Intelligence Power in Peace and War*.
52. Ibid., p. 269; emphasis added.
53. Ibid., p. 269 *infra*.

54. Ibid., p. 278, emphasis added.

55. The SIS began life primarily geared towards Imperial Germany; in 1919, its main priority became the new Soviet Union. In the early 1930s, it had to reorient itself to Nazi Germany, and, of course in 1945/46, it returned its attention to the USSR. Of course, since the end of the Cold War, the SIS has had to reorient itself and restructure production to suit the even more variable and uncertain New World (Dis)Order.

56. Heclo and Wildavsky, *The Private Government of Public Money*, pp. 118–19.

57. Herman, *Intelligence Power in Peace and War*, p. 332.

58. i-028.

59. Walter Laqueur, *A World of Secrets: The Uses and Limits of Intelligence* (New York: Basic Books, 1985), p. 21.

60. Herman, *Intelligence Power in Peace and War*, p. 295.

61. Ibid., p. 289.

62. Laqueur, *World of Secret*, p. 21, Herman, *Intelligence Power*, p. 292.

63. Herman, *Intelligence Power*, pp. 295–6; data overload, or so-called 'analysis paralysis' is a well established problem where technical intelligence methods are concerned. See also Laqueur, *A World of Secrets*, pp. 96–7, and, more recently, Alvin and Heidi Toffler, *War and Antiwar* (New York: Warner, 1995), p. 187.

64. In *Intelligence Power*, Herman refers throughout to TECHINT examples, as in the Gulf War, in which battlefield intelligence was predominantly technical (p. 296); overhead reconnaissance by U2s and satellites (p. 292); and Second World War SIGINT (p. 291).

65. Hardin's original study of the commons problem dealt with the traditional English common grazing land. Loosely speaking, as long as the number of cows is small enough that their grass consumption is less than the maximum yield of the grazing land, increasing the number of cattle gives a straight increase in, say, milk yield. However, once the number of cattle passes the threshold marked by how much grass is available, they start to eat into one another's grass supply, and the milk yield begins to drop, eventually to where they can live on the grass available, but cannot produce milk. At the point where they can no longer survive on the available commons, the benefit of grazing them on free land is nil and the farmer might as well take them home to graze on his own land. This model originally appeared in Garrett Hardin, 'The Tragedy of the Commons', *Science*, 162, 3859 (December 1968), pp. 1243–8. See also Thomas Schelling's retrospective on and summary of the model in his *Micromotives and Macrobehavior* (New York: W.W. Morton, 1978).

66. A pricing system was, in fact proposed during John Major's term as Chancellor of the Exchequer, in which the SIS would bill the costs of any requested operation to its consumer. The practice was not implemented during his term as Chancellor, nor was the proposal resurrected during his premiership. CHR.

67. Hinsley, et al., *British Intelligence*, vol. I, p. 18; Mike Smith of the *Daily Telegraph* brought this quotation to my attention.
68. Ibid., p. 55; see also pp. 50–1.
69. Hinsley et al., *British Intelligence*, vol. II, p. 18.
70. Ibid., vol. I, p. 18.
71. Davies, 'Organisational Politics', p. 124.
72. Hinsley et al., *British Intelligence*, vol. III, part 1, p. 472.
73. Cabinet Office, *Central Intelligence Machinery* (London: HMSO, 1993), p. 11.
74. Ibid., p. 13.
75. Private information.
76. Interviews with a senior UK intelligence official undertaken by Michael Smith and interview with a former SIS officer by the author.
77. i-028.
78. Cabinet Office, *Central Intelligence Machinery* (London: HMSO, 1993); *http://www.open.gov.uk/co/cim/cimrep2.htm*.
79. See, for example, Laqueur, *A World of Secrets*, p. 21; Herman, *Intelligence Power in Peace and War*, p. 292.
80. Geoffrey McDermott, *The New Diplomacy and Its Apparatus* (London: Plume, 1973), p. 138.
81. i-028.
82. Anthony Verrier, *Through the Looking-Glass: British Foreign Policy in an Age of Illusions* (London: Jonathan Cape, 1983), p. 10; former emphasis mine, latter in the original.
83. See, for example, Angus Mackenzie, *Secrets: the CIA's War at Home* (London: University of California Press, 1997), *passim*.
84. David Stafford and J.L. Granatstein, *Spy Wars: Espionage and Canada from Gouzenko to Glastnost* (Toronto: McLelland and Stewart, 1992), pp. 144–245.
85. K.G. Robertson, 'Accountable Intelligence: The British Experience', *Conflict Quarterly*, 8, 1 (Winter 1988), *passim*.
86. House of Commons, *Official Report*, 238, 52 (22 February 1994).

Glossary

SIS designations generally refer both to the office given the designation *and* the incumbent in that office at any given time.

A1	German A Section
A2	The Netherlands and Denmark A Section
A3	Belgium A Section
A4	Liaison with Free French and Polish Government in Exile
A5	Occupied France, Gibraltar and Tangier
Abwehr	German Military Intelligence
ACAS (I)	Assistant Chief of Air Staff, Intelligence (AI)
ACSS	Assistant Chief of Service
ADI (Science)	Assistant Director of Intelligence (Science)
ADNI	Assistant Director of Naval Intelligence
AFHQ	Allied Forces Headquarters
AI	Air Intelligence
AI1c	Air Ministry intelligence liaison to SIS
AIS	Aegean Intelligence Service
AIOC	Anglo-Iranian Oil Company
AO	Administrative Officer
A Section	Occupied Europe Section (1939–41)
AU	Auxiliary Unit (MIR)
AVO	Hungarian security service to the 1956 Soviet invasion
BCRA	*Bureau Central des Reseignements et d'Action*
BDCC	British Defence Coordinating Committee
BDCC (FE)	BDCC Far East
BDCC (ME)	BDCC Middle East
BLO	British Liaison Officer
BMH	British Military Hospital, Episkopi

BoT	Board of Trade
BSC	British Security Coordination
C	Chief of SIS (from Admiral Mansfield Smith-Cumming)
C/AF	Controller, Africa
CC/E	Chief Controller, Europe
C/CEE	Controller, Central and Eastern Europe
CC/FE	Chief Controller, Far East
CC/M	Chief Controller, Mediterranean
CC/ME	Chief Controller, Middle East
CC/P	Chief Controller, Pacific
CD	Head of SOE
CDI	Chief of Defence Intelligence (DIS)
CE	counter-espionage (penetration of hostile services; see CI)
C/EA	Controller, Eastern Area
C/EUR	Controller, Europe
CF	Cameron, Folkestone
C/FE	Controller, Far East
Cheka	See V-Cheka
C/GF	Controller, Global and Functional
CI	counter-intelligence (defensive action against hostile penetration)
CIA	Central Intelligence Agency
CID	Committee for Imperial Defence; Criminal Investigation Department
CIG	Current Intelligence Group
CI Section	Counter-Intelligence Section
C/ME	Controller, Middle East
C/NA	Controller, Northern Area
COCOM	Coordinating Committee on Strategic Exports
COMINT	Communications Intelligence
Comintern	Communist International
COMSEC	Communications Security
CoS	Chiefs of Staff Committee
CPA/CSS	Chief Personal Assistant to Chief of Secret Service
CPGB	Communist Party of Great Britain
CPO	Chief Passport Control Officer
C/PR	Controller, Production Research
CR	Central Registry

CRO	Commonwealth Relations Office
CRPO	Combined Research and Planning Organization
C Section	Circulating Section
CSO	Consular Security Officer
C/SOV	Controller, Soviet Bloc
C/SS	Chief of Secret Service
C/UK	Controller, UK
C/WA	Controller, Western Area
C/WH	Controller, Western Hemisphere
CX Report	SIS intelligence report to Whitehall
D	Designation of Head of Section D
D/C	Unidentified Section D subsection
D/CIS	Director, Counter-Intelligence and Security
DC/SS	Deputy Chief of Secret Service
D/D	Section D technical development subsection
DD/Admin	Deputy Director, Administration
DDMI(I)	Deputy Director, Military Intelligence (Information)
DDMI(O)	Deputy Director, Military Intelligence (Organization)
DDMI(S)	Deputy Director, Military Intelligence (Security)
DD/R	Deputy Director, Requirements
DDR	*Deutsche Demokratische Republik* (East Germany)
DD/SP	SIS Deputy Director responsible for counter-espionage and security, 1943–46
D/FA	Director, Finance and Administration
D/G	Section D Sweden subsection
DGI	Director General of Intelligence
DGSS	Director General of the Security Service
D/H	Section D subsection for Hungary, Balkans and Middle East
DI6	DIS designation of MoD liaison at SIS (see MODA)
DI6(A)	DIS designation of Army liaison to SIS
DI6(Air)	DIS designation of Air Force liaison to SIS
DI6(N)	DIS designation of Navy liaison to SIS
DIS	Defence Intelligence Staff
D/J	Section D Norway subsection
D/K	Section D subsection for Abyssinia (Ethiopia) and Middle East Propaganda
D/L	Section D subsection for clandestine postal interception abroad

DMI	Director of Military Intelligence
DNI	Director of Naval Intelligence
DOT	Department of Overseas Trade
D/P	Director of Production
DP1	Director of Production 1 (Western Europe)
DP2	Director of Production 2 (Middle East and Africa)
DP3	Director of Production 3 (Far East and Americas)
DP4	Director of Production 4 (UK, Soviet Bloc and Eastern Europe)
D/PA	Director of Personnel and Administration
D/R	Director of Requirements
DS Int	Directorate of Service Intelligence (DIS)
DSO	Defence Security Officer (Security Service)
D/SPA	Director, Security and Public Affairs
D/SS	Director, Support Services
DSTI	Directorate of Scientific and Technical Intelligence (JIB/DIS)
D/T	Assistant to D
D/TD	Director, Training and Development
DTI	Department of Trade and Industry
D/U	Section D planning subsection
DUS	Deputy Undersecretary
D/WP	Directorate/Director, War Planning
DWS	Diplomatic Wireless Service
D/X	Section D Laboratory
EMSIB	Eastern Mediterranean Special Intelligence Bureau
FBI	Federal Bureau of Investigation
FCI	Foreign Countries Industrial intelligence subcommittee of CID
FCO	Foreign and Commonwealth Office
FE	Far East
FEC	Far East Controller
FO	Foreign Office
FOA	Foreign Office Adviser
Force 136	SOE in the Far East
G2	Far East, North and South America (pre-1941)
G4	Aden, Iran, Iraq, East and West Africa (pre-1941)

G5	Spain and Portugal (pre-1941)
G7	Malta, Palestine, Egypt and Turkey (pre-1941)
G8	Sweden, Finland and USSR (pre-1941)
GC & CS	Government Codes and Cypher School
GCHQ	Government Communications Headquarters
Gestapo	*Geheime Staatspolizei*
GHQ	General Headquarters
GI	Global Issues
GKKNR	State Committee for the Coordination of Scientific Research
G Officer	Group Officer
GPU	*Gosudarstvennoye Politischeskoye Upravleniye* (State Political Directorate)
GRU	*Glavnoe Razvedyvatelnye Upravleniye* (Soviet/Federal Russian Military Intelligence)
G Section	Group Section
H/CI	Head of Counter-Intelligence
HD(S)E	Home Defence (Security) Executive
H/PD	Same as H/PS
H/PS	Head of Personnel Section (sometimes given as H/PD)
H/SECT	Head of Secretariat
H/TD	Head of Training and Development
H/TECH	Head of Technical Section
H/TS	Head of Training Section
HUMINT	human-source intelligence
I 3	Intelligence Section 3
IIC	Industrial Intelligence Centre
IId	SIS Scientific Intelligence section, 1939–46
IMINT	Imagery Intelligence
I/S	Inspectorate of Security
IONEC	Intelligence Officers' New Entry Course
I/Ops	Information Operations
IRD	Information Research Department (Foreign Office)
IS9	Intelligence School 9
IS9g	European field organization of MI9 (see P15)
ISA	Intelligence Services Act (1994)
ISC	Parliamentary Intelligence & Security Commitee

357

ISIC	Inter-Service Intelligence Committee (predecessor of JIC)
ISK	Intelligence Service, Knox
ISLD	Interservice Liaison Department
ISLD (FE)	ISLD (Far East)
ISO	Industrial Security Officer
ISOS	Intelligence Service, Oliver Strachey
ISRB	Interservice Research Bureau
JAS	Joint Assessments Staff
JIB	Joint Intelligence Bureau
JIC	Joint Intelligence Committee
JIO	Joint Intelligence Organization
JIS	Joint Intelligence Staff
JPS	Joint Planning staff
JSIC	Joint Scientific Intelligence Committee
JS/TIC	Joint Scientific and Technical Intelligence Committee
JTIC	Joint Technical Intelligence Committee
JTLS	Joint Technical Language Service
KGB	*Kommitet Gosudarstvennoe Besopasnostiye* (Committee for State Security)
LCS	London Controlling Section
LI	Liaison intelligence
LRC	London Receiving Centre
ME	Middle East
MEC	Middle East Controller; also Middle East Command
MECAS	Middle East Centre for Arabic Studies
MELO	Middle East Liaison Officer
MEW	Ministry of Economic Warfare
MGB	*Ministrenevoe Gosudarstvennoe Besopasnostiye* (Ministry of State Security)
MI	Military Intelligence
MI1c	First World War designation of SIS; later War Office Liaison at SIS
MI5	Security Service; War Office liaison with Security Service
MI6	War Office liaison to SIS during Second World War;

	also colloquial name for SIS after 1941
MI8	War Office Signal Interception Organization
MI9	War Office Escape and Evasion Organization
MID	Military Intelligence Directorate or Department
MIR	Military intelligence, Research
MIS	Ministerial Committee on the Intelligence Services
MO5	War Office 'Special Section'
MO5g	1915 designation of ex-SSB Home Section under mobilization
MO5j	1915 designation of ex-SSB Foreign Section under mobilization
MoD	Ministry of Defence
MODA/Air	Ministry of Defence Adviser, Air
MODA/Army	Ministry of Defence Adviser, Army
MODA/Navy	Ministry of Defence Adviser, Navy
MODA/SO	Ministry of Defence Adviser, Special Operations
NID	Naval Intelligence Directorate
NID(c)	RN designation for Section O
NKGB	*Narodniye Kommissariat Gosudarstvennoye Besopasnositiye* (People's Commissariat for State Security)
NKVD	*Narodniye Kommissariat Vutrenikh Del* (People's Commissariat of Internal Affairs)
OGPU	*Obedinennoe Gosudarstvennoe Politischeskoe Upravleniye* (Unified State Political Directorate)
OM	Oriental Mission
OSA	Official Secrets Act
OSINT	Open-source intelligence
OSS	Office of Strategic Services
P1	French Section (1941–45), Belgium, France, Italy and Iberian Peninsula (1946–56 approx.), France (1966–?)
P1a	French North Africa (1941–45)
P1b	Non-Free/Vichy France
P1c	Free French not covered by P5 (1941–45)
P2	Iberian Peninsula (1941–45), Scandinavia and The Netherlands (1946–56 approx.), Scandinavia (1966–?)

P3	Switzerland (1941–45), Austria, Germany and Switzerland (1946–56 approx.), Germany and Austria (1966–?)
P4	Italy (1941–45), Middle East (1946–56 approx.), Eastern Europe (1966–?)
P5	Liaison with exiled Polish *Deuxième Bureau* and Free French BCRA (1941–45), Balkans (1946–66 approx.), Soviet bloc (1966–?)
P6	Germany, liaison with exiled Czech *Deuxième Bureau* (1941–45), Greece, Turkey and Cyprus (1966–?)
P7	Belgium (1941–45), USA and Canada (1966–?)
P8	The Netherlands (1941–45), Latin America (1966–?)
P9	Scandinavia (1941–45), China (1966–?)
P10	Caribbean (1966–?)
P11	South-East Asia, Australasia (1966–?)
P12	Japan (1966–?)
P13	Baltics States (1939–45), India and Pakistan (1966–?)
P14	Africa (1966–?)
P15	MI9 liaison (IS9g) (1941–45), Africa (1966–?)
P16	Middle East (1966–?)
P17	Middle East (1966–?)
P18	Africa (1966–?)
P19	Africa (1966–?)
P20	UK (1966–?)
PCO	Passport Control Officer; Passport Control Organization; and Passport Control Office
P Division	SIS/SOE coordinating department at SEAC
PHOTINT	Photographic Intelligence
POMEF	Political Office to Middle East Forces
PRO	Public Record Office
P Section	Production Section
PRU	Photographic Reconnaissance Unit
PSO/CSS	Principle Staff Officer to Chief of Secret Service
PTCP	Production and Targeting, Counter-Proliferation
PUS/FCO	Permanent Undersecretary of the Foreign and Commonwealth Office
PWE	Political Warfare Executive
PWM	Political Warfare Mission
Q Device	Concealed tool, e.g. for escape and evasion

'Q Matters'	Counter-espionage liaison with OSS
R1	Political (Foreign Office) R Section
R2	Air Force R Section
R3	Admiralty Requirements Section
R4	War Office/Army Requirements Section
R5	Counter-Intelligence Section
R5 Com	Anti-Communist sub-section of R5
R5 Int	Counter-Intelligence sub-section of R5
R6	Industrial/Commercial and Financial Intelligence
R7	Scientific and Technical Intelligence Section
R8	GCHQ R Section
R9	Atomic or 'Tube Alloys' R Section
RAF	Royal Air Force
R/AF	Requirements, Africa
RCMP	Royal Canadian Mounted Police
'Red Book'	SIS Requirements Document; weekly JIC intelligence summary
R/ECON	Requirements, Economic Intelligence
R/EUR	Requirements, Europe
R/FE	Requirements, Far East
R/GC	GCHQ R Section post-1974, formerly R8.
RIS	Radio Intelligence Section
R/ME	Requirements, Middle East
RN	Royal Navy
R Section	Requirements Section
RSHA	*Reichsicherheithauptampt*
R/SOV	Requirements, Soviet Bloc
R/TECH	Requirements, Technical Intelligence
RSS	Radio Security Section or Service
RU	Research Unit
R/WH	Requirements, Western Hemisphere
SAC	Secret Activities Committee
SACSEA	Supreme Allied Commander, South-East Asia
SAM	SOE Moscow
SAS	Special Air Service
SB	Polish security service
SBO	Security Branch, Operations; Security Branch Officer
SBP	Security Branch, Personnel

SBS	Special Boat Service
SBV	Security Branch, Vetting
SCIU	Special Counter-Intelligence Unit
SCU	Special Communications Unit
SD	*Sicherheitsdienst*, Security Department of the RSHA
SD	Special duties
SEAC	South-East Asia Command
Section I	Political (FO) C Section
Section II	Air Ministry C Section
Section IId	Scientific Intelligence Section
Section III	Naval C Section
Section IV	War Office C Section
Section V	Counter-Espionage C Section
Section VI	MEW C Section
Section VIa	General Economic Intelligence
Section VIb	Banking and Finance
Section VIc	International Trade
Section VII	SIS Financial Officer
Section VIII	Communications Section
Section IX	Soviet Counter-Espionage Section
Section D	Sabotage and Subversion section of SIS
Section H	Wartime (1939–45) section handling postal censorship information to be used by SIS
Section N	Diplomatic bag opening section of SIS
Section O	'Operations' (wartime transport, including 'Shetland Bus', 1940–45)
Section Y	Telephone tap transcription and translation
SFU	Special Forces Unit
SHAEF	Supreme Headquarters, Allied European Forces
Sigurimi	Albanian secret police
SIFE	Security Intelligence Far East
SIGINT	Signals Intelligence, i.e. COMINT + ELINT
SIME	Security Intelligence Middle East
SIS	Secret Intelligence Service; sometimes also Special Intelligence Service
SLU	Special Liaison Unit
SO	Minister of Economic Warfare as head of SOE
SO1	Special Operations 1, predecessor of PWE
SO2	Special Operations 2, predecessor of SOE
SO3	Special Operations 3, planning section

SO/DWP	Special Operations Staff to Director, War Planning
SOE	Special Operations Executive
SOF	Special Operations Forces
SOM	Special Operations Middle East
SovBloc	Soviet bloc
Sov/Ops	Soviet Operations
SPA	Special Political Action Section
SS1	Metropolitan Special Branch section dealing with SIS on terms similar to a Service Intelligence Branch circulating section
SSA	Security Service Act
SSB	Secret Service Bureau
ST	Strategic Trade Section
STS	Special Training Schools
T Section	Targeting Section
TALS	Tube Alloys Liaison Section (see R7 and R9)
TCI Section	Targeting and Counter-Intelligence Section
TCS	Technical Coordinating Section (R7)
TECHINT	Technical Intelligence
UKUSA	UK–US system of SIGINT treaties
UKA	Eastern Europe natural cover section (post-Cold War)
UKB	Western Europe natural cover section
UKD	Middle East natural cover section (excluding Iran)
UKJ	Japan natural cover section
UKN	Section handling UK volunteer agents using 'natural cover'
UKO	India/Pakistan natural cover section
UKP	Iran natural cover section
ULTRA	Code name for product of Enigma cryptanalysis
V-Cheka	*Vse-Rosskaya Chrezvychaynaya Komissaya Po Borbe S Kontrrevolutisiye I Sabotazhem* (All-Russian Extraordinary Commission for Combating Counter-Revolution and Sabotage)
VC/SS	Vice-Chief of Secret Service
VI	Voluntary Interceptor
W Board	Committee supervising wartime deception

WL	Wallinger, London
WO	War Office
W/T	Wireless telegraphy
Y	General term for signals interception
Y Section	SIS communications interception and transcription unit
Y Service	Signal interception service
Z Network	SIS field organization parallel with PCO system 1935–39

Sources

INTERVIEWS

The nature of the work information provided by interviewees and legal constraints have made it necessary to treat the former SIS officers interviewed with strict confidentiality. Communications took the form of one or more interviews and/or correspondence. In most cases, interviews were supplemented by subsequent correspondence, and interview transcripts were submitted to the interviewee to ensure accuracy. In one case, circumstances prevented face-to-face interviews, and so a questionnaire was prepared and mailed to the former officer, followed by further correspondence on matters of detail. Three officers were still serving in official capacities in the Civil Service at the time research was undertaken, and two informants referred to copies of official papers either in their possession or to which they had access in the course of interviews and correspondence. Informant designations appear in the form of 'i-XY'. Whenever correspondence was commenced with a potential informant, a new 'interview' file was opened whether or not any interviews subsequently took place, as a result of which there are a number of gaps in the source numbers. Informant designations employed herein are as follows: i-01, i-03, i-08, i-10, i-11, i-015, i-17, i-19, i-20, i-21, i-28 and i-29. Information acquired from officials speaking in various fora under the Chatham House rule is cited as information under the Chatham House Rule, or ICHR.

In refences to documents in public archives, the Public Record Office is given as PRO, and the India Office Library of Records as IOLR.

PUBLISHED SOURCES

Adams, James, *The New Spies: Exploring the Frontiers of Espionage* (London: Hutchinson, 1994).

Aldrich, Richard, 'Britain's Secret Intelligence Service in Asia During the Second World War', *Modern Asian Studies*, 32, 1 (1998), pp. 179–217.

Aldrich, Richard, *Espionage, Security and Intelligence in Britain 1945–70* (Manchester: Manchester University Press, 1998).

Aldrich, Richard, 'Secret Intelligence for a Post-War World', in Richard Aldrich, (ed.), *British Intelligence, Strategy and the Cold War* (London: Routledge, 1993), pp. 15–41.

Aldrich, Richard, 'Unquiet in Death: The Post-War Survival of the "Special Operations Executive", 1945–51', in A. Gorst, L. Johnman and W. Scott Lucas (eds), *Contemporary British History, 1931–1961: Politics and the Limitations of Policy* (London: Pinter, 1991), pp. 193–210.

Andrew, Christopher, 'Churchill and Intelligence', *Intelligence and National Security*, 3, 3 (April 1988), pp. 181–93.

Andrew, Christopher, *For the President's Eyes Only* (London: Harper-Collins, 1995).

Andrew, Christopher, *Secret Service: The Making of the British Intelligence Community* (London: Sceptre, 1987).

Andrew, Christopher and Dilks, David, *The Missing Dimension: Governments and Intelligence Communities in the Twentieth Century* (Chicago: University of Chicago Press, 1984).

Bamford, James, *The Puzzle Palace* (London: Sidgwick & Jackson).

Beevor, J.G., *SOE: Recollections and Reflections* (London: Bodley Head, 1981).

Bennet, Gill, *History Notes: A Most Extraordinary and Mysterious Business: The Zinoviev Letter of 1924* (London: Foreign and Commonwealth Office, 1999).

Benton, Kenneth, 'The ISOS Years: Madrid 1941–3', *Journal of Contemporary History*, 30, 3 (July 1995), pp. 349–410.

Bethell, Nicholas, *The Great Betrayal: The Untold Story of Kim Philby's Greatest Coup* (London: Hodder & Stoughton, 1984).

Blake, George, *No Other Choice* (London: Jonathan Cape, 1990).

Blau, Peter M. and Meyer, Marshall W., *Bureaucracy in Modern Society* (New York: Random House, 1987).

Bower, Tom, *A Perfect English Spy: Sir Dick White and Secret War*

1935–90 (London: Heinemann, 1995).

Bower, Tom, *The Red Web: MI6 and the KGB Master Coup* (London: Mandarin, 1993).

Breckenridge, Scott D., *The CIA and the US Intelligence System* (Boulder, CO: Westview, 1986).

Bristow, Desmond, *A Game of Moles: The Deceptions of an MI6 Officer* (London: Little, Brown, 1993).

Brook-Shepherd, Gordon, *The Storm Birds: Soviet Cold-War Defectors* (London: Weidenfeld and Nicolson, 1988).

Brown, Anthony Cave, *C: The Secret Life of Stewart Graham Menzies, Spymaster to Winston Churchill* (New York: Macmillan, 1987).

Bunyan, Tony, *The History and Practice of Political Police in Britain* (London: Quartet, 1977).

Burch, Martin and Holliday, Ian, *The British Cabinet System* (London: Prentice-Hall/Harvester Wheatsheaf 1996).

Burnham, Peter, 'The Organisational View of the State', *Politics*, 14, 1 (June 1994), pp. 1–7.

Burns, T. and Stalker, G.M., *Management of Innovation* (London: Tavistock, 1961).

Cabinet Office, *Central Intelligence Machinery* (London: HMSO, 1993).

Cabinet Office, *Central Intelligence Machinery* (London: HMSO, 1995).

Cabinet Office, *Central Intelligence Machinery*, web version, at *http://www.open.gov.uk/co/ cim/cimrep2.htm*.

Campbell, Duncan, 'Friends and Others', *New Statesman and Society*, 26 November 1982, p. 6.

Cavendish, Anthony, *Inside Intelligence* (London: Collins, 1991).

Cecil, Robert, 'The Assessment and Acceptance of Intelligence: A Case Study', in K.G. Robertson (ed.), *British and American Approaches to Intelligence* (London: Macmillan, 1987), pp. 166–83.

Cecil, Robert, 'C's War', *Intelligence and National Security*, 1, 2 (April 1986), pp. 170–88.

Cecil, Robert, 'The Cambridge Comintern', in Christopher Andrew and David Dilks, *The Missing Dimension: Governments and Intelligence Communities in the Twentieth Century* (Chicago: University of Chicago Press, 1984), pp. 169–90.

Cecil, Robert, 'Five of Six at War', *Intelligence and National Security*, 9, 9 (April 1994).

Cecil, Robert, 'MI6', in I.C.B. Dear and M.R.D. Foot (eds), *Oxford Companion to the Second World War* (Oxford: Oxford University Press, 1994), pp. 345–52.

Central Intelligence Agency, *Analysis: Directorate of Intelligence in the 21st Century* (Washington, DC: Central Intelligence Agency, 1996).

Charters, David, 'Sir Maurice Oldfield Some Lessons for Canada', *Conflict Quarterly*, 2, 2 (Winter 1982), pp. 40–8.

Child, John, *Organisation: A Guide to Problems and Practice* (London: Paul Chapman, 1988).

Child, John, 'Organisational Structure, Environment and Performance: The Role of Strategic Choice', *Sociology*, 6, 1 (1972) pp. 1–22.

Clarke, Michael, 'The Policymaking Process', in Michael Smith, Steve Smith and Brian White (eds), *British Foreign Policy: Tradition, Change, Transformation* (London: Unwin Hyman, 1988) pp. 71–96.

Clive, Nigel, *A Greek Experience 1943–1948* (Wilton, Wiltshire: Michael Russell, 1985).

Cookridge, E.H., *George Blake: Double Agent* (New York: Ballantine, 1970).

Crozier, Michael, *The Bureaucratic Phenomenon* (London: Tavistock, 1964).

Cruickshank, Charles, *SOE in Scandinavia* (Oxford: Oxford University Press, 1986).

Curry, John, *The Security Service 1908–1945* (London: Public Record Office, 1999).

Dandeker, Christopher, *Surveillance, Power and Modernity* (Cambridge: Polity, 1990).

Darling, Donald, *Secret Sunday* (London: William Kimber, 1975).

Davies, Phillip H.J., 'Organizational Development of Britain's Intelligence Producer-consumer Interface', *Intelligence and National Security* 10, 4, pp. 113–32.

Deacon, Richard (Harold McCormick) *C: A Biography of Sir Maurice Oldfield, Head of MI6* (London: Futura, 1985).

Delmer, Sefton, *Black Boomerang* (London: Secker & Warburg 1962).

Delzell, Charles F., *Mussolini's Enemies: The Italian Anti-Fascist Resistance* (New York: Columbia University Press, 1988).

Denniston, A.G., 'The Government Code and Cypher School Between the Wars', *Intelligence and National Security*, 1, 1 (January 1986), pp. 48–70.

Deriabin, Peter and Schechter, Jerrold, *The Spy Who Saved the World: How a Soviet Colonel Changed the Course of the Cold War* (New York: Charles Scribner, 1992).

Dilks, David, 'Flashes of Intelligence: The Foreign Office, the SIS and Security Before the Second World War', in Christopher Andrew and David Dilks, *The Missing Dimension: Governments and Intelligence Communities in the Twentieth Century* (Chicago: University of Chicago Press, 1984) pp. 101–125.

Dorril, Stephen, *MI6: Fifty Years of Special Operations* (London: Fourth Estate, 2000).

Dukes, Paul, *The Story of ST 25: Adventure and Romance in Red Russia* (London: Cassell, 1938).

Dziak, John, *Chekisty: A History of the KGB* (New York: Ivy, 1988).

Elliott, Nicholas, *Never Judge a Man by his Umbrella* (Wilton, Wiltshire: Michael Russell, 1991).

Elliott Nicholas, *With My Little Eye* (Wilton, Wiltshire: Michael Russell, 1993).

Ellis, K., *The Post Office in the Eighteenth Century* (Oxford: Oxford University Press, 1958).

Farson, A. Stuart, 'Schools of Thought: National Perceptions of Intelligence', *Conflict Quarterly*, 9, 2 (Spring 1989) pp. 52–104.

Fergusson, Thomas, *British Military Intelligence 1870–1914* (Frederick, MD: University Publications of America, 1984).

Foot, M.R.D., *Resistance: An Analysis of European Resistance to Nazism 1940–1945* (London: Methuen, 1976).

Foot, M.R.D., *SOE: An Outline History* (London: BBC, 1985).

Foot, M.R.D., *SOE in France* (London: HMSO, 1966).

Foucault, Michel, *The Archeology of Knowledge* (New York: Pantheon, 1972).

Fourcade, Marie-Madeleine, *Noah's Ark: The Story of the Alliance Intelligence Network in Occupied France* (London: Allen and Unwin, 1973).

Fraser-Smith, Charles, McKnight, Gerald and Smith, Sandy, *The Secret War of Charles Fraser-Smith* (London: Michael Joseph, 1981).

Freedman, Lawrence, 'Intelligence Operations in the Falklands', *Intelligence and National Security*, 1, 3 (September 1986), pp. 309–31.

Garby-Czerniawksi, Roman, *The Big Network* (London: Ronald, 1961).

Gelber, Harry, review of Richelson and Ball's *Ties That Bind,*

Intelligence and National Security, 2, 1 (January 1987).

Gerth, Hans and Mills, C. Wright, *From Max Weber* (London: Routledge, 1991).

Gill, Peter, 'Reasserting Control: Recent Changes in the Oversight of the UK Intelligence, Community', *Intelligence and National Security*, 11, 2 (April 1996), pp. 3l3–31.

Golinkov, David, *The Secret War Against Soviet Russia* (Moscow: Novosti, 1981).

Gorka, Paul v., *Budapest Betrayed* (Wembley: Oak Tree, 1986).

Gorst, Anthony and Lucas, W. Scott, 'The Other Collusion: Operation Straggle and the Anglo-American Intervention in Syria 1955–56', *Intelligence and National Security*, 4, 3 (April 1989), pp. 576–93.

Gouldner, Alvin, 'Discussion of Industrial Sociology', *American Sociological Review*, 13 (1948) pp. 396–400.

Goulter, Christine, 'The Role of Intelligence in Coastal Command's Anti-Shipping Campaign, 1941–45', *Intelligence and National Security*, 5, 1, (January 1990) pp. 84–105.

Graham, Bill, *Break-In: Inside the Soviet Trade Delegation* (London: Bodley Head, 1987).

Habermas, Jürgen, *The Theory of Communicative Action. Volume 2. Lifeworld and System: A Critique of Functionalist Reasoning* (Boston, MA: Beacon, 1987).

Hannah, Michael T. and Freeman, John H., 'The Population Ecology of Organisations, *American Journal of Sociology*, 82, 5 (March 1977) pp. 929–964.

Hardin, Garrett, 'The Tragedy of the Commons', *Science*, 162, 3859 (December 1968).

Harrison, E.D.R., 'Some Reflections on Kim Philby's *My Silent War* as a Historical Resource', in Richard Aldrich (ed.), *Intelligence, Defence and Diplomacy: British Policy in the Post-War World* (London: Frank Cass, 1994).

Hasswell, Jock, *The First Respectable Spy: The Life and Times of Colquhoun Grant* (London: Hamish Hamilton, 1969).

Heclo, Hugh and Wildavsky, Aaron, *The Private Government of Public Money: Community and Policy Inside British Politics* (London: Macmillan, 1974).

Hennessy, Peter and Brownfield, Gail, 'Britain's Cold War Security Purge', *Historical Journal*, 25, 4 (1982), pp. 965–73.

Herman, Michael, *Intelligence Power in Peace and War* (Cambridge:

Cambridge University Press, 1996).

Hiley, Nicholas, 'The Failure of British Espionage Against Germany, 1907–1914', *Historical Journal*, 26, 4 (1983), pp. 867–89.

Hill, George, *Go Spy the Land* (London: Cassell, 1932).

Hinsley, F.H., Thomas, E.E., Ransom, C.F.G. and Knight, R.C., *British Intelligence in the Second World War: Its Influence on Strategy and Operations*, vol. I (London: HMSO, 1979).

Hinsley, F.H., Thomas, E.E., Ransom, C.F.G. and Knight, R.C., *British Intelligence in the Second World War: Its Influence on Strategy and Operations*, vol. II (London: HMSO, 1981).

Hinsley, F.H., Thomas, E.E., Ransom, C.F.G. and Knight, R.C., *British Intelligence in the Second World War: Its Influence on Strategy and Operations*, vol. III, part 1 (London: HMSO, 1984).

Hinsley, F.H. and Simkins, C.A.G., *British Intelligence in the Second World War: Security and Counterintelligence* vol. IV (London: HMSO, 1990).

House of Commons, *Official Report*, 238, 52 (22 February 1994).

Howard, Michael, *British Intelligence in the Second World War. Volume IV: Strategic and Operational Deception* (London: HMSO, 1990).

Howarth, Patrick, *Intelligence Chief Extraordinary: The Life of the Ninth Duke of Portland* (London: Bodley Head, 1986).

Howe, Ellic, *The Black Game: British Subversive Operations Against the Germans During the Second World War* (London: Queen Anne Press/Futura, 1982).

Hutton, J. Bernard, *Frogman Spy* (London: Neville Spearman, 1960).

Hutton, J. Bernard, *Commander Crabb is Alive* (Edinburgh: Mainstream, 1968).

Hutton, J. Bernard, *The Fake Defector* (London: Howard Baker, 1970).

Hyde, H. Montgomery, *George Blake: Superspy* (London: Futura, 1987).

Hyde, H. Montgomery, *The Quiet Canadian: The Secret Service Story of Sir William Stephenson* (London: Constable, 1989).

Jeffery, Keith, 'British Military Intelligence following World War I', in K.G. Robertson (ed.), *British and American Approaches to Intelligence* (London: Macmillan, 1987).

Johns, Philip, *Within Two Cloaks: Missions with SIS and SOE* (London: William Kimber, 1979).

Jones, R.V., *Most Secret War. British Scientific Intelligence 1939–1945* (London: Coronet, 1978).

Jones, R.V., *Reflections on Intelligence* (London: Jonathan Cape, 1989).

Jones, William, *Twelve Months with Tito's Partisans* (Bedford: Bedford Books, 1946).

Judd, Alan (Petty, Alan), *The Quest for C: Mansfield Cumming and the Founding of the Secret Service* (London: HarperCollins, 1999).

Kaufman, Stuart J. 'Organisational Politics and Change in Soviet Military Policy', *World Politics*, 46, 3 (April 1994) pp. 355–382.

Kemp, Peter, *Thorns of Memory* (London: Sinclair-Stevenson, 1990).

Kent, Sherman, *Strategic Intelligence for US World Policy* (Princeton: Princeton University Press, 1949).

Kettle, Michael, *Sidney Reilly: The True Story* (London: Corgi, 1983).

Kirkpatrick, Lyman B., *The US Intelligence Community: Foreign Policy and Domestic Activities* (New York: Hill and Wang, 1973).

Knight, Kenneth, 'The Compromise Organization', in Kenneth Knight (ed.), *Matrix Management* (London: Gower, 1977) pp. 1–12.

Kyle, Keith, *Suez* (London: Wiedenfeld & Nicolson, 1991).

Lampe, David, *The Last Ditch: The Secret of the Nationwide British Resistance Organisation* (London: Cassell, 1968).

Landau, Henry, *All's Fair: The Story of British Secret Service Behind German Lines* (New York: Putnam, 1934).

Lane, Jan-Erik, *The Public Sector: Concepts, Models and Approaches* (London: Sage, 1993).

Langley, James, *Fight Another Day* (London: Collins, 1974).

Lanning, Hugh and Norton-Taylor, Richard, *A Conflict of Loyalties: GCHQ 1980–1991* (Cheltenham: New Clarion, 1991).

Laqueur, Walter, *A World of Secrets: The Uses and Limits of Intelligence* (New York: Basic Books, 1985).

Lockhart, John Bruce 'Intelligence: A British View', in K.G. Robertson (ed.), *British and American Approaches to Intelligence* (London: Macmillan, 1987) pp. 37–59.

Lockhart, Robert Bruce, *Memoirs of a British Agent* (London: Putnam, 1932; Macmillan, 1985).

Lockhart, Robin Bruce, *Reilly, Ace of Spies* (London: Futura, 1983).

Lord Franks, *Falkland Islands Review* (London: HMSO, 1983).

Lorsch, J.W., *Managing Diversity and Interdependence: An Organisational Study of Multi-Divisional Businesses* (Boston, MA: Harvard University Press, 1973).

Lucas, W., Scott, W. and Morris, C.J., 'A Very British Crusade: The Information Warfare Department and the Beginning of the Cold

War', in Richard Aldrich (ed.), *British Intelligence Strategy and the Cold War* (London: Routledge, 1993), pp. 65–107.

Lustgarten, Lawrence, 'Learning from Peter Wright: A Response to D.C. Watt', *Political Quarterly*, 60 (1989) pp. 222–236.

Macdonnell, Francis, 'The Search for the Second Zimmermann Telegram: FDR, BSC and the Latin American Front', *International Journal of Intelligence and Counterintelligence*, 4, 4 (1988), pp. 487–505.

Mackenzie, Compton, *Aegean Memories* (London: Chatto & Windus, 1940).

Mackenzie, Compton, *First Athenian Memories* (London: Cassell, 1931).

Mackenzie, Compton, *Greek Memories* (London: Cassell, 1939).

Marshall-Cornwall, James, *Wars and Rumours of War* (London: Leo Cooper, 1984).

McCall, Gibb, *Flight Most Secret: Air Missions for the SOE and SIS* (London: William Kimber, 1981).

McDermott, Geoffrey, *The Eden Legacy and the Decline of British Diplomacy* (London: Leslie Frewin, 1969).

McDermott, Geoffrey, *The New Diplomacy and Its Apparatus* (London: Plume, 1973).

Medlicott, W.N., *The Economic Blockade*, vol. I (London: HMSO, 1952).

Medlicott, W.N., *The Economic Blockade*, vol. II (London: HMSO, 1959).

Mookerjee, Nanda, *The British Press, Intelligence and Parliament* (Calcutta: Jaysree Prakashan, 1981).

Naftali, Timothy, 'Intrepid's Last Deception: Documenting the Career of Sir William Stephenson', *Intelligence and National Security*, 9, 3 (1993) pp. 72–99.

NIMA (National Imagery and Mapping Agency) Public Homepage *http://www.164.214.2.53* (12 August 1997).

Neave, Airey, *Saturday at MI9* (London: Grafton, 1989).

Norton-Taylor, Richard, *In Defence of the Realm?* (London: Civil Liberties Trust, 1990).

Norton-Taylor, Richard, Obituary of Sir Dick White, *Guardian* (23 February 1993).

Norton-Taylor, Richard and Black, Ian, 'Spymasters Lift Veil To Meet the Press', *Guardian* (25 November 1993).

O'Brien, Terrence, *The Moonlight War: The Story of Clandestine*

Special Operations in Southeast Asia 1944–1945 (London: Collins, 1987).

Occleshaw, Michael, *Armour Against Fate: British Military Intelligence in the First World War* (London: Columbus, 1989).

Office of the Security Service Commissioner, *The Security Service* (London: HMSO, 1993).

O'Halpen, Eunan, 'Financing British Intelligence: The Evidence up to 1945', in K.G. Robertson (ed.), *British and American Approaches to Intelligence* (London: Macmillan, 1987) pp. 187–207.

Olsen, Mancur, *The Logic of Collective Action: Public Goods and the Theory of Groups* (London: Harvard University Press, 1971).

Olsen, Oluf Reed, *Two Eggs on My Plate* (London: Arrow, 1952).

Ostrovsky, Victor and Hoy, Claire, *By Way of Deception: A Devastating Insider's Portrait of the Mossad* (Toronto: Stoddart, 1990).

Page, Charles H., 'Bureaucracy's Other Face', *Social Forces*, 25 (1946).

Parris, Henry, *Constitutional Bureaucracy: The Development of British Central Administration Since the Eighteenth Century* (London: Allen and Unwin, 1969).

Peden, G.C., *British Rearmament and the Treasury 1932–1939* (Edinburgh: Scottish Academic Press, 1979).

Penkovsky, Oleg, *The Penkovsky Papers* (New York: Avon, 1965).

Philby, H.A.R. ('Kim') *My Silent War* (New York: Ballantine, 1983).

Pitt, D.C. and Smith B.C., *Government Departments: An Organisational Perspective* (London: Routledge, 1981).

Popplewell, Richard, *Intelligence and Imperial Defence: British Intelligence and the Defence of the Indian Empire 1904–1924* (London: Frank Cass, 1995).

Posen, Barry R., *Sources of Military Doctrine* (London: Cornell University Press, 1984).

Postan, M.M., *British War Production* (London: HMSO, 1952).

Powell, Walter W. and Dimaggio, Paul, *New Institutionalism and Organisational Analysis* (London: University of Chicago Press, 1991).

Pugh, Marshall, *Commander Crabb* (London: Macmillan, 1956).

Radcliffe, James, *The Reorganisation of British Central Government* (Aldershot: Dartmouth, 1981).

Ransom, Harry Howe, *The Intelligence Establishment* (Cambridge, MA: Harvard University Press, 1970).

Rathmell, Andrew, *Secret War in the Middle East: The Covert Struggle for Syria, 1949–1961* (London: Tauris, 1995).

Read, Anthony and Fisher, David, *Colonel Z: Secret Life of a Master of Spies* (London: Hodder & Stoughton, 1984).

Reilly, P., *The Adventures of Sidney Reilly* (London: Ellis, Matthews & Marot, 1931).

Rhodes R.A.W. and Marsh, David, 'Policy Networks in British Politics: A Critique of Existing Approaches', in R.A.W. Rhodes and David Marsh (eds), *Policy Networks in British Government* (Oxford: Clarendon, 1992).

Richelson, Jeffrey T., *Foreign Intelligence Organisations* (Cambridge, MA: Ballinger, 1988).

Richelson, Jeffrey T., *The US Intelligence Community* (Cambridge, MA: Ballinger, 1989).

Richelson, Jeffrey T. and Ball, Desmond, *The Ties that Bind* (Boston, MA: Unwin, 1985).

Robertson, K.G. (Ken), 'Accountable Intelligence: The British Experience', *Conflict Quarterly*, 8, 1 (Winter 1988), pp. 13–27.

Robertson, K.G., 'An Agenda for Intelligence Research', *Defence Analysis*, 3, 2 (1987) pp. 95–102.

Robertson, K.G., *Public Secrets* (London: Macmillan, 1982).

Robertson, K.G. 'Recent Reform of Intelligence in the United Kingdom: Democratization or Risk Management?', *Intelligence and National Security*, 13, 2, pp. 144–58.

Roosevelt, Kermit, *Countercoup: The Struggle for Control of Iran* (New York: McGraw-Hill, 1979).

Rose, Richard, *Understanding Big Government* (London: Sage, 1984).

Rowen, H.S, 'Reforming Intelligence: A Market Approach', in Roy Godson, Ernest R. May and Gary Schmitt (eds), *US Intelligence at the Crossroads: Agendas for Reform* (Washington, DC: Brassey's, 1995), pp. 233–42.

Rusbridger, James, *The Intelligence Game: Illusions and Delusions of International Espionage* (London: Bodley Head, 1989).

Sawatsky, John, *Men in the Shadows: The Shocking Truth about the RCMP Security Service* (Toronto: Doubleday, 1980).

Scharfman, Peter, 'Intelligence Analysis in the Age of Electronic Dissemination', in *Intelligence and National Security*, 10, 4 (October 1995) pp. 201–211.

Schelling, Thomas, *Micromotives & Macrobehaviour* 277 277 (New York: W.W. Morton 1978)

Scott, Richard, *Report of the Inquiry into Export of Defence Equipment and Dual-Use Goods to Iraq and Related Prosecutions*

(London: HMSO, 1996, 5 vols).

Security Commission, *Report of the Security Commission* (London: HMSO, 1985; Cmnd 9514).

Smith, Lyn, 'Covert British Propaganda: the Information Research Department 1947–1977', *Millennium*, 9, 1 (Spring 1981), pp. 67–82.

Smith, Michael, *Old Cloak, New Dagger: How Britain's Spies Came in from the Cold* (London: Gollancz, 1996).

Stafford, David, *Britain and European Resistance 1940–1945: A Survey of the Special Operations Executive, With Documents* (Toronto: University of Toronto Press, 1983).

Stafford, David, *Camp X: Canada's School for Secret Agents 1941–45* (Toronto: Lester & Orpen Dennys, 1986).

Stafford, David, 'Intrepid: Myth and Reality', *Journal of Contemporary History*, 22, 2 (April 1987), pp. 305–15.

Stewart, Rosemary, *The Reality of Management* (London: Heinemann, 1963).

Stoll, Clifford, *The Cuckoo's Egg* (London: Bodley Head, 1991).

Strang, Lord, *The Foreign Office* (London: Allen and Unwin, 1955).

Strawson, John, *History of the SAS Regiment* (London: Grafton, 1986).

Strong, Kenneth, *Intelligence at the Top: The Recollections of an Intelligence Officer* (London: Giniger, 1968).

Sweet-Escott, Bickham, *Baker Street Irregular* (London: Methuen, 1965).

Toffler, Alvin and Toffler, Heidi, *War and Antiwar* (New York: Warner, 1995).

Tomlinson, Richard, *The Big Breach: From Top Secret to Maximum Security* (Edinburgh: Cutting Edge, 2001).

Trevor-Roper, Hugh (Lord Dacre), *The Philby Affair: Espionage, Treason and Secret Services* (London: William Kimber, 1968).

Tullock, Gordon, *Politics of Bureaucracy* (Washington, DC: Public Affairs Press, 1965).

Urban, Mark, *UK Eyes Alpha: The Inside Story of British Intelligence* (London: Faber & Faber, 1986).

Verrier, Anthony, *Through the Looking-Glass: British Foreign Policy in an Age of Illusions* (London: Jonathan Cape, 1983).

Walker, David E., *Adventure in Diamonds* (London: Evans Brothers, 1955).

Wark, Welsey, 'Beyond Intelligence: The Study of British Strategy and the Norway Campaign, 1940', in Michael Graham Fry (ed.), *Power, Personalities and Policies: Essays in Honour of Donald Cameron Watt* (London: Frank Cass, 1982).

Wark, Wesley 'Our Man in Riga: Reflections on the Career and Writings of Leslie Nicholson, *Intelligence and National Security*, 11, 4 (October 1996).

Wark, Wesley, *The Ultimate Enemy* (Oxford: Oxford University Press, 1986).

Watt, Donald C., 'Fall-Out from Treachery: Peter Wright and the *Spycatcher* Case', *Political Quarterly*, 59 (1988).

Watt, Donald C., 'Learning from Peter Wright: A Reply', *Political Quarterly*, 60 (1989) pp. 237–238.

Weber, Max, *The Protestant Ethic and the Spirit of Capitalism* (London: Unwin University Books, 1967).

Weber, Max, *Economy and Society*, translated by Gunther Ross and Klaus Wittich, (London: University of California Press, 1978).

Welham, W.J. and Welham, A.J., *Frogman Spy* (London: W.H. Allen, 1990).

West, Nigel, *MI6: British Secret Intelligence Operations 1909–1945* (London: Grafton, 1988).

West, Nigel, *The Friends: British Post-War Secret Intelligence Operations* (London: Weidenfeld & Nicolson, 1988).

West, Nigel (Rupert Allason), *GCHQ: The Wireless War 1900–1986* (London: Weidenfeld & Nicolson, 1986).

West, Nigel, *A Matter of Trust: MI5 1945–72* (London: Weidenfeld & Nicolson 1982).

West, Nigel, *MI5: British Security Service Operations 1909–1945* (London: Triad/Granada, 1981).

West, Nigel, *Secret War* (London: Hodder and Stoughton, 1993).

West, Nigel, *The Secret War for the Falklands: The SAS, MI6 and the War Whitehall Nearly Lost* (London: Little, Brown, 1997).

West, Nigel and Tsarev, Oleg, *The Crown Jewels: The British Secrets Exposed by the KGB Archives* (London: HarperCollins, 1998).

White, Michael, 'Head of MI6 Is Named in Prime Minister's Move to Openness', *Guardian* (17 March 1992).

Whitwell, John (Leslie Nicholson), *British Agent* (London: William Kimber, 1966).

Wilson, F.M.G., *The Organisation of British Central Government* (London: Allen and Unwin, 1957).

Winterbotham, F.W., *The Nazi Connection: The Personal History of a Top-Level British Agent in Pre-War Germany* (London: Weidenfeld & Nicolson, 1978).

Winterbotham, F.W., *The Ultra Secret* (New York: Dell, 1974).

Woodhouse, C.M., *Something Ventured* (London: Granada, 1983).

Wright, Peter, *Spycatcher: The Candid Autobiography of a Senior Intelligence Officer* (Toronto: Hodder & Stoughton, 1987).

Young, John W., 'The Wilson Government's Reform of Intelligence Coordination, 1967–68', *Intelligence and National Security*, 16, 2 (Summer 2001).

Zifcak, Spencer, *New Managerialism: Administrative Reform in Whitehall and Canberra* (Buckingham: Open University Press, 1984).

Index